Multi-Agent Programming

Rafael H. Bordini · Mehdi Dastani ·
Jürgen Dix · Amal El Fallah Seghrouchni
Editors

Multi-Agent Programming

Languages, Tools and Applications

 Springer

Editors

Rafael H. Bordini
Department of Computer Science
University of Durham
South Road - Science Labs
Durham DH1 3LE
United Kingdom
R.Bordini@durham.ac.uk

and

Institute of Informatics
Federal University of Rio Grande do Sul
PO Box 15064
Porto Alegre, RS - 91501-970
Brazil
R.Bordini@inf.ufrgs.br

Mehdi Dastani
Department of Information
 & Computing Sciences
Utrecht University
Padualaan 14, 3584 CH Utrecht
De Uithof, Netherlands
mehdi@cs.uu.nl

Amal El Fallah Seghrouchni
Université Paris VI
Labo. Informatique
104 av. du President Kennedy
75016 Paris
France
amal.elfallah@lip6.fr

Jürgen Dix
Niedersächsische Technische Hochschule (NTH)
    Standort Clausthal Institut für Informatik
Julius-Albert. Str. 4
38678 Clausthal-Zellerfeld
Germany
dix@tu-clausthal.de

ISBN 978-1-4899-8359-6   ISBN 978-0-387-89299-3 (eBook)
DOI 10.1007/978-0-387-89299-3
Springer Dordrecht Heidelberg London New York

© Springer Science+Business Media, LLC 2009
Softcover re-print of the Hardcover 1st edition 2009

Printed on acid-free paper

Springer is part of Springer Science+Business Media (www.springer.com)

Foreword

This is the second book devoted to a state-of-the-art overview of multi-agent programming within five years. This in itself tells us something. To begin with, it
gives us the definite negative answer to the question Michael Wooldridge raises in
his foreword of the first book, viz. whether that book would be the final word on
agent-oriented programming... It was not!

The area of Multi-Agent Systems (MAS) in general is rapidly expanding: wit-
ness the attention the subject receives at prestigious international conferences
and numerous workshops. The expansion is even more accentuated in the sub-
area concerned with programming MAS using dedicated languages, platforms and
tools. Researchers are struggling to find the best way to program these highly complex but potentially very useful systems! In fact, by a very bold kind of induction
(1, 2, many!), I dare forecast that the present volume will not be the final word on
this matter either. It is my strong conviction that, as with so many things in life,
including programming in a broad sense, there is no unique best way to program
MAS, no unique language or platform that is evidently the optimal choice for every situation, and that, in the end, the best choice of language to use will heavily
depend on the application at hand.

What we see in this volume is on the one hand new proposals for generic
agent modeling and programming languages and tools. Here I use generic in the
sense that these languages and tools are not aimed at particular applications. But,
of course, they are not generic in the sense that they should be used for programming *any* possible system; as the term itself indicates, (multi) agent-oriented
programming concerns programming where certain special 'agent-like' cognitive
or social notions are taken as pivotal, such as goal-directedness, autonomy or, in
particular for MAS, coordination, and so this kind of programming is evidently
not meant to be used for just any conceivable application. On the other hand, we
see in this volume also a framework for a particular application.

Despite my remark about agent programming not being the panacea for programming all possible systems, I believe there are many potential applications for
creating intelligent systems where key agent notions *do* play a role! My predic-
tion is that we will see in the future both more variants of the 'generic' type of

languages and tools, and more application-dedicated ones. (A next overview may contain topics such as tools for MAS verification, organization-based programming and programming normative MAS, to mention just a few developments.) This is due to the natural dynamics of this area, and shows the field is alive and kicking! It is gradually building up an array of methods, techniques, models, languages and tools to design MAS. This book is the proof of this, and provides the community with an overview of new developments. I believe that a dynamic field such as multi-agent programming is served a great deal by such an overview.

Utrecht, The Netherlands,   *John-Jules Ch. Meyer*
March 2009   Intelligent Systems Group
Department of Information and Computing Sciences
Utrecht University

Preface

Agent technology currently plays an important role in complex software development. The underlying paradigm offers a large repertoire of original concepts, architectures, interaction protocols, and methodologies for the analysis and the specification of complex systems built as Multi-Agent Systems (MAS). In particular, MAS technology offers sensible alternatives for the design of distributed, open, intelligent systems. Several efforts, originating from academia, industry, and several standardisation consortia, have been made in order to provide new tools, methods, and frameworks aiming at establishing the necessary standards for widening the use of multi-agent systems techniques.

Beyond the standards, the significant level of maturity of MAS concepts and approaches has allowed the MAS research community to combine them in homogeneous frameworks so as to bridge the gap between theory and practice. As a result, practitioners have now at their disposal several efficient tools (such as languages and platforms) to build concrete systems and applications using MAS technology. Consequently, both the development and the deployment of MAS are today effective including at industrial level.

This book is the second volume in a series of books on Multi-Agent Programming (MAP) being co-edited by us; the first volume[1] was published in 2005. The aim of this series of books is to provide and maintain an updated state of the art related to programming multi-agent systems as well as presenting the main languages that contributed to its historical evolution (and are still themselves actively evolving). In fact, over the last few years — since around 2003, following a Dagstuhl Seminar (http://www.dagstuhl.de/02481) — we started a number of important initiatives aimed at providing both practitioners and researchers in the MAS field with the latest advances in the domain of programming languages and tools particularly target at MAS development. This effort includes, for example, the ProMAS workshop series (http://www.cs.uu.nl/ProMAS/) as well as an AgentLink III Technical Forum Group on Programming Multi-Agent Sys-

---

[1] Bordini, R., Dastani, M., Dix, J., El Fallah Seghrouchni, A. *Multi-Agent Programming: Languages, Platforms and Applications.* Springer (2005).

tems (http://www.agentlink.org/activities/al3-tf/), two Dagstuhl seminars (http://www.dagstuhl.de/06261; http://www.dagstuhl.de/08361),
and other related activities such the Multi-Agent Contest (http://www.
multiagentcontest.org/) and the series of LADS workshops (LADS'07 and
LADS'09) which take place with the MALLOW federated workshops event.

One of the driving motivations for promoting these activities related to *Programming Multi-Agent Systems* was the observation that the area of autonomous
agents and multi-agent systems had grown into a promising technology and that
the next step in furthering the achievement of the multi-agent systems project was
irrevocably associated with the development of programming languages and tools
that can effectively support multi-agent programming, including the implementation of key notions in multi-agent systems in a unified framework. We hope
that this second volume in the *Multi-Agent Programming* series will contribute
to enrich the panorama of languages, platforms and applications (as given also in
the first volume), now with addition of tools to support MAS development, thus
adding a new contribution towards surveying both state of the art and the history
of agent programming.

In this second volume of the MAP book series, we have invited several research
groups to report on their work on programming languages and tools for MAS, as
well as on multi-agent systems applications. Most importantly, as for the first volume, we have explicitly asked the authors of chapters on agent-oriented programming languages to follow a particular chapter structure, according to a template
we provided. More than that, we asked them to answer several key questions providing a summary of the main features of each agent development framework
(these can be found in the appendix of this book).

With this structure, and the appendix with brief summaries of the main features of each language, we aimed at providing the readers with a good basis for
comparison among the reported frameworks. The result is a book that can be
used to guide the choice of a particular framework for developing real-world
multi-agent systems or for teaching purposes and assigning practical coursework
when teaching multi-agent systems. This book has a sufficient level of detail to
introduce the reader to the use of some of the most prominent working agent
development frameworks currently available.

The Structure of Contributed Chapters

Chapters describing *Programming Languages* and their platforms discuss the functionality of the languages, the communication mechanisms they provide, their
underlying execution model or interpreters, their expressiveness and verification
possibilities, and the software engineering principles that they follow. These chapters discuss also the characteristics of the platforms that support these programming languages. The issues related to the platforms are: system deployment and
portability, any standards with which they comply, their extensibility, the tools

they provide, their technical interoperability, and their performance. Finally, each of these chapters explains which applications can be supported and implemented by the presented languages and their corresponding platforms. They discuss the typical application examples and any target application domains.

Chapters describing *Tools* cover different sorts of development tools such as debugging tools, testing tools, environment artifacts, integrated development environments (IDEs), modelling tools, etc. These chapters provide the necessary background to introduce the proposed tool, then describe it in some detail, and finally evaluate the tool. Because different types of development tools require different chapter structures, there is no single structure followed by all these chapters; each chapter discusses different important aspects of current techniques for MAS development.

There is also one chapter dedicated to the description of a specific application providing a multi-agent environment for negotiation. This chapter presents the application domain and explains the added value of multi-agent systems for this domain. It presents how the target multi-agent system has been designed and specified. Moreover, this chapter discusses which main features of agents were used in the applications, which methodology was used to design the agents, and how the designed agents were implemented. The chapter also discusses how the interaction between agents and their external shared environment are modelled and implemented. Finally, it presents some experimental results obtained using the application.

The Selected Frameworks and the Structure of the Book

The selection of the agent programming languages in this book is, of course, a matter of taste and reflects our own viewpoint. In the first volume, an important characteristic of all selected languages was that all of them had working implementations that users could download and use to develop their own applications. This time, we chose two languages that played an important role in the history of agent programming and are still being actively developed (METATEM and IndiGolog), languages that have been widely used in industrial applications (Brahms, JIAC, and Agent Factory), as well as a more recent agent programming language that we selected because it promotes understanding of the most important concepts of agent programming (GOAL).

As, we could not incorporate in the first book all frameworks and applications we considered interesting (that would be an encyclopedic task given the number of agent programming languages that appeared in the literature recently), we now present a sequel for the first book, and a third book is already in our plans, in which we shall survey and compare other existing agent programming languages and their platforms, as well as other industrial-strength applications. We hope to have started, in the first two books, with some useful material for researchers, students, and practitioners interested in theoretical aspects of agent frameworks as well as their application for practical purposes.

The book is structured in three parts, each described in detail below.

Part I: Languages

The first part of this book is dedicated to agent-oriented programming languages. Through six chapters, it presents a wide range of languages which, together with the ones in the first volume, provide a good overview of the main developments in the area of Multi-Agent Programming.

The first chapter in Part I, entitled "Executing Logical Agent Specifications", proposes an approach to capture, explicitly, the dynamic nature of agents. The approach presented here by *Michael Fisher and Anthony Hepple* is different from most agent-oriented programming languages which are based on Prolog-like logical goal-reduction techniques. In their work, the basic computational approach is that of model building for logical formulæ, but the underlying formalism is a *temporal logic*. In addition, the temporal basis allow them to consider multiple active goals and being able to achieve several at once. As in most agent-oriented languages, *deliberation* is used to choose between goals when not all can be satisfied at once. The basic execution of temporal formulæ provides the foundation for agent programming in the METATEM approach. In order to deal with multi-agent systems in an equally straightforward way, a simple and flexible model of organisational structuring has been incorporated into METATEM.

The second chapter, "IndiGolog: A High-Level Programming Language for Embedded Reasoning Agents", was written by *Giuseppe De Giacomo, Yves Lespérance, Hector J. Levesque, and Sebastian Sardina*. The authors discuss in that chapter the IndiGolog language, its implementation, and applications that have been realised with it. IndiGolog allows the programming of autonomous agents that sense their environment and do planning as they operate. It supports high-level program execution: the programmer provides a high-level nondeterministic program involving domain-specific actions and tests so as to execute the agents' tasks. The IndiGolog interpreter then reasons about the preconditions and effects of the actions in the program to find a (legal) terminating execution. Programmers provide a declarative specification of the domain using the Situation Calculus formalism and can control the amount of nondeterminism in the program. The language provides support for concurrent programming.

The third chapter presents "Brahms", a language currently used at NASA. In that chapter, *Maarten Sierhuis, William J. Clancey, and Ron J. J. van Hoof* report on an agent-oriented language for work practice simulation and multi-agent systems development. Brahms is a multi-agent modelling language for simulating human work practice that emerged from work processes in human organisations. The same Brahms language can be used to implement and execute distributed multi-agent systems, based on models of work practice that were first simulated. Brahms demonstrates how a multi-agent belief-desire-intention language, symbolic cognitive modelling, traditional business process modelling, activity and situated-cognition theories are all brought together in a coherent approach for analysis and design of organisations and human-centred systems.

The fourth chapter, "Programming Rational Agents in GOAL" by *Koen V. Hindriks*, proposes the language GOAL as a high-level language to program rational agents that derive their choice of action from their beliefs and goals. The language provides a set of programming constructs that allow and facilitate the manipulation of an agent's beliefs and goals and to structure its decision-making. The chapter also provides a formal semantics for the GOAL programming constructs.

The fifth chapter, "Merging Agents and Services — the JIAC Agent Platform" by *Benjamin Hirsch, Thomas Konnerth, and Axel Heßler*, presents a Java-based agent framework with an emphasis on industrial requirements such as software standards, security, management, and scalability. It has been developed within industry- and government-funded projects during the last two years. JIAC combines agent technology with a service-oriented approach. The chapter describes the main features of the framework, with focus on the language and the service-matching capabilities of JIAC V.

The sixth and final chapter of Part I is entitled "Towards Pervasive Intelligence: Reflections on the Evolution of the Agent Factory Framework". In that chapter, *Conor Muldoon, Gregory M. P. O'Hare, Rem W. Collier, and Michael J. O'Grady* report on Agent Factory framework, a cohesive framework for the development and deployment of multi-agent systems. The development of the framework started in the mid 1990s, but has gone through a significant redevelopment whereby several new extensions, revisions, and enhancements have been made. The chapter provides a discussion of the incremental developments in Agent Factory and provides motivations as to why such changes were necessary. The framework provides a practical and efficient approach to the development of intentional agent-oriented applications. This is combined with a methodology, integrated development environment support, and a suite of tools that aid the agent development process.

Part II: Tools

The second part of this book comprises three chapters describing tools for multi-agent programming. Development of real-world software applications requires a variety of tools, and it only recently that mature development tools are becoming available for practitioners. The chapters in this part provide a good overview of some such tools.

The first chapter in Part II, by *David Poutakidis, Michael Winikoff, Lin Padgham, and Zhiyong Zhang*, is entitled "Debugging and Testing of Multi-Agent Systems using Design Artefacts". It presents two tools: one for generating test cases for unit testing of agent-based systems, and one for debugging agent programs by monitoring a running system. Both tools are based on the idea that design artefacts can be valuable resources in testing and debugging. An empirical evaluation that was performed with the debugging tool showed that the debugging tool was useful to developers, providing a significant improvement in the number of bugs that were fixed, and in the amount of time taken.

The second chapter in Part II reports on "Environment Programming in CArtAgO". In that chapter, *Alessandro Ricci, Michele Piunti, Mirko Viroli, and Andrea Omicini* describe CArtAgO, a platform and infrastructure that provide a general-purpose programming model for building shared computational worlds (called 'work environments') that agents, possibly belonging to heterogeneous agent platforms, can exploit to work together within a Multi-Agent System. Being based on the *Agents and Artifacts* conceptual model, CArtAgO work environments are modelled and engineered in terms of set of artifacts programmed by MAS designers, collected in workspaces. From the agent viewpoint, artifacts are first-class entities representing resources and tools that agents can dynamically instantiate, share, and use to support their individual and collective activities. The chapter also provides an example using Jason as a reference platform for MAS programming.

Finally, the third chapter in Part II, by *Alexander Pokahr and Lars Braubach*, presents a "Survey of Agent-oriented Development Tools". As we mentioned before, development tools represent an important addition for the practical realisation of software applications, mainly because they help automating development activities and are able to hide some of the complexity so as to facilitate the tasks of the developers. In that chapter, the authors analyse the tool requirements for the various tasks that need to be performed in the different development phases. These requirements are the foundation for a detailed investigation of the landscape of available agent-oriented development tools. In order to assess the variety of tools systematically, existing surveys and evaluations have been used to isolate three important categories of tools, which are treated separately: modelling tools, IDEs, and phase-specific tools. For each of these categories, specific requirements are elaborated, an overview of existing tools is given, and one representative tool is presented in more detail.

Part III: Applications

The third part of this book comprises one chapter describing an interesting application; the chapter is entitled "A Multi-Agent Environment for Negotiation". In that chapter, *Koen V. Hindriks, Catholijn M. Jonker, and Dmytro Tykhonov* introduce the System for Analysis of Multi-Issue Negotiation (SAMIN). SAMIN offers a negotiation environment that supports and facilitates the setup of various negotiation setups. The environment has been designed to analyse negotiation processes between human negotiators, between human and software agents, and between software agents. It offers a range of different agents, domains, and other options useful for defining a negotiation setup. The environment has been used to test and evaluate a range of negotiation strategies in various domains, where one can play against other negotiating agents as well as humans. The chapter also discusses some of the experimental results.

Finally, we provide, in an appendix, the summaries of each of the six agent programming languages presented in the book. Appendix A starts with a section showing the criteria we consider appropriate for comparing agent platforms; they are introduced in the form of objective questions we posed to the authors. Each of the following sections after that contains the short answers, provided by the contributing authors, relative to each of the programming languages (and their platforms) presented in the book.

Acknowledgements

We are much grateful to all members of the Programming Multi-Agent Systems community who have given much support throughout the last seven years to our initiatives, for example the programme committee members of the ProMAS and LADS workshop series as well as the attendants of the Dagstuhl seminars and the participants of the Multi-Agent Contest. Their thorough work has done a great service to the area of Programming Multi-Agent Systems in general. We thank Tristan M. Behrens for his help in typesetting this book. Most importantly, we thank all the authors of contributed chapters for their excellent work and patience during the long and complex process of putting a book together.

Durham, Utrecht, Clausthal, Paris,   *Rafael H. Bordini*
March 2009   *Mehdi Dastani*
                                                                                   Jürgen Dix
                                                     Amal El Fallah Seghrouchni

Contents

List of Contributors

Lars Braubach
Distributed Systems and Information Systems Group, Computer Science Department, University of Hamburg, Hamburg, Germany
e-mail: braubach@informatik.uni-hamburg.de

Dr. Lars Braubach is, since 2007, a project leader within the VSIS group at Hamburg University. He earned his Diploma in Informatics in 2003 and his Dr. rer.nat. in Informatics in the area of distributed (multi-agent) systems with focus on architectures and methodologies for realizing intelligent systems in 2007. Since 2003, he worked in the DFG funded project MedPAge as part of the priority research program (SPP) 1083. As part of MedPAge, he co-develops the Jadex agent framework since 2003 together with Alexander Pokahr. Since 2007, he co-acquired and manages two DFG-funded research projects. The SodekoVS project deals with fundamental research in the area of self-organizing systems, whereby in the technology transfer project, Go4Flex, in cooperation with the industry partner Daimler, agile workflow descriptions are explored. He has published over 45 peer-reviewed scientific publications and has co-organized a number of workshops and conferences – mostly in the area of multi-agent systems.

William J. Clancey
NASA Ames Research Center, Moffett Field, CA 94035
IHMC, Pensacola, FL
e-mail: william.j.clancey@nasa.gov

William J. Clancey is the Chief Scientist for Human-Centered Computing in the Intelligent Systems Division at NASA Ames Research Center. He is on an intergovernment appointment from the Florida Institute for Human and Machine Cognition (Pensacola), where he is a Senior Computer Scientist. Clancey holds a doctorate in computer science from Stanford University (1979), in which he developed the first computer program to use an expert system for teaching. He also has a BA degree in mathematical sciences from Rice University, Houston (1974). Prior to joining NASA, Clancey was Senior Research Scientist and founding member of the Institute for Research on Learning (1987-1997); earlier he was at the Knowledge Systems Lab in the Computer Science Department at Stanford University (1979-1987). He holds five software patents involving instruction, finance, and work practice simulation. Clancey has published more than 50 journal articles, 35 book chapters, and six books, including Situated Cognition: On Human Knowledge and Computer Representations (1997). He has presented invited tutorials and keynote addresses in 20 countries. He is currently writing a NASA Special Publication for the History Division on how working with the Mars Exploration Rover has changed the nature of field science. For more information, please visit: http://bill.clancey.name.

Rem W. Collier
CLARITY: The Centre for Sensor Web Technologies, School of Computer Science & Informatics, University College Dublin, Belfield, Dublin 4, Ireland
e-mail: rem.collier@ucd.ie

Rem Collier is a lecturer in the School of Computer Science and Informatics at University College Dublin. His research interests focus on the area of Agent-Oriented Software Engineering and on the design and implementation of Agent Factory, a software engineering framework that provides structured support for the fabrication of large-scale multi-agent systems. He was formerly a postdoctoral research fellow on the 'E = mC2: Empowering the mobile Citizen Creatively' project.

Giuseppe De Giacomo
Dipartimento di Informatica e Sistemistica, Università di Roma "La Sapienza", Rome, Italy
e-mail: degiacomo@dis.uniroma1.it

Giuseppe De Giacomo (http://www.dis.uniroma1.it/~degiacomo) is a Full Professor in Computer Science and Engineering at the SAPIENZA Università di Roma, in Rome, Italy. His main research interests are in knowledge representation and reasoning, reasoning about action, cognitive robotics, description logics, conceptual and data modeling, information integration, service composition and verification, and object-oriented methodologies. He is currently involved in national and international research projects on knowledge representation and reasoning, information integration, and service composition. He is the author of several publications in international conferences and journals. He regularly serves as a PC member for many international conferences and workshops, including IJCAI, KR, AAAI, ICAPS, PODS, ICDT.

Michael Fisher
University of Liverpool, Liverpool, UK
e-mail: MFisher@liverpool.ac.uk

Michael Fisher (http://www.csc.liv.ac.uk/~michael) is a Professor of Computer Science at the University of Liverpool, where he heads the Logic and

Computation research group and is Director of the Liverpool Verification Laboratory. His main research interests concern the use of Logic in Computer Science and Artificial Intelligence, particularly temporal reasoning, theorem-proving, programming languages, formal verification, and autonomous and agent-based systems. He has been active in research for over 20 years, having produced over 100 research papers, and has been developing agent programming languages with a strong formal basis since 1995. This has involved investigation of a range of languages tackling multi-agent aspects, coordination, resource-boundedness, deliberation and context-awareness. He is currently on the editorial boards of both the Journal of Applied Logic and Annals of Mathematics and Artificial Intelligence, is a corner editor for the Journal of Logic and Computation, and is a member of the steering committees for the CLIMA, JELIA, and TIME conferences.

Anthony Hepple
University of Liverpool, Liverpool, UK
e-mail: A.J.Hepple@liverpool.ac.uk

Anthony Hepple (http://www.csc.liv.ac.uk/~anthony) is a PhD student in the Department of Computer Science at the University of Liverpool, where he is a member of the Logic and Computation research group. His interest in multi-agent programming languages involves theory, implementation and application to the high-level programming of pervasive systems. Prior to this he obtained a Master's degree, also from the University of Liverpool and gained many years of experience teaching a range of computer science subjects.

Axel Heßler
DAI Labor, Technische Universität Berlin
e-mail: Axel.Hessler@dai-labor.de

Dipl.-Inform. Axel Heßler studied computer science at the Technische Universität Berlin. He works as a researcher at the DAI-Labor of TU Berlin. He has worked on a number of projects within the laboratory, including the JIAC IV agent-platform. Currently, he is finalising his PhD thesis about agent-oriented methodologies in the context of complex projects.

Koen V. Hindriks
Man-Machine Interaction group, Delft University of Technology, Mekelweg 4,
2628 CD, Delft, The Netherlands
e-mail: K.V.Hindriks@tudelft.nl

Koen Hindriks (1971) is Assistant Professor at the Man-Machine Interaction group at the Faculty of Electrical Engineering, Mathematics and Computer Science of the Delft University of Technology. He studied computing science, and finished his PhD at Utrecht University on agent programming languages. His research interests include common-sense reasoning, agent-oriented programming based on common sense concepts like beliefs and goals, and the verification and specification of agent programs. He has designed and developed several agent programming languages, including 3APL and GOAL. He is also interested in the design and development of negotiating agents, which involves among others research on representation, strategies and learning techniques and evaluation techniques that can be usefully applied in the development of such agents.

Benjamin Hirsch
DAI Labor, Technische Universität Berlin
e-mail: Benjamin.Hirsch@dai-labor.de

Dr. Benjamin Hirsch studied Artificial Intelligence at the University of Amsterdam, and obtained his PhD in 2005 at the University of Liverpool. His thesis has been nominated for the "distinguished dissertation award 2006" of the British computer science society. Dr. Hirsch is director of the Competence Center Agent Core Technologies at the DAI Labor, which is part of the Technische Universität Berlin. The competence center consists of roughly 10 doctoral students as well as 5 graduate students, and focuses on next generation service-centric software. Under his supervision, the competence center staffs several projects related to serviceware frameworks and service engineering.

Ron J. J. van Hoof
Perot Systems/NASA Ames Research Center, Moffett Field, CA 94035
e-mail: ronnie.j.vanhoof@nasa.gov

Ron van Hoof is a computer scientist with a Master's degree in Knowledge Engineering from the University of Middlesex, London, England and a Bachelor's degree in Computer Science from the Hogeschool West-Brabant in the Netherlands. Currently Ron works for Perot Systems Government Services at NASA Ames Research Center where his work involves the development of a multi-agent modeling language, simulation environment and real-time agent execution environment used to both simulate and support work practice (BRAHMS). Brahms is a data driven (forward chaining) discrete event multi-agent environment. Ron's responsibilities include being the development lead, system architect and software engineer responsible for the Brahms language, Brahms virtual machine, the integration of the Brahms components and to both develop and support the development of Brahms-based distributed agent systems.

Catholijn M. Jonker
Man-Machine Interaction group, Delft University of Technology, Mekelweg 4,
2628 CD, Delft, The Netherlands
e-mail: C.M.Jonker@tudelft.nl

Catholijn Jonker (1967) is full professor of Man-Machine Interaction at the Faculty of Electrical Engineering, Mathematics and Computer Science of the Delft University of Technology. She studied computer science, and did her PhD studies at Utrecht University. After a post-doc position in Bern, Switzerland, she became assistant (later associate) professor at the Department of Artificial Intelligence of the Vrije Universiteit Amsterdam. From september 2004 unitl september 2006 she was a full professor of Artificial Intelligence / Cognitive Science at the Nijmegen Institute of Cognition and Information of the Radboud University Nijmegen. She chaired De Jonge Akademie (Young Academy) of the KNAW (The Royal Netherlands Society of Arts and Sciences) in 2005 and 2006, and she is a member of the same organisation from 2005 through 2010. Her recent publications address cognitive processes and concepts such as trust, negotiation, and the dynamics of individual agents and organisations. In Delft she works with an interdisciplinary team to engineer human experience through multi-modal interaction between natural and artificial actors in a social dynamic context. In the prestigious VICI innovation project Pocket Negotiator she develops intelligent decision support systems for negotiation.

Thomas Konnerth
DAI Labor, Technische Universität Berlin
e-mail: Thomas.Konnerth@dai-labor.de

Dipl.-Inform. Thomas Konnerth studied computer science at the Technische Universität Berlin. Since finishing his Diploma, he has been working as a Researcher at the DAI-Labor on several projects including the JIAC IV agent-platform. Currently he is wrapping up his PhD thesis which is focuses on the subject of integrating agent-oriented techniques with service oriented approaches.

Yves Lespérance
Department of Computer Science and Engineering, York University, Toronto, Canada
e-mail: lesperan@cse.yorku.ca

Yves Lespérance (http://www.cse.yorku.ca/~lesperan) is an Associate Professor in the Department of Computer Science and Engineering at York University, in Toronto, Canada. He received a Ph.D. in Computer Science from the University of Toronto in 1991. His research is in the areas of knowledge representation and reasoning, multiagent systems, and cognitive robotics. He is the author of over 70 scholarly publications. He is currently a member of the Board of Directors of IFAAMAS and was Co-Chair of the ATAL workshop in 1999 and 2000. He is also a member of the editorial board of the Journal of Applied Non-Classical Logics, and has served on the PC of many international conferences and workshops, including IJCAI, AAAI, ECAI, KR, and AAMAS.

Hector J. Levesque
Department of Computer Science, University of Toronto, Toronto, Canada
e-mail: hector@cs.toronto.edu

Hector J. Levesque (http://www.cs.toronto.edu/~hector) received his Ph.D. from the University of Toronto in 1981. After graduation, he accepted a position at the Fairchild Lab for AI Research in Palo Alto, and then joined the faculty at the University of Toronto where he has remained since 1984. Dr. Levesque has published over 60 research papers, and is the co-author of a 2004 textbook on knowledge representation and reasoning. In 1985, he received the Computers and Thought Award given by IJCAI. He is a founding fellow of the AAAI, and was a co-founder of the International Conference on Principles of Knowledge Representation and Reasoning. In 2001, Dr. Levesque was the Conference Chair of IJCAI-01, and served as President of the Board of Trustees of IJCAI from 2001 to 2003.

Conor Muldoon

CLARITY: The Centre for Sensor Web Technologies, School of Computer Science & Informatics, University College Dublin, Belfield, Dublin 4, Ireland
e-mail: conor.muldoon@ucd.ie

Conor Muldoon is an IRCSET Postdoctoral Research Fellow in the School of Computer Science and Informatics, University College Dublin (UCD). His research interests include Distributed Artificial Intelligence, Multi-Agent Systems and Mobile Computing. He is a former winner of the 'CIA System Innovation Award' at Cooperative Information Agents (CIA), Helsinki, Finland, 2003.

Michael J. O'Grady

CLARITY: The Centre for Sensor Web Technologies, School of Computer Science & Informatics, University College Dublin, Belfield, Dublin 4, Ireland
e-mail: michael.j.ogrady@ucd.ie

Michael O'Grady is an SFI Postdoctoral Research fellow within the School of Computer Science & Informatics at University College Dublin. His research interests included mobile computing and Ambient Intelligence. Prior to joining the school, he worked in the commercial software and telecommunications industries. He has served as a reviewer for a number of international journals and conferences, and to date, he has published in excess of 50 journal and conference papers.

Gregory M. P. O'Hare

CLARITY: The Centre for Sensor Web Technologies, School of Computer Science & Informatics, University College Dublin, Belfield, Dublin 4, Ireland
e-mail: gregory.ohare@ucd.ie

Gregory O'Hare is a Senior Lecturer in the School of Computer Science and Informatics at University College Dublin. His research focuses upon Multi-Agent Systems (MAS) and Mobile and Ubiquitous computing. He has published over 200 journal and conference papers in these areas together with two text books. He is a PI with CLARITY: the Centre for Sensor Web Technologies, a CSET funded by SFI to the tune of a 16 million euro.

Andrea Omicini

DEIS, Università di Bologna, Italy
e-mail: andrea.omicini@unibo.it

Andrea Omicini is Professor at the DEIS, Department of Electronics, Informatics and Systems of the Alma Mater Studiorum – Università di Bologna, Italy. He has written over 180 articles on agent-based systems, coordination, programming languages, software infrastructures, Internet technologies, artificial intelligence, and software engineering, published in international journals, books, conferences and workshops. He has edited 10 books and guest-edited 15 international journal special issues on agent-related issues.

Lin Padgham
School of Computer Science & IT, RMIT University, Melbourne, Australia
e-mail: lin.padgham@rmit.edu.au

Lin Padgham is a Professor in Artificial Intelligence at RMIT University, Australia. She has spent more than 10 years researching intelligent multi-agent systems and has developed (with colleagues) the Prometheus design methodology for building agent systems, and co-authored the first detailed book (published 2004) on a methodology for building multi-agent systems. In 2005, the supporting tool for this methodology, the Prometheus Design Tool, won the award for the best demonstration at AAMAS'05. Lin serves on the editorial board of Autonomous Agents and Multi-Agent Systems, and was Program Co-Chair for AAMAS 2008.

Michele Piunti
Istituto di Scienze e Tecnologie della Cognizione (ISTC-CNR), Roma, Italy
DEIS, Università di Bologna, Italy
e-mail: michele.piunti@unibo.it

Michele Piunti main research interests are in the context of Multi Agent Systems, Cognitive Models of Agency, Interactions and Coordination. He is now attending PhD school in Electronics, Computer Science and Telecomunications at Dipartimento di Elettronica Informatica e Sistemistica (DEIS), Università di Bologna. He previously had a research grant from Istituto di Scienze e Tecnologie della Cognizione (ISTC-CNR, Rome), where he worked in the context of anticipatory cognitive embodied systems. At the time of writing of this chapter Michele Piunti was a visiting researcher at the Division for Industrial Engineering and Computer Sciences of École Nationale Supérieure des Mines de Saint-Étienne.

Alexander Pokahr
Distributed Systems and Information Systems Group, Computer Science Department, University of Hamburg, Hamburg, Germany
e-mail: pokahr@informatik.uni-hamburg.de

Dr. Alexander Pokahr is, since 2007, a project leader within the VSIS group at Hamburg University. He earned his Diploma in Informatics in 2003 and his Dr. rer.nat. in Informatics in the area of programming languages and development tools for distributed intelligent software systems. Together with Lars Braubach he worked on the MedPAge project and in the DFG priority research program SPP 1083 "Intelligent Agents in Real-World Business Applications" for the last 5 years and co-developed the Jadex agent framework. Currently he manages two co-acquired DFG-funded research projects. In the SodekoVS project it is aimed at making self-organizing mechanisms generically software technically usable, whereas in the 2009 starting Go4Flex project workflows will be made more flexible by using goal-oriented concepts. He has published over 45 peer-reviewed scientific publications and has co-organized a number of workshops and conferences – mostly in the area of multi-agent systems.

David Poutakidis
Adaptive Intelligent Systems, Melbourne, Australia
School of Computer Science & IT, RMIT University, Melbourne, Australia
e-mail: davpout@cs.rmit.edu.au

Dr David Poutakidis has extensive experience with intelligent agents and artificial intelligence. His recently completed doctoral research examined debugging and testing methodologies for agent-oriented systems. David is also an experienced individual with industrial and academic experience as a solutions architect, business analyst and scientist. He is currently working as a consultant for a specialist software testing company in Melbourne, Australia.

Alessandro Ricci
DEIS, Università di Bologna, Italy
e-mail: a.ricci@unibo.it

Alessandro Ricci is a researcher associate at DEIS (Department of Electronics, Informatics and Systems), Alma Mater Studiorum – Università di Bologna and lecturer at the Second Faculty of Engineering, located in Cesena. He got his laurea degree and PhD in Computer Science and Engineering from Alma Mater, with a PhD thesis entitled "Engineering Agent Societies with Coordination Artifacts and Supporting Infrastructures". After working on coordination models and infrastructures for multi-agent systems, his main research activities currently concern agents and multi-agent systems as a paradigm for computer programming and software engineering.

Sebastian Sardina
School of Computer Science and Information Technology, RMIT University, Melbourne, Australia
e-mail: sebastian.sardina@rmit.edu.au

Sebastian Sardina (http://www.cs.rmit.edu.au/~ssardina) is a Research Fellow of Artificial Intelligence in the School of Computer Science and Information Technology at RMIT University, Melbourne, Australia. He received his M.Sc. and Ph.D. from the University of Toronto in 2000 and 2005, respectively, and his Bachelor degree from the Universidad Nacional del Sur, Argentina, in 1997. Sebastian's current research interests include intelligent multi-agent systems, reasoning about action and change, cognitive robotics, planning, and knowledge representation and reasoning in general.

Maarten Sierhuis

Carnegie Mellon University Silicon Valley/NASA Ames Research Center, Moffett Field, CA 94035
Man-Machine Interaction Group, Delft University of Technology, Mekelweg 4, 2628 CD Delft, The Netherlands
e-mail: maarten.sierhuis@nasa.gov

Maarten Sierhuis is senior scientist at NASA Ames Research Center and adjunct professor at Carnegie Mellon University's Silicon Valley campus. He currently is also a visiting professor in the Man-Machine Interaction group at Delft University of Technology. He is co-principal investigator for the Brahms project in the Work Systems Design & Evaluation group in the Collaborative and Assistant Systems area within the Intelligent Systems Division. Sierhuis holds a doctorate in social science informatics from the University of Amsterdam (2001), in which he developed a theory for modeling and simulating work practice and researched the Brahms agent-oriented language for that purpose. He also has a BSc. degree in informatics from the Polytechnic University in The Hague, The Netherlands (1986). Prior to joining NASA, Sierhuis was a member of technical staff at NYNEX Science & Technology (1990-1997); earlier he was at IBM in New York and Sema Group in The Netherlands (1986-1990). He has presented invited lectures on Brahms, has published widely in this area and holds two software patents involving work practice simulation and hypertext databases. For more information, please visit: http://homepage.mac.com/msierhuis.

Dmytro Tykhonov

Man-Machine Interaction group, Delft University of Technology, Mekelweg 4, 2628 CD, Delft, The Netherlands
e-mail: D.Tykhonov@tudelft.nl

Dmytro Tykhonov (1982) is a PhD researcher at the Man-Machine Interaction Group, Delft University of Technology, The Netherlands. He studied artificial intelligence at Vrije Universiteit Amsterdam where he received his Master of Science diploma. He works on design and implementation of negotiation systems with a focus on opponent modelling and design of efficient negotiation strategies. This includes research questions such as learning an opponent model in single-shot negotiations, analysis of negotiation performance, computational complexity of preferences and negotiation strategies. His research interests include multi-agent simulations of social phenomena such as trust and deception in trade environments and the influence of national cultures on the development of trust-based trade relations. He is also interested in the art of practical software engineering.

Mirko Viroli

DEIS, Università di Bologna, Italy
e-mail: mirko.viroli@unibo.it

Mirko Viroli has been a research associate at DEIS, Alma Mater Studiorum – Università di Bologna, since 2002. His main research areas cover multiagent systems, coordination models, self-organizing systems and programming languages.

He has published more than 100 papers in peer-reviewed journals and conference proceedings, and served as editor of special issues of refereed journals and organizer of several workshops and conferences. Among the many research activities, he co-designed the artifact abstraction for multiagent systems and the wildcard mechanism of Java generics. His main current interest is the design of new computational models leading to the implementation of infrastructures for the coordination of complex systems.

Michael Winikoff
University of Otago, Dunedin, New Zealand,
School of Computer Science & IT, RMIT University, Melbourne, Australia
e-mail: michael.winikoff@otago.ac.nz

Michael Winikoff was Associate Professor at RMIT University (in Australia) until the end of 2008. He is now working with the Higher Education Development Centre at the University of Otago (in New Zealand). Michael's research interests concern notations for specifying and constructing software. In particular, he is interested in agent oriented software engineering methodologies, and developed (with colleagues) the Prometheus design methodology for building agent systems, and co-authored the first detailed book (published 2004) on a methodology for building multi-agent systems. In 2005, the supporting tool for this methodology, the Prometheus Design Tool, won the award for the best demonstration at AAMAS'05. Michael serves on the editorial board of the International Journal of Agent-Oriented Software Engineering.

Zhiyong Zhang
School of Computer Science & IT, RMIT University, Melbourne, Australia
e-mail: zhzhang@cs.rmit.edu.au

Zhiyong Zhang is a PhD candidate at RMIT (Australia). His research area is automated testing for multi agent systems. Zhiyong obtained his bachelor degree of computer software at BITI (Beijing, P.R.China), and masters degree in A.I. at K.U.Leuven (Belgium). He has over five years of industry experience in software development and project management.

Part I
Languages

Chapter 1
Executing Logical Agent Specifications

Michael Fisher and Anthony Hepple

Abstract Many agent-oriented programming languages are based on the Prolog-like logical goal reduction approach where rules are used to reduce, in a depth-first way, a selected goal. The ability of agents to change between goals means that such languages often overlay the basic computational engine with a mechanism for dynamically changing which goal is selected.

Our approach is different. The basic computational approach we use is that of model building for logical formulae, but the underlying formulae are *temporal*. This allows us to capture the dynamic nature of the agent explicitly. In addition, the temporal basis provides us with ways of having multiple active 'goals' and being able to achieve several at once. As in most agent-oriented languages *deliberation* is used to choose between goals when not all can be satisfied at once.

This basic execution of temporal formulae provides us with the foundation for agent programming. In order to deal with multi-agent systems in an equally straightforward way we also incorporate a very simple, but flexible, model of organisational structuring.

These two aspects provide the core of the language implemented. There are, however, many extensions that have been proposed, some of which have been implemented, and all of which are mentioned in this article. These include varieties of agent belief, resource-bounded reasoning, the language's use as a coordination language, and the use of contextual constraints.

Michael Fisher
University of Liverpool, Liverpool, UK, e-mail: MFisher@liverpool.ac.uk

Anthony Hepple
University of Liverpool, Liverpool, UK, e-mail: A.J.Hepple@liverpool.ac.uk

R.H. Bordini et al. (eds.), *Multi-Agent Programming*,
DOI 10.1007/978-0-387-89299-3_1, © Springer Science+Business Media, LLC 2009

1.1 Motivation

What does an agent do? It has a number of choices of how to proceed, most simply represented by a finite-state machine, for example:

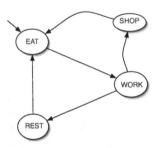

Here the agent begins in the 'EAT' state and can take any transition to move to another state. But the agent also has *choices*. In the example above, when the agent is in the 'WORK' state it can then either move to the 'REST' state or to the 'SHOP' state. How shall the agent decide what to do at these choice states? The agent could act randomly, effectively tossing a coin to see which branch to take. Or we could fix the order in which choices are made, effectively modifying the state machine to capture a fixed set of choices, for example:

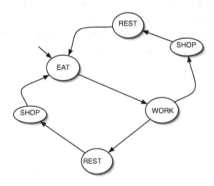

Here, we are restricted about which choices to take, for example being disallowed from following the sequence

EAT $\longrightarrow$ WORK $\longrightarrow$ REST $\longrightarrow$ EAT $\longrightarrow$ WORK $\longrightarrow$ REST $\longrightarrow$ EAT $\longrightarrow$ ...

which was allowed in the original state machine. Not only is this prescription of choices against the spirit of agent-oriented computing, where choices are made dynamically based on the prevailing conditions, but this is also very inflexible. State machines become large and complex if we try to capture all possible legal sequences of choices within them.

Thus, agents, particularly *rational* agents, have various *motivational attitudes* such as goals, intentions, or desires, which help them make choices at any point in their computation. These motivations not only help direct an agent's choices, but are dynamic themselves with new motivations being able to be added at any time. Thus, if we consider the first state machine and provide some additional motivations (let us call them *goals* here) then we can avoid 'bad' sequences just by using these goals to direct our choice. If the agent's main goals are to REST and SHOP then, at the WORK state the most important goal will direct the choice of next state. For example, let us say we move to the REST state. When we again come back to the WORK state, we still have a goal to SHOP, and so we may well choose that branch. And so on. Each time we visit the WORK state, the current goals modify which choices we take.

This is not only a simple view, but it is also a very flexible one. These ideas are at the heart of, for example, BDI languages where the desires and intentions act as motivations for choosing between options [29, 30].

We choose to use a *formal logic* to capture exactly this fundamental choice. This simple view allows us to describe both the potential choices and the agent motivations. If we recall the first state machine above, then we can actually capture what is happening via a set of logical formulae, as follows.

$$\text{EAT} \Rightarrow \bigcirc \text{WORK}$$
$$\text{WORK} \Rightarrow \bigcirc (\text{REST} \vee \text{SHOP})$$
$$\text{REST} \Rightarrow \bigcirc \text{EAT}$$
$$\text{SHOP} \Rightarrow \bigcirc \text{EAT}$$

These are actually *temporal logic* formulae, with the temporal operator '$\bigcirc$' meaning "at the next moment in time". As you can see from the formulae above, we can treat these as being 'rules' telling us what to do next. However, we can go beyond just simple modelling of finite-state machines. (Note that, to precisely model the state machine we also need to add rules ensuring that exactly one of EAT, WORK, REST, or SHOP is true at any moment in time.) As we have the full power of temporal logic (propositional temporal logic, in this case) we can define additional propositions and use them to define other aspects of the computation. For example, rather than

$$\text{WORK} \Rightarrow \bigcirc (\text{REST} \vee \text{SHOP})$$

we might instead have

$$(\text{WORK} \wedge tired) \Rightarrow \bigcirc \text{REST}$$
$$(\text{WORK} \wedge \neg tired \wedge rich) \Rightarrow \bigcirc \text{SHOP}$$
$$(\text{WORK} \wedge \neg tired \wedge \neg rich) \Rightarrow \bigcirc (\text{REST} \vee \text{SHOP})$$

Importantly, all of *tired*, SHOP, etc., are propositions within the language.

As described above, as well as the basic structure of choices, a core component of agent computation is some representation of motivations such as goals. Fortunately, temporal logic provides an operator that can be used to give a simple form of motivation, namely the "sometime in the future" operator '$\Diamond$'. This operator is used to ensure that some property becomes true at *some* point in the future; possibly now, possibly in the next moment, possibly in 5 moments time, possibly in 400 moments time, but it will definitely happen. Consider again our original example, but now with such *eventualities* added:

$$\text{WORK} \Rightarrow \Diamond \text{REST}$$
$$\text{WORK} \Rightarrow \Diamond \text{SHOP}$$
$$\text{WORK} \Rightarrow \bigcirc (\text{REST} \vee \text{SHOP})$$

These formulae describe the fact that there is still a choice between REST or SHOP, once the WORK state is reached, but also ensures that eventually (since we keep on visiting the WORK state) REST will become true and eventually SHOP will become true. Importantly, we can never take the same choice forever.

Thus, the above is the basic motivation for our agent language. There are clearly many other aspects involved in the programming of rational agents (and, indeed, we will discuss these below) but the use of temporal logic formulae of the above form to describe computation, and the execution of such formulae in order to implement agents, is the underlying metaphor.

1.2 Language

The basic 'METATEM' approach was developed many years ago as part of research into formal methods for developing software systems [2]. Here, the idea is to *execute* a formal specification by building a concrete model for the specification; since the specifications are given in temporal logic, model-building for temporal formulae was developed. Throughout, the *imperative future* view was followed [24, 1], essentially comprising forward chaining from initial conditions and building the future state by state.

1.2.1 Syntactical Aspects

Thus, the core language we use is essentially that of *temporal logic* [11, 17]. This is a formal logic based on the idea that propositions/predicates can be true/false *de-*

pending on what moment in time they are evaluated. Thus, the temporal structure linking moments in time is important. While there are many different possibilities for such temporal structures [17], we adopt one of the simplest, namely a linear sequence of discrete moments in time with a distinguished 'start' moment (finite past).

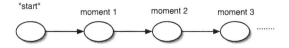

This sequence of moments can go on for ever. Importantly, the basic propositions/predicates within the language can have different truth values at different moments. Thus, a proposition '*hungry*' might be false in the 'start' moment, true in moment 1, true in moment 2, false in moment 3, etc.

Obviously we need a language to be able to describe such situations. Again, there are many varieties of temporal language, even for the simple model above. So, we choose a basic, but flexible, variety involving the logical operators:

'$\bigcirc$' . . . . "in the next moment in time";
'$\square$' . . . . "at every future moment";
'$\diamondsuit$' . . . ."at some future moment".

These operators give us useful expressive power and, even with such a simple temporal logic as a basis, we are able to describe both an agent's individual dynamic behaviour, and also (see later) how an agent's beliefs or goals evolve. As is demonstrated by the following simple example of conversational behaviour, which captures a subtle preference for listening over speaking by allowing models with repeated listening states but preventing uninterrupted speaking!

$\square$(SPEAK $\vee$ LISTEN)
$\square\neg$(SPEAK $\wedge$ LISTEN)
LISTEN $\Rightarrow$ $\diamondsuit$SPEAK
SPEAK $\Rightarrow$ $\bigcirc$LISTEN

1.2.1.1 Basic Execution

Given a temporal description, using the above language, we adopt the following basic execution approach:

- transform the temporal specification into a *normal form* [13];
- from the initial constraints, *forward chain* through the set of temporal rules constraining the *next* state of the agent; and
- constrain the execution by attempting to satisfy eventualities (aka goals), such as $\Diamond g$ (i.e. g eventually becomes true). (This, in turn, involves some strategy for choosing between such eventualities, where necessary.)

The basic normal form, called Separated Normal Form (SNF) [13], essentially categorises formulae into 3 varieties: *initial rules*, of the form **start** $\Rightarrow \varphi$, which indicate properties of the initial state; *step rules*, of the form $\psi \Rightarrow \bigcirc\varphi$, which indicate properties of the *next* state; and *sometime rules*, of the form $\psi \Rightarrow \Diamond\phi$, which indicate properties of the future. In each case φ is a disjunction of literals, ψ is a conjunction of literals and ϕ is a positive literal. In summary, the transformation to this normal form ensures that all negations apply only to literals, that all temporal operators other than $\bigcirc$ and $\Diamond$ are removed, and that all occurrences of the $\Diamond$ operator apply only to literals.

Since we allow first-order predicates, implied quantification of variables, and non-temporal rules, the specific normal form used is more complex. Below, we provide the normal form of each rule type implemented, a corresponding example in first-order temporal logic and, with the implied quantification, an equivalent example in the implemented METATEM syntax.

START RULE:

General $start \Rightarrow \exists\overline{x}. \bigvee_{i=1}^{a} p_i(\overline{x})$

Example $start \Rightarrow \exists x.[p(x) \vee q(x)]$

Code   ```start => p(X) | q(X);```

STEP RULE:

General $\forall\overline{x}.\left[\left[\bigwedge_{i=1}^{a} p_i(\overline{x}) \wedge \exists\overline{y}. \bigwedge_{j=0}^{b} q_j(\overline{y},\overline{x})\right] \Rightarrow \bigcirc \exists\overline{z}. \bigvee_{k=1}^{c} r_k(\overline{z},\overline{x})\right]$

Example $\forall x.\left[[p(x) \wedge \exists y.q(y,x)] \Rightarrow \bigcirc\exists z.[r(z,x) \vee s(z,x)]\right]$

Code   ```p(X) & q(Y,X) => NEXT r(Z,X) | s(Z,X);```

SOMETIME RULE:

General $\forall \overline{x}. \left[\left[\bigwedge_{i=1}^{a} p_i(\overline{x}) \wedge \exists \overline{y}. \bigwedge_{j=0}^{b} q_j(\overline{y}, \overline{x}) \right] \Rightarrow \Diamond \exists \overline{z}. r(\overline{z}, \overline{x}) \right]$

Example $\forall x. \left[[p(x) \wedge \exists y. q(y, x)] \Rightarrow \Diamond \exists z. r(z, x) \right]$

Code   `p(X) & q(Y,X) => SOMETIME r(Z,X);`

NON-TEMPORAL (PRESENT-TIME) RULE:

General $\forall \overline{x}. \left[\left[\bigwedge_{i=1}^{a} p_i(\overline{x}) \wedge \exists \overline{y}. \bigwedge_{j=0}^{b} q_j(\overline{y}, \overline{x}) \right] \Rightarrow \bigvee_{k=1}^{c} r_k(\overline{x}) \right]$

Example $\forall x. \left[[p(x) \wedge \exists y. q(y)] \Rightarrow [r(x) \vee s(x)] \right]$

Code   `p(X) & q(y) => r(X) | s(X);`

We are able to omit explicit quantification symbols from the program code by making the following interpretations.

- Any variable appearing positively in the antecedents is universally quantified.
- Any variables that remain after substitution of matching, and removal of non-matching, universal variables are existentially quantified.
- Of the existentially quantified variables, those that appear only negatively in the antecedents are ignored.
- Existential variables in the consequent of an otherwise grounded rule, which cannot be matched are grounded by Skolemisation.

Existentially quantified variables are not allowed in the consequent of a present-time rule, preventing circumstances in which present-time rules fire repeatedly (possibly infinitely) as a result of new terms generated by repeated grounding by Skolemisation.
Next, we consider a number of examples, exhibiting the basic execution mechanism.

Examples of Basic Execution

We now consider several basic examples, describing how execution of such scenarios occurs.

Example 1

Consider a machine capable of converting a raw material into useful widgets, that has a hopper for its raw material feed which, when empty, prevents the machine from producing widgets. A simple specification for such a machine, presented in the normal form described above, is as follows (each rule is followed by an informal description of its meaning):

```
start => hopper_empty;
```
The hopper is initially empty.

```
true => power;
```
The machine has uninterrupted power.

```
hopper_empty => NEXT fill_hopper;
```
If the hopper is empty, then it must be refilled in the next moment in time.

```
fill_hopper => NEXT ( material | hopper_empty ) ;
```
Filling the hopper is *not* always successful.

```
( material & power ) => NEXT widget;
```
If the machine has power and raw material then, in the next moment in time a widget will be produced.

Execution begins with the construction of an initial state which is constrained by the start rules and any present-time rules. Thus, in the *start* state our machine has an empty hopper and power:

The interpretation of each state is used to derive constraints on the next state. Applying the above rules to this initial state produces the constraint `fill_hopper`, which must be true in any successor state. The METATEM execution algorithm now attempts to build a state that satisfies this constraint and is logically consistent with the agent's present-time rules. In this example we have only one present-time rule, which does not contradict our constraints but does introduce another constraint, hence state 1 is built:

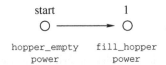

State 1 provides the METATEM agent with its first choice point. Evaluation of the agent's rules constrains the next state to satisfy the disjunction

$$((\text{material} \wedge \text{power}) \vee (\text{hopper\_empty} \wedge \text{power})).$$

Without any preferences or goals to guide its decision, the METATEM agent is able to choose either alternative and makes a non-deterministic choice between disjuncts. For this example we will assume that `material` is made true in state 2:

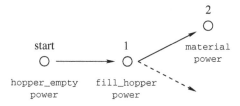

In this state, our machine has both the power and material necessary to produce a widget in the next state:

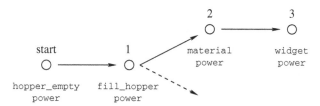

Note. Without explicit rules, be they temporal or non-temporal, the machine no longer believes it has its raw material. Hence, evaluation of the agent's temporal rules with the interpretation of state 3 produces no constraints and the agent will produce no further states.

Example 2

This example illustrates the backtracking nature of the METATEM algorithm when it encounters a state that has no logically consistent future. Staying with our widget machine, we modify its non-temporal rule and provide an additional rule:

```
true => power | ~power;
```
Power can now be switched 'on' or 'off'.

```
( fill_hopper & power ) => NEXT false;
```
Filling the hopper with the power switched on causes irrecoverable problems in the next state!

Execution now begins in one of two states,

$$(\text{hopper\_empty} \wedge \text{power}) \text{ or } (\text{hopper\_empty} \wedge \neg \text{power})$$

due to the conjunction introduced by the modified present-time rule. Let us assume that the former is chosen, though it is inconsequential to our example. Again our agent has a choice when constructing the next state, it can fill the hopper with the power on or with the power off. Each of these choices has a consistent present but only one has a consistent future! Let us assume that the 'wrong' choice is made and the 'correct' choice is retained for future exploration;

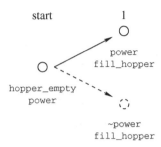

Now, evaluation of state 1's interpretation constrains all future states to include false — this state has no future. It is at this point, when no consistent choices remain, that METATEM backtracks to a previous state in order to explore any remaining choices[1]. Execution then completes in much the same way as the previous example:

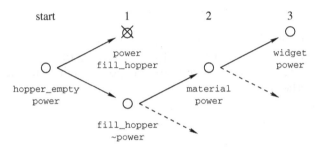

At this point it should be emphasised that the above executions are, in each case, only one of many possible models that satisfy the given temporal specification. Indeed, many models exist that produce no widgets at all. To ensure the productivity of our widget machine we must introduce a goal in the form of an eventuality. For the next example we return to our conversational agent to demonstrate the use of temporal eventualities.

Example 3

For this example, we re-write the specification presented at the end of Section 1.2.1 into the executable normal form, removing all necessity operators ($\Box$), and conjunctions from the consequents of all rules. The result of which is:

```
true => NEXT ( speak | listen );
```
Always speaking or listening...

---

[1] In this example, the agent's ability to fill its hopper is considered to be internal and *reversible*. However, the current METATEM implementation does distinguish between internal and external (those that cannot be reversed and hence cannot be backtracked over) abilities. The sending of messages is an important example of an external ability.

```
speak => ~listen;
listen => ~speak
```
...but never at the same time.

```
listen => SOMETIME speak;
```
Eventually speak after listening.

```
speak => NEXT listen;
```
Always pause to listen, after speaking.

The model resulting from execution of this specification is one which alternates between listening and speaking in successive states;

Although intuitively we may expect to see multiple listening states between each speaking state, the METATEM algorithm endeavours to satisfy outstanding eventualities *at the earliest opportunity*. That is, providing it is logically consistent to do so, an eventuality (such as "$\Diamond speak$") will be made true without being explicitly stated in the consequents of a *next* rule. There are no conflicting commitments and therefore there is no need to delay its achievement.

1.2.1.2 Strategies and Deliberation

Where there are multiple outstanding eventualities, and where only a subset of these can be satisfied at the same time, then some strategy for deciding which eventualities to satisfy now, and which to hold over until future states, is required. As we have seen in the previous section, we are not able to require both speak and listen to be true at the same point in time. Thus, if we require both "sometime listen" and "sometime speak" to be made true many times, then we must decide when to make speak true, when to make listen true, and when to make neither true.

The basic strategy for deciding between conflicting eventualities is provided directly by the original METATEM execution algorithm. This is to choose to satisfy the eventuality that has been outstanding (i.e. needing to be satisfied, but as yet unsatisfied) the longest. This has the benefit that it ensures that no eventuality remains outstanding forever, unless it is the case that the specification is unsatisfiable [1].

There are, however, a number of other mechanisms for handling such strategies that have been developed. The most general is that described in [14]. To explain this, let us view the outstanding eventualities at any moment in time as a list. The eventualities will then be attempted in list-order. Thus, in the basic METATEM case we would order the list based on the age of the eventuality. When an eventuality is satisfied, it is removed from the list; when a new eventuality is generated, we add this to the end of the list.

With this list view, our strategy for deciding which eventualities to satisfy next is just based on the order of eventualities within a list. Thus, if the agent can *re-order* this list between states then it can have a quite sophisticated strategy for *deliberation*, i.e. for dynamically choosing what to tackle next. This approach is discussed further in [14, 18] but, unless we put some constraints on the re-ordering we might apply, then there is a strong danger that the completeness of the execution mechanism will be lost [18].

In the current implementation, rather than using this quite strong, but dangerous, approach we adopt simpler, and more easily analysable, mechanisms for controlling (or at least influencing) the choice of eventuality to satisfy. These mechanisms are characterised by the predicates/directives `atLeast`, `atMost` and `prefer`.

The `atLeast` predicate places a minimum constraint on the number of instances of positive predicates, whilst `atMost` places a maximum constraint on the number of instances of positive predicates in a given temporal state, in the style of the capacity constraints described by [10]. Besides providing the developer with the ability to influence an agent's reasoning, when applied judiciously `atMost` and `atLeast` can simplify the fragment of the logic considered and hence can increase the execution performance of a METATEM agent.

As an example of the use of predicate constraints we provide some code snippets from an example included with the METATEM download, which specifies the behaviour of a lift. The lift responds to calls from floors above and below it and, when more than one call remains outstanding, must decide which call to serve first, changing direction if necessary. Each discrete moment in time of our temporal model denotes the lift's arrival at a floor and the transition between temporal states is analogous to the lift's transition between floors. The following rules specify that the lift starts at the ground floor and must satisfy all calls before it can achieve the `waiting` state:

```
start => atFloor(0);
true => SOMETIME waiting;
call(X) => ~waiting;
```

Clearly, it is desirable that the lift visits a floor in each state of our model. This behaviour could be specified by the rule

```
true => NEXT atFloor(X);
```

which states that there must exist an X such that `atFloor(X)` is satisfied in each moment in time. However, our lift must visit *one and only one* of a limited number of *valid* floors. The above rule is logically too general as it allows multiple x's in any moment in time and implies an infinite domain of x [2]. Therefore our

---

[2] Indeed, the current implementation considers existential variables on the right-hand side of future rules on an open-world principle, implementing a form of Skolemisation by, when necessary, creating new terms. In this example our lift could disappear to an imaginary floor!

lift specification does not use the rule given immediately above, but instead employs predicate constraints. These ensures that the lift visits one and only one floor at each moment, without introducing an existential variable. The following declarations in an agent description file achieve this.

```
at_most 1 atFloor true;
at_least 1 atFloor true;
```

The construction of each temporal state during the execution of a METATEM specification generates a logical interpretation that is used to evaluate the antecedents of each temporal rule. The consequents of all the rules that fire are conjoined (and transformed into disjunctive normal form) to represent the agent's choices for the next temporal state, each conjunction being a distinct choice, one of which is chosen and becomes the interpretation of the next temporal state, from which the next set of choices are derived. This process is repeated, and conjunctions that are not chosen are retained as alternative choices to be taken in the event of backtracking. As mentioned earlier, a number of fundamental properties of the formulae in each conjunction affect the choice made. For example, an agent will always satisfy a commitment if it is consistent to do so, and will avoid introducing commitments (temporal 'sometime' formula) if able to, by making a choice containing only literal predicates. These preferences are built-in to METATEM, however the prefer construct allows the developer to modify the outcome of METATEM's choice procedure by re-ordering the list of choices according to a declared pair of predicates (e.g. prefer(win, lose)) after the fundamental ordering has been applied. We refer to the prefer construct as a deliberation meta-predicate and the architecture of the current METATEM allows the implementation of further deliberation meta-predicates as 'plug-ins'.

Each of these constructs can be declared as applicable in all circumstances or as context dependent, that is, only applicable when a given formula is true. Typically this formula might be an inContext/1 or inContent/1 predicate when one is expressing an agent's preferences or constraints when acting under the influence of another agent (the concept and purpose of Context/Content is explained in Section 1.2.1.3). Furthermore, each preference is assigned an integer weighting, within the (arbitrary) range of 1–99, which allows a fine-grained ordering of preferences[3].

For example, the following snippets are two alternative applications of the prefer construct to the lift example described above, to encourage the lift to continue moving in the same direction when appropriate;

```
prefer downTo to upTo when moving(down) weight 50;
prefer upTo to downTo when moving(up) weight 50;

prefer("downTo","upTo","moving(down)",50)
prefer("upTo","downTo","moving(up)",50)
```

---

[3] We reserve the weighting values 0 and 100 for built-in preferences.

The first two directives above are examples of those that appear in the preamble of an agent definition file[4], these preferences apply from time, $t = 0$. The latter two directives are examples of meta-predicates that, when appearing in the consequents of a temporal NEXT rule, will provide the agent with the declared preference from the temporal state following the state in which the rule was fired. The former type is simply a syntactic convenience for a rule of the type

```
start => prefer("downTo","upTo","moving(down)",50)
```

Once a preference is applied it is upheld for all future states and there is no mechanism for explicitly deleting it, instead preferences can be *overridden* by an otherwise identical preference which declares a higher priority value or *counteracted* by an opposing preference. However, the use of context dependent preferences is encouraged as leaving a context provides the effect of deleting a preference but with the benefit that the preference will be reinstated upon entering the relevant context. We believe this is a natural interpretation of preferences.

1.2.1.3 Multiple Agents

METATEM supports the asynchronous, concurrent execution of multiple agents which are able to send one another messages that are guaranteed to arrive at some future moment in time. Each agent has its own concept of time and the duration of each time step for an individual agent is neither fixed nor constant throughout execution. Conceptually then, the transition of multiple agents between successive temporal states is as depicted in Fig. 1.1.

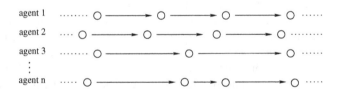

Fig. 1.1 Typical asynchronous agent execution.

Note. The form of asynchronous execution seen in Fig. 1.1 is a little problematic for propositional temporal logic to represent straight-forwardly. However, as described in [12] a temporal logic based on the *Real Numbers* rather than the Natural Numbers, provides an appropriate semantic basis. Importantly, the propositional fragment of such a *Temporal Logic of the Reals* required still remains decidable [26]. An agent sends a message to another agent by making the action predicate *send(Recipient, Message)* true in one of its own states. This guarantees that at some future moment the predicate *receive(From, Message)* will be true in

---

[4] A more detailed description of the agent file is given in Section 1.3

at least one state of the recipient agent (where *Recipient*, *From* and *Message* are all terms and are substituted by the recipient agent's name, the sending agent's name and the message content, respectively). The *send* predicate is an example of a special 'action' predicate which, when made true, prevents subsequent backtracking over the state in which it holds. For this reason, the use of a deliberate–act style of programming is encouraged in which an agent explores multiple execution paths, performing only retractable internal actions, backtracking when necessary, before taking a non-retractable action.

Although METATEM agents exist as individual threads within a single Java™ virtual machine there are no other predefined agent containers or agent spaces that maintain a centralised structuring of multiple agents. Instead METATEM follows an agent-centred approach to multi-agent development with the only implemented interactions between autonomous agents being message passing. Support for the abstract structuring of agent societies is provided by internal (to each agent) constructs and is discussed in detail in the next section.

Agent structuring: Content and Context.

At the implementation level, and as the default abstraction, agents occupy a single flat structure (potentially physically distributed). However, each agent maintains two sets of agent references named 'Content' and 'Context' which provide the flexibility to represent a wide range of inter-agent relationships and multi-agent structuring [22, 8], as can be represented as in Fig. 1.2.

Fig. 1.2 An abstract representation of a single METATEM agent.

The actual meaning of a relationship between an agent and the members of its Content and its counterpart Context is entirely flexible and dependent on the application being tackled. That is, during the initial analysis stage of an agent-oriented software engineering process when the most appropriate abstraction(s) are determined, it may be declared that the Content set of an agent who acts as a team leader are the agents that comprise its team. Alternatively, an agent may be declared to represent an aspect of the environment, and those agents who have the 'environment' agent in their Content set have that aspect of the environment within their sphere of influence. An agent specification then, contains its temporal specification (its behaviour) along with its Content and Context sets.

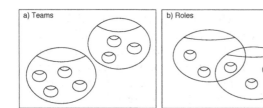 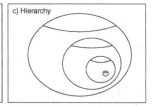

Fig. 1.3 A selection of METATEM agent structures, with possible interpretations; a) two teams of agents, b) five agents fulfilling two roles (one agent fulfils both roles), and c) a nested hierarchy of agents.

Structurally, an agent's Content set are those agents an agent is said to "contain" and its Context are those it is "contained by". But abstractly, and capturing the social nature of multi-agent systems, an agent's Context should be viewed as the set of agents that influence its own behaviour and its Content as those agents whose behaviour it has some influence over. These agents sets are used to store the multi-agent structure in a truly distributed manner that not only allows a wide range of structures and abstractions to be implemented (as illustrated in Fig. 1.3) but also allows dynamic structural changes at run-time without central organisation.

Predicates	Actions
inContent(Agent)	addToContent(Agent)
inContext(Agent)	enterContext(Agent)
enteredContent(Agent)	removeFromContent(Agent)
enteredContext(Agent)	leaveContext(Agent)
leftContent(Agent)	
leftContext(Agent)	

Table 1.1 Some of the system predicates and actions that can be used by METATEM agents to reason about, and modify, their Content and Context sets.

Crucially, an agent is able to reason about, and modify, its relationship with other agents at any given moment in time using the system predicates and action predicates listed in Table 1.1. In the case of the inContent/1 and inContext/1 predicates, they hold true for all agents that are members of Content (and Context respectively) and for all moments in time that they remain members. The actions listed can only be made true by the agent whose Content (and Context respectively) is modified; in each case making the action true entails that in the next moment in time the modification has taken effect, i.e. for Content, the following rules apply.

```
addToContent(a) => NEXT inContent(a);

removeContent(a) => NEXT ~inContent(a);.
```

Multicast message passing

One of the most advantageous practical benefits of the Context/Content grouping described above, is their use in message passing. For, as well as sending messages to individual named agents, a METATEM agent can address messages to sets of agents using a number of supported set expressions. The terms `Content` and `Context` are in fact literal set expressions which can be used to build larger expressions using the operators `UNION`, `INTERSECTION` and `WITHOUT`, for instance an agent can send a message to the set `Content UNION Context`. Additionally, an agent can send a message to all agents who share the same Context, *without maintaining an explicit reference to those agents*. The three fundamental multicasts are depicted in Fig. 1.4.

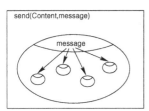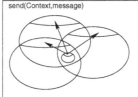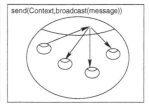

Fig. 1.4 The three fundamental forms of multicast messaging across METATEM's multi-agent structure.

It is expected that the membership of an agent's Content and Context sets changes at runtime, as is appropriate for the agent's activity in the modelled system. The inclusion of a third set of agents called the `Known` set contains all agents an agent has ever encountered. It retains a references to those agents who once belonged to `Content` or `Context` sets after they have left [5].

1.2.2 Semantics and Verification

Programs in METATEM essentially comprise formulae in SNF normal form [13], together with annotations concerning communication and organisation. It is important to note that *any* temporal logic formula can be translated to an equivalent one in SNF (be it propositional, or first-order) in polynomial time. Once we have a set of SNF formulae representing the behaviour of an agent, we can begin execution. Without external interaction, such execution essentially corresponds to model construction for the formulae. Thus, an important theorem from [2, 1] concerning propositional temporal logic is

---

[5] The intended purpose of an agent's `Known` set is that of a list of contacts or address book and is partly implemented for efficiency reasons.

Theorem 1.1. *If a set of SNF rules, R, is executed using the* METATEM *algorithm, with the proviso that the oldest outstanding eventualities are attempted first at each step, then a model for R will be generated if, and only if, R is satisfiable.*

Once we add deliberation, for example re-ordering of outstanding eventualities, then this theorem becomes:

Theorem 1.2. *If a set of SNF rules, R, is executed using the* METATEM *algorithm, with a fair[6] ordering strategy for outstanding eventualities, then a model for R will be generated if, and only if, R is satisfiable.*

Thus, the *fair ordering strategy* restriction imposes a form of *fairness* on the eventuality choice mechanism [18].

It is also important to note that, once we move to either the execution of full first-order temporal specifications, or we consider the execution of an agent in an unknown environment, then completeness *can not* be guaranteed. At this stage we are only *attempting* to build a model for the temporal formula captured within the program.

If, however, we have specifications of all the participants in the multi-agent system, together with a strong specification of the communication and execution aspects, then we can, in principle, develop a full specification for the whole system. If this specification is within a decidable fragment, then we can analyse such specifications automatically.

An alternative approach is to consider the *operational semantics* of METATEM and use model checking. In [7] a common semantic basis for many agent programming languages was given, with METATEM being one of the languages considered. In [3], a model checker was developed for this common core and so, in principle, METATEM agents can be verified via this route also (although model-checking for METATEM agents has not yet been carried out).

1.2.3 Software Engineering Issues

In common with many agent-oriented languages, the aim of METATEM is to capture the highest level of deliberative behaviour required of a system and to provide a clear and concise set of constructs with which to express it. It is anticipated that METATEM code will account for only a small minority of a given system's code-base, whilst the majority of functionality will be engineered with whichever traditional (or otherwise) technique is most appropriate for the application domain concerned. Software engineering issues for METATEM therefore reduce to the following questions. Which methodologies are recommended/suited to the engineering of systems that employ METATEM agents? Can a METATEM agent

---

[6] By *fair* we mean a strategy that ensures that if an eventuality is outstanding for an inﬁﬁÄnite number of steps, then at some point in the execution that eventuality will continually be attempted.

be interfaced with other technologies? In this section we attempt to answer these questions.

1.2.3.1 Methodology

Although much work can be done to improve our understanding of this important aspect of agent technology, we are able to make some constructive comments about techniques that have been employed during METATEM's evolution. The METATEM approach can be considered a generalisation of a number of programming techniques, for instance, from object-oriented programming; agents can be readily organised into access-controlled groups [21] (akin to packages) and a type system that implements a kind of inheritance has been adopted as a method of ensuring that certain behavioural contracts are fulfilled.

Whilst informal agent-oriented design methodologies such as Gaia [31] and Prometheus [28] are well suited to capturing global system behaviour and agent interactions, we feel that the behaviour of an individual METATEM agent requires a more formal design approach if the principle benefit of the execution method is to be realised (that of direct execution of a logical specification). One way to arrive at a precise representation of an individual agent's behaviour is to model it as a finite-state machine [16]. The derivation of temporal formulae from such a model is a largely mechanical process.

In other work [15], an iterative approach to system design has been explored that makes use of the agent grouping structures to make iterative refinement of a design, by decomposing atomic agents into groups of sub-ordinate agents. In this way, by adopting appropriate organisation abstractions during each iteration, complex structures and relationships are developed. This is a promising approach but needs further development.

1.2.3.2 Integration

A truly agent centred philosophy has been adopted throughout the evolution of the METATEM approach to multi-agent programming, that considers all entities to be an agent with an associated temporal specification. Thus, system components that are developed and implemented with technology other than agent-oriented technology[7] must be wrapped inside a METATEM agent. A straightforward method for achieving this via a Java API is provided, such that any technology that can be interfaced with Java, can also be interfaced with METATEM.

---

[7] In fact, any technology other than METATEM!

1.2.4 Extensions

A number of extensions to METATEM have been explored, by the authors and others, all of which have previously published theory and some of which have benefited from an implementation. However, as none are yet included in the current METATEM implementation we simply provide a list and refer the reader to relevant publications.

1. Belief predicates and epistemic properties have been explored in [14] and are expected to be included in the current METATEM implementation in the future.
2. Bounded belief and resource-bounded reasoning is described in [19, 20] and it is intended that this is implemented alongside item 1 above.
3. Probabilistic belief was explored by Ferreira et al. in [6, 5].
4. The use of METATEM as a high-level process coordination language has been explored in [25].
5. More recently, the notion of context and its applicability to agent organisation is the subject of ongoing research [8, 9].

1.3 Platform

A METATEM implementation, its documentation and some simple examples are available from the following URL.

```
http://www.csc.liv.ac.uk/~anthony/metatem.html
```

1.3.1 Defining Programs

The METATEM system is a `Java` application that has no dependencies other than a `Java` Runtime Environment that supports `Java 6.0` code. Defining a multi-agent system with METATEM involves creating the following source files (each are plain-text files):

1. System file;
2. Agent file;
3. Rule file.

System file. The system file declares the agents and the initial relationships between agents. For each agent, a name is declared and a type is given that corresponds with an agent file. Any initial relationships between the declared agents are declared by enumerating the members of each agent's `Content`, `Context` and `Known` sets. An example system file is shown below.

```
agent fred : "example/robot.agent";
agent Barney : "example/robot.agent";
agent wilma : "example/boss.agent";

fred {
Context : wilma;
}

barney {
Known : wilma, barney;
}

wilma {
Content : wilma;
Known : barney;
}
```

Agent file. An agent file is defined for each agent type. It defines a METATEM program by declaring and importing a series of temporal constraints and rule blocks. In most cases, the majority of an agent file's content will be any number of rule blocks, each containing the runtime behaviour of an agent and described using the three rule types described in Section 1.2.1. In the preamble to these rule blocks a number of abilities, runtime options, meta-predicates and include statements can be declared. An example agent file is shown below.

```
// a traffic light controller
type agent;

ability timer: metatem.agent.ability.Timer;

at_least 1 red;
at_most 1 green;
at_most 1 amber;

startblock: {
 start => red(east_west);
 start => red(north_south);
}

ruleblock: {

 // illegal combinations
 amber(X) => ~green(X);
 red(X) => ~green(X);
```

```
// when red it must at some time turn to amber...
red(X) => SOMETIME amber(X);

//... but not before the other light is red only
red(X) & amber(Y) & X\=Y => NEXT ~amber(X);
red(X) & green(Y) & X\=Y => NEXT ~amber(X);

// red must hold when amber is shown
red(X) & ~amber(X) => NEXT red(X);

// once amber is shown, green can be displayed
amber(X) & red(X) => NEXT green(X);
amber(X) & red(X) => NEXT ~amber(X);

// amber follows green
green(X) => NEXT amber(X) | green(X);
green(X) => NEXT ~red(X);

// red follows a single amber
amber(X) & ~red(X) => NEXT red(X);
}
```

Rule file. Rule files are a programming convenience that allows multiple agent types to re-use rule-blocks via 'include' statements. They contain only rule blocks.

The full syntax of each file type, in Backus-Naur form, is provided in the system documentation.

1.3.1.1 Built-in predicates

On top of the support for first order logic, METATEM provides a number of constructs commonly found in Prolog implementations and sometimes known as built-in predicates. Arithmetic is supported by the is/2 and lessThan/2 predicates. The declaration and manipulation of sets is achieved with set expressions that support *set union*, *set intersection* and *set difference* operators. Finally, *quoted* terms are supported along with a number of built-in predicates that allow a formula to be represented as a term if required.

1.3.1.2 Agent abilities

METATEM's mechanism for giving agents the ability to act on their environment is achieved via special predicates we call *abilities*. The platform provides send and `timer` abilities which allow agents to send messages to other agents immediately and to themselves after a period of delay, respectively. Application specific actions are supported by the METATEM API and involve the creation of a `Java` class that extends the API's `AgentAbility` class for each action. Once declared in the header of an agent file, abilities may appear wherever it is valid for a conventional predicate to appear. Abilities have the same logical semantics, on a state by state basis, as conventional predicates. However, a special 'external' ability type exists which, when executed in a state, prevents the METATEM interpreter from backtracking over that state. Characterisation of abilities as internal or external is of course dependent upon the application but as an example, a database select query might be implemented as an internal ability whereas an update query might be considered external. Internal abilities are reversible in the sense that it is safe to backtrack over them without the need for an equal and opposite action—as the action is deemed to have no side-effects.

1.3.2 Available tools and documentation

The current version of METATEM has a default command-line execution and output, however a basic graphical visualisation tool is also provided that provides a dynamic visualisation of the relationships between agents during execution and a monitoring facility that provides the ability to isolate individual agents and monitor their logical state. Proposals for the near future include a web interface for online demonstration and teaching purposes. A screen-shot of the tool showing the visualisation of example multi-agent structures is given in Fig. 1.5.

Developer's documentation is included in the download available from the project web page.

1.3.3 Standards compliance, interoperability and portability

The current METATEM implementation is written entirely in `Java` using no platform dependent APIs and is thus portable to any platform supporting a `Java` `1.6` (or later) runtime environment. Although METATEM does not support heterogeneous agents directly, the creation of METATEM wrapper agents for heterogeneous agents is possible and covered by the developers' documentation.

METATEM agents are executed concurrently, each having a thread of their own in the same virtual machine. There are no plans to distribute agents across a network but the current implementation does not preclude this extension if it were required.

It is important to note that the use of logical notations, together with strong notions of execution and completeness, ensure that the language has a close relationship with its semantics. The flexibility of general first-order predicates, and

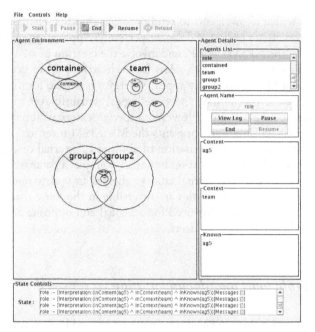

Fig. 1.5 A visualisation tool for the control and monitoring of METATEM agents.

of the content/context structures, ensures that semantics are both user definable and transparent.

1.3.4 Other features of the platform

METATEM's most distinctive feature is the inclusion of structuring constructs in the core of the language (Context and Content sets) which enable agent organisation techniques that have the flexibility to be user-definable.

The nature of the declarative logic that describes the behaviour of a METATEM agent can lead, in cases where agents are faced with many choices, to slow execution. In these cases, one can often ameliorate the effects of logical complexity by appropriate use of the deliberation meta predicates discussed in Section 1.2.1.2.

1.4 Applications supported by the language and/or the platform

We should make it clear that the current METATEM implementation is a prototype implementation that has been put to experimental use and has not been used for any real-world applications, though we now feel it is mature enough to be considered for use in the wider academic world. Its formal underpinnings and strong semantics make it a natural choice for application areas that require a high degree of clarity at a high-level of abstraction, particularly where time features prominently in the specification or where verification of system properties may be required. Features of the implementation such as meta-deliberation make METATEM a candidate language when agents must have the ability to reason about and/or modify their own reasoning, whilst the built-in agent grouping mechanism aims to support applications that comprise a significant number of agents with overlapping concerns. The natural handling of concurrency as autonomous METATEM agents, each defined by a formal temporal specification, lends itself to use as a language for coordinating processes between which dependencies exist—the specification of a coordination model [25]. The authors believe that METATEM will prove useful for the specifcation of highly distributed systems such as those found in pervasive computing scenarios, this is therefore the focus of their current application research.

Though the current platform has not been applied widely, the METATEM language itself has been used in (or at least has inspired work in) several areas. For example, in tackling planning, temporal logics have been increasingly used to control search. In [27] direct execution of temporal formula is used to directly implement planning. METATEM, and specifically the underlying normal form, provide a concise description of temporal behaviours and this has been used in [4] to implement a form of agent verification. Similarly, the encoding of verification problems using the METATEM rule form has been shown to be beneficial to the efficiency of model checkers [23].

Acknowledgements Many people have influenced the current METATEM implementation but Benjamin Hirsch and Chiara Ghidini must be thanked for their significant contribution to the current implementation and agent grouping strategies, respectively. In addition, thanks go to Michael Cieslar for developing the graphical visualisation tool.

References

1. Barringer, H., Fisher, M., Gabbay, D., Owens, R., Reynolds, M. (eds.): The Imperative Future: Principles of Executable Temporal Logics. John Wiley & Sons, Inc., New York, NY, USA (1996)
2. Barringer, H., Fisher, M., Gabbay, D.M., Gough, G., Owens, R.: METATEM: An introduction. Formal Aspects of Computing 7(5), 533–549 (1995)

3. Bordini, R.H., Dennis, L.A., Farwer, B., Fisher, M.: Automated Verification of Multi-Agent Programs. In: Proc. 23rd IEEE/ACM International Conference on Automated Software Engineering (ASE), pp. 69–78 (2008)
4. Costantini, S., Dell'Acqua, P., Pereira, L.M., Tsintza, P.: Specification and Dynamic Verification of Agent Properties. In: Proc. Ninth International Conference on Computational Logic in Multi-Agent Systems (2008)
5. de Carvalho Ferreira, N., Fisher, M., van der Hoek, W.: Specifying and Reasoning about Uncertain Agents. International Journal of Approximate Reasoning **49**(1), 35–51 (2008)
6. de Carvalho Ferreira, N., Fisher, M., van der Hoek, W.: Logical Implementation of Uncertain Agents. In: Proceedings of 12th Portuguese Conference on Artificial Intelligence (EPIA), *Lecture Notes in Computer Science*, vol. 3808. Springer (2005)
7. Dennis, L.A., Farwer, B., Bordini, R.H., Fisher, M., Wooldridge, M.: A Common Semantic Basis for BDI Languages. In: Proc. Seventh International Workshop on Programming Multiagent Systems (ProMAS), *Lecture Notes in Artificial Intelligence*, vol. 4908, pp. 124–139. Springer Verlag (2008)
8. Dennis, L.A., Fisher, M., Hepple, A.: A Common Basis for Agent Organisation in BDI Languages. In: Proc. 1st International Workshop on LAnguages, methodologies and Development tools for multi-agent Systems (LADS), *Lecture Notes in Computer Science*, vol. 5118, pp. 171–188. Springer (2008)
9. Dennis, L.A., Fisher, M., Hepple, A.: Language Constructs for Multi-Agent Programming. In: Proc. 8th Workshop on Computational Logic in Multi-Agent Systems (CLIMA), *Lecture Notes in Artificial Intelligence*, vol. 5056, pp. 137–156. Springer (2008)
10. Dixon, C., Fisher, M., Konev, B.: Temporal Logic with Capacity Constraints. In: Proc. 6th International Symposium on Frontiers of Combining Systems, *Lecture Notes in Computer Science*, vol. 4720, pp. 163–177. Springer (2007)
11. Emerson, E.A.: Temporal and Modal Logic. In: J. van Leeuwen (ed.) Handbook of Theoretical Computer Science, pp. 996–1072. Elsevier (1990)
12. Fisher, M.: A Temporal Semantics for Concurrent METATEM. Journal of Symbolic Computation **22**(5/6), 627–648 (1996)
13. Fisher, M.: A Normal Form for Temporal Logic and its Application in Theorem-Proving and Execution. Journal of Logic and Computation **7**(4), 429–456 (1997)
14. Fisher, M.: Implementing BDI-like systems by direct execution. In: Proceedings of the 15th International Joint Conference on Artificial Intelligence (IJCAI), vol. 1, pp. 316–321. Morgan Kaufmann, San Fransisco, CA, USA (1997)
15. Fisher, M.: Towards the Refinement of Executable Temporal Objects. In: H. Bowman, J. Derrick (eds.) Formal Methods for Open Object-Based Distributed Systems. Chapman & Hall (1997)
16. Fisher, M.: Temporal Development Methods for Agent-Based Systems. Journal of Autonomous Agents and Multi-Agent Systems **10**(1), 41–66 (2005)
17. Fisher, M.: Temporal Representation and Reasoning. In: F. van Harmelen, B. Porter, V. Lifschitz (eds.) Handbook of Knowledge Representation, *Foundations of Artificial Intelligence*, vol. 2. Elsevier Press (2007)
18. Fisher, M.: Agent Deliberation in an Executable Temporal Framework. Technical Report ULCS-08-014, Department of Computer Science, University of Liverpool, UK (2008)
19. Fisher, M., Ghidini, C.: Programming Resource-Bounded Deliberative Agents. In: Proc. 16th International Joint Conference on Artificial Intelligence (IJCAI), pp. 200–205. Morgan Kaufmann (1999)
20. Fisher, M., Ghidini, C.: Exploring the Future with Resource-Bounded Agents. Journal of Logic, Language and Information **18**(1), 3–21 (2009)
21. Fisher, M., Ghidini, C., Hirsch, B.: Programming Groups of Rational Agents. In: Proc, International Workshop on Computational Logic in Multi-Agent Systems IV (CLIMA), *Lecture Notes in Artificial Intelligence*, vol. 3259, pp. 16–33. Springer-Verlag, Heidelberg, Germany (2004)

22. Fisher, M., Kakoudakis, T.: Flexible Agent Grouping in Executable Temporal Logic. In: Proceedings of Twelfth International Symposium on Languages for Intensional Programming (ISLIP). World Scientific Press (1999)
23. Frisch, A.M., Sheridan, D., Walsh, T.: A Fixpoint Based Encoding for Bounded Model Checking. In: Proc. 4th International Conference on Formal Methods in Computer-Aided Design (FMCAD), *Lecture Notes in Computer Science*, vol. 2517, pp. 238–255. Springer (2002)
24. Gabbay, D.: Declarative Past and Imperative Future: Executable Temporal Logic for Interactive Systems. In: B. Banieqbal, H. Barringer, A. Pnueli (eds.) Proceedings of Colloquium on Temporal Logic in Specification, pp. 402–450. Altrincham, U.K. (1987). (Published in *Lecture Notes in Computer Science*, volume 398, Springer-Verlag)
25. Kellett, A., Fisher, M.: Concurrent METATEM as a Coordination Language. In: Coordination Languages and Models, *Lecture Notes in Computer Science*, vol. 1282. Springer-Verlag (1997)
26. Kesten, Y., Manna, Z., Pnueli, A.: Temporal Verification of Simulation and Refinement. In: A Decade of Concurrency, *Lecture Notes in Computer Science*, vol. 803, pp. 273–346. Springer-Verlag (1994)
27. Mayer, M.C., Limongelli, C., Orlandini, A., Poggioni, V.: Linear Temporal Logic as an Executable Semantics for Planning Languages. Journal of Logic, Language and Information **16**(1) (2007)
28. Padgham, L., Winikoff, M.: Developing Intelligent Agent Systems: A Practical Guide. John Wiley and Sons (2004)
29. Rao, A.S., Georgeff, M.P.: Modeling rational agents within a BDI-architecture. In: Proceedings of the 2nd International Conference on Principles of Knowledge Representation and Reasoning (KR), pp. 473–484. Morgan Kaufmann, San Fransisco, CA, USA (1991)
30. Rao, A.S., Georgeff, M.P.: BDI agents: From theory to practice. In: Proceedings of the 1st International Conference on Multi-Agent Systems (ICMAS), pp. 312–319. IEEE Press, Washington, DC, USA (1995)
31. Wooldridge, M., Jennings, N.R., Kinny, D.: The gaia methodology for agent-oriented analysis and design. Journal of Autonomous Agents and Multi-Agent Systems **3**(3), 285–312 (2000)

Chapter 2
IndiGolog: A High-Level Programming Language for Embedded Reasoning Agents

Giuseppe De Giacomo, Yves Lespérance, Hector J. Levesque, and Sebastian Sardina

Abstract IndiGolog is a programming language for autonomous agents that sense their environment and do planning as they operate. Instead of classical planning, it supports *high-level program execution*. The programmer provides a high-level nondeterministic program involving domain-specific actions and tests to perform the agent's tasks. The IndiGolog interpreter then reasons about the preconditions and effects of the actions in the program to find a legal terminating execution. To support this, the programmer provides a declarative specification of the domain (i.e., primitive actions, preconditions and effects, what is known about the initial state) in the situation calculus. The programmer can control the amount of non-determinism in the program and how much of it is searched over. The language is rich and supports concurrent programming. Programs are executed online together with sensing the environment and monitoring for events, thus supporting the development of reactive agents. We discuss the language, its implementation, and applications that have been realized with it.

Giuseppe De Giacomo
Dipartimento di Informatica e Sistemistica, Università di Roma "La Sapienza", Rome, Italy, e-mail: degiacomo@dis.uniroma1.it

Yves Lespérance
Department of Computer Science and Engineering, York University, Toronto, Canada, e-mail: lesperan@cse.yorku.ca

Hector J. Levesque
Department of Computer Science, University of Toronto, Toronto, Canada, e-mail: hector@cs.toronto.edu

Sebastian Sardina
School of Computer Science and Information Technology, RMIT University, Melbourne, Australia, e-mail: sebastian.sardina@rmit.edu.au

R.H. Bordini et al. (eds.), *Multi-Agent Programming*,
DOI 10.1007/978-0-387-89299-3_2, © Springer Science+Business Media, LLC 2009

2.1 Motivation

Designing autonomous agents that do the right thing in changing and incompletely known environments is challenging. The agent needs to adapt to changing environment conditions and user objectives. Architectures based on classical planning can provide flexibility and adaptability, but they often end up being too demanding computationally. Our approach of *high-level program execution* [61] aims for a middle ground between classical planning and normal programming. The idea, roughly, is that instead of searching for a sequence of actions that would take the agent from an initial state to some goal state, the task is to find a sequence of actions that constitutes a legal execution of some sketchy high-level non-deterministic program involving domain specific actions and tests. As in planning, to find a sequence that constitutes a legal execution of a high-level program, it is necessary to reason about the preconditions and effects of the actions within the body of the program. However, if the program happens to be almost deterministic, very little searching is required; as more and more non-determinism is included, the search task begins to resemble traditional planning. Thus, in formulating a high-level program, the programmer gets to control the search effort required.

The high-level program execution approach to agent programming was concretely realized in the Golog programming language [62], a procedural language defined on top of the situation calculus [71, 82], a predicate logic framework for reasoning about action. Golog (the name stands for "alGOl in LOGic") provides a full set of procedural constructs including conditionals, loops, recursive procedures, as well as several nondeterministic choice constructs. The interpreter for the language uses a situation calculus action theory representing the agent's beliefs about the state of the environment and the preconditions and effects of the actions to reason and find a provably correct execution of the program.

An extension of Golog called ConGolog (Concurrent Golog) [24] was later developed to provide concurrent programming facilities. Then, more recently, in IndiGolog (incremental deterministic Golog) [26, 87, 28], the framework was generalized to allow the programmer to control planning/lookahead and support online execution, sensing the environment, and execution monitoring.

In addition to these, there have been other proposals of languages based on the high-level program execution approach. One is Thielscher's FLUX language [99], which uses the fluent calculus as its formal foundation. As well, decision theoretic versions of the approach have been proposed yielding languages such as DTGolog [14, 97, 34].

In this chapter, we will focus our presentation on IndiGolog, briefly mentioning how it differs from Golog and ConGolog as we go along. The high-level program execution approach is related to work on planning with domain specific control information, such as hierarchical task network (HTN) planning [33], and planning with temporal logic control specifications [3].

The Golog family of high level agent programming languages can be contrasted with the more mainstream BDI agent programming languages/architectures, such as PRS [39] and its various successors, such as AgentSpeak [78], Jason [11], Jack [17], and JAM [45], as well as the closely related 3APL [44]. These were developed as a way of enabling *abstract plans* written by programmers to be combined and used in real-time, in a way that was both flexible and robust. These BDI agent programming languages were conceived as a simplified and operationalized version of the BDI (Belief, Desire, Intention) model of agency, which is rooted in philosophical work such as Bratman's [15] theory of practical reasoning and Dennet's theory of intentional systems [31]. In the BDI paradigm, agents are viewed, as well as built, as entities whose (rational) actions are a consequence of their mental attitudes, beliefs, desires, obligations, intentions, etc. Theoretical work on the BDI model has focused on the formal specification of the complex logical relationships among these mental attitudes (e.g., [22, 79]). But more practical work in the area has sought to develop BDI agent programming languages that incorporate a simplified BDI semantics basis that has a computational interpretation.

An important feature of BDI-style programming languages and platforms is their interleaved account of sensing, deliberation, and execution [76]. In BDI systems, *abstract plans* written by programmers are combined and executed in real-time. By executing as they reason, BDI agents reduce the likelihood that decisions will be made on the basis of outdated beliefs and remain responsive to the environment by making adjustments in the steps chosen as they proceed. Because of this, BDI agent programming languages are well suited to implementing systems that need to operate more or less in real time (e.g., air traffic control and unmanned aerial vehicles (UAVs), space shuttle monitoring, search and rescue co-ordination, internet electronic business, and automated manufacturing [66, 7, 32, 9]). Unlike in classical planning-based architectures, *execution* happens at each step, and there is no lookahead to check that the selected plan can be successfully expanded and executed. The assumption is that the careful crafting of plans' preconditions to ensure the selection of appropriate plans at execution time, together with a built-in mechanism for trying alternative options, will usually ensure that a successful execution is found, even in the context of a changing environment. The approach works well if good plans can be specified for all objectives that the agent may acquire and all contingencies that may arise. However, there are often too many possible objectives and contingencies for this to be practical. Trying alternative options may not work in an environment where choices cannot be "undone." Thus supplying some form of lookahead planning in an agent programming language remains valuable provided it can be effectively controlled.

Various proposals have been made to incorporate planning (at execution time) in BDI agent programming languages. [89, 90] have proposed the CANPlan and CanPlan2 languages, that incorporate an HTN planning mechanism [33] into a classical BDI agent programming language. Earlier less formal work on this topic is reviewed in [89]. We will come back to the relationship between our high level agent programming approach and other work on agent programming languages in the final section of the chapter.

The rest of the chapter is organized as follows. In the next section, we present the syntax and semantics of IndiGolog and discuss the basis of the whole approach. In

Section 2.3, we discuss in details our platform for high-level program execution supporting IndiGolog. In Section 2.4, we briefly survey some of the applications that have been developed using it. After that, we conclude by discussing the distinguishing features of our approach and issues for future work.

2.2 Language

2.2.1 Syntactical Aspects

The Situation Calculus and Basic Action Theories

Our approach to agent programming relies on the agent being able to reason about its world and how it can change, whether for planning/lookahead, for updating its knowledge after executing an action or observing an exogenous action/event, for monitoring whether its actions are having the expected effects, etc. More specifically, we assume that the agent has a theory of action for the domain in which it operates, a theory which is specified in the situation calculus [71], a popular predicate logic formalism for representing dynamic domains and reasoning about action.

We will not go over the situation calculus in detail. We merely note the following components. There is a special constant S_0 used to denote the *initial situation*, namely that situation in which no actions have yet occurred. There is a distinguished binary function symbol do, where $do(a, s)$ denotes the successor situation to s resulting from performing the action a. For example, in a Blocks World, the situation term $do(put(A, B), do(put(B, C), S_0))$, could denote the situation where the agent has done the actions of first putting block B on block C and then putting block A on block B, after starting in the initial situation S_0. Relations (resp. functions) whose values vary from situation to situation, are called *fluents*, and are denoted by predicate (resp. function) symbols taking a situation term as their last argument. Thus, for example, we might have that block B was initially on the table, i.e. $OnTable(B, S_0)$, and after the agent put it on C, it no longer was, i.e. $\neg OnTable(B, do(put(B, C), S_0))$. There is also a special predicate $Poss(a, s)$ used to state that action a is executable in situation s.

Within this language, we can formulate action theories which describe how the world changes as the result of the available actions in the domain. Here, we use *basic action theories* [82], which include the following types of axioms:

- Axioms describing the initial situation, S_0.
- Action precondition axioms, one for each primitive action a, characterizing $Poss(a, s)$.
- Successor state axioms, one for each relational fluent F (resp. functional fluent f), which characterize the conditions under which $F(\mathbf{x}, do(a, s))$ holds (resp. $f(\mathbf{x}, do(a, s)) = v$) in terms of what holds in situation s; these axioms may

be compiled from effects axioms, but provide a solution to the frame problem [81].

- Unique names axioms for the primitive actions.
- A set of foundational, domain independent axioms for situations Σ as in [82].

Various ways of modeling sensing in the situation calculus have been proposed. One is to introduce a special fluent $SF(a, s)$ (for *sensed fluent value*) and axioms describing how the truth value of SF becomes correlated with those aspects of a situation which are being sensed by action a [58]. For example, the axiom

$$SF(senseDoor(d), s) \equiv Open(d, s)$$

states that the action *senseDoor(d)* tells the agent whether the door is open in situation s. For actions with no useful sensing information, one writes $SF(a, s) \equiv True$. In general, of course, sensing results are not binary. For example, reading the temperature could mean returning an integer or real number. See [93] on how these can be represented.

To describe an execution of a sequence of actions together with their sensing results, one can use the notion of a *history*, i.e., a sequence of pairs (a, μ) where a is a primitive action and μ is 1 or 0, a sensing result. Intuitively, the history $\sigma = (a_1, \mu_1) \cdot \ldots \cdot (a_n, \mu_n)$ is one where actions $a_1, \ldots, a_n$ happen starting in some initial situation, and each action a_i returns sensing result μ_i. We can use *end*$[\sigma]$ to denote the situation term corresponding to the history σ, and *Sensed*$[\sigma]$ to denote the formula of the situation calculus stating all sensing results of the history σ. Formally,

end$[\epsilon] = S_0$, where ϵ is the empty history; and
end$[\sigma \cdot (a, \mu)] = do(a, end[\sigma])$.

Sensed$[\epsilon] = True$;
Sensed$[\sigma \cdot (a, 1)] = Sensed[\sigma] \wedge SF(a, end[\sigma])$;
Sensed$[\sigma \cdot (a, 0)] = Sensed[\sigma] \wedge \neg SF(a, end[\sigma])$.

We illustrate how a domain is specified by giving a partial specification of the Wumpus World domain [92]:

$LocAgent(S_0) = \langle 1, 1 \rangle$,
$HasArrow(S_0)$,
$DirAgent(S_0) = right$,

$Poss(pickGold, s) \equiv IsGold(LocAgent(s), s)$,

$DirAgent(do(a, s)) = y \equiv$
$\qquad (a = turnRight \wedge DirAgent(s) = down \wedge y = left) \vee$
$\qquad \ldots \vee (a \neq turnRight \wedge a \neq turnLeft \wedge DirAgent(s) = y)$.

Thus, the agent is initially on the $\langle 1, 1 \rangle$ square, facing in the *right* direction, and it has some arrows to shoot at the Wumpus. It is possible for the agent to perform the *pickGold* action in a situation s if there is a gold coin where the agent is located in s. The direction of the agent is y in the situation that results from action a being performed in situation s if and only if the action was to turn in the right direction (i.e. clockwise) and the agent was facing *down* in s and the new direction y is *left*, or any of several other cases of the agent doing a turning action (we leave out the details), or the agent's direction was already y in s and the action a is neither turning right nor turning left.

The IndiGolog Programming Constructs

Next we turn to programs. IndiGolog provides the following rich set of programming constructs (most of which are inherited from Golog [62] and ConGolog [24]):

a,	primitive action
$\phi?$,	test/wait for a condition
$\delta_1; \delta_2$,	sequence
$\delta_1 \mid \delta_2$,	nondeterministic branch
$\pi\, x.\, \delta$,	nondeterministic choice of argument
δ^*,	nondeterministic iteration
if ϕ **then** δ_1 **else** δ_2 **endIf**,	conditional
while ϕ **do** δ **endWhile**,	while loop
$\delta_1 \parallel \delta_2$,	concurrency with equal priority
$\delta_1 \rangle\!\rangle \delta_2$,	concurrency with δ_1 at a higher priority
$\delta^\parallel$,	concurrent iteration
$\langle \phi \rightarrow \delta \rangle$,	interrupt
proc $P(\mathbf{x})\ \delta$ **endProc**,	procedure definition
$P(\boldsymbol{\theta})$,	procedure call
$\Sigma(\delta)$,	search operator

In the first line, a stands for a situation calculus action term where the special situation constant *now* may be used to refer to the current situation (i.e. that where a is to be executed). Similarly, in the line below, ϕ stands for a situation calculus formula where *now* may be used to refer to the current situation, for example $OnTable(block, now)$. We use $a[s]$ ($\phi[s]$) for the action (formula) obtained by substituting the situation variable s for all occurrences of *now* in functional fluents appearing in a (functional and predicate fluents appearing in ϕ). Moreover when no confusion can arise, we often leave out the *now* argument from fluents altogether; e.g. write $OnTable(block)$ instead of $OnTable(block, now)$. In such cases, the situation suppressed version of the action or formula should be understood as an abbreviation for the version with *now*.

Among the constructs listed, we notice the presence of nondeterministic constructs. These include ($\delta_1 \mid \delta_2$), which nondeterministically chooses between programs δ_1 and δ_2, $\pi\, x.\, \delta$, which nondeterministically picks a binding for the variable x and performs the program δ for this binding of x, and δ^*, which performs δ zero or more times. $\pi\, x_1, \ldots, x_n.\, \delta$ is an abbreviation for $\pi\, x_1. \ldots .\pi\, x_n\, \delta$.

Test actions ϕ? can be used to control which branches may be executed, e.g., $[(\phi?; \delta_1) \mid (\neg\phi?; \delta_2)]$ will perform δ_1 when ϕ is true and δ_2 when ϕ is false (we use [...] and (...) interchangeably to disambiguate structure in programs). A test can also be used to constrain the value of a nondeterministically bound variable, e.g., $\pi\, x.\, [\phi(x)?; \delta(x)]$ will perform $\delta(x)$ with x bound to a value that satisfies $\phi(x)$ (or fail if no such value exists). Finally, as we discuss below, tests can also be used to synchronize concurrent processes.

The constructs if ϕ then δ_1 else δ_2 endIf and while ϕ do δ endWhile are the synchronized versions of the usual if-then-else and while-loop. They are synchronized in the sense that testing the condition ϕ does not involve a transition per se: the evaluation of the condition and the first action of the branch chosen are executed as an atomic unit. So these constructs behave in a similar way to the test-and-set atomic instructions used to build semaphores in concurrent programming.[1]

We also have constructs for concurrent programming. In particular $(\delta_1 \parallel \delta_2)$ expresses the concurrent execution (interpreted as interleaving) of the programs/processes δ_1 and δ_2. Observe that a process may become blocked when it reaches a primitive action whose preconditions are false or a test/wait action ϕ? whose condition ϕ is false. Then, execution of the program may continue provided that another process executes next. When the condition causing the blocking becomes true, the no longer blocked process can resume execution.

Another concurrent programming construct is $(\delta_1 \rangle\!\rangle \delta_2)$, where δ_1 has higher priority than δ_2, and δ_2 may only execute when δ_1 is done or blocked. $\delta^{\parallel}$ is like nondeterministic iteration δ^*, but the instances of δ are executed concurrently rather than in sequence.

Finally, one may include interrupts in a concurrent program to immediately "react" to a condition becoming true. An interrupt $\langle \phi \rightarrow \delta \rangle$ has a trigger condition ϕ, and a body δ. If the interrupt gets control from higher priority processes and the condition ϕ is true, the interrupt triggers and the body is executed, suspending any lower priority processes that may have been executing. Once the interrupt body completes execution, the suspended lower priority processes may resume. The interrupt may also trigger again (when its condition becomes true). $\langle \mathbf{x} : \phi \rightarrow \delta \rangle$ is an abbreviation for $\langle \exists\mathbf{x}.\phi \rightarrow \pi\mathbf{x}.[\phi?; \delta] \rangle$. The language also allows for recursive procedures, and other convenient constructs can easily be defined, usually as abbreviations.

Finally, the *search operator* $\Sigma(\delta)$ is used to specify that lookahead should be performed over the (nondeterministic) program δ to ensure that nondeterministic choices are resolved in a way that guarantees its successful completion. When a program is not in a search block, nondeterministic choices are resolved externally from the program executor, and hence, to the executor, look like they are made in an arbitrary way. The search operator can thus be used by the programmer to

---

[1] In [62], non-synchronized versions of if-then-elses and while-loops are introduced by defining: if ϕ then δ_1 else δ_2 endIf $\overset{\text{def}}{=} [(\phi?; \delta_1) \mid (\neg\phi?; \delta_2)]$ and while ϕ do δ endWhile $\overset{\text{def}}{=} [(\phi?; \delta)^*; \neg\phi?]$. The synchronized versions of these constructs introduced here behave essentially as the non-synchronized ones in absence of concurrency. However the difference is significant when concurrency is allowed.

control the scope of lookahead search (this is a new feature in IndiGolog [26, 87]; in Golog and ConGolog lookahead search over the whole program is automatically performed). We discuss the semantics of the search operator in the next section.

Some Examples

We illustrate how one specifies an agent's behavior in IndiGolog with some examples from the Wumpus World application [92]. If the Wumpus is known to be alive at a location l which is aligned with the agent's location, then the agent executes procedure shoot(d) with the direction d at which the Wumpus is known to be. The procedure is in charge of aiming and shooting the arrow at direction d; it is defined using a search block as follows:

> **proc** shoot(d)
> $\Sigma[(turnRight^* \mid turnLeft^*); (DirAgent = d)?; shootFwd]$
> **endProc**

The agent's main control procedure, which is to be executed online is as follows:

> **proc** mainControl
> $\langle d, l : LocWumpus = l \land AliveWumpus = \texttt{true} \land$
> $\qquad Aligned(LocAgent, d, LocWumpus) \longrightarrow$ shoot(d)$\rangle$
> $\rangle\rangle$
> $\langle IsGold(LocAgent) = \texttt{true} \longrightarrow pickGold\rangle$
> $\rangle\rangle$
> $\langle InDungeon = \texttt{true} \longrightarrow$
> $\qquad smell; senseBreeze; senseGold;$
> $\qquad [(\neg HoldingGold?; \text{explore}) \mid (HoldingGold?; goto(\langle 1, 1 \rangle); climb)]\rangle$
> **endProc**

Here, we use a set of prioritized interrupts to ensure that the agent reacts immediately to threats/opportunities: if the agent comes to know that the Wumpus is in shooting range (highest priority interrupt), it interrupts whatever it was doing and immediately executes the procedure "shoot" with the appropriate direction argument; otherwise, if it comes to know that there is gold at the current location (medium priority interrupt), it immediately picks it up; otherwise, finally, if it is in the dungeon (lowest priority interrupt), it senses its surroundings and then either executes the "explore" procedure when it is not yet carrying gold or exits the dungeon otherwise. The program terminates when the conditions of all the interrupts become false, i.e., when the agent is no longer in the dungeon.

To further illustrate how the search operator can be used, consider the following example (adapted from one in [57]) of an iterative deepening search procedure to find a robot delivery schedule/route that serves all clients and minimizes the distance traveled by the robot; one calls the procedure using $\Sigma(\text{minimizeDistance}(0))$:

proc minimizeDistance($dist$)

```
        serveAllClientsWithin(dist)        % try to serve all clients in at most dist
        | minimizeDistance(dist + 1)       % otherwise increment dist
endProc
```

```
proc serveAllClientsWithin(dist)
        ((¬∃c)ClientToServe(c))?           % when all clients served, exit
        |                                  % otherwise pick a client
        π c, d.[ (ClientToServe(c) ∧ DistanceTo(c) = d ∧ d ≤ dist)?;
            goTo(c); serve(c);             % serve selected client
            serveAllClientsWithin(dist − d)]   % serve remaining clients
endProc
```

Note that in "minimizeDistance," we rely on the fact that the IndiGolog implementation tries nondeterministic branches left-to-right, in Prolog fashion. It is possible to define a "try δ_1 otherwise δ_2" construct that eliminates the need for this assumption.

As a final example of the use of the search operator, consider the following procedures, which implement a generic iterative deepening planner (adapted from [82]):

```
proc IDPlan(maxl) % main iterative deepening planning procedure
        IDPlan2(0, maxl)
endProc
```

```
proc IDPlan2(l, maxl)
        BDFPlan(l)                    % try to find a plan of length l
        | [(l < maxl)?; IDPlan2(l + 1, maxl)] % else increment l up to maxl
endProc
```

```
procBDFPlan(l) % a bounded depth first planning procedure
        (Goal)? |
        [(l > 0)?; π a.(Acceptable(a))?; a; BDFPlan(l − 1)]
endProc
```

One calls the planning procedure using $\Sigma(\text{IDPlan}(N))$ where N is a plan length bound; *Goal* is a defined predicate specifying the goal and *Acceptable* is another defined predicate that can be used to filter what actions are considered in a given situation.

2.2.2 Semantics and Verification

Reasoning about Action: Projection via Regression and Progression

Our "high level program execution" framework requires reasoning about action. The executor must reason to check that its actions are possible and to determine whether the tests in the high-level program hold. This reasoning is required whether the agent is actually executing the program online or performing looka-head/planning to find a successful execution offline. So let's begin by discussing reasoning about action.

There are two well known reasoning tasks that our executor must perform. The main one is called the (temporal) *projection task*: determining whether or not some condition will hold after a sequence of actions has been performed starting in some initial state. The second one is called the *legality task*: determining whether a sequence of actions *can* be performed starting in some initial state. Assuming we have access to the preconditions of actions, legality reduces to projection, since we can determine legality by verifying that the preconditions of each action in the sequence are satisfied in the state just before the action is executed. Projection is a very basic task since it is necessary for a number of other larger tasks, including planning and high-level program execution, as we will see later in the chapter.

We can define projection in the situation calculus as follows: given an action the-ory $\mathcal{D}$, a sequence of ground action terms, $\mathbf{a} = [a_1, \ldots, a_n]$, and a formula $\phi[s]$ that is uniform in s (i.e. roughly where the only situation term that appears is s), the task is to determine whether or not

$$\mathcal{D} \models \phi[do(\mathbf{a}, S_0)].$$

Reiter [81] has shown that the projection problem can be solved by *regression*: when $\mathcal{D}$ is an action theory (as specified earlier), there is a regression operator $\mathcal{R}$, such that for any ϕ uniform in s,

$$\mathcal{D} \models \phi[do(\mathbf{a}, S_0)] \quad \text{iff} \quad \mathcal{D}_{una} \cup \mathcal{D}_{S_0} \models \phi'[S_0],$$

where $\mathcal{D}_{S_0}$ is the part of $\mathcal{D}$ that characterizes S_0, $\mathcal{D}_{una}$ is the set of unique name axioms for primitive actions, and $\phi' = \mathcal{R}(\phi, \mathbf{a})$. So to solve the projection prob-lem, it is sufficient, to regress the formula using the given actions, and then to determine whether result holds in the initial situation, a much simpler entailment. Regression has proved to be a powerful method for reasoning about a dynamic world, reducing it to reasoning about a static initial situation. However, it does have a serious drawback. Imagine a long-lived agent that has performed thousands or even millions of actions in its lifetime, and which at some point, needs to deter-mine whether some condition currently holds. Regression involves transforming this condition back through those many actions, and then determining whether the transformed condition held initially. This is not an ideal way of staying up to date.

The alternative to regression is *progression* [65]. In this case, we look for a progres-sion operator $\mathcal{P}$ that can transform an initial database $\mathcal{D}_{S_0}$ into the database that results after performing an action. More precisely, we want to have that

$$\mathcal{D} \models \phi[do(\mathbf{a}, S_0)] \quad \text{iff} \quad \mathcal{D}_{una} \cup \mathcal{D}'_0 \models \phi[S_0],$$

where $\mathcal{D}_{S_0}$ is the part of $\mathcal{D}$ that characterizes S_0, $\mathcal{D}_{una}$ is the set of unique name axioms for primitive actions, and $\mathcal{D}'_0 = \mathcal{P}(\mathcal{D}_{S_0}, \mathbf{a})$. The idea is that as actions are performed, an agent would change its database about the initial situation, so that to determine if ϕ held after doing actions $\mathbf{a}$, it would be sufficient to determine if ϕ held in the progressed situation (with no further actions), again a much simpler entailment. Moreover, unlike the case with regression, an agent can use its *mental idle time* (for example, while it is performing physical actions) to keep its database up to date. If it is unable to keep up, it is easy to imagine using regression until the database is fully progressed.

There are, however, drawbacks with progression as well. For one thing, it is geared to answering questions about the *current* situation only. In progressing a database forward, we effectively lose the historical information about what held in the past. It is, in other words, a form of *forgetting* [64, 47]. While questions about a current situation can reasonably be expected to be the most common, they are not the only meaningful ones.

A more serious concern with progression is that it is not always possible. As Lin and Reiter show [65], there are simple cases of basic action theories where there is no operator $\mathcal{P}$ with the properties we want. (More precisely, the desired $\mathcal{D}'_0$ would not be first-order definable.) To have a well-defined projection operator, it is necessary to impose further restrictions on the sorts of action theories we use, as we will see below.

Reasoning with Closed and Open World Knowledge Bases

So far, we have assumed like Reiter, that $\mathcal{D}_{S_0}$ is any collection of formulas uniform in S_0. Regression reduces the projection problem to that of calculating logical consequences of $\mathcal{D}_{S_0}$. In practice, however, we would like to reduce it to a much more tractable problem than ordinary first-order logical entailment. It it is quite common for applications to assume that $\mathcal{D}_{S_0}$ satisfies additional constraints: domain closure, unique names, and the closed-word assumption [80]. With these, for all practical purposes, $\mathcal{D}_{S_0}$ does behave like a database, and the entailment problem becomes one of database query evaluation. Furthermore, progression is well defined, and behaves like an ordinary database transaction.

Even without using (relational) database technology, the advantage of having a $\mathcal{D}_{S_0}$ constrained in this way is significant. For example, it allows us to use Prolog technology directly to perform projection. For example, to find out if $(\phi \vee \psi)$ holds, it is sufficient to determine if ϕ holds or if ψ holds; to find out if $\neg\phi$ holds, it is sufficient to determine if ϕ does not hold (using negation as failure), and so on. None of these are possible with an unconstrained $\mathcal{D}_{S_0}$.

This comes at a price, however. The unique name, domain closure and closed-world assumptions amount to assuming that we have *complete knowledge* about S_0: anytime we cannot infer that ϕ holds, it will be because we are inferring that $\neg\phi$ holds. We will never have the status of ϕ undecided. This is obviously a very strong assumption. Indeed we would expect that a typical agent might start with incomplete knowledge, and only acquire the information it needs by actively *sensing* its environment as necessary.

A proposal for modifying Reiter's proposal for the projection problem along these lines was made by De Giacomo and Levesque [27]. They show that a modified version of regression can be made to work with sensing information. They also consider how closed-world reasoning can be used in an open world using what they call *just-in-time queries*. In a nutshell, they require that queries be evaluated only in situations where enough sensing has taken place to give complete information about the query. Overall, the knowledge can be incomplete, but it will be locally complete, and allow us to use closed-world techniques.

Another independent proposal for dealing effectively with open-world reasoning is that of Liu and Levesque [106]. (Related proposals are made by Son and Baral [96] and by Amir and Russell [2].) They show that what they call *proper knowledge bases* represent open-world knowledge. They define a form of progression for these knowledge bases that provides an efficient solution to the projection problem that is always logically sound, and under certain circumstances, also logically complete. The restrictions involve the type of successor-state axioms that appear in the action theory $\mathcal{D}$: they require action theories that are *local-effect* (actions only change the properties of the objects that are parameters of the action) and *context-complete* (either the actions are context-free or there is complete knowledge about the context of the context-dependent ones). Vassos and Levesque [102] extended this approach to more general theories, while relying on the assumption that there is a finite domain and a restricted form of disjunctive knowledge in the initial database in order to remain first-order and tractable. In [103], they also show that an alternative definition of progression that is always first-order is nonetheless correct for reasoning about a large class of sentences. As well, in [101] they reconsider Lin and Reiter's progression (actually a slight variant that solves a few problems) and show that in case actions have only local effects, this form of progression is always first-order representable; moreover, for a restricted class of local-effect axioms they show how to construct a progressed database that remains finite.

The Offline Execution Semantics

Now let's return to the formal semantics of IndiGolog. This semantics is based on that of ConGolog, so we will go over the latter first. In [24], a single step structural operational (transition system) semantics in the style of [75] is defined for ConGolog programs. Two special predicates $Trans$ and $Final$ are introduced. $Trans(\delta, s, \delta', s')$ means that by executing program δ starting in situation s, one can get to situation s' in one elementary step with the program δ' remaining to be executed. $Final(\delta, s)$ means that program δ may successfully terminate in situation s.

Note that this semantics requires quantification over programs. To allow for this, [24] develops an encoding of programs as first-order terms in the logical language (observe that programs as such, cannot in general be first-order terms, since they mention formulas in tests, and the operator π in $\pi x.\delta$ is a sort of quantifier, hence an encoding is needed).[2] Encoding programs as first-order terms, although it requires some care (e.g. introducing constants denoting variables and defining substitution explicitly in the language), does not pose any major problem.[3] In the following we abstract from the details of the encoding as much as possible, and essentially use programs within formulas as if they were already first-order terms. The full encoding is given in [24]. (In [36], an approach to handling ConGolog programs that does not rely on any type of encoding is presented. There, high-level programs are compiled into standard situation calculus basic action theories such that the executable situations are exactly those that are permitted by the program.) The predicate $Trans$ for programs without procedures is characterized by the following set of axioms $\mathcal{T}$ (here as in the rest of the chapter, free variables are assumed to be universally quantified):

1. Empty program:
$$Trans(nil, s, \delta', s') \equiv False.$$

2. Primitive actions:
$$Trans(a, s, \delta', s') \equiv Poss(a[s], s) \land \delta' = nil \land s' = do(a[s], s).$$

3. Test/wait actions:
$$Trans(\phi?, s, \delta', s') \equiv \phi[s] \land \delta' = nil \land s' = s.$$

4. Sequence:
$$Trans(\delta_1; \delta_2, s, \delta', s') \equiv$$
$$\exists \gamma.\delta' = (\gamma; \delta_2) \land Trans(\delta_1, s, \gamma, s') \lor Final(\delta_1, s) \land Trans(\delta_2, s, \delta', s').$$

5. Nondeterministic branch:
$$Trans(\delta_1 \mid \delta_2, s, \delta', s') \equiv Trans(\delta_1, s, \delta', s') \lor Trans(\delta_2, s, \delta', s').$$

6. Nondeterministic choice of argument:
$$Trans(\pi v.\delta, s, \delta', s') \equiv \exists x. Trans(\delta^v_x, s, \delta', s').$$

7. Nondeterministic iteration:
$$Trans(\delta^*, s, \delta', s') \equiv \exists \gamma.(\delta' = \gamma; \delta^*) \land Trans(\delta, s, \gamma, s').$$

---

[2] In the original presentation of Golog [62], a simpler semantics was given where $Do(\delta, s, s')$ was only an abbreviation for a formula $\Phi(s, s')$ that did not mention the program δ (or any other programs), thus avoiding the need to reify programs. However, when dealing with concurrency, it is more convenient to use a transition semantics.

[3] Observe that we assume that formulas that occur in tests never mention programs, so it is impossible to build self-referential sentences.

8. Synchronized conditional:

$$Trans(\textbf{if } \phi \textbf{ then } \delta_1 \textbf{ else } \delta_2 \textbf{ endIf}, s, \delta', s') \equiv$$
$$\phi[s] \wedge Trans(\delta_1, s, \delta', s') \vee \neg\phi[s] \wedge Trans(\delta_2, s, \delta', s').$$

9. Synchronized loop:

$$Trans(\textbf{while } \phi \textbf{ do } \delta \textbf{ endWhile}, s, \delta', s') \equiv$$
$$\exists\gamma.(\delta' = \gamma; \textbf{while } \phi \textbf{ do } \delta) \wedge \phi[s] \wedge Trans(\delta, s, \gamma, s').$$

10. Concurrent execution:

$$Trans(\delta_1 \parallel \delta_2, s, \delta', s') \equiv$$
$$\exists\gamma.\delta' = (\gamma \parallel \delta_2) \wedge Trans(\delta_1, s, \gamma, s') \vee \exists\gamma.\delta' = (\delta_1 \parallel \gamma) \wedge Trans(\delta_2, s, \gamma, s').$$

11. Prioritized concurrency:

$$Trans(\delta_1 \,\rangle\!\rangle\, \delta_2, s, \delta', s') \equiv$$
$$\exists\gamma.\delta' = (\gamma \,\rangle\!\rangle\, \delta_2) \wedge Trans(\delta_1, s, \gamma, s') \vee$$
$$\exists\gamma.\delta' = (\delta_1 \,\rangle\!\rangle\, \gamma) \wedge Trans(\delta_2, s, \gamma, s') \wedge \neg\exists\zeta, s''.Trans(\delta_1, s, \zeta, s'').$$

12. Concurrent iteration:

$$Trans(\delta^{\parallel}, s, \delta', s') \equiv \exists\gamma.\delta' = (\gamma \parallel \delta^{\parallel}) \wedge Trans(\delta, s, \gamma, s').$$

The assertions above characterize when a configuration (δ, s) can evolve (in a single step) to a configuration (δ', s'). Intuitively they can be read as follows:

1. (nil, s) cannot evolve to any configuration.
2. (a, s) evolves to $(nil, do(a[s], s))$, provided that $a[s]$ is possible in s. After having performed a, nothing remains to be performed and hence nil is returned. Note that in $Trans(a, s, \delta', s')$, a stands for the program term encoding the corresponding situation calculus action, while $Poss$ and do take the latter as argument; we take the function $\cdot[\cdot]$ as mapping the program term a into the corresponding situation calculus action $a[s]$, as well as replacing now by the situation s. The details of how this function is defined are in [24].
3. $(\phi?, s)$ evolves to (nil, s), provided that $\phi[s]$ holds, otherwise it cannot proceed. Note that the situation remains unchanged. Analogously to the previous case, we take the function $\cdot[\cdot]$ as mapping the program term for condition ϕ into the corresponding situation calculus formulas $\phi[s]$, as well as replacing now by the situation s (see [24] for details).
4. $(\delta_1; \delta_2, s)$ can evolve to $(\delta_1'; \delta_2, s')$, provided that (δ_1, s) can evolve to (δ_1', s'). Moreover it can also evolve to (δ_2', s'), provided that (δ_1, s) is a final configuration and (δ_2, s) can evolve to (δ_2', s').
5. $(\delta_1 \mid \delta_2, s)$ can evolve to (δ', s'), provided that either (δ_1, s) or (δ_2, s) can do so.

6. $(\pi v.\delta, s)$ can evolve to (δ', s'), provided that there exists an x such that (δ^v_x, s) can evolve to (δ', s'). Here δ^v_x is the program resulting from δ by substituting v with the variable x.[4]

7. (δ^*, s) can evolve to $(\delta'; \delta^*, s')$ provided that (δ, s) can evolve to (δ', s'). Observe that (δ^*, s) can also not evolve at all, (δ^*, s) being final by definition (see below).

8. (if ϕ then δ_1 else δ_2 endIf, s) can evolve to (δ', s'), if either $\phi[s]$ holds and (δ_1, s) can do so, or $\neg\phi[s]$ holds and (δ_2, s) can do so.

9. (while ϕ do δ endWhile, s) can evolve to $(\delta'; \text{while } \phi \text{ do } \delta \text{ endWhile}, s')$, if $\phi[s]$ holds and (δ, s) can evolve to (δ', s').

10. You single step $(\delta_1 \parallel \delta_2)$ by single stepping either δ_1 or δ_2 and leaving the other process unchanged.

11. The $(\delta_1 \rangle\!\rangle \delta_2)$ construct is identical, except that you are only allowed to single step δ_2 if there is no legal step for δ_1. This ensures that δ_1 will execute as long as it is possible for it to do so.

12. Finally, you single step $\delta^{\parallel}$ by single stepping δ, and what is left is the remainder of δ as well as $\delta^{\parallel}$ itself. This allows an unbounded number of instances of δ to be running.

Observe that with $(\delta_1 \parallel \delta_2)$, if both δ_1 and δ_2 are always able to execute, the amount of interleaving between them is left completely open. It is legal to execute one of them completely before even starting the other, and it also legal to switch back and forth after each primitive or wait action.[5]

Final(δ, s) tells us whether a program δ can be considered to be already in a *final* state (legally terminated) in the situation s. Obviously we have *Final*(nil, s), but also *Final*(δ^*, s) since δ^* requires 0 or more repetitions of δ and so it is possible to not execute δ at all, the program completing immediately.

The predicate *Final* for programs without procedures is characterized by the set of axioms $\mathcal{F}$:

1. Empty program:
$$Final(nil, s) \equiv True.$$

2. Primitive action:
$$Final(a, s) \equiv False.$$

3. Test/wait action:
$$Final(\phi?, s) \equiv False.$$

4. Sequence:
$$Final(\delta_1; \delta_2, s) \equiv Final(\delta_1, s) \wedge Final(\delta_2, s).$$

5. Nondeterministic branch:

---

[4] More formally, in the program term δ, v is substituted by a term of the form *nameOf*(x), where *nameOf* is used to convert situation calculus objects/actions into program terms of the corresponding sort (see [24]).

[5] It is not hard to define new concurrency constructs $\parallel_{min}$ and $\parallel_{max}$ that require the amount of interleaving to be minimized or maximized respectively.

$$Final(\delta_1 \mid \delta_2, s) \equiv Final(\delta_1, s) \vee Final(\delta_2, s).$$

6. Nondeterministic choice of argument:

$$Final(\pi v.\delta, s) \equiv \exists x.Final(\delta_x^v, s).$$

7. Nondeterministic iteration:

$$Final(\delta^*, s) \equiv True.$$

8. Synchronized conditional:

$$Final(\textbf{if } \phi \textbf{ then } \delta_1 \textbf{ else } \delta_2 \textbf{ endIf}, s) \equiv$$
$$\phi[s] \wedge Final(\delta_1, s) \vee \neg\phi[s] \wedge Final(\delta_2, s).$$

9. Synchronized loop:

$$Final(\textbf{while } \phi \textbf{ do } \delta \textbf{ endWhile}, s) \equiv \neg\phi[s] \vee Final(\delta, s).$$

10. Concurrent execution:

$$Final(\delta_1 \parallel \delta_2, s) \equiv Final(\delta_1, s) \wedge Final(\delta_2, s).$$

11. Prioritized concurrency:

$$Final(\delta_1 \rangle\!\rangle \delta_2, s) \equiv Final(\delta_1, s) \wedge Final(\delta_2, s).$$

12. Concurrent iteration:
$$Final(\delta^\parallel, s) \equiv True.$$

The assertions above can be read as follows:

1. (nil, s) is a final configuration.
2. (a, s) is not final, indeed the program consisting of the primitive action a cannot be considered completed until it has performed a.
3. $(\phi?, s)$ is not final, indeed the program consisting of the test action $\phi?$ cannot be considered completed until it has performed the test $\phi?$.
4. $(\delta_1; \delta_2, s)$ can be considered completed if both (δ_1, s) and (δ_2, s) are final.
5. $(\delta_1 \mid \delta_2, s)$ can be considered completed if either (δ_1, s) or (δ_2, s) is final.
6. $(\pi v.\delta, s)$ can be considered completed, provided that there exists an x such that (δ_x^v, s) is final, where δ_x^v is obtained from δ by substituting v with x.
7. (δ^*, s) is a final configuration, since δ^* is allowed to execute 0 times.
8. $(\textbf{if } \phi \textbf{ then } \delta_1 \textbf{ else } \delta_2 \textbf{ endIf}, s)$ can be considered completed, if either $\phi[s]$ holds and (δ_1, s) is final, or if $\neg\phi[s]$ holds and (δ_2, s) is final.
9. $(\textbf{while } \phi \textbf{ do } \delta \textbf{ endWhile}, s)$ can be considered completed if either $\neg\phi[s]$ holds or (δ, s) is final.
10. $(\delta_1 \parallel \delta_2)$ can be considered completed if both δ_1 and δ_2 are final.
11. $(\delta_1 \rangle\!\rangle \delta_2)$ is handled identically with the previous case.

12. $\delta^\|$ is a final configuration, since $\delta^\|$ is allowed to execute 0 instances of δ.

The ConGolog semantics handles procedure definitions and procedure calls in a standard way with call-by-value parameter passing and lexical scoping. We leave out the axioms that handle this; they can be found in [24].[6]

In the following we denote by $\mathcal{C}$ the set of axioms for *Trans* and *Final* plus those needed for the encoding of programs as first-order terms.

Regarding interrupts, it turns out that these can be explained using other constructs of ConGolog:

$$\langle \, \phi \rightarrow \delta \, \rangle \overset{\text{def}}{=} \textbf{while } Interrupts\_running \textbf{ do}$$
$$\textbf{if } \phi \textbf{ then } \delta \textbf{ else } False? \textbf{ endIf}$$
$$\textbf{endWhile}$$

To see how this works, first assume that the special fluent $Interrupts\_running$ is identically *True*. When an interrupt $\langle \phi \rightarrow \delta \rangle$ gets control, it repeatedly executes δ until ϕ becomes false, at which point it blocks, releasing control to any other process in the program that is able to execute. Note that according to the above definition of *Trans*, no transition occurs between the test condition in a while-loop or an if-then-else and the body. In effect, if ϕ becomes false, the process blocks right at the beginning of the loop, until some other action makes ϕ true and resumes the loop. To actually terminate the loop, we use a special primitive action $stop\_interrupts$, whose only effect is to make $Interrupts\_running$ false. Thus, we imagine that to execute a program δ containing interrupts, we would actually execute the program $\{start\_interrupts\,;\,(\delta \,\rangle\!\rangle\, stop\_interrupts)\}$ which has the effect of stopping all blocked interrupt loops in δ at the lowest priority, *i.e.* when there are no more actions in δ that can be executed.

Offline executions of programs, which are the kind of executions originally proposed for Golog [62] and ConGolog [24], are characterized using the $Do(\delta, s, s')$ predicate, which means that there is an execution of program δ that starts in situation s and terminates in situation s':

$$Do(\delta, s, s') \overset{\text{def}}{=} \exists \delta'.Trans^*(\delta, s, \delta', s') \wedge Final(\delta', s'),$$

where $Trans^*$ is the reflexive transitive closure of $Trans$.[7] Thus there is an execution of program δ that starts in situation s and terminates in situation s' if

---

[6] Note that when the number of recursive calls is unbounded, this requires defining *Trans* and *Final* using a second order formula. In ConGolog a procedure call is not a transition (only primitive actions and tests are), so one must allow for an arbitrarily large but finite number of procedure calls in a transition; see [24].

[7] $Trans^*$ can be defined as the (second-order) situation calculus formula:

$$Trans^*(\delta, s, \delta', s') \overset{\text{def}}{=} \forall T.[\ldots \; \supset \; T(\delta, s, \delta', s')],$$

where ... stands for the conjunction of the universal closure of the following implications:

$$True \; \supset \; T(\delta, s, \delta, s),$$
$$Trans(\delta, s, \delta'', s'') \wedge T(\delta'', s'', \delta', s') \; \supset \; T(\delta, s, \delta', s').$$

and only if we can perform 0 or more transitions from program δ in situation s to reach situation s' with program δ' remaining, at which point one may legally terminate.

An *offline execution* of δ from s is a sequence of actions $a_1, \ldots, a_n$ such that: $\mathcal{D} \cup \mathcal{C} \models Do(\delta, s, do(a_n, \ldots, do(a_1, s) \ldots))$, where $\mathcal{D}$ is an action theory as mentioned above, and $\mathcal{C}$ is a set of axioms defining the predicates $Trans$ and $Final$ and the encoding of programs as first-order terms [24].

The Online Execution Semantics

The offline execution model of Golog and ConGolog requires the executor to search over the whole program to find a complete execution before performing any action. As mentioned earlier, this is problematic for agents that are long lived or need to sense their environment as they operate. The *online execution* model of IndiGolog [26, 87] addresses this. Imagine that we started with some program δ_0 in S_0, and that at some later point we have executed certain actions $a_1, \ldots a_k$ and have obtained sensing results $\mu_1, \ldots \mu_k$ from them, i.e. we are now in history $\sigma = (a_1, \mu_1) \cdot \ldots \cdot (a_k, \mu_k)$, with program δ remaining to be executed. The *online high-level program execution task* then is to find out what to do next, defined by:

- stop, if $\mathcal{D} \cup \mathcal{C} \cup \{Sensed[\sigma]\} \models Final(\delta, end[\sigma])$;
- return the remaining program δ', if

$$\mathcal{D} \cup \mathcal{C} \cup \{Sensed[\sigma]\} \models Trans(\delta, end[\sigma], \delta', end[\sigma]),$$

  and no action is required in this step;
- return action a and δ', if

$$\mathcal{D} \cup \mathcal{C} \cup \{Sensed[\sigma]\} \models Trans(\delta, end[\sigma], \delta', do(a, end[\sigma])).$$

So the online version of program execution uses the sensing information that has been accumulated so far to decide if it should terminate, take a step of the program with no action required, or take a step with a single action required. In the case that an action is required, the agent can be instructed to perform the action, gather any sensing information this provides, and the online execution process iterates. As part of this online execution cycle, one can also monitor for the occurrence of exogenous actions/events. When an exogenous action is detected it can be added to the history σ, possibly causing an update in the values of various fluents. The program can then monitor for this and execute a "reaction" when appropriate (e.g. using an interrupt). The IndiGolog semantics of [26] defines an *online execution* of a program δ starting from a history σ, as a sequence of *online configurations*

$$(\delta_0 = \delta, \sigma_0 = \sigma), \ldots, (\delta_n, \sigma_n)$$

such that for $i = 0, \ldots, n-1$:

$$\mathcal{D} \cup \mathcal{C} \cup \{Sensed[\sigma_i]\} \models Trans(\delta_i, end[\sigma_i], \delta_{i+1}, end[\sigma_{i+1}]),$$

$$\sigma_{i+1} = \begin{cases} \sigma_i & \text{if } end[\sigma_{i+1}] = end[\sigma_i], \\ \sigma_i \cdot (a, \mu) & \text{if } end[\sigma_{i+1}] = do(a, end[\sigma_i]) \text{ and } a \text{ returns } \mu. \end{cases}$$

An *online execution successfully terminates* if

$$\mathcal{D} \cup \mathcal{C} \cup \{Sensed[\sigma_n]\} \models Final(\delta_n, end[\sigma_n]).$$

Note that this definition assumes that exogenous actions do not occur; one can easily generalize the definition to allow them.

The Search Operator

The online execution of a high-level program does not require a reasoner to determine a lengthy course of action, formed perhaps of millions of actions, before executing the first step in the world. It also gets to use the sensing information provided by the first n actions performed so far in deciding what the $(n + 1)$'th action should be. On the other hand, once an action has been executed in the world, there may be no way of backtracking if it is later found out that a nondeterministic choice was resolved incorrectly. As a result, an online execution of a program may fail where an offline execution would succeed.

To cope with the fact that it may be impossible to backtrack on actions executed in the real world, IndiGolog incorporates a new programming construct, namely the *search operator*. The idea is that given any program δ the program $\Sigma(\delta)$ executes online just like δ does offline. In other words, before taking any action, it first ensures using offline reasoning that this step can be followed successfully by the rest of δ. More precisely, according to [26], the semantics of the search operator is that

$$Trans(\Sigma(\delta), s, \Sigma(\delta'), s') \equiv Trans(\delta, s, \delta', s') \wedge \exists s^*.Do(\delta', s', s^*).$$

If δ is the entire program under consideration, $\Sigma(\delta)$ emulates complete offline execution. But consider $[\delta_1 ; \delta_2]$. The execution of $\Sigma([\delta_1 ; \delta_2])$ would make any choice in δ_1 depend on the ability to successfully complete δ_2. But $[\Sigma(\delta_1) ; \delta_2]$ would allow the execution of the two pieces to be done separately: it would be necessary to ensure the successful completion of δ_1 before taking any steps, but consideration of δ_2 is deferred. If we imagine, for example, that δ_2 is a large high-level program, with hundreds of pages of code, perhaps containing Σ operators of its own, this can make the difference between a scheme that is practical and one that is only of theoretical interest.

Being able to search still raises the question of how much offline reasoning should be performed in an online system. The more offline reasoning we do, the safer the execution will be, as we get to look further into the future in deciding what choices to make now. On the other hand, in spending time doing this reasoning, we are detached from the world and will not be as responsive. This issue is very clearly evident in time-critical applications such as robot soccer [34] where there is very little time between action choices to contemplate the future. Sardina has cast this problem as the choice between deliberation and reactivity [86], and see also [6].

Another issue that arises in this setting is the form of the offline reasoning. Since an online system allows for a robot to *acquire information during execution* (via sensing actions, or passive sensors, or exogenous events), how should the agent deal with this during offline deliberation [23]. The simplest possibility is to say that it ignores any such information in the plan for the future that it is constructing. This is essentially what the semantics for the search operator given above does. It ensures that there exist a complete execution of the program (in the absence of exogenous actions), but it does not ensure that the agent has enough information to know what to do. For example, consider the program

$$\Sigma((a \mid sense_P); \text{if } P \text{ then } b \text{ else } c \text{ endIf})$$

and an agent that does not know initially whether P hold. The search semantics given above says that the agent may do action a, since it knows that afterwards there will be some way to successfully complete the execution. But in fact the agent will then get stuck not knowing which branch to take. A more adequate deliberation mechanism would require the execution of $sense_P$ as the first step, since it does guarantee the complete executability of the program, unlike action a.

An even more sophisticated deliberation approach would have the agent construct a plan that would prescribe different behaviors depending on the information acquired during execution. This is *conditional planning* (see, for example, [10, 73]). For the example above, this would produce a plan that requires the agent to first do $sense_P$, and then if it had sensed that P held, to do b and otherwise to do c; then the agent is guaranteed to always know what action to perform to complete the execution. One form of this has been incorporated in high-level execution by Lakemeyer [48] and Sardina [84]. In [87], a semantics for such a sophisticated search operator is axiomatized in a version of the situation calculus extended with a possible-world model of knowledge. [25] and [88] develop non-epistemic, metatheoretic accounts of this kind of deliberation, and discuss difficulties that arise with programs involving unbounded iteration.

Another possibility is to attempt to *simulate* what will happen external to the agent *including exogenous events*, and use this information during the deliberation [56]. This is a kind of contingency planning [77]. In [41], this idea is taken even further: at deliberation time a robot uses, for example, a model of its navigation system by computing, say, piece-wise linear approximations of its trajectory; at execution time, this model is then replaced by the real navigation system, which provides position updates as exogenous actions. [54] develops an account of deliberation where the agent's high level program must be executed against a dynamic environment also modeled as a nondeterministic program. Deliberation must produce a deterministic conditional plan that can be successfully executed against all possible executions of the environment program.

Another issue arises whenever an agent performs at least some amount of lookahead in deciding what to do. What should the agent do when the world (as determined by its sensors) does not conform to its predictions (as determined by its action theory)? First steps in logically formalizing this possibility were taken by De Giacomo et al. [30] in what they call *execution monitoring*. The deliberation model formalized in [87] incorporates execution monitoring and replanning. Lastly, a search operator that deliberates on a program relative to a set of goals is described in [91].

As we have seen, it is possible to define different search/deliberation constructs with varying degrees of sophistication. For many cases, however, the simple search operator defined above suffices, and implementations for it can easily be developed; these are provably correct under some plausible assumptions (for instance, when the truth value of all tests in a program will be known by the time they are evaluated, as in the "just-in-time histories" of [26, 28]).

We close the section by noting that Shapiro et. al [95, 94] have developed a verification environment, CASLve, for an extension of ConGolog that supports multiagent plans and modeling agents' knowledge and goals, based on the PVS theorem proving/verification system.[8] Some non-trivial programs have been formally verified.

2.2.3 Software Engineering Issues and Other Features of the Language

At this point, our language offers only limited support for building large software systems. It supports procedural abstraction, but not modules. Very complex agents can be decomposed into simpler agents that cooperate, and each can be implemented separately. One important feature that we do offer is that the agent's beliefs are automatically updated based on a declarative action theory, which supports the use of complex domain models, and helps avoid the errors that typically occur when such models are manually updated.

Our language/platform is implemented in SWI-Prolog, which provides flexible mechanisms for interfacing with other programming languages such as Java or C, and for socket communication. There are also libraries for interfacing with the JADE and OAA multiagent platforms; see the end of Section 3 for details.

Note that ConGolog has been used as a formal specification/modeling language for software requirements engineering [50, 104]. Such ConGolog specifications can be validated by simulated execution or verification. One may even use them for early prototyping. IndiGolog could be used in a requirements-driven approach to software development such as Tropos [19].

---

[8] http://pvs.csl.sri.com/

Our approach provides for a high degree of extensibility. The declarative language definition supports the easy addition of new programming constructs. The underlying situation calculus framework supports many extensions in the way change is modeled, e.g. continuous change, stochastic effects, simultaneous actions, etc. [82] Evidence for this extensibility is that the language has been extended numerous times. Note that there is currently no specific built-in support for mobile agents. What we have seen so far, is the formal specification of our language. If one wants to actually run an agent programmed in IndiGolog in the real-world, one needs to address many practical issues that are not dealt with in the formal account. For instance, when an action transition step is performed in an online execution, the action ought to be carried out in the environment where it is supposed to occur, and its sensing outcome needs to be extracted as well. Similarly, a mechanism for recognizing and assimilating external exogenous events needs to be developed. All this requires a framework in which an online execution is realized in the context of a real (external) environment. In the next section, we describe a platform that does exactly this.

2.3 Platform

We now turn to describing what is probably the most advanced IndiGolog based platform currently available. This platform[9] was originally developed at the University of Toronto and is based on LeGolog [60], which is in turn based on a proof-of-concept simple implementation originally written by Hector Levesque. The platform is a *logic-programming* implementation of IndiGolog that allows the incremental execution of high-level Golog-like programs [85]. This is the only implementation of IndiGolog that is modular and easily extensible so as to deal with any external platform, as long as the suitable interfacing modules are programmed (see below). Among others, the system has been used to control the LEGO MINDSTORM [60] and the ER1 Evolution[10] robots, as well as other software agents [92], to coordinate mobile actors in pervasive scenarios [52], and to incorporate automated planning into cognitive agents [21, 20].

Although most of the code is written in vanilla Prolog, the overall architecture is written in the well-known open source SWI-Prolog[11] [105]. SWI-Prolog provides flexible mechanisms for interfacing with other programming languages such as Java or C, allows the development of multi-threaded applications, and provides support for socket communication and constraint solving.

Generally speaking, the IndiGolog implementation provides an incremental interpreter of high-level programs as well as a framework for dealing with the *real* execution of these programs on *concrete* platforms or devices. This amounts to

---

[9] Available at http://sourceforge.net/projects/indigolog/.

[10] http://www.evolution.com/er1/

[11] http://www.swi-prolog.org/

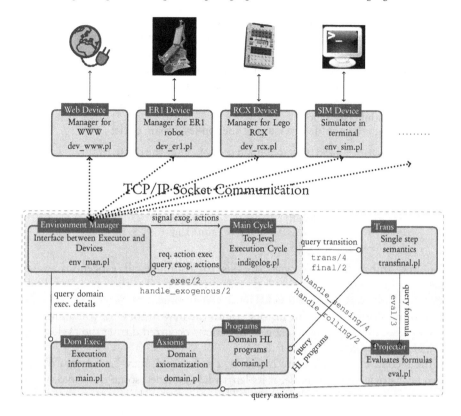

Fig. 2.1 The IndiGolog implementation architecture. Links with a circle ending represent goal posted to the circled module.

handling the real execution of actions on concrete devices (e.g., a real robot plat-form), the collection of sensing outcome information (e.g., retrieving some sen-sor's output), and the detection of exogenous events happening in the world. To that end, the architecture is modularly divided into six parts, namely, *(i)* the top-level main cycle; *(ii)* the language semantics; *(iii)* the temporal projector; *(vi)* the environment manager; *(v)* the set of device managers; and finally *(vi)* the domain application. The first four modules are completely domain independent, whereas the last two are designed for a specific domain. The architecture is depicted in Figure 2.1.

The Top-Level Main Cycle and Language Semantics

The top-level main cycle implements the IndiGolog online execution account ex-plained in Section 2.2.2. It realizes the *sense-think-act* loop well-known in the agent community [46].

The main predicate of the main cycle is `indigo/2`; a goal of the form `indigo(E,H)` states that the high-level program `E` is to be executed online at history `H`. As in the definition of online executions, the main cycle strongly relies on the meaning of the language constructs. Hence, clauses for relations *Trans* and *Final* are needed for each of the constructs. These two relations are modeled with Prolog predicates `trans/4` and `final/2` and are defined in the language semantics module (see below).

The following is a simplified version of the top-level main cycle:

```
indigo(E,H):- handle_exogenous(H,H2), !, indigo(E,H2).
indigo(E,H):- handle_rolling(H,H2), !, indigo(E,H2).
indigo(E,H):- catch(final(E,H), exog, indigo(E,H)).
indigo(E,H):- catch(trans(E,H,E1,H1), exog, indigo(E,H)),
  (var(H1) -> true ;
   H1=H -> indigo(E1,H) ;
   H1=[A|H] -> exec(A,S), handle_sensing(H,A,S,H2),
       indigo(E1,H2)).
```

The first thing the main cycle does is to assimilate all exogenous events that have occurred since the last execution step. To that end, predicate `handle_exogenous/2`, provided by the environment manager (see below), is used to transform the current history `H` into the new history `H2` containing the new exogenous events—if no exogenous actions occurred during the cycle, then `handle_exogenous/2` just fails.

In the second clause, predicate `handle_rolling/2` may "roll forward" the current history `H`, for example, if its length has exceeded some threshold, yielding then the new (shorter) history `H2`. This amounts to doing *progression* of the current history [65, 101]. Since progressing the current history is a task related to the background action theory being used to execute the program, the predicate `handle_rolling/2` is implemented by the temporal projector (see below).

After all exogenous actions have been assimilated and the history progressed as needed, the main cycle goes on to actually executing the high-level program `E`. First, if the current program to be executed is terminating in the current history, then the top-level goal `indigo/2` simply succeeds (third clause). Otherwise, the interpreter checks whether the program can evolve a single step (fourth clause) by relying on predicate `trans/4` (explained below). If the program evolves without executing any action, then the history remains unchanged and we continue to execute the remaining program from the same history. If, however, the step involves performing an action, then this action is executed and incorporated into the current history, together with its sensing result (if any), before continuing the execution of the remaining program. The actual execution of the action is implemented via predicate `exec/2`, provided by the environment manager (described below), which returns the sensing outcome of the action. Finally, `handle_sensing/4` returns the new history obtained by incorporating the executed action and its sensing outcome into the current history (this predicate is provided by the temporal projector, to allow for alternative implementations, e.g. through progression).

Note that, in the third and fourth clauses above, goals `final/2` and `trans/4` are posted within a `catch/3` extra-logical predicate.[12] The point is that proving `final/2` or `trans/4` could be time consuming, as there may be substantial reasoning involved. If, during such reasoning, an exogenous event happens, such reasoning is not guaranteed to be adequate anymore, as the history of events has changed. In that case, the interpreter simply *aborts* the single-step reasoning (i.e., goal `final/2` or `trans/4`) and re-starts the cycle, which in turn will first assimilate the just observed events.

As mentioned above, the top-level loop relies on two central predicates, namely, `final/2` and `trans/4`. These predicates implement relations *Trans* and *Final*, giving the single step semantics for each of the constructs in the language. It is convenient, however, to use an implementation of these predicates defined over histories instead of situations. So, for example, these are the corresponding clauses for sequence (represented as a list), nondeterministic choice of programs, tests, and primitive actions:

```
final([E|L],H) :- final(E,H), final(L,H).
trans([E|L],H,E1,H1) :- final(E,H), trans(L,H,E1,H1).
trans([E|L],H,[E1|L],H1) :- trans(E,H,E1,H1).

final(ndet(E1,E2),H) :- final(E1,H) ; final(E2,H).
trans(ndet(E1,E2),H,E,H1) :- trans(E1,H,E,H1).
trans(ndet(E1,E2),H,E,H1) :- trans(E2,H,E,H1).

trans(?(P),H,[],H) :- eval(P,H,true).
trans(E,H,[],[E|H]) :- action(E), poss(E,P),
    eval(P,H,true).
/* Obs: no final/2 clauses for action and test
programs */
```

As is easy to observe, these Prolog clauses are almost directly "lifted" from the corresponding axioms for *Trans* and *Final*. Predicates `action/1` and `poss/2` specify the actions of the domain and their corresponding precondition axioms; both are defined in the domain axiomatization (see below). More importantly, `eval/3` is used to check the truth of a condition at a certain history, and is provided by the temporal projector, described next.

A naive implementation of the search operator would deliberate from scratch at every point of its incremental execution. It is clear, however, that one can do better than that, and cache the successful plan obtained and avoid replanning in most cases:

```
final(search(E),H) :- final(E,H).
trans(search(E),H,path(E1,L),H1) :-
    trans(E,H,E1,H1), findpath(E1,H1,L).

/* findpath(E,H,L): solve (E,H) and store the path in list L */
/* L = list of configurations (Ei,Hi) expected along the path */
```

---

[12] `catch(:Goal, +Catcher, :Recover)` behaves as `call/1`, except that if an exception is raised while `Goal` executes, and the `Catcher` unifies with the exception's name, then `Goal` is aborted and `Recover` is called.

```
findpath(E,H,[(E,H)])  :- final(E,H).
findpath(E,H,[(E,H)|L])  :- trans(E,H,E1,H1), findpath(E1,H1,L).

/* When we have a path(E,L), try to advance using list L */
final(path(E,[(E,H)]),H) :- !.  /* last step */
final(path(E,_),H) :- final(E,H). /* off path; re-check */
trans(path(E,[(E,H),(E1,H1)|L]),H,path(E1,[(E1,H1)|L]),H1) :- !.
trans(path(E,_),H,E1,H1) :-
    trans(search(E),H,E1,H1).  /* redo search */
```

So, when a search block is first solved, the whole solution path found is stored as the sequence of configurations that are expected. If the actual configurations reached match, then steps are performed without any reasoning (first final/2 and trans/4 clauses for program path(E,L)). If, on the other hand, the actual configuration does not match the one expected next, for example, because an exogenous action occurred and the history thus changed, replanning is performed to look for an alternative path (second final/2 and trans/4 clauses for program path(E,L)). Other variants of the search operator are provided, such as a searchc(E) construct in the spirit of [48, 84] that constructs a conditional plan that solves E.

Finally, we point out that by decoupling trans/4 and final/2 from the main cycle and the temporal projector, one can change the actual high-level programming language used. In that way, one could use the architecture to execute any agent language with a single-step operational semantics. For example, one could use the architecture to execute AgentSpeak agents [78], by suitably recasting the derivation rules of such BDI languages into trans/4 and final/2 clauses—in this case, the program E would stand for the agent's current active intentions and H for the history of executed actions and external events.

The Temporal Projector

The temporal projector is in charge of maintaining the agent's beliefs about the world and evaluating a formula relative to a history. It could be realized with standard database technology (see [29]) or with an evaluation procedure for some reasoning about action formalism. In the context of the situation calculus, for instance, one could use temporal projectors for basic action theories [74], guarded theories [27], or even fluent calculus theories of action [98]. The only requirement for the projector module is to provide an implementation of predicate eval/3: goal eval(+F,+H,?B) states that formula F has truth value B, usually true or false, at history H.

Within the architecture, the projector is used in two places. First, predicate eval/3 is used to define trans/4 and final/2, as the legal evolutions of high-level programs may often depend on what things are believed true or false. Furthermore, as seen above, the temporal projector provides a number of auxiliary tools used by the top-level loop for bookkeeping tasks. For instance, the top-level cycle is agnostic on how sensing results are incorporated into the belief structure of the agent; this is handled by the `handle_sensing/4` predicate defined in the projector. Similarly, the projector may provide progression facilities by implementing the predicate `handle_rolling/2`.

We illustrate the projector module by briefly describing the one used for modeling the Wumpus World domain [92]. This projector is an extension of the classical formula evaluator used for Golog in [62, 24], so as to handle some limited forms of incomplete knowledge. To that end, the evaluator deals with the so-called *possible values* that (functional) fluents may take at a certain history. We say that a fluent is *known* at h only when it has exactly one possible value at h. For a detailed description and semantics of this type of knowledge-based theories we refer to [100, 59].

We assume then that users provide definitions for each of the following predicates for fluent f, action a, sensing result r, formula w, and arbitrary value v:

- `fluent`(f), f is a ground fluent;
- `action`(a), a is a ground action;
- `init`(f, v),   initially, v is a possible value for f;
- `poss`(a, w),   it is possible to execute action a provided formula w is known to be true;
- `causes`(a, f, v, w),   action a affects the value of f: when a occurs and w is possibly true, v is a possible value for f;
- `settles`(a, r, f, v, w), action a with result r provides sensing information about f: when this happens and w is known to be true, v is the only possible value for f;
- `rejects`(a, r, f, v, w), action a with result r provides sensing information about f: when w is known to be true, v is not a possible value for f.

Formulas are represented in Prolog using the obvious names for the logical operators and with all situations suppressed; histories are represented by lists of the form $o(a, r)$ where a represents an action and r a sensing result. We will not go over how formulas are recursively evaluated, but just note that the procedure is implemented using the following four predicates: *(i)* kTrue(w, h) is the main and top-level predicate and it tests if the formula w is *known to be true* in history h; *(ii)* mTrue(w, h) is used to test if w is *possibly true* at h; *(iii)* subf(w_1, w_2, h) holds when w_2 is the result of replacing each fluent in w_1 by one of its *possible values* in history h; and *(iv)* mval(f, v, h) calculates the *possible* values v for fluent f in history h and is implemented as follows:

```
mval(F,V,[]) :- init(F,V).
mval(F,V,[o(A,R)|H]) :-
      causes(A,F,_,_), !, causes(A,F,V,W), mTrue(W,H).
mval(F,V,[o(A,R)|H]) :- settles(A,R,F,V1,W), kTrue(W,H), !,
      V=V1.
mval(F,V,[o(A,R)|H]) :-
      mval(F,V,H), \+(rejects(A,R,F,V,W), kTrue(W,H)).
```

So for the empty history, we use the initial possible values. Otherwise, for histories whose last action is a with result r, if f is changed by a with result r, we return any value v for which the condition w is possibly true; if a with result r senses the value of f, we return the value v for which the condition is known; otherwise, we return any value v that was a possible value in the previous history h and that is not rejected by action a with result r. This provides a solution to the frame problem: if a is an action that does not affect or sense for fluent f, then the possible values for f after doing a are the same as before.

Finally, the interface of the module is defined as follows:

```
eval(F,H,true)  :- kTrue(F,H).
eval(F,H,false) :- kTrue(neg(F),H).
```

The Environment Manager and the Device Managers

Because the architecture is meant to be used with concrete agent/robotic plat-forms, as well as with software/simulation environments, the online execution of IndiGolog programs must be linked with the external world. To that end, the *environment manager* (EM) provides a complete interface with all the external devices, platforms, and real-world environments that the application needs to in-teract with.

In turn, each external device or platform that is expected to interact with the ap-plication (e.g., a robot, a software module, or even a user interface) is assumed to have a corresponding *device manager*, a piece of software that is able to talk to the actual device, instruct it to execute actions, as well as gather information and events from it. The device manager understands the "hardware" of the cor-responding device and provides a high-level interface to the EM. For example, the device manager for the Wumpus World application is the code responsible for "simulating" an actual Wumpus World environment. It provides an interface for the execution of actions (e.g., moveFwd, smell, etc.), the retrieval of sens-ing outcomes for action smell, and the detection of occurrences of exogenous events (e.g., scream). In our case, the device is also in charge of depicting the world configuration in a Java applet.

Because actual devices are independent of the IndiGolog application and may be in remote locations, device managers are meant to run in different processes and, possibly, on different machines; they communicate then with the EM via TCP/IP sockets. The EM, in contrast, is part of the IndiGolog agent architecture and is tightly coupled with the main cycle. Still, since the EM needs to be open to the external world regardless of any computation happening in the main cycle, the EM and the main cycle run in different (but interacting) threads, though in the same process and Prolog run-time engine.[13]

So, in a nutshell, the EM is responsible of executing actions in the real world and gathering information from it in the form of sensing outcome and exogenous events by communicating with the different device managers. More concretely,

---

[13] SWI-Prolog provides a clean and efficient way of programming multi-threaded Prolog appli-cations.

given a domain high-level action (e.g., *moveFwd*(2*m*)), the EM is in charge of: *(i)* deciding which actual "device" should execute the action; *(ii)* ordering its execution by the device via its corresponding device manager; and finally *(iii)* collecting the corresponding sensing outcome. To realize the execution of actions, the EM provides an implementation of `exec/2` to the top-level main cycle: `exec(+A,-S)` orders the execution of action A, returning S as its sensing outcome.

Besides the execution of actions, the EM continuously listens to the external devices, that is to their managers, for the occurrence of exogenous events. When a device manager reports the occurrence of one or more exogenous actions in its device (e.g., the robot bumped into an object), the EM stores these events in the Prolog database so that the main cycle can later assimilate them all. Moreover, if the main cycle is currently reasoning about a possible program transition (i.e., it is trying to prove a `trans/4` or `final/2` goal), the EM raises an exception named "`exog`" in the main cycle thread. As already mentioned, this will cause the main cycle to abort its reasoning efforts, re-start its loop, and assimilate the pending events.

The Domain Application

From the user perspective, probably the most relevant aspect of the architecture is the specification of the domain application. Any domain application must provide:

1. An *axiomatization of the dynamics of the world*. The exact form of such an axiomatization would depend on the temporal projector used.
2. One or more *high-level agent programs* that specify the different agent behaviors available. In general, these will be IndiGolog programs, but they could be other types of programs under different implementations of `trans/4` and `final/2`.
3. All the necessary *execution information* to *run* the application in the external world. This amounts to specifying which external devices the application relies on (e.g., the device manager for the ER1 robot), and how high-level actions are actually executed on these devices (that is, by which device each high-level action is to be executed). Information on how to translate high-level symbolic actions and sensing results into the device managers' low-level representations, and vice-versa, could also be provided.

We illustrate the modeling of an application domain using our running example for the Wumpus domain (we only give a partial specification for the sake of brevity):

```
fluent(locAgent).
fluent(isGold(L)) :- loc(L).
init(locAgent,cell(1,1)).
init(hasArrow,true).
```

```
init(locWumpus,L):- loc(L), not L=cell(1,1).

action(pickGold).
poss(pickGold, isGold(locAgent)=true).

causes(moveFwd, locAgent, Y, and(dirAgent=up,
    up(locAgent,Y))).
causes(moveFwd, locWumpus, Y, or(Y=locWumpus,
    adj(locWumpus,Y))).

rejects(smell, 0, locW, Y, adj(locAgent, Y)).
rejects(smell, 1, locW, Y, neg(adj(locAgent, Y))).
settles(senseGold, 1, isGold(L), true, locAgent=L).
settles(senseGold, 0, isGold(L), false, locAgent=L).
```

The first block defines two (functional) fluents: `locAgent` stands for the current location of the agent; `isGold(L)` states whether location L is known to have gold. Initially, the agent is in location `cell(1,1)` and is holding an arrow. More interestingly, the Wumpus is believed to be somewhere in the grid but not in `cell(1,1)`. The second block defines the action of picking up gold, which is possible only if the agent believes that there is gold at its current location. The two clauses shown for `causes/4` state possible ways fluents `locAgent` and `locWumpus` may change when the agent moves forward. First, if the agent is aiming north, then the new location of the agent is updated accordingly. Second, whenever the agent moves, the Wumpus will either stay still or move to an adjacent cell. Observe that even if at some point the agent knows exactly where the Wumpus is located (that is, there is only one possible value for fluent `locWumpus`), after moving forward the agent considers several possible values for the location of the Wumpus. The remaining clauses specify how sensing actions affect the possible values of the relevant fluents. Fluent `locWumpus` is sensed by the `smell` action: if there is no stench (i.e., the sensing result is 0) then each of the agent's adjacent locations is not a possible value for fluent `locWumpus`, otherwise the opposite holds. Fluent `isGoldL` is sensed by the `senseGold` action which settles the value of the fluent depending on the sensing result.

Available Tools and Documentation

The platform distribution includes documentation and examples that, though simple, have allowed new users to learn how to effectively develop new applications. Currently, there are no tools developed specifically for the platform. For debugging, tracing facilities are provided; Prolog facilities can also be used. This is an area where more work is needed.

Standards Compliance, Interoperability and Portability

There has been some work on interfacing IndiGolog with commonly used multiagent platforms and supporting the use of standard agent communication languages. This can support the development of multiagent systems that incorporate planning and reasoning agents implemented in IndiGolog. The IG-OAAlib library [49] supports the inclusion of IndiGolog agents in systems running under SRI's Open-Agent Architecture (OAA) [67]. Another library, IG-JADE-PKSlib [69, 68] supports the inclusion of IndiGolog agents in systems running under JADE [8], which is FIPA-compliant and more scalable. This library allows IndiGolog agents to use the FIPA agent communication language and run standard agent interaction protocols (e.g. contract net).

Other Features of the Platform

Our platform is an advanced stable prototype and is currently hosted as an open source project at SourceForge (http://sourceforge.net/projects/indigolog/). It is designed in a modular way and is easily extensible, though this requires expertise in Prolog.

No detailed analysis regarding the number of agents that could be run efficiently or the number of messages that could be handled has been performed so far. For use in robotic architectures or workflow management, performance has not been a problem.

2.4 Applications Supported by the Language and/or the Platform

Among some of the applications built using the "high level program execution approach", we can mention an automated banking agent that involved a 40-page Golog program [55, 83]. This is an example of high-level specification that would have been completely infeasible formulated as a planning problem.

A number of cognitive robotic systems have been implemented on a variety of robotic platforms, using Golog-family languages. For a sampling of these systems, see [57, 34, 18, 35]. Perhaps the most impressive demonstration to date was that of the museum tour-guide robot reported in [16]. Borzenko et al. [13] have used IndiGolog to develop a high-level controller for a vision-based pose estimation system. They have also developed an IndiGolog library for knowledge-based control of vision systems called INVICON [12].

McIlraith and Son [72] have adapted ConGolog to obtain a framework for performing web service composition and customization, an approach that has been very influential. Martinez and Lespérance [69, 68, 70] have developed a library and toolkit that combines IndiGolog, the JADE multiagent platform [8], and the PKS planner [73] for performing web service composition. As well, [38] used a version of ConGolog to support the modeling and analysis of trust in social networks. To get a better idea of how IndiGolog can be used in applications, let us briefly discuss some work using IndiGolog in the area of pervasive computing.

2.4.1 Using IndiGolog to Coordinate Mobile Actors in Pervasive Computing Scenarios

In [51, 52], de Leoni *et al.* use the IndiGolog platform described in Section 2.3 to build a process management system (PMS) that coordinates mobile actors in pervasive computing scenarios. PMSs ([63, 1]) are widely used for the management of business processes that have a clear and well-defined structure. In de Leoni et al.'s work, the authors argue that PMSs can also be used in mobile and highly dynamic situations to coordinate, for instance, operators, devices, robots, or sensors. To that end, they show how to realize PMSs in IndiGolog, and how to operationalize the framework proposed in [53] for automatically adapting a process when a gap is sensed between the internal world representation (i.e., the virtual reality) and the actual external reality (i.e., the physical reality).

As an example, consider one of the scenarios investigated in [51, 52, 53]. This scenario concerns an emergency response operation involving various activities that may need to be adapted on-the-fly to react to unexpected exogenous events that could arise during the operation. Figure 2.2 depicts an Activity Diagram of a process consisting of two concurrent branches; the final task is *send data* and can only be executed after the branches have successfully completed. The left branch, abstracted out from the diagram, is built from several concurrent processes involving *rescue*, *evacuation*, and *census* tasks. The right branch begins with the concurrent execution of three sequences of tasks: *go*, *photo*, and *survey*. When all survey tasks have been completed, the task *evaluate pictures* is executed. Then, a condition is evaluated on the resulting state at a decision point (i.e., whether the pictures taken are of sufficient quality). If the condition holds, the right branch is considered finished; otherwise, the whole branch should be repeated.

When using IndiGolog for process management, *tasks* are taken to be predefined sequences of actions and *processes* to be IndiGolog programs. The objective of the PMS is to carry out the specified processes by assigning tasks to actors, monitoring the progress of the overall process, and adapting its execution when required. Thus, after each action, the PMS may need to align the internal world representation with the actual external reality. In Figure 2.2, parts of the IndiGolog program implementing the PMS for the emergency response example are shown ([52]). The main procedure, called pms, involves three interrupts running at different priorities. The first highest priority interrupt fires when an exogenous event has happened (i.e., condition exogEvent is true). In such a case, the monitor procedure is executed, evaluating whether or not adaptation is required (see below).

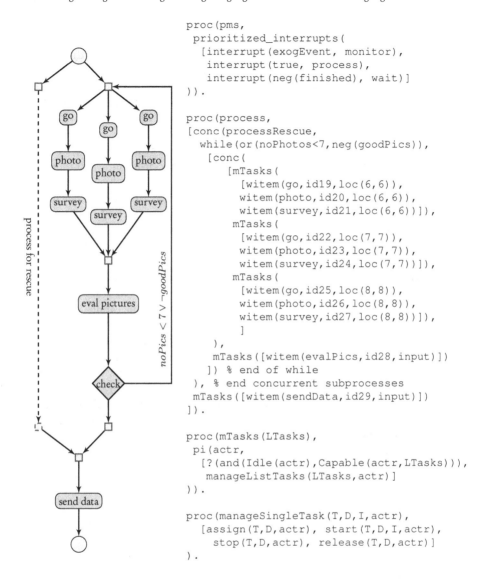

```
proc(pms,
  prioritized_interrupts(
    [interrupt(exogEvent, monitor),
     interrupt(true, process),
     interrupt(neg(finished), wait)]
)).

proc(process,
  [conc(processRescue,
    while(or(noPhotos<7,neg(goodPics)),
      [conc(
         [mTasks(
            [witem(go,id19,loc(6,6)),
             witem(photo,id20,loc(6,6)),
             witem(survey,id21,loc(6,6))]),
          mTasks(
            [witem(go,id22,loc(7,7)),
             witem(photo,id23,loc(7,7)),
             witem(survey,id24,loc(7,7))]),
          mTasks(
            [witem(go,id25,loc(8,8)),
             witem(photo,id26,loc(8,8)),
             witem(survey,id27,loc(8,8))]),
          ]
       ),
       mTasks([witem(evalPics,id28,input)])
      ]) % end of while
  ), % end concurrent subprocesses
  mTasks([witem(sendData,id29,input)])
]).

proc(mTasks(LTasks),
  pi(actr,
    [?(and(Idle(actr),Capable(actr,LTasks))),
     manageListTasks(LTasks,actr)]
)).

proc(manageSingleTask(T,D,I,actr),
  [assign(T,D,actr), start(T,D,I,actr),
    stop(T,D,actr), release(T,D,actr)]
).
```

Fig. 2.2 An example of process management with IndiGolog.

If no exogenous event has occurred (or the ones that occurred were expected), then the second interrupt triggers and execution of the actual emergency response process is attempted. Procedure process, also shown in the figure, encodes the Activity Diagram of the example process. It relies, in turn, on procedure mTasks(LTasks), where LTasks is a sequence of elements witem(T,I,D), each one representing a task T, with identifier I, and input data D that needs to be performed. This procedure is meant to carry out all tasks in the list by assigning them to a *single* actor that can perform all of them.

Of course, to assign tasks to an actor, the PMS needs to reason about the available actors, their current state (e.g., their location), and their capabilities, as not every actor is capable of performing a task. In fact, before assigning the first task in any task list, a *pick* operation is done to choose an actor `actr` that is idle (i.e., fluent `Idle(actr)` holds), and able to execute the whole task list (we leave out the definition of `Capable(actr,LTasks)`).

Once a suitable actor has been chosen, procedure `manageSingleTask(T, I,D)` will be called with each task `T` in the list (with identifier `I` and input data `D`). This procedure will first execute `assign(T,D,actr)`, which, among other things, makes fluent `Idle(actr)` false. The actor is then instructed to start working on the task when the PMS executes the action `start(T,D,I,actr)`, which also provides the required information to the actor. When an actor finishes executing an assigned task, it alerts the PMS via exogenous action `finishedTask(T,actr)`; the PMS notes the completion of the task by performing `stop(T,D,actr)` and releases the actor by executing the action `release(T,D,actr)`, after which fluent `Idle(actr)` becomes true.

It is worth mentioning that, if the process being carried out cannot execute further, for instance, because it is waiting for actors to complete their current tasks, the lowest priority interrupt fires and the PMS just waits.

The execution of the process being carried out by the PMS can be interrupted by the `monitor` module when a misalignment between the expected reality and the actual reality is discovered. In this case, the monitor *adapts* the (current) process to deal with the discrepancy. To do this, the monitor procedure uses the IndiGolog lookahead operator Σ to search for a plan that would bring the actual reality back into alignment with the expected reality. To that end, the PMS keeps a "copy" of the expected value of each relevant fluent so that when an exogenous action is sensed, it can check whether the action has altered the value of some relevant fluent. If so, the monitor looks for a plan that would bring all fluents to their expected values using a program along the lines of $\Sigma([(\pi a.a)^*; ExpectedState?])$. It is easily noted that this kind of adaptation amounts to solving a classical planning problem, and hence, that a state-of-the-art automated planner could be used to perform the required search. In many cases though, a domain expert would be able to provide information on how the *adaptation* should be performed, thus reducing the complexity of the planning task. For instance, when the mismatch involves a team of mobile actors becoming *disconnected* (e.g., because some actor moved too far away), then the whole process can be adapted by running a search program along the lines of $\Sigma([\pi\, actr, loc.Idle(actr)?; moveTo(actr, loc)]^*; TeamConnected?)$, which tries to relocate idle actors so that the whole team is re-connected (the actual program used would in fact implement a better search strategy). IndiGolog is well suited for realizing this kind of domain-specific planning and execution monitoring.

2.5 Final Remarks

IndiGolog is a rich programming language for developing autonomous agents. Agents programmed in IndiGolog have a situation calculus action theory that they use to model their domain and its dynamics. The theory is used to automatically update their beliefs after actions are performed or events occur. This supports the use of complex domain models and helps avoid the errors that typically occur when such models are manually updated. Moreover it can be used for performing planning/lookahead. The language supports "high level program execution", where the programmer provides a sketchy nondeterministic program and the system searches for a way to execute it. This is usually much less computationally demanding than planning, as the sketchy program constrains the search. As well, programs are executed online and the agent can acquire information at execution time by performing sensing actions or by observing exogenous actions. The language supports concurrent programming, and reactive behaviors can easily be programmed. The language has a classical predicate logic semantics specified through a transition system account defined on top of the situation calculus. One can make statements about offline executions of programs within the logical language and reason about properties of programs in the logic. Online executions of programs are formalized metatheoretically in terms of entailment in the situation calculus theory.

Compared to the mainstream BDI agent programming languages, IndiGolog seems to have several advantages: support for planning/lookahead, automatic belief update, built-in reasoning capabilities, and clean logical semantics. The downside is that these reasoning capabilities can slow the agent's response to events. But with suitable programming of control knowledge, adequate responsiveness can usually be achieved.

Perhaps one weakness of IndiGolog in comparison to BDI agent programming languages is that in the former, plans/procedures are not associated with goals/events; there is no "goal directed invocation". This can make it harder to organize the agent's plan library and to find alternative plans to achieve a goal when a selected plan fails.

There has only been limited work on relating "Golog-like" high-level programming languages and BDI agent programming languages. Hindriks et al. [43, 42] show that ConGolog can be bisimulated by the agent language 3APL under some conditions, which include the agent having complete knowledge; ConGolog's lookahead search mechanism is also ignored as are sensing actions and exogenous events. Also related is the work of Gabaldon [37] on encoding Hierarchical Task Network (HTN) libraries in ConGolog. Much work remains to be done in order to better understand how our approach relates to the BDI approach and others. It would be very interesting to develop an agent programming framework that combines the best features of the IndiGolog and BDI approaches.

More work is necessary to improve the effectiveness of the IndiGolog platform as a programming tool. The platform currently provides little built-in support for programming multiagent systems, interfacing with other agent platforms, or using standard communication languages. But this can be circumvented by using a library like IG-JADE-PKSlib [69, 68], which supports the inclusion of IndiGolog agents in systems running under JADE [8] and allows IndiGolog agents to use the FIPA agent communication language and run standard agent interaction protocols. An integrated development environment with good monitoring and debugging facilities would also be highly desirable. Work is also required on facilities to support large-scale agent programming, e.g. the use of modules.

Another limitation of our platform is that it uses a simple, relatively inefficient planning/lookahead mechanism implemented in Prolog. But it should be possible to address this by doing planning with Golog-style task specifications using state-of-the-art planners. Some authors have addressed this problem. [5] develops an approach for compiling Golog-like task specifications together with the associated domain definition into a PDDL 2.1 planning problem that can be solved by any PDDL 2.1 compliant planner. [4] describes techniques for compiling Golog programs that include sensing actions into domain descriptions that can be handled by operator-based planners. [36] shows how a ConGolog task specification involving concurrent processes together with the associated domain definition can be compiled into an ordinary situation calculus basic action theory; moreover it show how the specification can be complied into PDDL under some assumptions. Classen et al. [21, 20] have also used the IndiGolog architecture to integrate automated planning systems into cognitive agents and tested the performance of the integrated system in typical planning domain benchmarks [40].

Acknowledgements The late Ray Reiter was a major contributor to Golog and to our approach to agent programming. Gerhard Lakemeyer helped us with the sections on reasoning about action and robotics applications. Stavros Vassos helped develop the Wumpus World application. Massimiliano de Leoni helped us with the section on applications involving mobile actors in pervasive computing scenarios. We thank everyone who contributed to developing the approach and platform over the years.

References

1. van der Aalst, W., van Hee, K.: Workflow Management. Models, Methods, and Systems. MIT Press (2004)
2. Amir, E., Russell, S.: Logical filtering. In: Proceedings of the International Joint Conference on Artificial Intelligence (IJCAI), pp. 75–82. Acapulco, Mexico (2003)
3. Bacchus, F., Kabanza, F.: Planning for temporally extended goals. Annals of Mathematics and Artificial Intelligence **22**, 5–27 (1998)
4. Baier, J., McIlraith, S.: On planning with programs that sense. In: Proceedings of Principles of Knowledge Representation and Reasoning (KR), pp. 492–502. Lake District, UK (2006)
5. Baier, J.A., Fritz, C., McIlraith, S.A.: Exploiting procedural domain control knowledge in state-of-the-art planners. In: Proceedings of the International Conference on Automated Planning and Scheduling (ICAPS), pp. 26–33. Providence, Rhode Island (2007)
6. Baral, C., Son, T.C.: Relating theories of actions and reactive control. Electronic Transactions on Artificial Intelligence **2**(3-4), 211–271 (1998)
7. Belecheanu, R.A., Munroe, S., Luck, M., Payne, T., Miller, T., McBurney, P., Pechoucek, M.: Commercial applications of agents: Lessons, experiences and challenges. In: Proceed-

ings of Autonomous Agents and Multi-Agent Systems (AAMAS), pp. 1549–1555. ACM Press (2006)

8. Bellifemine, F., Claire, G., Greenwood, D.: Developing Multi-Agent Systems with JADE. Wiley (2007)

9. Benfield, S.S., Hendrickson, J., Galanti, D.: Making a strong business case for multiagent technology. In: Proceedings of Autonomous Agents and Multi-Agent Systems (AAMAS), pp. 10–15. ACM Press, New York, NY, USA (2006)

10. Bertoli, P., Cimatti, A., Roveri, M., Traverso, P.: Planning in nondeterministic domains under partial observability via symbolic model checking. In: Proceedings of the International Joint Conference on Artificial Intelligence (IJCAI), pp. 473–478 (2001)

11. Bordini, R.H., Hübner, J.F., Wooldridge, M.: Programming Multi-agent Systems in AgentSpeak Using Jason. Wiley Series in Agent Technology. Wiley (2007). Series in Agent Technology

12. Borzenko, O., Lespérance, Y., Jenkin., M.: INVICON: a toolkit for knowledge-based control of vision systems. In: Proc. of the 4th Canadian Conference on Computer and Robot Vision (CRV'07), pp. 387–394. Montréal, QC, Canada (2007)

13. Borzenko, O., Xu, W., Obsniuk, M., Chopra, A., Jasiobedzki, P., Jenkin, M., Lespérance, Y.: Lights and camera: Intelligently controlled multi-channel pose estimation system. In: Proc. of the IEEE International Conference on Vision Systems (ICVS'06). New York, NY, USA (2006). Paper 42 (8 pages)

14. Boutilier, C., Reiter, R., Soutchanski, M., Thrun, S.: Decision-theoretic, high-level agent programming in the situation calculus. In: Proceedings of the National Conference on Artificial Intelligence (AAAI), pp. 355–362. AAAI Press, Menlo Park, CA (2000)

15. Bratman, M.E.: Intentions, Plans, and Practical Reason. Harvard University Press (1987)

16. Burgard, W., Cremers, A., Fox, D., Hähnel, D., Lakemeyer, G., Schulz, D., Steiner, W., Thrun, S.: Experiences with an interactive museum tour-guide robot. Artificial Intelligence 114(1–2), 3–55 (1999)

17. Busetta, P., Rönnquist, R., Hodgson, A., Lucas, A.: JACK intelligent agents: Components for intelligent agents in Java. AgentLink Newsletter 2 (1999). Agent Oriented Software Pty. Ltd.

18. Carbone, A., Finzi, A., Orlandini, A., Pirri, F., Ugazio, G.: Augmenting situation awareness via model-based control in rescue robots. In: Proceedings of the IEEE/RSJ International Conference on Intelligent Robots and Systems (IROS), pp. 3699–3705. Edmonton, AB, Canada (2005)

19. Castro, J., Kolp, M., Mylopoulos, J.: Towards requirements-driven information systems engineering: The Tropos project. Information Systems 27(6), 365–389 (2002)

20. Classen, J., Engelmann, V., Lakemeyer, G., Röger, G.: Integrating Golog and planning: An empirical evaluation. In: Non-Monotonic Reasoning Workshop. Sydney, Australia (2008)

21. Classen, J., Eyerich, P., Lakemeyer, G., Nebel, B.: Towards an integration of planning and Golog. In: Proceedings of the International Joint Conference on Artificial Intelligence (IJCAI), pp. 1846–1851. Hyderabad, India (2007)

22. Cohen, P.R., Levesque, H.J.: Intention is choice with commitment. Artificial Intelligence Journal 42, 213–261 (1990)

23. Dastani, M., de Boer, F.S., Dignum, F., van der Hoek, W., Kroese, M., Meyer, J.J.: Programming the deliberation cycle of cognitive robots. In: Proceedings of the International Cognitive Robotics Workshop (COGROBO). Edmonton, Canada (2002)

24. De Giacomo, G., Lespérance, Y., Levesque, H.J.: ConGolog, a concurrent programming language based on the situation calculus. Artificial Intelligence Journal 121(1–2), 109–169 (2000)

25. De Giacomo, G., Lespérance, Y., Levesque, H.J., Sardina, S.: On deliberation under incomplete information and the inadequacy of entailment and consistency-based formalizations. In: Proceedings of the Programming Multiagent Systems Languages, Frameworks, Techniques and Tools workshop (PROMAS). Melbourne, Australia (2003)

26. De Giacomo, G., Levesque, H.J.: An incremental interpreter for high-level programs with sensing. In: H.J. Levesque, F. Pirri (eds.) Logical Foundations for Cognitive Agents: Contributions in Honor of Ray Reiter, pp. 86–102. Springer, Berlin (1999)

27. De Giacomo, G., Levesque, H.J.: Projection using regression and sensors. In: Proceedings of the International Joint Conference on Artificial Intelligence (IJCAI), pp. 160–165. Stockholm, Sweden (1999)

28. De Giacomo, G., Levesque, H.J., Sardina, S.: Incremental execution of guarded theories. ACM Transactions on Computational Logic (TOCL) 2(4), 495–525 (2001)

29. De Giacomo, G., Mancini, T.: Scaling up reasoning about actions using relational database technology. In: Proceedings of the National Conference on Artificial Intelligence (AAAI), pp. 245–256 (2004)

30. De Giacomo, G., Reiter, R., Soutchanski, M.: Execution monitoring of high-level robot programs. In: Proceedings of Principles of Knowledge Representation and Reasoning (KR), pp. 453–465 (1998)

31. Dennett, D.: The Intentional Stance. The MIT Press (1987)

32. Doherty, P.: Advanced research with autonomous unmanned aerial vehicles. In: Proceedings of Principles of Knowledge Representation and Reasoning (KR) (2004). Extended abstract for Plenary Talk

33. Erol, K., Hendler, J.A., Nau, D.S.: HTN planning: Complexity and expressivity. In: Proceedings of the National Conference on Artificial Intelligence (AAAI), pp. 1123–1228 (1994)

34. Ferrein, A., Fritz, C., Lakemeyer, G.: On-line decision-theoretic Golog for unpredictable domains. In: Proc. of 27th German Conference on Artificial Intelligence, pp. 322–336. Ulm, Germany, UK (2004)

35. Finzi, A., Pirri, F., Pirrone, M., Romano, M.: Autonomous mobile manipulators managing perception and failures. In: Proceedings of the Annual Conference on Autonomous Agents (AGENTS), pp. 196–201. Montréal, QC, Canada (2001)

36. Fritz, C., Baier, J.A., McIlraith, S.A.: ConGolog, Sin Trans: Compiling ConGolog into basic action theories for planning and beyond. In: Proceedings of Principles of Knowledge Representation and Reasoning (KR), pp. 600–610. Sydney, Australia (2008)

37. Gabaldon, A.: Programming hierarchical task networks in the situation calculus. In: AIPS'02 Workshop on On-line Planning and Scheduling. Toulouse, France (2002)

38. Gans, G., Jarke, M., Kethers, S., Lakemeyer, G., Ellrich, L., Funken, C., Meister, M.: Requirements modeling for organization networks: A (dis-)trust-based approach. In: Proc. of IEEE Int. Requirements Engineering Conf., pp. 154–163 (2001)

39. Georgeff, M.P., Lansky, A.L.: Reactive reasoning and planning. In: Proceedings of the National Conference on Artificial Intelligence (AAAI), pp. 677–682. Seattle, USA (1987)

40. Gerevini, A., Bonet, B., Givan, B. (eds.): Booklet of 4th International Planning Competition. Lake District, UK (2006). URL http://www.ldc.usb.ve/ bonet/ipc5/

41. Grosskreutz, H., Lakemeyer, G.: ccGolog: an action language with continuous change. Logic Journal of the IGPL (2003)

42. Hindriks, K., Lespérance, Y., Levesque, H.: An embedding of ConGolog in 3APL. Tech. Rep. UU-CS-2000-13, Department of Computer Science, Utrecht University (2000)

43. Hindriks, K., Lespérance, Y., Levesque, H.J.: A formal embedding of ConGolog in 3APL. In: Proceedings of the European Conference in Artificial Intelligence (ECAI), pp. 558–562. Berlin, Germany (2000)

44. Hindriks, K.V., de Boer, F.S., van der Hoek, W., Meyer, J.J.C.: Agent programming in 3APL. Autonomous Agents and Multi-Agent Systems 2, 357–401 (1999)

45. Huber, M.J.: JAM: A BDI-theoretic mobile agent architecture. In: Proceedings of the Annual Conference on Autonomous Agents (AGENTS), pp. 236–243. ACM Press, New York, NY, USA (1999)

46. Kowalski, R.A.: Using meta-logic to reconcile reactive with rational agents. In: K.R. Apt, F. Turini (eds.) Meta-Logics and Logic Programming, pp. 227–242. The MIT Press (1995)

47. Lakemeyer, G.: Relevance from an epistemic perspective. Artificial Intelligence 97(1–2), 137–167 (1997)

48. Lakemeyer, G.: On sensing and off-line interpreting in Golog. In: H. Levesque, F. Pirri (eds.) Logical Foundations for Cognitive Agents: Contributions in Honor of Ray Reiter, pp. 173–187. Springer, Berlin (1999)
49. Lapouchnian, A., Lespérance, Y.: Interfacing IndiGolog and OAA — a toolkit for advanced multiagent applications. Applied Artificial Intelligence **16**(9-10), 813–829 (2002)
50. Lapouchnian, A., Lespérance, Y.: Modeling mental states in agent-oriented requirements engineering. In: Proc. of the 18th Conference on Advanced Information Systems Engineering (CAiSE'06), pp. 480–494. Luxembourg (2006)
51. de Leoni, M.: Adaptive Process Management in Pervasive and Highly Dynamic Scenarios. Ph.D. thesis, SAPIENZA - University of Rome (2009)
52. de Leoni, M., Marrella, A., Mecella, M., Valentini, S., Sardina, S.: Coordinating mobile actors in pervasive and mobile scenarios: An AI-based approach. In: Proceedings of the 17th IEEE International Workshops on Enabling Technologies: Infrastructures for Collaborative Enterprises (WETICE); CoMA sub-workshop. IEEE Computer Society, Rome, Italy (2008)
53. de Leoni, M., Mecella, M., De Giacomo, G.: Highly dynamic adaptation in process management systems through execution monitoring. In: Proceedings of the Fifth International Conference on Business Process Management (BPM'07), *Lecture Notes in Computer Science*, vol. 4714, pp. 182–197. Springer, Brisbane, Australia (2007)
54. Lespérance, Y., De Giacomo, G., Ozgovde, A.N.: A model of contingent planning for agent programming languages. In: Proceedings of Autonomous Agents and Multi-Agent Systems (AAMAS), pp. 477–484. Estoril, Portugal (2008)
55. Lespérance, Y., Levesque, H.J., Ruman, S.J.: An experiment in using Golog to build a personal banking assistant. In: L. Cavedon, A. Rao, W. Wobcke (eds.) Intelligent Agent Systems: Theoretical and Practical Issues (Based on a Workshop Held at PRICAI '96 Cairns, Australia, August 1996),, *LNAI*, vol. 1209, pp. 27–43. Springer-Verlag (1997)
56. Lespérance, Y., Ng, H.K.: Integrating planning into reactive high-level robot programs. In: Proceedings of the International Cognitive Robotics Workshop (COGROBO), pp. 49–54. Berlin, Germany (2000)
57. Lespérance, Y., Tam, K., Jenkin, M.: Reactivity in a logic-based robot programming framework. In: N. Jennings, Y. Lespérance (eds.) Intelligent Agents VI — Agent Theories, Architectures, and Languages, 6th International Workshop, ATAL'99, Proceedings, *LNAI*, vol. 1757, pp. 173–187. Springer-Verlag, Berlin (2000)
58. Levesque, H.J.: What is planning in the presence of sensing? In: Proceedings of the National Conference on Artificial Intelligence (AAAI), pp. 1139–1146. American Association for Artificial Intelligence, Portland, Oregon (1996)
59. Levesque, H.J.: Planning with loops. In: Proceedings of the International Joint Conference on Artificial Intelligence (IJCAI), pp. 509–515 (2005)
60. Levesque, H.J., Pagnucco, M.: LeGolog: Inexpensive experiments in cognitive robotics. In: Proceedings of the International Cognitive Robotics Workshop (COGROBO), pp. 104–109. Berlin, Germany (2000)
61. Levesque, H.J., Reiter, R.: High-level robotic control: Beyond planning. A position paper. In: AAAI 1998 Spring Symposium: Integrating Robotics Research: Taking the Next Big Leap (1998)
62. Levesque, H.J., Reiter, R., Lespérance, Y., Lin, F., Scherl, R.B.: GOLOG: A logic programming language for dynamic domains. Journal of Logic Programming **31**, 59–84 (1997)
63. Leymann, F., Roller, D.: Production Workflow: Concepts and Techniques. Prentice Hall PTR (1999)
64. Lin, F., Reiter, R.: Forget it! In: Proceedings of AAAI Fall Symposium on Relevance. New Orleans, USA (1994)
65. Lin, F., Reiter, R.: How to progress a database. Artificial Intelligence Journal **92**, 131–167 (1997)
66. Ljungberg, M., Lucas, A.: The OASIS air-traffic management system. In: Proceedings of the Pacific Rim International Conference on Artificial Intelligence (PRICAI). Seoul, Korea (1992)

67. Martin, D., Cheyer A, J., Moran, D.: The open agent architecture: A framework for building distributed software systems. Applied Artificial Intelligence **13**, 91–128 (1999)
68. Martinez, E.: Web service composition as a planning task: An agent oriented framework. Master's thesis, Department of Computer Science, York University, Toronto, ON, Canada (2005)
69. Martinez, E., Lespérance, Y.: IG-JADE-PKSlib: an agent-based framework for advanced web service composition and provisioning. In: Proc. of the AAMAS 2004 Workshop on Web-services and Agent-based Engineering, pp. 2–10. New York, NY, USA (2004)
70. Martinez, E., Lespérance, Y.: Web service composition as a planning task: Experiments using knowledge-based planning. In: Proc. of the ICAPS-2004 Workshop on Planning and Scheduling for Web and Grid Services, pp. 62–69. Whistler, BC, Canada (2004)
71. McCarthy, J., Hayes, P.J.: Some philosophical problems from the standpoint of artificial intelligence. Machine Intelligence **4**, 463–502 (1969)
72. McIlraith, S., Son, T.C.: Adapting Golog for programming the semantic web. In: Proceedings of the Eighth International Conference on Knowledge Representation and Reasoning (KR2002), pp. 482–493. Toulouse, France (2002)
73. Petrick, R., Bacchus, F.: A knowledge-based approach to planning with incomplete information and sensing. In: Proceedings of the International Conference on AI Planning & Scheduling (AIPS), pp. 212–221 (2002)
74. Pirri, F., Reiter, R.: Some contributions to the metatheory of the situation calculus. Journal of the ACM **46**(3), 261–325 (1999)
75. Plotkin, G.D.: A structural approach to operational semantics. Tech. Rep. DAIMI-FN-19, Computer Science Department, Aarhus University, Denmark (1981)
76. Pollack, M.E.: The uses of plans. Artificial Intelligence Journal **57**(1), 43–68 (1992)
77. Pryor, L., Collins, G.: Planning for contingencies: A decision-based approach. J. of Artificial Intelligence Research **4**, 287–339 (1996)
78. Rao, A.S.: AgentSpeak(L): BDI agents speak out in a logical computable language. In: W.V. Velde, J.W. Perram (eds.) Proceedings of the Seventh European Workshop on Modelling Autonomous Agents in a Multi-Agent World. (Agents Breaking Away), *Lecture Notes in Computer Science (LNCS)*, vol. 1038, pp. 42–55. Springer-Verlag (1996)
79. Rao, A.S., Georgeff, M.P.: Modeling rational agents within a BDI-architecture. In: Proceedings of Principles of Knowledge Representation and Reasoning (KR), pp. 473–484 (1991)
80. Reiter, R.: On closed world data bases. In: Logic and Data Bases, pp. 55–76 (1977)
81. Reiter, R.: The frame problem in the situation calculus: A simple solution (sometimes) and a completeness result for goal regression. In: V. Lifschitz (ed.) Artificial Intelligence and Mathematical Theory of Computation: Papers in Honor of John McCarthy, pp. 359–380. Academic Press, San Diego, CA (1991)
82. Reiter, R.: Knowledge in Action. Logical Foundations for Specifying and Implementing Dynamical Systems. The MIT Press (2001)
83. Ruman, S.J.: GOLOG as an agent-programming language: Experiments in developing banking applications. Master's thesis, Department of Computer Science, University of Toronto (1996)
84. Sardina, S.: Local conditional high-level robot programs. In: R. Nieuwenhuis, A. Voronkov (eds.) Proceedings of the International Conference on Logic for Programming, Artificial Intelligence, and Reasoning (LPAR), *Lecture Notes in Computer Science (LNCS)*, vol. 2250, pp. 110–124. Springer, La Habana, Cuba (2001)
85. Sardina, S.: IndiGolog: An Integrated Agent Arquitecture: Programmer and User Manual. University of Toronto (2004). URL http://sourceforge.net/projects/indigolog/
86. Sardina, S.: Deliberation in agent programming languages. Ph.D. thesis, Department of Computer Science (2005)
87. Sardina, S., De Giacomo, G., Lespérance, Y., Levesque, H.J.: On the semantics of deliberation in IndiGolog – from theory to implementation. Annals of Mathematics and Artificial Intelligence **41**(2–4), 259–299 (2004)

88. Sardina, S., De Giacomo, G., Lespérance, Y., Levesque, H.J.: On the limits of planning over belief states. In: Proceedings of Principles of Knowledge Representation and Reasoning (KR), pp. 463–471. Lake District, UK (2005)
89. Sardina, S., de Silva, L.P., Padgham, L.: Hierarchical planning in BDI agent programming languages: A formal approach. In: H. Nakashima, M.P. Wellman, G. Weiss, P. Stone (eds.) Proceedings of Autonomous Agents and Multi-Agent Systems (AAMAS), pp. 1001–1008. ACM Press, Hakodate, Japan (2006)
90. Sardina, S., Padgham, L.: Goals in the context of BDI plan failure and planning. In: E.H. Durfee, M. Yokoo, M.N. Huhns, O. Shehory (eds.) Proceedings of Autonomous Agents and Multi-Agent Systems (AAMAS). ACM Press, Hawaii, USA (2007)
91. Sardina, S., Shapiro, S.: Rational action in agent programs with prioritized goals. In: J.S. Rosenschein, M. Wooldridge, T. Sandholm, M. Yokoo (eds.) Proceedings of Autonomous Agents and Multi-Agent Systems (AAMAS), pp. 417–424. ACM Press, Melbourne, Australia (2003)
92. Sardina, S., Vassos, S.: The Wumpus World in IndiGolog: A preliminary report. In: L. Morgenstern, M. Pagnucco (eds.) Proceedings of the Workshop on Non-monotonic Reasoning, Action and Change at IJCAI (NRAC-05), pp. 90–95 (2005)
93. Scherl, R.B., Levesque, H.J.: Knowledge, action, and the frame problem. Artificial Intelligence Journal 144(1–2), 1–39 (2003)
94. Shapiro, S.: Specifying and verifying multiagent systems using the cognitive agents specification language (CASL). Ph.D. thesis, Department of Computer Science, University of Toronto (2005)
95. Shapiro, S., Lespérance, Y., Levesque, H.J.: The cognitive agents specification language and verification environment for multiagent systems. In: C. Castelfranchi, W.L. Johnson (eds.) Proceedings of Autonomous Agents and Multi-Agent Systems (AAMAS), pp. 19–26. ACM Press (2002)
96. Son, T.C., Baral, C.: Formalizing sensing actions — A transition function based approach. Artificial Intelligence 125(1–2), 19–91 (2001)
97. Soutchanski, M.: An on-line decision-theoretic Golog interpreter. In: Proceedings of the International Joint Conference on Artificial Intelligence (IJCAI), pp. 19–26. Seattle, WA, USA (2001)
98. Thielscher, M.: The fluent calculus. Tech. Rep. CL-2000-01, Computational Logic Group, Artificial Intelligence Institute, Department of Computer Science, Dresden University of Technology (2000)
99. Thielscher, M.: FLUX: A logic programming method for reasoning agents. Theory and Practice of Logic Programming 5(4–5), 533–565 (2005). Special Issue of Theory and Practice of Logic Programming on Constraint Handling Rules
100. Vassos, S.: A feasible approach to disjunctive knowledge in situation calculus. Master's thesis, Department of Computer Science (2005)
101. Vassos, S., Lakemeyer, G., Levesque, H.: First-order strong progression for local-effect basic action theories. In: Proceedings of Principles of Knowledge Representation and Reasoning (KR), pp. 662–672. Sydney, Australia (2008)
102. Vassos, S., Levesque, H.: Progression of situation calculus action theories with incomplete information. In: Proceedings of the International Joint Conference on Artificial Intelligence (IJCAI), pp. 2024–2029. Hyderabad, India (2007)
103. Vassos, S., Levesque, H.: On the progression of situation calculus basic action theories: Resolving a 10-year-old conjecture. In: Proceedings of the National Conference on Artificial Intelligence (AAAI), pp. 1004–1009. Chicago, Illinois, USA (2008)
104. Wang, X., Lespérance, Y.: Agent-oriented requirements engineering using ConGolog and i*. In: G. Wagner, K. Karlapalem, Y. Lespérance, E. Yu (eds.) Agent-Oriented Information Systems 2001, Proceedings of the 3rd International Bi-Conference Workshop AOIS-2001, pp. 59–78. iCue Publishing, Berlin, Germany (2001)
105. Wielemaker, J.: An overview of the SWI-Prolog programming environment. In: F. Mesnard, A. Serebenik (eds.) Proceedings of the 13th International Workshop on Logic Programming Environments, pp. 1–16. Katholieke Universiteit Leuven, Heverlee, Belgium (2003). CW 371

106. Yongmei Liu, H.J.L.: Tractable reasoning with incomplete first-order knowledge in dynamic systems with context-dependent actions. In: Proceedings of the International Joint Conference on Artificial Intelligence (IJCAI), pp. 522–527. Edinburgh, UK (2005)

Chapter 3
Brahms
An Agent-Oriented Language for Work Practice Simulation and Multi-Agent Systems Development

Maarten Sierhuis, William J. Clancey, and Ron J. J. van Hoof

Abstract Brahms is a multi-agent modeling language for simulating human work practice that emerges from work processes in organizations. The same Brahms language can be used to implement and execute distributed multi-agent systems, based on models of work practice that were first simulated. Brahms demonstrates how a multi-agent belief-desire-intention language, symbolic cognitive modeling, traditional business process modeling, activity- and situated cognition theories are brought together in a coherent approach for analysis and design of organizations and human-centered systems.

3.1 Motivation

Brahms was developed as a multiagent modeling and simulation language to visualize the social systems of work for business redesign projects [25]. In the early years (1992-1999), Brahms was purely a modeling and simulation language and tool designed to model people's work practice, i.e. the cultural, circumstantial, interactional influences on how work actually gets done, as opposed to an abstract

Maarten Sierhuis
Carnegie Mellon University Silicon Valley/NASA Ames Research Center, Moffett Field, CA 94035,
Man-Machine Interaction Group, Delft University of Technology, Mekelweg 4, 2628 CD Delft, The Netherlands
e-mail: maarten.sierhuis@nasa.gov

William J. Clancey
NASA Ames Research Center, Moffett Field, CA 94035,
IHMC, Pensacola, FL
e-mail: william.j.clancey@nasa.gov

Ron J. J. van Hoof
Perot Systems/NASA Ames Research Center, Moffett Field, CA 94035,
e-mail: ronnie.j.vanhoof@nasa.gov

R.H. Bordini et al. (eds.), *Multi-Agent Programming*,
DOI 10.1007/978-0-387-89299-3_3, © Springer Science+Business Media, LLC 2009

top-down functional description of an organization's work process. In more recent years (2000-2003) we developed the Brahms language also as an agent-oriented language (AOL) for developing multi-agent systems (MAS). Besides running the Brahms virtual machine (BVM) as a simulation engine, by turning off the simulation clock, the BVM can execute its agents in real-time enabling the execution of a MAS. To couple human activity with external systems, there is an extensive Java application interface (JAPI) allowing the developer to integrate Brahms agents with external software applications, real-time devices, networks, etc, and develop agents completely in Java.

The Brahms language was originally conceived of as a language for modeling[1] contextual behavior of groups of people, called work practice.

> *Work Practice:* The collective performance of contextually situated activities of a group of people who coordinate, cooperate and collaborate while performing these activities synchronously or asynchronously, making use of knowledge previously gained through experiences in performing similar activities.

This created two very important ideas for the language; First, to model a group of people it is very natural to model them as software agents. Second, modeling situated behavior of a group imposes a constraint on the level of detail that is useful in modeling the dependent and independent behavior of the individuals. The right level is a representational level that falls between functional process models and individual cognitive models [6]. If we are interested in modeling a day-in-the-life of say ten or more people, modeling the individual behavior at the level of cognitive task models will be very time consuming, because these models are generally at the millisecond decision-making level. To overcome this kind of detail, the Brahms language uses a more abstract level of behavioral modeling that is derived from Activity Theory [27, 14] and Situated Action [26]. An individual's behavior is represented in terms of activities that take an amount of discrete time and can be decomposed into more detailed subactivities if necessary.

Brahms demonstrates how a multiagent belief-desire-intention (BDI) language, symbolic cognitive modeling, traditional business process modeling, activity- and situated cognition theories are brought together in a coherent approach for analysis and design of organizations and human-centered systems. The Brahms environment consists of different tools to develop, simulate or execute Brahms models and display agent and object interactions. Brahms is freely available for research purposes at the Brahms project website[2].

---

[1] We refer to Brahms programmers as modelers and Brahms programming as modeling, because we feel that Brahms is a fifth-generation multiagent model description language, rather than a third- or fourth-generation programming language.

[2] http://www.agentisolutions.com

3.2 Language

This section provides a detailed description of the Brahms language according to the specific criteria used to compare the different agent-oriented languages in this book. We first discuss the *specifications and syntactical aspects* of the Brahms language. This section discusses all major representational capabilities. Then, we discuss *semantics and verification*. Brahms is a practical language used in many applications at NASA. Brahms was not developed as a formal specification language for BDI and it does not have a formal semantic specification. One could be developed if desired. Brahms is a compiled language and does have a formal syntactic representation, which we will discuss. Next, we discuss *software engineering issues*. As a practical modeling and programming language, Brahms has many influences from object-oriented and rule-based languages. There is a definite influence from the Java programming language. The section ends with some more discussion of *other features of the language*, which focusses on modeling geographical environments.

The Brahms language is a pure AOL. It is *not* a set of Java libraries enabling agent-based programming in the Java language. Instead, Brahms is a full-fledged multiagent language allowing the modeler to easily and naturally represent *multiple agents*. The grammar of the Brahms language in this chapter is provided in EBNF (Extended Backus Naur Form) grammar rules. The notation used in these grammar rules is as in Table 3.1.

Table 3.1 Synopsis of the notation used in EBNF grammar rules

Construct	Interpretation
`::=` `*` `+` `{}` `[]` `|` `.`	Symbols part of the BNF formalism
`X ::= Y`	The syntax of X is defined by Y
`{X}`	Zero or one occurrence of X
`X*`	Zero or more occurrences of X
`X+`	One or more occurrences of X
`X	Y`	One of X or Y (exclusive or)
`[X]`	Grouping construct for specifying scope of operators, e.g. `[X|Y]` or `[X]*`
symbol	Predefined terminal symbol of the language
symbol	User-defined terminal symbol of the language
symbol	Non-terminal symbol

3.2.1 Syntactical Aspects

This subsection answers the question; Does the Brahms language support various agent concepts such as, mental attitudes, deliberation, adaptation, social abilities, and reactive as well as cognitive-based behaviour?

Although Brahms was originally developed for modeling people's behavior, the Brahms language is a *domain independent* language. This means that the modeler decides what a Brahms model represents. Agents can represent whatever autonomous entity the modeler wants to represent, such as a person, an animal, or an autonomous or intelligent system. The following Brahms language features are discussed:

- Mental attributes: attributes, relations, beliefs and facts, no explicit desires, frame instantiations (intentions).
- Deliberation: concluding new beliefs, and use of thoughtframes for reasoning.
- Adaptation: changing beliefs, execution activity behavior and reasoning based on context.
- Social Abilities: groups and group inheritance, communication, and modeling the environment (objects, geography and location).
- Reactive and Cognitive-based behavior: modeling activity behavior, versus pure cognitive behavior, detectables, workframe-activity subsumption.
- Communication: communication activities, and communicative acts.

Brahms is an agent-oriented BDI-like language. It allows easy creation of groups of agents that execute activities based on local beliefs. Below is a simple taxonomy of some of the language concepts discussed in this section:

```
    GROUPS are composed of
       AGENTS having
         BELIEFS and doing
         ACTIVITIES executed by
           WORKFRAMES defined by
             PRECONDITIONS, matching agent's beliefs
             PRIMITIVE ACTIVITIES
             COMPOSITE ACTIVITIES, decomposing the activity
             DETECTABLES, including INTERUPTS, IMPASSES
             CONSEQUENCES, creating new beliefs and/or facts
           DELIBERATION implemented with
             THOUGHTFRAMES defined by
               PRECONDITIONS, matching agent's beliefs
               CONSEQUENCES, creating new beliefs
```

3.2.1.1 Agents, Groups, and Attributes

Agents. A Brahms model is always about the activities of agents. An agent is therefore the most central construct in a Brahms model. Agents adhere to the standard attributes we associate with agency. They are autonomous, can be deliberative, as well as reactive and proactive, and are bounded rational.

```
agent ::=
    agent agent-name { group-membership }
    {
        { display: literal-string ; }
        { cost: number ; }
        { time_unit: number ; }
        { location: area-name ; }
        { icon : literal-string ; }
        { attributes }
        { relations }
        { initial-beliefs }
        { initial-facts }
        { activities }
        { workframes }
        { thoughtframes }
    }

    group-membership ::= memberof group-name [, group-name ]*

    externalagt ::= external agent agent-name ;
```

In the Brahms language, an agent is defined by the keyword *agent*, followed by the agent's name and its *group-membership*. Just as in object-oriented modeling where the concept of an object class enables one to define a type of object, Brahms includes an agent *group* concept to define a group of multiple agents with a similar make-up and behavior (see below). An agent has a number of possible facets or elements that are optional (see agent syntax above).

Group and Group Membership. The concept of a *group* in Brahms is similar to the concept of a template or class in object-oriented programming. A group represents a collection of agents that can perform similar work and have similar properties. A group defines the *attributes* and *relations*, the *initial-beliefs* and *initial-facts*, and the *activities*, *workframes* and *thoughtframes* of members in the group. The difference with classes in object-oriented programming is that the relationship between a group and its members is not an IS-A relationship, but a MEMBER-OF relationship. This is why we speak of "*a member of a group*" instead of "an instance of a group." An agent can be a member of one or more groups. An agent will inherit attributes, relations, initial-beliefs, initial-facts, activities, workframes and thoughtframes from the group(s) it is a member of.

```
group ::=
    group group-name { group-membership }
    {
        { display: literal-string ; }
        { cost: number ; }
        { time_unit: number ; }
        { icon : literal-string ; }
        { attributes }
        { relations }
        { initial-beliefs }
        { initial-facts }
        { activities }
        { workframes }
        { thoughtframes }
    }
```

Using group membership and inheritance, we can model agent organization:

- *Functional Roles*
  Groups are similar to that of functional roles in an organization. A group in Brahms could represent a typical role in an organization and the work activities that someone performs when playing that role. For example, we could represent the role of Maintenance Technician or Flight Controller as a group.
- *Structural or Organizational Groupings*
  A group can also depict an organizational group. For example, we can define a group as "members of the Work System Design & Evaluation group at NASA Ames Research Center." We could now describe the work-activities, and initial-beliefs of members of the WSD&E group, such as when they have group meetings, etc.
- *Informal and Social Groupings*
  We can also create informal and social groups related to conceptual definitions that make sense in the modeling activity. For instance, in modeling the people at work we could create a social group "all people meeting at the water cooler." We can now describe the activities, workframes, thoughtframes and initial-beliefs that people meeting at the water cooler have in common. This might not be that interesting, but in modeling people's interactions, with for example, legacy systems we could define an informal group of "system-xyz users." In this group we can describe how people interact with system-xyz, and

what initial-beliefs the system users have (e.g. the initial-belief that the system contains specific data).

The group inheritance diagram from figure 3.1 is written in the Brahms language as follows:

```
jimport gov.nasa.arc.brahms.modat.kfx.KfxFile;

group Student {
    attributes:
        public string name;
        public boolean male;
        private int howHungry;
        private double preferredCashOut;
        private long perceivedtime;
        public symbol colorHair;
        public BaseGroup spouse;
        public relation(Student) studyFriend;
}

group BrahmsModeler {
    attributes:
        public map myIntIndexMap;
        public map myStringIndexMap;
        public Group myGroup;
        public java(KfxFile) javaKfxFile;
}

agent Alex_Agent memberof Student, BrahmsModeler { }
agent Kim_Agent memberof Student { }
agent Joyce_Agent { }
```

The BaseGroup definition does not have to be made, because it is part of the Base Model library that is always imported. All groups are by definition a member of BaseGroup (see Fig. 3.1).

Attributes. After the optional agent (and group) facets, there are a number of sections in an agent (and group). First, the *attributes section* defines the attributes for the agent. Attributes represent a property of a group or agent. Figure 3.1 and the Brahms code above show the attribute definitions for the two groups Student and BrahmsModeler. Attributes do not have values as in object-oriented programming. Instead, attributes have values as part of the beliefs of an agent or facts in the world. Attribute values are assigned or changed by asserting new beliefs or facts (see section 3.2.1.2).

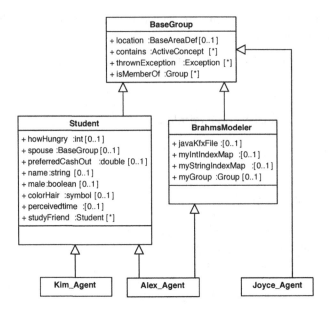

Fig. 3.1 **Group membership and multiple-inheritance**

Relations: Relations, defined in the *relations section*, represent a relationship between two objects, two agents, or an agent and an object. The scope of a relation is similar to that of an attribute. Relations are assigned or changed by asserting new beliefs or facts. Relations are unary relations between the left-hand side and the right-hand side in the relation (see fig. 3.2 and the source code below).

Fig. 3.2 **Relations**

```
class Song { ... }

object WhatAWonderfulWorld instanceof Song { ... }

object LaVieEnRose instanceof Song { ... }
```

```
group Artist {
    relations:
        public Song Performs;
}

agent LuisArmstrong memberof Artist {
    initial_beliefs:
        (current Performs WhatAWonderfulWorld);
        (current Performs LaVieEnRose);
}
```

3.2.1.2 Facts and Beliefs

In Brahms an agent acts according to its beliefs and its ability to deduce new beliefs from its current beliefs. In this section we describe the intentional notions of Brahms agents. The state of the world and that of agents in Brahms is stored in informational units called *facts* and *beliefs*.

Facts. A fact is meant to represent some physical state of the world or an attribute of some object or agent. Facts are globally true. Unlike objects, agents cannot reason with or act directly on facts, however, agents can detect facts in the world (representing noticing or sensing) turning them into beliefs for the agent (see section 3.2.1.7). Each BVM contains its own world fact-set containing all facts that are created during runtime by agents and objects running in that particular BVM. By representing part of the context of the agent as facts in the world, we are able to have agents react to the same facts in different ways, depending on their beliefs about these facts. Konolige defines a common fact, CF, as a fact that is known by all agents [13]. In Brahms, it is not necessary that an agent has any belief, right or wrong, about a fact. Although it is easily possible to have all agents inherit an initial-belief that corresponds to an initial-fact, or have all agents detect a particular fact at initialization, if it exists.

Beliefs. A belief represents an agent's interpretation of a fact in the world. A belief held by an agent may differ from the corresponding fact. For example, from our above example, if Alex is studying in South Hall he could believe "South Hall is 65 degrees" while the fact is that "South Hall is 80 degrees." A belief can also represent an agentÃÕs conception of the world (s)he lives in. For example, our student Alex could believe "I am a student at University of California, Berkeley"—a belief about locations, or geography of the world the agents is located in, is modeled using the Brahms geography model described in section 3.2.4. Beliefs are local to an agent. Agents can reason about their beliefs and create new beliefs, and agents can communicate their beliefs to other agents and objects.

Beliefs and facts can be defined as initial beliefs and facts at the group, agent, class and object level. Initial facts can also be defined for area-definitions and areas. An agent or object can also create beliefs and facts while performing an activity. A belief or fact can be thought of as an object-attribute-value triplet.

initial-belieforfact ::= ([value-expression | relational-expression]);

value-expression ::= obj-attr equality-operator value |
    obj-attr equality-operator sgl-object-ref

equality-operator ::= = | !=

relational-expression ::=
    tuple-object-ref relation-name sgl-object-ref { is truth-value }

value ::= literal-string | number | param-name | **unknown**

obj-attr ::=
    tuple-object-ref . attribute-name {(collection-index)}

tuple-object-ref ::= agent-name | object-name |
    conceptual-object-name | area-name |
    variable-name | param-name |
    current

sgl-object-ref ::= tuple-object-ref | **unknown**

Initial beliefs and facts are a way to populate agents and objects with an initial set of beliefs and create an initial set of facts in the world at agent initialization time. However, an agent can not do much if its belief-set or the world's fact-set cannot change. Agents and object can change beliefs and facts in the world by performing some behavior. How an agent or object can behave will be explained later on. Here we explain the command an agent or object can use to create new or change previously asserted beliefs and/or facts.

Facts and beliefs are created using a *conclude* statement. An agent or object can create or change either a belief for itself, or a fact in the world, or both. The syntax of the conclude statement is as follows.

consequence ::= **conclude(**(resultcomparison){, belief-certainty}
    {, fact-certainty)};

resultcomparison ::= [result-val-comp | rel-comp]

result-val-comp ::=
    obj-attr equality-operator expression |
    obj-attr equality-operator literal-symbol |
    obj-attr equality-operator literal-string |
    obj-attr equality-operator sgl-object-ref |
    tuple-object-ref equality-operator sgl-object-ref

belief-certainty ::= **bc:** unsigned
fact-certainty ::= **fc:** unsigned

The conclude statement has two variables that can be specified after the result-comparison. These are the belief-certainty (bc) and fact-certainty (fc) variables. These variables specify with what certainty the agent creates the belief or fact respectively. The value of these variables can be an unsigned integer between the interval [0, 100], and specifies with what percent certainty the belief or fact is created. For example the following conclude statement states that the agent will get a belief "(current.male = true)" with 100% certainty, thus in all cases, and a fact with 0% certainty, thus never.

conclude((current.male = true), bc:100, fc:0);

3.2.1.3 Thoughtframes

Thoughtframes (thoughtframe! TFR) define deductions, mostly referred to as production rules. TFRs are taken to be inferences an agent makes. TFRs do not perform actions, consume no time, and cannot be interrupted. The only allowable statements in a TFR is one or more consequences, concluding new beliefs. Because TFRs represent reasoning, the agent cannot create or change facts in the world in a TFR. Therefore, no matter the value of the fact-certainty in a consequence in a TFR, a fact will never be created. A TFR consists of a variable declaration section, one or more preconditions and one or more consequences. The syntax of a TFR is given below.

```
thoughtframe ::=
    thoughtframe thoughtframe-name {
        { display : literal-string ; }
        { repeat : truth-value ; }
        { priority : unsigned ; }
        { variable-decl }
        { [ precondition-decl thoughtframe-body-decl ] |
        thoughtframe-body-decl }
    }

variable-decl ::= variables : [ variable ]*

precondition-decl ::=
    when ( { [ precondition ] [ and precondition ]* } )

thoughtframe-body-decl ::=
    do { [ thoughtframe-body-element ; ]* }

thoughtframe-body-element ::= consequence
```

As we will see later on, TFRs can be placed within composite activities, allowing for modeling problem-solving activities that take time. This is seen as: while the agent is 'in' the activity, the agent reasons using its TFRs. Conclusions of new beliefs in TFRs can execute new TFRs and/or workframes (WFR). Preconditions are similar for TFRs and WFRs.

Preconditions. When the preconditions of a TFR match the beliefs of the agent or object, its consequences are immediately executed, similar to forward-chaining production rules. An important point is that preconditions for agents only match with the beliefs of the agent. The syntax for preconditions is as follows.

```
precondition ::= [ known | unknown ] ( novalcomparison ) |
    [ knownval | not ] ( evalcomparison )

novalcomparison ::= obj-attr |
    obj-attr relation-name |
    tuple-object-ref relation-name
```

```
        evalcomparison ::= eval-val-comp | rel-comp

    eval-val-comp ::=
        expression evaluation-operator expression |
        obj-attr equality-operator literal-symbol |
        obj-attr equality-operator literal-string |
        obj-attr equality-operator sgl-object-ref |

        sgl-object-ref equality-operator sgl-object-ref

    rel-comp ::=
        obj-attr relation-name obj-attr { is truth-value } |
        obj-attr relation-name sgl-object-ref { is truth-value } |
        tuple-object-ref relation-name sgl-object-ref { is truth-value }
```

The agent's inference engine (part of the BVM) is implemented based on the well-known RETE algorithm [11]. However, unlike in OPS5 [3], each agent has two types of reasoning state networks (RSN); one for beliefs and one for facts. At this moment Brahms only supports conjunctions (AND) in its preconditions, but we will be adding disjunctions (OR) soon, because, even though you do not need disjunctions, it is sometimes easier for rule maintenance to be able to write rules more compactly using disjunctions.

Precondition Operators. There are four types of preconditions. The precondition types are operators that evaluate to *true* or *false*, depending on evaluating the belief-condition in each operator to match on one or more beliefs in the agent's belief-set.

knownval(evalcomparison) precondition operator evaluates to true iff:

Exists(belief b) [Matches(b, evalcomparison)]

This means that there exists a belief in the agent's belief-set that matches the evalcomparison. Given the below *TFR for agent Alex* and assuming the *belief-set for agent Alex*, both preconditions evaluate to *true*, firing the TFR.

```
thoughtframe tf_HowMuchMoneyToGet_HungryEQhigh_1 {
    when (knownval(current.needCash = true) and
          knownval(current.hungryness = high))
    do {
        conclude((current.preferredCashOut = 15), bc:100, fc:0);
    }
```

```
}
Alex' belief-set:
{
   (Alex.needCash = true);
   (Alex.hungryness = high);
}
```

The keyword *current* matches on the agent itself, and because the TFR is for agent Alex the two beliefs match on the preconditions. Both *knownval* preconditions return true, making the entire *when-clause* true and thus firing the TFR executing the *body-statement*. After the TFR execution, agent Alex' belief-set will now include the belief *(Alex.preferredCashOut = 15)*, because the belief-certainty is 100%. Unlike traditional production-rule systems (such as OPS5), the created belief will have a timestamp. This timestamp equals the simulation-clock time at which the TFR was fired (or system-clock time in case of real-time execution).

not(evalcomparison) precondition operator evaluates to true iff:

not(Exists(belief b) [Matches(b, evalcomparison)])

This means that none of the beliefs in the agent's belief-set match on the evalcomparison, similar to all beliefs do not match on the evalcomparison, and is the way to express that the precondition evaluates to true if the agent does not have a belief that matches the evalcomparison.

```
thoughtframe tf_HowMuchMoneyToGet_HungryEQhigh_2 {
   when (not(current.needCash = true) and
         knownval(current.hungryness = high))
   do {
         conclude((current.preferredCashOut = 10), bc:100, fc:0);
   }
}
Alex' belief-set:
{
   (Alex.needCash = false);
   (Alex.hungryness = high);
}
```

In this case all preconditions also match the beliefs of agent Alex. The *not* precondition evaluates to true, because even though the agent has a belief about the attribute needCash, the value of that belief is 'false' while the precondition tries to match on the value 'true'. Therefore, the precondition evaluates to true. After firing of the above TFR, agent Alex will have the belief *(current.preferredCashOut = 10)*.

One might ask what would have happened if agent Alex does not have any belief about the attribute needCash for Alex, would the *not* precondition evaluate to true? The answer to this question is, yes it would, because it still would hold true that all of agent Alex' beliefs do not match the evalcomparison of the precondition.

Known precondition operator evaluates to true iff:

Exists(belief b) [Matches(b, novalcomparison)]

This means that there exists a belief in the agent's belief-set that matches the novalcomparison. A novalcomparison is a precondition expression that matches on any belief the agent has about the specified attribute or relation, without providing a necessary right-hand side value. Thus, regardless of the right-hand side value of the belief (whether for an attribute or a relation), if a belief exists the *known* precondition evaluates to *true*. Given the below TFR for agent Alex and assuming the belief-set for agent Alex, both preconditions evaluate to true, firing the TFR.

```
thoughtframe tf_HowMuchMoneyToGet_HungryEQhigh_3 {
    when (known(current.needCash) and
          knownval(current.hungryness = high))
    do {
          conclude((current.preferredCashOut = 15), bc:100, fc:0);
    }
}
Alex' belief-set:
{
    (Alex.needCash = false);
    (Alex.hungryness = high);
}
```

In this case all preconditions still also match the beliefs of agent Alex. The *known* precondition evaluates to true, because the agent has a belief about the attribute needCash, even though the value of that belief is 'false'. The precondition matches on any belief of the form *(Alex.needCash = <any-value>)*. After firing of the above TFR, agent Alex will have the belief *(current.preferredCashOut = 15)*.

unknown(novalcomparison) evaluates to true iff:

not(Exists(belief b) [Matches(b, novalcomparison))]

This means that none of the beliefs in the agent's belief-set match on the novalcomparison, similar to all beliefs do not match on the novalcomparison. Thus, regardless of the right-hand side value of the belief (whether for an attribute or a relation), if a belief exists the *unknown* precondition evaluates to *false*. This is a way to express that the precondition evaluates to true if the agent does not have a belief about a given attribute or relation. Given the below TFR for agent Alex and assuming the belief-set for agent Alex, the *unknown* preconditions evaluates to *false*, preventing the TFR from firing.

```
thoughtframe tf_HowMuchMoneyToGet_HungryEQhigh_4 {
    when (unknown(current.needCash) and
          knownval(current.hungryness = high))
    do {
          conclude((current.preferredCashOut = 5), bc:100, fc:0);
    }
}
Alex' belief-set:
{
    (Alex.needCash = true);
    (Alex.hungryness = high);
}
```

The *unknown* precondition's novalcomparison still matches on the needCash attribute belief for agent Alex. The *unknown* precondition thus evaluates to false, because the agent has a belief about the attribute needCash. The *unknown* precondition returns false for any belief of the form *(Alex.needCash = <any-value>)*. One might ask what would happen if the right-hand side value of the belief is 'unknown', would the *unknown* precondition evaluate to true? The answer is no, in such a case the precondition would evaluate to false, because having a belief of the form *(Alex.needCash = unknown)* means that the agent knows about the attribute needCase, even though it does not know its specific boolean value.

Defining Thoughtframes. Thoughtframes can be defined at the "top-level" of a group, agent, class and/or object. Thoughtframes defined at the top-level are always active, meaning that their preconditions will be evaluated at each change in the agent's belief-set.

```
group Student {
    ...
    thoughtframes:
        thoughtframe tf_HowMuchMoneyToGet_HungryEQhigh_1 {
```

```
                    when (knownval(current.needCash = true) and
                        knownval(current.hungryness = high))
                    do {
                            conclude((current.preferredCashOut = 15), bc:100, fc:0);
                    }//do
            }//tf_HowMuchMoneyToGet_HungryEQhigh_1
    }//Student
```

It is also possible to define thoughtframes within a *composite activity*. In this case the thoughtframes will only be active when the agent is executing the composite activity, and is the way to model problem-solving as an activity taking time. For an explanation of composite activities see section 3.2.1.6.

```
group Student {
    ...
    activities:
        composite_activity SolveCashOutProblem( ) {
            ...
            thoughtframes:
                thoughtframe tf_HowMuchMoneyToGet_HungryEQhigh_1 {
                    when (knownval(current.needCash = true) and
                        knownval(current.hungryness = high))
                    do {
                            conclude((current.preferredCashOut = 15), fc:0);
                    }//do
                }//tf_HowMuchMoneyToGet_HungryEQhigh_1
            ...
        }//composite_activity SolveCashOutProblem
    ...
}//Student
```

Variables. Variables can be used to write more generic rules (TFRs) or templates for activities (WFRs). Variables have quantifiers, as will be described below. Before a variable can be used it has to be declared, and the scope of the variable is bound to the frame it is declared in. There are three quantifiers for variables: *foreach*, *collectall*, and *forone*. Variables are used in preconditions to be bound to agents, objects or values. When bound in preconditions, variables can be used in consequences, detectables, and pass-by-reference parameters for activities. The syntax for defining a variable in a TFR or WFR is as follows.

```
variable ::=
    [foreach | collectall | forone ] ( type-def ) variable-name ;
```

The quantifier affects the way a variable is bound to a specific instance of the defined type of the variable.

Foreach quantifier. A foreach variable is bound to only one instance of its type definition, but for each instance that can be bound to the variable a separate frame instantiation is created. Consider, for example, the following thoughtframe with a foreach variable.

```
thoughtframe tf_CountOrders {
    variables:
        foreach(Order) order;
    when (knownval(order is-assigned-to current))
    do {
        conclude((current.numberOfOrders = current.numberOfOrders + 1));
    }
}
```

If three orders are assigned to agent Alex_Agent and the agent has beliefs for all three of the orders matching the precondition, the agent's engine creates three TFR instantiations (TFI), and in each TFI the foreach variable is bound to one of the three orders.

Collectall quantifier. A collectall variable can be bound to more then one instance as a list. The variable is bound to all matching agent or object instances (depending on its type), and only one TFI is created. Consider the previous example with a collectall variable declaration:

```
variables:
    collectall(Order) order;
```

In this situation the agent's engine creates one TFI and binds the collectall variable to a list of all three orders.

Forone quantifier. A forone variable can be bound to only one instance or value, and only one TFI is created. A forone variable binds to a random belief-instance found and ignores other possible matches. In the previous example, the variable declaration would look like:

```
variables:
    forone(Order) order;
```

In this situation, similar to the collectall, only one TFI gets created, but, unlike in the collectall case, only one of the three orders gets bound to the variable.

Unbound variables. A declared variable need not be used in a precondition. In that case the variable is unbound (that is, it does not get a value) when a frame instantiation is created. An unbound variable can be bound in an activity. Note that an unbound variable may not be used in a consequence statement, which will always result in a runtime error.

Repeat. A TFR can be executed one or more times depending on the value of the *repeat* facet. In case the repeat facet is set to false, the TFR can only be performed one time for a specific binding of the variables, called a thoughtframe instantiation (TFI). The scope of the repeat facet of a TFR defined as part of a composite activity is limited to the time the activity is active, meaning that the TFR with a specific variable binding and a repeat facet set to false will not execute repeatedly while the composite activity is active.

Priority. Setting a TFR's *priority* facet allows control over the execution sequence of TFRs when more then one TFR is available at the same time. The priority facet can be set with a value greater or equal to zero. When two TFRs are available to be fired at the same time, the one with the highest priority will fire first. When both priorities are the same the sequence of execution is undefined. The default value for the priority facet, when it is not specified, is zero. Note that it is not recommended to use priorities to control the sequence of thoughtframe execution. A better modeling practice is to define preconditions controling TFR execution [5].

3.2.1.4 Primitive Activities

The central concept in Brahms, for the main purpose of modeling human behavior, is the concept of *activity*. An activity is an abstraction of real-life actions that help accomplish a daily task. A model of an agent's activities describes what the agent actually does over time (i.e. its behavior), based on the causal relationship between the decision to perform an activity and the past and present state of its context. In describing people's real-life activities, each activitiy in the world takes time no matter how short. A person is always within an activity taking action. Sleeping is an activity, waiting for the bus is an activity, simply doing nothing is an activity. Indeed, being alive is an activity. The following key points can be made about activities:

1. Reasoning is an activity taking time, not just an inference or deduction. Thus logical inferences happen within an activity.
2. Activities might not involve goals and tasks. For example, answering the phone is an activity that might not be part of any specific task that is being accomplished. In fact, it might be an activity that is interrupting the task being worked on.
3. Modeling activity behavior involves more than logical inferencing, namely the representation of chronological activities that agents do.
4. The activation of an activity is constrained by preconditions that are associated with an activity template it is part of. For example, activities may have preferential start times, as expressed in preconditions for the template, which may refer to the time in hours, minutes, seconds, day of the year, and/or day of the week.
5. An activity may be interrupted by a scheduled activity, such as going to lunch at noon. Time may change the priorities of activities and different people might do the same activities at different times.

In summary, activities are socially constructed engagements, situated in the real world, taking time, effort and application of knowledge, with a defined beginning and end, while not necessarily needing goals in the sense of problem-solving tasks, and being interruptable, resumable and able to be impassed. In this chapter we only describe the syntax and semantics of the Brahms activity language. For more discussion about the theory behind activities in Brahms, we refer the reader to [8, 19]. Brahms has different types of primitive activities.

- *Primitive activities*: These are the lowest level activities in an activity model. They are user-defined, take some time, but are not further specified in any detail. Parameters are time and resources. At any time during execution an agent is always executing some primitive activity. If an agent is not executing a primitive activity, one can say that the human-behavior model is underspecified.
- *Predefined activities*: These are language-level primitive activities with predefined semantics (e.g. communicate, move, get, put).
- *Java activities*: A Brahms Java activity is an user-defined primitive activity that is implemented as a Java class, using the Brahms JAPI. Java code may cause an action to happen completely outside the BVM (e.g. pop-up a dialog that says "hello world"). A Java activity can also do things within the BVM. Java code can generate output parameter values and assign them to unbound variables in a WFR, or generate new agents or objects within the Brahms model being executed. Java activities can also create new beliefs and facts, as well as interface to external systems.

activities ::= **activities :** [activity]*

activity ::=

```
        primitive-activity |
        predefined-activity |
        java-activity |
        composite-activity

    predefined-activity ::=
        move-activity |
        create-agent-activity |
        create-object-activity |
        communicate-activity |
        broadcast-activity |
        get-activity |
        put-activity
```

All activities have to be declared in the activities section of either a group, agent, class, object, or composite activity. The declared activities can then be referenced in the workframes (WFRs) defined for the group, agent, class or object. It is possible to define input parameters for primitive activities. These input parameters can be used to make activities more generic. Activities can be assigned a priority. The priorities of activities in a workframe are used to define the priority of a workframe. The workframe will get the priority of the activity with the highest priority defined in the workframe. Activities and thus workframes have a duration. The duration of the activity can be defined to be a fixed amount of time or a random amount of time. For a fixed amount of time, the random facet has to be set to false and the max-duration attribute has to be set to the maximum duration in seconds. The duration of the activity can also be defined to be a random amount of time. To define a random amount of time the random facet has to be set to true, the min-duration facet has to be set to the minimum duration of the activity in seconds and the max-duration facet has to be set to the maximum duration of the activity in seconds.

```
primitive-activity ::=
primitive_activity activity-name ({param−decl [, param−decl ]*})
{
    { prim-act-facets }
}
```

```
prim-act-facets ::=
{ display : ID.literal-string ; }
{ priority : [ ID.unsigned | param-name ] ; }
{ random : [ ID.truth-value | param-name ] ; }
{ min_duration : [ ID.unsigned | param-name ] ; }
{ max_duration : [ ID.unsigned | param-name ] ; }
{ resources : [ param-name | OBJ.object-name ]
              [ , [ param-name | OBJ.object-name ]* ; }
```

Below is the definition of a Study primitive activity. The primitive activity takes a Book object as a parameter, which is used as a resource in the activity. The activity has a random duration between 30 minutes and 2 hours. The durations are given in seconds.

```
primitive_activity Study (Book course_book)
{
    display : "Study for a Cours" ;
    priority : 10 ;
    random : true ;
    min_duration : 1800 ; /* 30 mins */
    max_duration : 7200 ; /* 2 hours */
    resources : course_book;
}
```

3.2.1.5 Workframes

An agent cannot always apply all its available activities, given the agent's belief-state and the location it is in. Each activity is therefore associated with a conditional statement or constraint, representing a condition/activity template called *workframe* (WFR). WFRs are situation-action rules taking time. A WFR defines conditions under which an agent or object can perform an activity (or activities). WFRs are similar to TFRs, with similar syntax. They have preconditions that are matched against the belief-set of the agent or object. In short, activities describe *what* agents do, workframes describe *when* agents do what they do, thus defining when activities are executed. Workframes can be associated with groups/agents and classes/object. Having two agents with different workframes performing the same activity, can represent individual differences.

```
workframe ::=
workframe workframe-name
{
    { display : ID.literal-string ; }
    { type : factframe | dataframe ; }
    { repeat : truth-value ; }
    { priority : unsigned ; }
    { variable-decl }
    { detectable-decl }
    { [ precondition-decl workframe-body-decl ] |
         workframe-body-decl }
}

workframe-name ::= ID.name

variable-decl ::= variables : [ variable ]*

detectable-decl ::= detectables : [ detectable ]*

precondition-decl ::= when ({[precondition] [and precondition]*})

workframe-body-decl ::= do {[workframe-body-element]*}

workframe-body-element ::= [activity-ref | consequence |
         delete-operation]

activity-ref ::= activity-name({param-expr[, param-expr]*});

delete-operation ::= delete [ variable-name | param-name ];
```

A workframe is a more important unit than the simple precondition-activity-consequence design might suggest, because a workframe may model relationships involving location, object resources such as tools and documents, required information, other agents the agent is working and communicating with, and the state of previous or ongoing work. Active workframes may establish a context of activities for the agent and thereby model the agent's intentions, e.g., calling person X to give or get information, or going to the fax machine to look for document Y. In this way, behavior may be modeled as continuous across time, and not merely reactive.

```
group PrimitiveActivityPerformer {
    attributes:
        public boolean execute_PAC_1;

    activities:
        primitive_activity PAC_1(int pri) {
            display: "PAC 1";
            priority: pri;
            max_duration: 900;
        }


        primitive_activity PAC_2(int pri, int dur) {
            display: "PAC 2";
            priority: pri;
            max_duration: dur;
        }

    workframes:
        workframe wf_PAC_1 {
            repeat: true;
            when (knownval(current.execute_PAC_1 = true))
            do {
                PAC_1(1);
                conclude((current.execute_PAC_1 = false));
            }
        }

        workframe wf_PAC_2 {
            repeat: true;
            do {
                PAC_2(0, 1800);
                conclude((current.execute_PAC_1 = true), bc:25);
                PAC_2(0, 600);
            }
        }
}
```

Workframes can be interrupted and resumed, based on the priorities of activity references within. Priorities of activities can be dynamically assigned through parameters passed in. The above example shows two WFRs in the group PrimitiveActivityPerformer. WFR *wf_PAC_2* has no preconditions and *repeat = true*. This workframe will therefore always fire in an endless loop. WFR *wf_PAC_1* has one precondition, which at the start of execution will always be false, since the agent will not have a belief that will match it.

On closer examination of the body of WFR *wf_PAC_2* we see that the WFR first calls activity *PAC_2* with priority zero and duration 1800 seconds and later on again with priority zero with a duration of 600 seconds. Given that the priorities of both activity-references in the WFR are zero, the WFR itself gets a priority of zero at instantiation (WFI).

However, in between the two activity-references the activity concludes a belief that will match the precondition for WFR *wf_PAC_1*. A match on this precondition would create a WFI for *wf_PAC_1* with priority one due to the fact that it calls activity *PAC_1* with priority one, and always has a duration of 900 seconds after which the conclude statement sets the belief to false, which stops the repeat=true and ends the WFI. Thus, WFR *wf_PAC_1* always only fires ones, even though the repeat is set to true.

Because the WFI for *wf_PAC_1* gets priority one its priority is higher than that of WFR *wf_PAC_2*. This *interrupts* the WFI for *wf_PAC_2* after the conclude statement, and starts a WFI for *wf_PAC_1* for 900 seconds. After the WFI for *wf_PAC_1* is completed, the WFI for *wf_PAC_2* again becomes the only WFI and thus automatically the highest priority WFI, and thus *wf_PAC_2* continues execution at the point it was interrupted, which is at the start of the second *PAC_2* activity-reference.

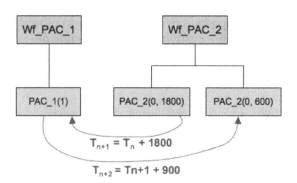

Fig. 3.3 Interrupted Workframe-Activity Hierarchy

As you can see in Fig. 3.3 WFR *wf_PAC_2* gets interrupted after the first call to activity *PAC_2*, at time $T_n + 1800$. At that time activity *PAC_1* starts executing. The next event is the end of activity *PAC_1* and thus of WFI *wf_PAC_1*. At time $T_{n+1} + 900$ WFI *wf_PAC_2* comes out of being interrupted and again becomes the current WFI, and the second activity *PAC_2* starts execution.

There is one more point to make about WFR *wf_PAC_2*; the conclude statement has a belief-certainty of 25. This means that the belief in the conclude statement is only created in 25% of the time. This means that the interruption of *wf_PAC_2* only occurs once in four executions on average.

Primitive activities take time, which may be specified by the modeler as a definite quantity or a random quantity within a range. However, because WFIs can be interrupted and never resumed, when an activity will actually finish cannot be predicted from its start time.

3.2.1.6 Composite Activities

Composite activities are user-defined detailed activities that are decomposed into sub-activities. The lowest activity in a composite activity is always either a primitive-, predefined-, or a Java activity. A composite activity describes what an agent does while it is "in" the activity. A composite activity can be interrupted, when one of its lower-level activities gets interrupted, or one of its contained workframes gets interrupted.

A composite activity requires one or more workframes to execute. Since activities are called within the do-part of a workframe, each is performed at a certain time within the workframe. The body of a workframe has a top-down, left-to-right execution sequence (see Fig. 3.4). Preference or relative priority of workframes can be modeled by grouping them into ordered composite activities. The workframes within a composite activity, however, can be performed in any order depending on when their preconditions are satisfied. In this way, workframes can explicitly control executions of composite activities, and execution of workframes depend not on their order, but on the satisfiability of their preconditions and the priorities of their activities.

```
composite-activity :: =
composite-activity activity-name( { param-decl [ , param-decl ]* } )
{
    { display : literal-string ; }
    { priority : [ unsigned | param-name ] ; }
    { end_condition : [ detectable | nowork ] ; }
    { detectable-decl }
    { activities }
    { workframes }
    { thoughtframes }
}
```

A composite activity can terminate in the following three ways:

1. A composite activity terminates whenever the WFR in which it is executed terminates, due to a WFR detectable of type complete or abort (see section 3.2.1.7).

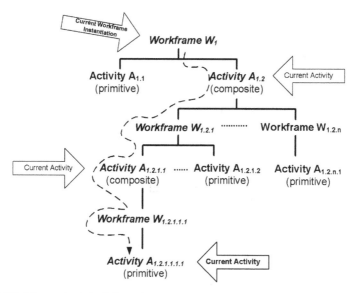

Fig. 3.4 Workframe-Activity Hierarchy

2. A composite activity terminates immediately whenever its *end_condition* is declared to be a *detectable*, and a detectable with an *end_activity* action is declared within the composite activity and is activated.
3. A composite activity terminates when the modeler has defined the *end_condition* to be *nowork*, and there is no workframe in the composite activity that is either available or is the current workframe being executed.

During the execution of a composite activity, the engine continuously checks whether the agent has received a belief that matches any detectables.

3.2.1.7 Detectables

A detectable is a language construct used within an activity or WFR by which an agent may notice facts in the world. The noticing of the fact may cause the agent to continue, impasse, stop, or to finish the activity or WFR. Detectables are used for detecting facts and reacting to beliefs that are created based on the fact detection, while the agent is executing a WFR and an activity. It allows for modeling contextual awareness of the agent, which means that the agent only detects relevant facts for the current activity. This enables modeling of reactive behavior that is constrained by the agent's activity, i.e. what it is currently doing.

```
detectable :: =
detectable detectable-name {
    { when ( [ whenever | unsigned ] ) }
        detect ( ( resultcomparison ) { , detect-certainty } )
    { then [ workframe-det | activity-det ] } ;
}

detect-certainty :: = dc : unsigned

workframe-det :: = continue | impasse | abort | complete

activity-det :: = end_activity
```

A detectable is defined in a workframe (see workframe-det) or in a composite activity (see activity-det). A detectable is active while a workframe/activity is active. It is used for noticing states of the world, and being able to act upon those.

When-condition: For each detectable it needs to be specified when the detectable is active in the workframe or activity. There are two options:

- *Whenever*: This means that, when the workframe or activity in which the detectable is defined is active, the detectable is checked every time a new fact is asserted and also every time a new belief is asserted for the agent.
- *At a specified percent completion time*: An unsigned integer specifies that, when the workframe or activity in which the detectable is defined is active, the detectable needs to be checked at the percentage completion of the workframe or activity, varying from 0% (start) to 100% (end) completion. These kind of detectables are only checked once.

The default, if the when-condition is not specified, is *whenever*.

Detect-condition: There is a two-step process for the activation of detactables:

1. Fact Detection: This step is subdivided into two parts:
    a. Notice fact: Facts are matched on only the left-hand side of the detect condition.
    b. Create belief: fact becomes a belief, regardless of the right-hand side of the detect condition.

2. Trigger action: Execute the detectable-type action, when the detect condition is *true*, based solely on the existence of the belief(s) in the agent's belief-set that match the detect-condition.

Detect-certainty: The fact detect-certainty is a number ranging from 0 to 100 and represents the probability that the fact(s) will be detected, based on the detect-condition. A detect-certainty of 0% means that the fact(s) will never be detected. A detect-certainty of 100% means that a fact will always be detected, based on the left-hand side of the detect-condition in the detectable. Any detect-certainty in between means that the fact(s) will be detected given a probability with a normal distribution between 0 and 1. The default, if the detect-certainty is not specified, is 100. Note, however, that the detect-certainty has no influence on the agent getting the fact as a belief by other means then the detectable. For instance, the agent can get the belief(s) through reasoning (TFRs), or through a communication with other agents. In that case, the detectable action can fire, regardless of the fact detect-certainty

Detectable-action: An agent never reacts directly to the facts it detects, only to the beliefs that match the detect condition. A detectable merely causes a belief to be asserted as part of its fact detection. The action portion or trigger is activated by matching against the beliefs; i.e. it is possible to trigger the action of a detectable by only asserting a belief without the same fact being present in the world state. Detection and triggers are evaluated independent of one another. There are five different detectable actions possible, the first four are only valid for detectables in WFRs and the last one is only valid for detectables in composite activities:

- *continue*: This action has no effect, and only used for having agents detect facts and turn them into beliefs (i.e. only noticing, and no action). If no detectable-action is specified, this is the default action.
- *impasse*: This action impasses the workframe until the impasse is resolved. The detect-condition is the impasse condition. What this means is that as long as the agent has a belief that matches the detect-condition in the impasse-detectable, the WFI is impassed. As soon as the agent gets a belief that makes the detect-condition false, the impasse is resolved and the WFI becomes interrupted, vying for becoming the current WFI again, based on priority.
- *abort*: This action terminates the workframe immediately.
- *complete*: This action terminates the current activity and skips all remaining activities in the workframe, but still executes all remaining consequences.
- *end_activity*: This action is only meaningful when used in a detectable for a composite activities. It causes the composite activity to be ended immediately, regardless if there are workframes or thoughtframes in it that are or can become active.

3.2.1.8 Classes and Objects

In Brahms, agents are intentional. However we also want to be able to describe artifacts in the real world as action-oriented systems, but unintentional at the same time. We model such an artifact as an object. An example of an object in Brahms is a fax machine. If we want to describe the behavior of a fax machine, we could argue that we could describe a fax machine as an intentional agent. However, in the real world we would never ascribe intention to the actions of a fax machine. A fax machine mainly reacts to facts in the world; such as a person pushing the start button on the fax machine that makes the fax machine start faxing a document. Since in Brahms we are interested in describing the world with its animate and inanimate entities, we want the capability to make a difference between an intentional entity (an agent), like a person, and an unintentional entity (an object) like a fax machine.

An object, in Brahms, is a construct that generally represents an artifact or data. Objects could be data objects (e.g. a database record), inanimate objects (e.g. a table) or computational objects (e.g. a computer system). The key properties of objects are facts, beliefs, thoughtframes, workframes and activities, which together represent the state and causal behaviors of objects. Some objects may have internal states, such as information in a computer, that are modeled as beliefs. Other artifact states such as the fact that a phone is off the hook are facts about the artifact in the world.

Classes: Classes in Brahms represent an abstraction of one or more object instances. The concept of a class in Brahms is similar to the concept of a template or class in object-oriented programming (Rumbaugh et al. 1998). It defines the thoughtframes, activities and workframes, initial-facts and initial-beliefs for instances of that class (objects). Brahms does not allow multiple inheritance for objects.

Objects: Objects in Brahms have all of the elements that an agent has, plus two additional elements; conceptual-object membership and resource. Furthermore, instead of having group-membership (MEMBER-OF) relationships, an object can have class-inheritance (IS-A) relationships with classes.

Objects can have a belief-set. Beliefs in an object can model data encoded within the object. Beliefs can be seen as the information that an object carries, such as the text written on a piece of paper.

Objects can act on Facts or on Beliefs: By default, WFR preconditions in objects match on facts, not on the beliefs inside the object. TFR preconditions in objects match on beliefs inside the object, similar to agents. The problem becomes how to do data processing within an object? In other words, how to conclude a belief in a TFR that triggers an activity in a WFR? Concluding a fact in a TFR is not allowed and since a WFR in an object can only react to facts this seems impossible. To solve this problem, WFRs in objects can specify a workframe-type:

- Factframe: Preconditions match on facts. This is the default type in objects.
- Dataframe: Preconditions match on beliefs

```
class ::=
class class-name { extends class-name [ , class-name ]* }
{
    { class-facets }
}

object ::=
object object-name instanceof class-name
    {partof conceptual-object-name [, conceptual-object-name ]*}
{
    { class-facets }
}

class-facets ::=
{ display : literal-string ; }
{ cost : number ; }
{ time_unit : number ; }
{ resource : truth-value ; }
{ icon : literal-string ; }
{ attributes }
{ relations }
{ initial-beliefs }
{ initial-facts }
{ activities }
{ workframes }
{ thoughtframes}
```

3.2.1.9 Communications

In Brahms communication between agents and objects is done by communicating beliefs. The communication of beliefs is done with a *communication* activity that transfers beliefs to/from one agent to one or several other agents, or to/from an (information carrier) object. A communication activity is used to model different types of communications that can be observed in the world. Examples are: face to face conversations, reading or writing a document, or data entered into computers.

An agent or object has to have the belief before it can communicate (i.e. tell) the belief to another agent or object. The recipient agent or object will have its original beliefs overwritten with the communicated beliefs. The syntax of a communication activity is as follows:

```
communicate-activity ::=
communicate activity-name ( { param-decl [ , param-decl ]* } )
{
    { display : literal-string ; }
    { priority : [ unsigned | param-name ] ; }
    { random : [ truth-value | param-name ] ; }
    { min_duration : [ unsigned | param-name ] ; }
    { max_duration : [ unsigned | param-name ] ; }
    { resources }
    { type : [ phone | fax | email | face2face | terminal |
            pager | none | param-name ] ; }
    with : [ [ agent-name | object-name | param-name ]
            [ , [ agent-name | object-name | param-name ] ]* ;
    about : transfer-definition [ , transfer-definition ]* ;
    { when : [ start | end | param-name ] ; }
}

transfer-definition ::=
transfer-action ( communicative-act | resultcomparison )

transfer-action ::= send | receive
communicative-act ::= object-name | param-name
```

The direction of communication is defined by the transfer-definition:

- send: The agent communicated with will *always* receive the belief.
- receive: The agent from which the beliefs are received does not know it is being communicated with. Also, that agent needs to have the belief.
- Transfer of beliefs happens either at the start or at the end of the activity.

Another way of communication is using the *Communicator library*. The Communicator library can be used to send and receive FIPA (Foundation of Intelligent Physical Agents) communicative acts[3]. The Communicator library implements external activities for agents to communicate with other agents through communicative acts. These activities can be used to create, read, manipulate, retract, and send communicative-act objects.

The library defines the class *CommunicativeAct*. CommunicativeAct objects are serializable objects that are communicated between agents. A CommunicativeAct object needs an *envelope* with the address information (from, to, date, ...) and transport hints, and a *payload* for the message content and content properties according to the FIPA definition:

---

[3] http://www.fipa.org/specs/fipa00037/index.html

```
class CommunicativeAct extends SerializableObject {
    attributes:
        public map envelope;
        public map payload;
        public Exception raisedException;
}//CommunicativeAct
```

Serializable objects are objects that can be efficiently communicated between agents either running toghether in one BVM, or distributed over the network between multiple BVMs. The BVM uses an efficient dedicated protocol for communicating serializable objects between agents distributed over a network.

3.2.2 Semantics and Verification

In this section we briefly discuss the preciseness, expressiveness, and the verifiability of the Brahms language.

Brahms is a strongly typed compiled BDI agent language. As the reader has seen in the previous sections, Brahms has a well-defined grammar specified in EBNF and a clear, but not formally defined, semantics.

The Brahms compiler's lexer and parser are generated using JavaCC[4]. JavaCC generates a top-down (recursive descent) parser. The parser and lexer work together to parse the source files and to identify the appropriate tokens for use by the parser. The parser generates a parse tree in the first pass which is also where syntactic analysis takes place. In the second pass the compiler performs the semantic analysis which includes type checking. In the last pass the compiler generates an internal object model with the compiled code and uses that model to then generate compiled code for the BVM. Brahms' compiled code is generated as XML-based Brahms compiled concept files that have the extension '.bcc'. At the moment, the compiler does not have an optimizer.

Brahms has a clear and precise semantics that is part of the second pass of the compiler. Currently, there is work in progress to be able to make formal verification of Brahms models possible. The approach taken is to re-generate a Brahms model into a Jason program [2]. Since *Jason* is a pure BDI language with a clear defined semantics a Brahms model will be verifiable as a Jason program [10].

---

[4] https://javacc.dev.java.net/doc/features.html

3.2.3 Software Engineering Issues

In this section we discuss some of the software engineering and programming language principles, such as abstraction, inheritance, modularity, overloading, overriding, information hiding, error handling, generic programming, etc., that have been considered or adopted within design of the Brahms language.

3.2.3.1 Agent-oriented versus object-oriented.

With belief-based agent-oriented languages, such as Brahms, people often confuse groups and agents with classes and objects in an object-oriented language (OOP), such as Java. Object-oriented programming includes features such as encapsulation, polymorphism, and inheritance, enabling the notion of information-hiding. In OOP encapsulation is created by definition of member attributes in a class. The purpose of encapsulation of information is to hide the physical implementation of data, so that if it is changed, the change is restricted to the class definition. Encapsulation takes a different form in belief-based agents. In belief-based agent-oriented programming, the issue is not about hiding the physical data storage definition, but rather hiding the internal belief-state of an agent, so that the agent can use it to act upon and change it independent from other agents. Agents are autonomous behavioral entities, whereas objects are simply encapsulated data and function containers that can be accessed by others, through well-defined interfaces. Agents can only interact through the use of communication protocols.

Polymorphism and inheritance in OOP is the abstraction of similar types and functionalities of objects into an inheritance hierarchy of abstract types to more specific types. It is about inheritance of similar properties and functions, as well as about function or method overloading, where we redefine a function or method at a more specific level if needed, so that others can interface with objects of similar types in the hierarchy in similar ways. Although these capabilities are useful in software engineering in general, and are thus also useful also in agent-oriented programming, they are not the key differences between agent-oriented and object-oriented. The Brahms language also has inheritance of properties, etc, in groups. Brahms also has polymorphism in the form of activity overloading (see below). However, the notion of groups and inheritance in Brahms is not about abstract class types, but about group membership. In other words, the behavior of agents is defined by the different groups an agent belongs to. These so-called *communities of practice* define what the agent knows and when and how it will behave as a member of that group, independently from others. This is because the agent is a member of that group and not because the agent is of a particular type. These differences are subtle, but very important in distinguishing belief-based agent-oriented programming from object-oriented programming.

3.2.3.2 Activity overriding and overloading

The Brahms language allows polymorphism by providing both activitiy overriding and overloading (ad-hoc polymorphism). This makes it possible to write a workframe in a high-level group that is inherited by subgroups that override/overload an activity referenced in the workframe. In the example below the subgroups *LunarRobot* and *LunarAstronaut* each override the activity *LunarActivity* as a composite activity. Both groups also inherit the WFR *wf_PerformLunarActivity* from the group *LunarExplorer*. This WFR will call the overridden activity for each subgroup, and thus lunar robot and lunar astronaut agents execute their lunar activity appropriately.

```
group LunarExplorer {
    activities:
        primitive_activity LunarActivity(map input) {
            max_duration: 10;
        }

    workframes:
        workframe wf_PerformLunarActivity {
            when (...)
            do {
                LunarActivity(map input);
            }
        }
}

group LunarRobot memberof LunarExplorer {
    activities:
        composite_activity LunarActivity(map input) {
            ...
        }
}

    group LunarAstronaut memberof LunarExplorer {
    activities:
        composite_activity LunarActivity(map input) {

            ...
        }
}
```

3.2.3.3 Java integration

The ultimate objective is to completely integrate Brahms with the Java language, which would allow the Brahms modeler/programmer to write pure Java code as part of a Brahms model/program. However, at the moment this is not possible yet. Brahms currently has two ways of interfacing with Java using the Brahms JAPI:

- **Java activities** are primitive activities written in Java. To write a Java activity you will need to define the Java activity in the Brahms model, and implement the activity by writing the activity using the Brahms JAPI. To do this you need to create a Java class that extends from the *AbstractExternalActivity* abstract class in the JAPI. The AbstractExternalActivity is an interface for external activities implemented in Java, called by Brahms Java activities. The external activity can perform any Java action. This abstract class provides access to parameters passed to Brahms Java activities, and allows for adding bindings to unbound variables passed to Brahms java activities through parameters. Most importantly, you need to define the *doActivity* method to execute the Java activity.

- **External agents** are Brahms agents written in the Java programming language. To write an external agent you will need to define the agent as an external agent in the Brahms model and then write the external agent in Java using the Brahms JAPI. To do this you need to create a Java class that extends from the *AbstractExternalAgent* abstract class in the JAPI. The AbstractExternalAgent is an interface for external agents implemented in Java, loaded into the virtual machine to participate in a Brahms simulation or real-time agent execution. The external agent can perform any Java action. This abstract implementation provides access to the concepts loaded in the virtual machine and the world state to allow for communications with these concepts and to allow for world state changes to be triggered by this agent.

- **Java objects** can be referenced using Java class types as Brahms attribute types. This allows referencing Java objects from within the Brahms language.

3.2.4 Other features of the language: geography model

In Brahms agents and objects can be situated in a model of the physical world. The world is represented independent of the capability of agents. An *areadefinition* is used for defining a class of *area* instances used for representing geographical locations. Areadefinitions are similar to classes in their use. Examples of areadefinitions are "Building", and "City". An example of an area is "Berkeley". Areas can be decomposed into sub-areas. For example, a building can be decomposed into one or more floors. A floor can be decomposed into offices. The decomposition can be modeled using the PART-OF relationship. A *path* connects two areas and represents a route that can be taken by an agent or object to travel from one area to another. The modeler may specify distance as the time it takes to move from area1 to area2 via the path. The BVM automatically generates location facts and beliefs for agents and objects moving from one area to another.

Agents and objects can be located in an initial location (i.e. areas). Agents and objects can move to and from areas. When agents and/or objects come into a location, the BVM automatically creates a location fact *(agent.location = <current-area>)*. Agents always know where they are and they notice other agents and objects. When agents come into a location, the BVM automatically gives the agent a belief about its new location (same as the location fact), and also gives the agent a location belief for all other agents and objects currently in that location. When an agent or object leaves a location, the location fact and beliefs are retracted from all agents that are in that location the moment the agent or object leaves. Agents and objects can carry (through the *containment* relation) other agents and objects. Contained agents and objects are not "noticed" until they are put into the area by the containing agent or object.

```
areadef ::=
areadef areadef-name { areadef-inheritance }
{
    { display : literal-string ; }
    { icon : literal-string ; }
    { attributes }
    { relations }
    { initial-facts }
}
areadef-inheritance ::= extends areadef-name[, areadef-name ]*

area ::=
area area-name instanceof areadef-name { partof area-name }
{
    { display : literal-string ; }
    { icon : literal-string ; }
    { attributes }
    { relations }
    { initial-facts }
}
```

The geography model is a conceptual model, meaning that it does not represent the geography as a graphical three-dimentional model. Areas can have attributes and relations, and define initial facts. Facts about areas can represent the state of a location, e.g. the temperature in an area. The BVM automatically generates facts about the 'partof' relationships in the geography. Agents can detect these facts and thus learn (i.e. get beliefs) about the areas in their environment.

The example geography model below, defines a simple geography for the University of Berkeley in Berkeley, CA. This model defines the university buildings SouthHall and SpraulHall, where two students (Kim and Alex) are initially located. Furthermore, the model defines two bank branches and two restaurants in the city of Berkeley.

```
// Area defintions
areadef University extends BaseAreaDef { }
areadef UniversityHall extends Building { }
areadef BankBranch extends Building { }
areadef Restaurant extends Building { }

// ATM World
area AtmGeography instanceof World { }

// Berkeley
area Berkeley instanceof City partof AtmGeography { }

// inside Berkeley
area UCB instanceof University partof Berkeley { }
area SouthHall instanceof UniversityHall partof UCB { }
area SpraulHall instanceof UniversityHall partof UCB { }
area Telegraph_Av_113 instanceof BankBranch partof Berkeley { }
area Bancroft_Av_77 instanceof BankBranch partof Berkeley { }
area Telegraph_Av_2405 instanceof Restaurant partof Berkeley { }
area Telegraph_Av_2134 instanceof Restaurant partof Berkeley { }

// initial location
agent Kim_Agent memberof Student {
    location: SouthHall;

agent Alex_Agent memberof Student {
    location: SouthHall;
}
```

Agents and objects can move within the geography model. To have an agent move from one location to another you can do the following:

- Use a *move(to_location)* activity in a WFR.
- Specify the duration of the move in clock-ticks. By default the duration is zero, unless,
- There is a define a *Path* object between two areas. A path defines a duration to move from area1 to area2. A path object defines a bi-directional path.

- The BVM creates and retracts location facts and beliefs automatically.
- Agents in an area will detect arrivals and departures of other agents and objects (by the creation and retraction of location beliefs for agents located in the area).
- In the move activity you can specify (sub-)area arrival and departure detection for the agents.
- The BVM calculates the shortest path between areas, given a geography model.
- Contained objects and agents move with the agent or object that is moving. However, they will not get noticed by other agents, until they are placed in the destination area by the agent (using a put activity).

3.3 Platform

The Brahms Agent Environment (BAE) is a collection of tools for developing complex models of agents, objects and areas for the purpose of simulating work practice, or for developing MAS solutions to support the people that are part of a work system. The BAE also supports the development of distributed agent-based solutions in support of an organization's workflow. In this section we describe the BAE tools, available documentation, standards compliance, and interoperability and portability features of Brahms.

3.3.1 Available tools and documentation

The Brahms tools and documentation that are included in the BAE are:

- **The Brahms Compiler** (BC). The BC is a compiler for the Brahms language. The compiler compiles .b source files into .bcc byte-code files.
- **The Brahms Virtual Machine** (BVM. The BVM is both a simulation engine for simulating Brahms models, and a MAS execution environment for real-time agents.
- **The Composer**. The Composer is a dedicated integrated development environment (IDE) for Brahms. It provides a project editor, model editors, a source code editor, and several post-execution displays. The modeler can both compile and run a model from within the Composer. The Composer is a useful tool for those who use Brahms for modeling and simulating work practice.
- **The Brahms Eclipse Plugin**. The Brahms Eclipse Plugin is a plugin for the Eclipse development environment. The plugin is useful for those who use Brahms as a MAS development tool, and also develop and integrate with Java code.
- **The AgentViewer**. The AgentViewer is a post-execution event timeline viewer for agent and object beliefs, workframes, activities and thoughtframes, as well as inter-agent and -object communications. The AgentViewer is a kind of debugging tool, although it is used after executing the model and is not an in-

teractive debugging environment. During the execution of the model (either in simulation mode or in real-time mode), all events are stored by the event-logger of the BVM in an ascii-formated history file. Using the AgentViewer application, this history file can be parsed into a MySQL database that the AgentViewer uses to generate a TimeLine view.

- **The Communication Display**. The Communication Displayprovides a spring diagram of the agent and object communications. It shows the to and from communications, as well as the number of beliefs and/or Communicative-Acts communicated. The Communication Display is integrated with the AgentViewer application and uses the same MySQL database to retrieve its data.
- **Documentation**. Brahms documentation is provided on the Brahms website[5]. The documentation available via this website can be easily accessed through Quick Links on the home page.

3.3.2 *Standards compliance, interoperability and portability*

All the tools that are part of the BAE are written in the Java language and require the Java Runtime Environment version 6. Currently, the BAE is supported on Windows 2000/XP, Linux, OS X, and Solaris. The AgentViewer and Communication Display require MySQL (either version 4.1, 5.0.51 or later) to be installed. In its simulation mode, agents cannot be distributed over multiple BVMs, and the BAE uses a Brahms native communication protocol. In simulation as well as in real-time execution mode Brahms agents can be integrated with other agent systems through the use of external agents (see section 3.2.1.1).

In its real-time execution mode, the BAE uses a custom architecture for its communication, naming/directory service and agent-life cycle management. This custom architecure is called the Collaborative Infrastructure (CI). It is a Java-based communication framework for agent-based communications loosely based on FIPA. The CI is an open agent communication framework and has a Java and C++ API, allowing Brahms agents to be integrated with Java, C++ and C programs that also use the CI as their agent communications architecture. The CI includes a directory service for registering and finding CI agents. The CI uses a Brahms native protocol using sockets as its transport layer for communication between distributed agents.

---

[5] http://www.agentisolutions.com

3.3.3 Other features of the platfrom

The BAE has been extensively tested over the years in both simulation mode and in real-time execution mode. We do not have any specific performance metrics available, but BAE version 1.2.7 is currently running the OCAMS application 24x7 in NASA's Mission Control (see section 3.4).

3.4 Applications supported by the language and/or the platform

In this section we describe a number of the most prominent applications of Brahms. We categorize Brahms applications into those that primarily use Brahms as a simulation environment, and those that use Brahms as a real-time (distributed) MAS execution environment.

Brahms has been used in many simulation projects at the NYNEX and Bell Atlantic phone companies [6], NASA (see below), the Universities of Twente [4], Amsterdam [15] and Utrecht [16], and by several research organizations throughout the world. At NASA, Brahms has been used to develop a distributed multi-agent human-robot exploration system (see below), simulation of collaborative traffic flow management for future concepts of the US National Airspace [28, 29], and most recently to simulate and implement an intelligent workflow application for NASA's Mission Control (see below). Following is a description of a number of NASA simulation and MAS applications developed with Brahms.

Apollo EVA Simulations
From 1998 until 2001, Sierhuis developed Brahms simulations of the Apollo 12, 14, 15 & 16 Apollo Lunar Surface Exploration Package offload and deployment extra-vehicular activities (EVA) on the Moon [18].

Day-in-the-life Simulation onboard the ISS
The International Space Station (ISS) is one the most complex projects ever, with numerous interdependent constraints affecting productivity and crew safety. This requires planning years before crew expeditions, and the use of sophisticated scheduling tools. We presented an agent-based model and simulation of the activities and work practices of astronauts onboard the ISS based on an agent-oriented approach. Between 2001 and 2003 we developed a Brahms simulation model of a day-in-the-life onboard of the ISS Alpha crew [1, 20].

MER Mission Operations Simulation
Mission operations systems for space missions are comprised of a complex network of human organizations, information and deep-space network systems and

spacecraft hardware. Similar to the operations within traditional organizations, one of the problems in mission operations is the management of the mission information systems related to the human work processes. Brahms was used to model and simulate NASA's Mars Exploration Rover (MER) mission operation work process [24, 21, 17].

Shuttle Mission Operations Simulation
In this project we used the Brahms environment to model and simulate JSC's Mission Operations Directorate (MOD) organization, and the work performed during the Shuttle pre-launch through docking phases with the International Space Station [23]. The output of the simulation is a detailed time line of the flight controllers activities and communication and metrics of different work activity and workload.

Mobile Agents MAS
We have developed and tested an advanced EVA communications and computing system to increase astronaut self-reliance and safety, reducing dependence on continuous monitoring and advising from mission control on Earth. This system, called the Mobile Agents Architecture (MAA), is voice controlled and provides information verbally to the astronauts through programs called personal agents. The system partly automates the role of CapCom in Apollo including monitoring and managing EVA navigation, scheduling, equipment deployment, telemetry, health tracking, and scientific data collection [7, 12].

OCA ISS Flight Control Simulation and Intelligent Workflow MAS
The OCA Mirroring System (OCAMS) is a practical engineering application of multi-agent systems technology, involving redesign of the tools and practices in a complex, distributed system. OCAMS is designed to assist flight controllers in managing interactions with the file system onboard the ISS. The simulation-to-implementation engineering methodology combines ethnography, participatory design, multiagent simulation, and agent-based systems integration [9]. The OCAMS system is currently deployed in the ISS Mission Control at NASA Johnson Space Center (JSC) in Houston. OCAMS supports the ISS OCA officer 24x7 in their uplinking, downlinking, mirroring, archiving and distributing of files to and from the ISS.

3.5 Final Remarks

In this chapter we described the Brahms language and environment. Brahms has been in development as an agent simulation language since 1992, and has matured to a full-fledged AOL. Brahms is well-tested and stable. This is proven by the fact that Brahms is used in NASA Mission Control for the development of operational multi-agent systems.

Brahms contributes to the multi-agent languages community in at least two ways:
1) Brahms is both an agent-based simulation language and a MAS development environment. This allowed us to develop a *from simulation to implementation* agent-
oriented software engineer methodology that has been applied at NASA [22], 2)
the Brahms language was the first AOL language that integrated a BDI architecture with a reactive activity-based subsumption architecture, all the way back to
the early nineties [19].

In the near future, we are working on integrating the Brahms and the Java language more. The next release of Brahms will have a seamless integration of Java
objects. Preconditions in workframes and thoughtframes will allow matching on
Java object members, without them becoming beliefs. This will optimize the use
of Java objects from within the Brahms language. We are also in the process of
adding the use of lists in preconditions. Our ultimate objective is to completely
combine the Brahms and Java languages, allowing the Brahms programmer to
write Java code within their Brahms program, without the need for using a Java
API. Brahms will support both Java objects, methods and agent activities, and
the ability to call Java object methods directly from a workframe. This will combine the benefit of both object-oriented and agent-oriented programming in one
language.

The BAE has a stable and free release available for research purposes from the
Brahms website at http://www.agentisolutions.com. Brahms does not (as of now)
provide an open-source distribution, but is available for free download under the
Brahms Research license agreement.

Acknowledgements Brahms development started in 1992 as a collaboration between the former R&D center of the then NYNEX corporation (NYNEX Science and Technology) and the
former Institute for Research on Learning (IRL), a spinoff of Xerox PARC. Since 1998, Brahms
has been developed and used by the Work Systems Design and Evaluation group in NASA
Ames' Intelligent Systems division. We thank all our NYNEX, IRL and NASA funders over
the past sixteen years. In particular, we like to thank Jim Euchner (NYNEX) and Mike Shafto
(NASA) for their continued support of Brahms and our Brahms research team.

References

1. Acquisti, A., Sierhuis, M., Clancey, W.J., Bradshaw, J.M.: Agent based modeling of collaboration and work practices onboard the international space station. In: 11th Computer-
   Generated Forces and Behavior Representation Conference, pp. p.181–188. Orlando, Fl.
   (2002)
2. Bordini, R.H., H§bner, J.F., Wooldridge, M.: Programming multi-agent systems in AgentS-
   peak using Jason. Series in Agent Technology. Wiley (2007)
3. Brownston, L., Farrell, R., Kant, E., Martin, N.: Programming Expert Systems in OPS5.
   Addison-Wesley (1985)
4. Bruinsma, G., de Hoog, R.: Exploring protocols for multidisciplinary disaster response using adaptive workflow simulation. In: B.V.d. Walle, M. M. Turoff (eds.) International Conference on Information System for Crisis Response and Management (ISCRAM). Newark,
   New Jersey (2006)

5. Clancey, W.: Heuristic classification. Artificial Intelligence **27**(3), 289–350 (1985)
6. Clancey, W., Sachs, P., Sierhuis, M., Hoof, R.v.: Brahms: Simulating practice for work systems design. International Journal on Human-Computer Studies **49**, 831–865 (1998)
7. Clancey, W., Sierhuis, M., Alena, R., Berrios, D., Dowding, J., Graham, J., Tyree, K., Hirsh, R., Garry, W., Semple, A., Buckingham Shum, S., Shadbolt, N., Rupert, S.: Automating capcom using mobile agents and robotic assistants (2007)
8. Clancey, W.J.: Simulating activities: Relating motives, deliberation, and attentive coordination. Cognitive Systems Research **3**(3), 471–499 (2002)
9. Clancey, W.J., Sierhuis, M., Seah, C., Reynolds, F., Hall, T., Scott, M.: Multi-agent simulation to implementation: A practical engineering methodology for designing space flight operations. In: A. Artikis, G. O'Hare, K. Stathis, G. Vouros (eds.) The Eighth Annual International Workshop "Engineering Societies in the Agents World" (ESAW 07), vol. LNAI. Springer, London (2008)
10. Fisher, M., Pearce, E., Wooldridge, M., Sierhuis, M., Visser, W., Bordini, R.H.: Towards the verifications of human-robot teams. In: IEEE ISoLA Workshop on Leveraging Applications of Formal Methods, Verification, and Validation. Loyola College Graduate Center, Columbia, MD (2005)
11. Forgy, C.: Rete: A fast algorithm for the many pattern/many object pattern match problem. Artificial Intelligence **19**, 17–37 (1982)
12. Hirsh, R., Graham, J., Tyree, K., Sierhuis, M., Clancey, W.J.: Intelligence for human-robotic planetary surface robots. In: A.M. Howard, E.W. Tunstel (eds.) Intelligence for Space Robotics. TSI Press, Albuquerque (2006)
13. Konolige, K.: A Deduction Model of Belief. Morgan Kaufmann, San Mateo, CA (1986)
14. Leont'ev, A.N.: Activity, Consciousness and Personality. Prentice-Hall, Englewood Cliffs, NJ (1978)
15. Netten, N., Bruinsma, G., van Someren, M., de Hoog, R.: Task-adaptive information distribution for synamic collaborative emergency response. International Journal of Intelligent Control and Systems **11**(4), 238–247 (2007)
16. van Putten, B.J., Dignum, V., Sierhuis, M., Wolfe, S.R.: Opera and brahms: a symphony? In: Agent-Oriented Software Engineering (AOSE) 2008 at The Sixth International Joint Conference on Autonomous Agents & Multi-Agent Systems (AAMAS 2008), vol. Forthcoming LNCS Proceedings. Springer, Estoril, Portugal (2008)
17. Seah, C., Sierhuis, M., Clancey, W.: Multi-agent modeling and simulation approach for design and analysis of mer mission operations. In: 2005 International Conference on Human-Computer Interface Advances for Modeling and Simulation (SIMCHI'05). 2005 Western Simulation Multiconference (WMC'05), New Orleans, Louisiana (2005)
18. Sierhuis, M.: Modeling and simulating work practice; brahms: A multiagent modeling and simulation language for work system analysis and design. Ph.d. thesis, University of Amsterdam, SIKS Dissertation Series No. 2001-10 (2001)
19. Sierhuis, M.: "it's not just goals all the way down"– "it's activities all the way down". In: G.M.P. O'Hare, A. Ricci, M.J. O'Grady, O. Dikenelli (eds.) Engineering Societies in the Agents World VII, 7th International, Workshop, ESAW 2006, Dublin, Ireland, September 6-8, 2006, Revised Selected and Invited Papers, *Lecture Notes in Computer Science*, vol. LNCS 4457/2007, pp. 1–24. Springer, Dublin, Ireland (2007)
20. Sierhuis, M., Acquisti, A., Clancey, W.: Multiagent plan execution and work practice: Modeling plans and practices onboard the iss. In: 3rd International NASA Workshop on Planning and Scheduling for Space. Houston, TX (2002)
21. Sierhuis, M., Clancey, W., Seah, C., Trimble, J., Sims, M.H.: Modeling and simulation for mission operations work system design. Journal of Management Information Systems **Vol. 19**(No. 4), 85–129 (2003)
22. Sierhuis, M., Clancey, W.J., Seah, C.H.: Organization and work systems design and engineering; from simulation to implementation of multi-agent systems. In: Agent Directed Simulation, chap. 13. Wiley (To Appear)

23. Sierhuis, M., Diegelman, T.E., Seah, C., Shalin, V., Clancey, W.J., Selvin, A.M.: Agent-based simulation of shuttle mission operations. In: Agent-Directed Simulation 2007 part of the 2007 Spring Simulation Multiconference, pp. 53–60. The Society for Modeling and Simulation International, ACM/SIGSIM, Norfolk, VA (2007)

24. Sierhuis, M., Sims, M., Clancey, W., Lee, P.: Applying multiagent simulation to planetary surface operations. In: L. Chaudron (ed.) COOP'2000 workshop on Modelling Human Activity, pp. 19–28. Sophia Antipolis, France (2000)

25. Suchman, L.: Representations of work. Communications of the ACM/Special Issue 38(9) (1995)

26. Suchman, L.A.: Plans and Situated Action: The Problem of Human Machine Communication. Cambridge University Press, Cambridge, MA (1987)

27. Vygotsky, L.S.: Mind in Society: The Development of Higher Psychological Processes. Harvard University Press, Cambridge, MA (1978)

28. Wolfe, S.R., Jarvis, P.A., Enomoto, F.Y., Sierhuis, M.: Comparing route selection strategies in collaborative traffic flow management. In: Intelligent Agent Technology (IAT 2007). IEEE press, Fremont, CA, USA (2007)

29. Wolfe, S.R., Sierhuis, M., Jarvis, P.A.: To bdi, or not to bdi: Design choices in an agent-based traffic flow management simulation. In: Agent Directed Simulation 2008 held at the SpringSim Multi-Conference 2008. ACM, Ottawa, Canada (2008)

Chapter 4
Programming Rational Agents in GOAL

Koen V. Hindriks

Abstract The agent programming language GOAL is a high-level programming language to program *rational agents* that derive their *choice of action* from their *beliefs* and *goals*. The language provides the basic building blocks to design and implement rational agents by means of a set of programming constructs. These programming constructs allow and facilitate the manipulation of an agent's beliefs and goals and to structure its decision-making. GOAL agents are called rational because they satisfy a number of basic *rationality constraints* and because they decide to perform actions to further their goals based upon a reasoning scheme derived from *practical reasoning*. The programming concepts of belief and goal incorporated into GOAL provide the basis for this form of reasoning and are similar to their common sense counterparts used everyday to explain the actions that we perform. In addition, GOAL provides the means for agents to *focus their attention* on specific goals and to *communicate* at the *knowledge level*. This provides an intuitive basis for writing high-level agent programs. At the same time these concepts and programming constructs have a *well-defined, formal semantics*. The formal semantics provides the basis for defining a *verification framework* for GOAL for verifying and reasoning about GOAL agents which is similar to some of the well-known agent logics introduced in the literature.

4.1 Motivation

The concept of a *goal* lies at the basis of our understanding of why we perform actions. It is common sense to explain the things we do in terms of beliefs and goals. I started writing this chapter with the goal of explaining the programming language GOAL. The *reasons* for performing actions are derived from our moti-

Koen V. Hindriks
EEMCS, Delft University of Technology, Mekelweg 4, Delft
e-mail: k.v.hindriks@tudelft.nl

R.H. Bordini et al. (eds.), *Multi-Agent Programming,*
DOI 10.1007/978-0-387-89299-3_4, © Springer Science+Business Media, LLC 2009

vations and the notion of *rational behaviour* is typically explained in terms of actions that are produced in order to further our goals [5, 14, 16]. A researcher that has a goal to have finished a book chapter but is going on a holiday instead is not considered to behave rationally because holidays do not further the goal of writing a book chapter.

The idea to use common sense notions to build programs can be traced back to the beginnings of Artificial Intelligence. Shoham, who was one of the first to propose a new programming paradigm that he called *agent-oriented programming*, cites McCarthy about the usefulness of ascribing such notions to machines [29, 39]. One of the first papers on Artificial Intelligence, also written by McCarthy, is called *Programs with Common Sense* [28]. It has been realized that in order to have machines compute with such notions it is imperative to precisely specify their meaning [39]. To this end, various logical accounts have been proposed, mainly using modal logic, to clarify the core common sense meaning of these notions [10, 25, 34]. These accounts have aimed to precisely capture the essence of a conceptual scheme based on common sense that may also be useful and applicable in specifying rational agent programs. The first challenge thus is to provide a well-defined semantics for the notions of belief, goal and action which can also provide a computational interpretation of these notions useful for programming agents.

One of the differences between our approach and earlier attempts to put common sense concepts to good use in Artificial Intelligence is that we take a definite *engineering stance* (contrast [28] and [39]). The concepts are used to introduce a new agent programming language that provides useful programming constructs to develop agent programs. The second challenge is to provide agent programming language that is practical, transparent, and useful. It must be practical in the sense of being easy to use, transparent in the sense of being easy to understand, and useful in the sense of providing a language that can solve real problems.

4.1.1 The GOAL Agent Programming Language

The agent programming language GOAL that we will introduce and discuss meets both of the challenges identified above [3, 22]. The distinguishing feature of the language GOAL is its notion of *declarative goals* and the way agents derive their choice of actions from such goals.[1] The beliefs and goals of a GOAL agent are called its *mental state*. Various constraints are placed on the mental state of an agent, which roughly correspond to constraints on their common sense counterparts. On top of the mental attitudes a GOAL agent also has so-called action rules to guide the action selection mechanism.

---

[1] GOAL is an acronym for Goal-Oriented Agent Language.

The main features of GOAL include:

- *Declarative beliefs*: Agents use a symbolic, logical language to represent the information they have, and their beliefs or knowledge about the environment they act upon in order to achieve their goals. This *knowledge representation language* is not fixed by GOAL but, in principle, may be varied according to the needs of the programmer.
- *Declarative goals*: Agents may have multiple goals that specify *what* the agent wants to achieve at some moment in the near or distant future. Declarative goals specify a state of the environment that the agent wants to establish, they do not specify actions or procedures how to achieve such states.
- *Blind commitment strategy*: Agents commit to their goals and drop goals only when they have been achieved. This commitment strategy, called a *blind* commitment strategy in the literature [34], is the *default* strategy used by GOAL agents. Rational agents thus do not have goals that they believe are already achieved, a constraint which has been built into GOAL agents.
- *Rule-based action selection*: Agents use so-called *action rules* to select actions, given their beliefs and goals. Such rules may *underspecify* the choice of action in the sense that multiple actions may be performed at any time given the action rules of the agent. In that case, a GOAL agent will select an arbitrary action for execution.
- *Policy-based intention modules*: Agents may focus their attention and put all their efforts on achieving a subset of their goals, using a subset of their actions, using only knowledge relevant to achieving those goals. GOAL provides modules to structure action rules and knowledge dedicated to achieving specific goals. Informally, modules can be viewed as policy-based intentions in the sense of [6].
- *Communication at the knowledge level* [31]: Agents may communicate with each other to exchange information, and to coordinate their actions. GOAL agents communicate using the knowledge representation language that is also used to represent their beliefs and goals.

This brief but comprehensive overview of the GOAL language illustrates the range of concepts that are available to program rational agents. GOAL is a high-level and expressive language that facilitates programming agents that derive their choice of action from their beliefs and goals. Arguably, as the reader may convince his or herself by means of the examples provided below, the language is easy to understand, which is achieved by a careful balance between the rich common sense intuitions associated with these concepts and their formal counterparts that have been incorporated into GOAL. Moreover, transparency is achieved since the programming contructs available do not aim at capturing all the subtle nuances of the rich common sense concepts but only their core meaning.

4.2 Language

In Section 4.2.1, the GOAL language is firstly introduced by means of a number of examples that illustrate what a GOAL agent program looks like. A classical and well-known domain called the *Blocks World* has been used for this purpose. We like to think of the Blocks World as the "hello world" example of agent programming (see also [40]). It is both simple and rich enough to demonstrate various of the available programming constructs in GOAL. In Section 4.2.2 the operational semantics of GOAL is introduced as well as a program logic to verify properties of GOAL agents.

4.2.1 Syntactical Aspects

A GOAL agent decides which action to perform next based on its beliefs and goals. In a Blocks World the decision amounts to where to move a block, in a robotics domain it might be where to move to or whether to pick up something with a gripper or not. Such a decision typically depends on the current state of the agent's environment as well as general knowledge about this environment. In the Blocks World an agent needs to know what the current configuration of blocks is and needs to have basic knowledge about such configurations (e.g. when is a block part of a tower) to make a good decision. The former type of knowledge is typically *dynamic* and changes over time, whereas the latter typically is *static* and does not change over time. In line with this distinction, two types of knowledge of an agent are distinguished: conceptual or domain knowledge stored in a *knowledge base* and beliefs about the current state of the environment stored in a *belief base*. A decision to act will usually also depend on the goals of the agent. In the Blocks World a decision to move a block on top of an existing tower of blocks would be made, for example, if it is a goal of the agent to have the block on top of that tower. In a robotics domain it might be that the robot has a goal to bring a package somewhere and therefore picks it up. Goals of an agent are stored in a *goal base*. The goals of an agent may change over time, for example, when the agent adopts a new goal or drops one of its goals. As a rational agent should not pursue goals that it already believes to be achieved, such goals need to be removed. GOAL provides a built-in mechanism for doing so based on a so-called *blind commitment strategy*. We will discuss this built-in goal update mechanism in more detail below. Together, the knowledge, beliefs and goals of an agent make up its *mental state*. A GOAL agent inspects and modifies this state at runtime analogously as a Java method operates on the state of an object. Agent programming in GOAL therefore can also be viewed as *programming with mental states*.

To select an action a GOAL agent needs to be able to *inspect* its knowledge, beliefs and goals. An action may or may not be selected if certain things follow from an agent's mental state. For example, if a block is misplaced, that is, the current position of the block does not correspond with the agent's goals, the agent may decide to move it to the table. A GOAL programmer needs to write special conditions called *mental state conditions* in order to verify whether the appropriate conditions for selecting an action are met. In essence, writing such conditions means specifying a *strategy* for action selection that will be used by the GOAL agent. Such a strategy is coded in GOAL by means of *action rules* which define when an action may or may not be selected. After selecting an action, an agent needs to *perform* the action. Performing an action in GOAL means changing the agent's mental state. An action to move a block, for example, will change the agent's beliefs about the current position of the block. The effects of an action on the mental state of an agent need to be specified explicitly in a GOAL agent program by the programmer except for a few built-in actions. Whether or not a real (or simulated) block will also be moved in an (simulated) environment depends on whether the GOAL agent has been adequately connected to such an environment. Although there are many interesting things to say about this connection (related to e.g. failure of actions and percepts obtained through sensors), in this chapter we will not discuss this in any detail.

We are now ready to define more precisely what a GOAL agent is. A *basic* GOAL *agent program* consists of five sections: (1) a set of domain rules, which is optional, collectively called the *knowledge base* of the agent, (2) a set of beliefs, collectively called the *belief base*, (3) a set of goals, called the *goal base*, (4) a *program section* which consists of a set of action rules, and (5) an *action specification* that consists of a specification of the pre- and post-conditions of the actions available to the agent. To avoid confusion of the program section with the agent program itself, from now on, the agent program will simply be called *agent*. The term agent will be used both to refer to the program text itself as well as to the execution of such a program. It should be clear from the context which of the two senses is intended. An Extended Backus-Naur Form syntax definition (cf. [38]) of a GOAL program is provided in Table 4.1.[2] The syntax specification of GOAL also contains references to modules. Modules are discussed in Section 4.2.1.2.

4.2.1.1 A GOAL Blocks World Agent

In order to explain how a GOAL agent works, we will design an agent that is able to effectively solve Blocks World problems. To this end, we now briefly introduce the Blocks World domain. The Blocks World is a simple environment that consists of a finite number of blocks that are stacked into *towers* on a table of *unlimited* size. It is assumed that each block has a unique label or name $a, b, c, \ldots$. Labelling

---

[2] Here, boldface is used to indicate *terminal symbols*, i.e. symbols that are part of an actual program. Italic is used to indicate *nonterminal symbols*. [...] is used to indicate that ... is optional, | is used to indicate a choice, and * and + denote zero or more repetitions or one or more repetitions of a symbol, respectively. The nonterminal *clause* refers to arbitrary Prolog clauses, which is dependent on the Prolog system used. The current implementation of GOAL uses SWI-Prolog [42]. It is only allowed, however, to use a subset of the built-in predicates available in SWI-Prolog; in particular, for example, no meta-predicates can be used.

program	::=	**main** *id* {
		[**knowledge** { *clause** }]
		beliefs { *clause** }
		goals { *poslitconj** }
		program { (*actionrule* | *module*)+ }
		action-spec {*actionspecification*}
		}
module	::=	**module** *id* {
		context { *mentalstatecond* }
		[**knowledge** { *clause** }]
		[**goals** { *poslitconj** }]
		program { (*actionrule* | *module*)+ }
		[**action-spec** {*actionspecification*}]
		}
clause	::=	any legal Prolog clause .
poslitconj	::=	*atom* {, *atom*}* .
litconj	::=	[**not**]*atom* {, [**not**]*atom*}*
atom	::=	*predicate*[*parameters*]
parameters	::=	(*id*{ ,*id*}*)
actionrule	::=	**if** *mentalstatecond* **then** *action* .
mentalstatecond	::=	*mentalatom* { , mentalatom }* | **not**(*mentalstatecond*)
mentalatom	::=	true | **bel** (*litconj*) | **goal** (*litconj*)
actionspec	::=	action { **pre**{*litconj*} **post**{*litconj*} }
action	::=	*user-def action* | *built-in action*
user-def action	::=	*id*[parameters]
built-in action	::=	**insert**(*poslitconj*) | **delete**(*poslitconj*) |
		adopt(*poslitconj*) | **drop**(*poslitconj*) |
		send(*id* , *poslitconj*)
id	::=	(a..z | A..Z | _ | \$) { (a..z | A..Z | _ | 0..9 | \$) }*

Table 4.1 Backus Naur Syntax Definition

blocks is useful because it allows us to identify a block uniquely by its name. This is much simpler than having to identify a block by means of its position with respect to other blocks, for example. Typically, labels of blocks are used to specify the current as well as goal configurations of blocks, a convention that we will also use here. Observe that in that case labels define a unique feature of each block and they cannot be used interchangeably as would have been the case if only the colour of a block would be a relevant feature in any (goal) configuration. In addition, blocks need to obey the following "laws" of the Blocks World: (i) a block is either on top of another block or it is located somewhere on the table; (ii) a block can be directly on top of at most one other block; and, (iii) there is at most one block directly on top of any other block (cf. [11]).[3] Although the Blocks World domain defines a rather simple environment it is sufficiently rich to illustrate various features of GOAL and to demonstrate that GOAL allows to program simple and elegant agent programs to solve such problems.

---

[3] For other, somewhat more realistic presentations of this domain that consider e.g., limited table size, and varying sizes of blocks, see e.g. [18].

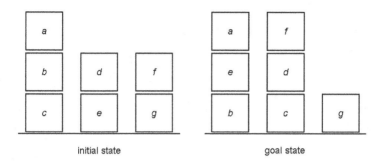

Fig. 4.1 Example Blocks World problem taken from [40].

A *Blocks World problem* is the problem of which actions to perform to transform an initial state or configuration of towers into a goal configuration, where the exact positioning of towers on the table is irrelevant. A Blocks World problem thus defines an action selection problem which is useful to illustrate the action selection mechanism of GOAL. See Figure 4.1 for an example problem. Here we assume that the only action available to the agent is the action of moving one block that is on top of a tower onto the top of another tower or to the table. A block on top of a tower, that is, a block without any block on top of it, is said to be *clear*. As there is always room to move a block onto the table, the table is also said to be clear.

The performance of a Blocks World agent can be measured by means of the number of moves it needs to transform an initial state or configuration into a goal state. An agent performs optimally if it is not possible to improve on the number of moves it uses to reach a goal state.[4] Some basic insights that help solving a Blocks World problem and that are used below in the design of an agent that can solve such problems are briefly introduced next. A block is said to be *in position* if the block in the current state is on top of a block or on the table and this corresponds with the goal state, and all blocks (if any) below it are also in position. A block that is not in position is said to be *misplaced*. In Figure 4.1 all blocks except block c and g are misplaced. Observe that only misplaced blocks have to be moved in order to solve a Blocks World problem. The action of moving a block is called *constructive* if in the resulting state that block is in position. It should be noted that in a Blocks World where the table has unlimited size in order to reach

---

[4] The problem of finding a minimal number of moves to a goal state is also called the *optimal* Blocks World problem. This problem is NP-hard [18]. It is not within the scope of this chapter to discuss either the complexity or heuristics proposed to obtain near-optimal behaviour in the Blocks World; see [13] for an approach to define such heuristics in GOAL.

the goal state it is only useful to move a block onto another block if the move is constructive, that is, if the move puts the block in position. Also observe that a constructive move always decreases the number of misplaced blocks.[5]

Representing Knowledge, Beliefs and Goals

One of the first steps in developing and writing a GOAL agent is to design and write the knowledge, beliefs and goals that an agent needs to meet its design objectives. The process of doing so need not be finished in one go but may need several iterations during the design of an agent before completing the **knowledge**, **beliefs**, and **goals** sections of a GOAL agent. It is however important to get the representation of the agent's knowledge, beliefs and goals right as both the action specifications and action rules also depend on it. To do so we need a *knowledge representation language* that we can use to describe the content of the various mental attitudes of the agent. Although, as will be explained in Section 4.2.2, GOAL is not married to any particular knowledge representation language, here, *Prolog* will be used to present an example GOAL agent. We assume the reader to be familiar with the basics of Prolog (see [41] for a classic introduction), although familiarity with first-order logic probably will be sufficient to understand the example.

In the Blocks World, first of all we need to be able to represent the configuration of blocks. That means we need to be able to represent which block is on another block and which blocks are clear. In order to do so, the expressions on(X,Y) and clear(X) are introduced. The predicate on is used to express that block X is on Y, where Y may be either another block or the table. For example, on(a,b) is used to represent the fact that block a is on block b and on(b,table) is used to represent that block b is on the table. The predicate clear is used to represent that nothing is on top of a block and to express that the table is clear, i.e. there is always an empty spot on the table where a block can be moved to. It is possible to derive that a block is clear from the facts expressed in terms of the on predicate and we will introduce a logical rule to do so below. It is not possible to similarly derive that the table is always clear (because it is a basic assumption we have made) and we need to represent this fact explicitly by means of the expression clear(table). Finally, to be able to distinguish blocks from the table, the expression block(X) is introduced to express that X is a block.

Using the on predicate makes it possible to define the states a Blocks World can be in. A *state* is defined as a set of facts of the form on(X,Y) that is consistent with the basic "laws" of the Blocks World introduced above. Assuming that the set of blocks is given, a state that contains a fact on(X,Y) for each block X in that set is called *complete*, otherwise it is called a *partial* state. In the remainder, we only consider complete states. It is now also possible to formally define a Blocks World problem. A Blocks World problem is a pair $\langle B_{initial}, G \rangle$ where $B_{initial}$ denotes

---

[5] It is not always possible to make a constructive move, which explains why it is sometimes hard to solve a Blocks World problem optimally. In that case the state of the Blocks World is said to be in a *deadlock*, see [40] for a detailed explanation.

the initial state and G denotes the goal state. The labels $B_{initial}$ and G have been intentionally used here to indicate that the set of facts that represent the initial state correspond with the initial beliefs and the set of facts that represent the goal state correspond with the goal of an agent that has as its main aim to solve a Blocks World problem.

```
1   main BlocksWorldAgent
2   { This agent solves the Blocks World problem of Figure 1.
3      knowledge{
4         block(a), block(b), block(c), block(d), block(e), block(f), block(g).
5         clear(table).
6         clear(X) :- block(X), not(on(Y,X)).
7         tower([X]) :- on(X,table).
8         tower([X,Y|T]) :- on(X,Y), tower([Y|T]).
9      }
10     beliefs{
11        on(a,b), on(b,c), on(c,table), on(d,e), on(e,table), on(f,g), on(g,table).
12     }
13     goals{
14        on(a,e), on(b,table), on(c,table), on(d,c), on(e,b), on(f,d), on(g,table).
15     }
16     program{
17        if a-goal(tower([X,Y|T])), bel(tower([Y|T])) then move(X,Y).
18        if a-goal(tower([X|T])) then move(X,table).
19     }
20     action-spec{
21        move(X,Y) {
22           pre{ clear(X), clear(Y), on(X,Z) }
23           post{ not(on(X,Z)), on(X,Y) }
24        }
25     }
26  }
```

Table 4.2 GOAL Agent Program for solving the Blocks World Problem of Figure 4.1

In the agent program listed in Table 4.2 the **beliefs** section consists of the facts that represent the initial state of the Blocks World problem of Figure 4.1. These facts are represented in the program as a single conjunction (where the comma-symbol denotes conjunction in Prolog). It would not have made a difference if each of these facts would have been represented as individual clauses separated here by the period-symbol. Similarly, the goal state corresponding with Figure 4.1 is represented as a single conjunction in the **goals** section in the program. In the **goals** section, however, it is important to represent the goal to be achieved as a single conjunction. The reason is that each of the facts present in the **goals** section need to be achieved *simultaneously*. If these facts would have been included as clauses separated by the period-symbol this would have indicated that the agent has *multiple, independent goals*. Observe that it is not the same to have two separate goals on(a,b) and on(b,c) instead of a single goal on(a,b), on(b,c) as in the first case we may put a on top of b, remove a again from b, and put b on top of c which would not achieve a state where a is on top of b which is on top of c simultaneously.[6] It thus is important to keep in mind that, from a logical point of view, the period-symbol separator in the **beliefs** (and **knowledge** section) means the same as the conjunction operator represented by the comma-symbol, but that the meaning of these separators is different in the **goals** section. In the **goals** section the conjunction operator is used to indicate that facts are part of a *single* goal whereas the period-symbol separator is used to represent that an agent has *several different* goals that need not be achieved simultaneously. As separate goals may be achieved at different times it is also allowed that single goals when they are taken together are *inconsistent*, where this is not allowed in the **beliefs** section of an agent. For example, an agent might have the two goals on(a,b) and on(b,a). Obviously these cannot be achieved simultaneously, but they can be achieved one after the other.

Facts that may change at runtime should be put in the **beliefs** section. They are used to initialise the belief base of a GOAL agent that may change when a GOAL agent performs actions. Facts that do not change may be put in the **knowledge** section of a GOAL agent. These are used to initialise the knowledge base of the agent which is never modified at runtime. For this reason, the facts of the form block(X) representing the blocks present in the Blocks World are put in the **knowledge** section in Table 4.2. All blocks present in Figure 4.1 are enumerated in this section. The fact that the table is clear is also put in the **knowledge** section. In addition, domain knowledge related to the Blocks World is represented here. For example, the rule clear(X) :- block(X), not(on(Y,X)) can be read as defining when a block X is clear, which is the case whenever there is no other block on top of X. Observe that this rule is only correct if a state represented by the agent's beliefs is complete, as the negation of Prolog succeeds whenever no proof can be constructed for on(Y,X) *(negation as failure)*. That is, Prolog supports the *closed world assumption* which is the presumption that what is not currently known to be true is false.

A GOAL agent derives conclusions by combining its knowledge and beliefs. This allows an agent to draw conclusions about the current state it believes it is in using the rules present in the **knowledge** section. For example, the agent in Table 4.2 may derive that clear(a), which expresses that block a is clear, by means of the rule clear(X) :- block(X), not(on(Y,X)). This follows since we have block(a) according to the knowledge base of the agent and the belief base does not contain a fact on(X,a) for any X.

Although a programmer may also include rules in the **beliefs** section it is a better practice to include these in the **knowledge** section. One reason is that GOAL does not allow to modify such rules at runtime. Another reason is that rules present in the **knowledge** section may also be used when reasoning with goals. The definition of the predicate tower in the **knowledge** section in Table 4.2 provides

---

[6] Incidentally, note that these observations are related to the famous *Sussman anomaly*. Early planners were not able to solve simple Blocks World problems because they constructed plans for subgoals (parts of the larger goal) that could not be combined into a plan to achieve the main goal. The Sussman anomaly provides an example of a Blocks World problem that such planners could not solve, see e.g. [17].

an example where this is useful. The rules that define this predicate define when a list of blocks [X|T] is a tower. The first rule tower([X]) :- on(X,table) requires that the basis of a tower is grounded on the table. The second rule recursively defines that whenever [Y|T] is a tower, extending this tower with a block X on top of Y also yields a tower, that is, [X,Y|T] is a tower. Observe that it is not required that block X is clear and a stack of blocks that is part of a larger tower also is considered to be a tower. For example, it is possible to derive tower([b,c]) using the facts representing the initial state depicted in Figure 4.1.

It turns out that the concept of a tower is particularly useful for defining when a block is in position or misplaced. In order to provide such a definition, however, we need to be able to derive that an agent has the goal of realizing a particular tower. This cannot be derived from the information present in the goal base of the example agent but requires additional conceptual knowledge which defines the notion of a tower. In combination with the conceptual knowledge present in the knowledge base it is possible, however, to derive such a goal, which illustrates that it is useful to derive conclusions from a *single* goal in combination with the knowledge base. By doing so, for example, it is possible for the example agent of Table 4.2 to derive that tower([e,b]) is a (sub)goal. It can do so by means of the rules that define the predicate tower in the knowledge base of the agent and the (sub)goals on(b,table) and on(e,b) in the goal base.

Mental State Conditions

Agents that derive their choice of action from their beliefs and goals need the ability to inspect their mental state. In GOAL, *mental state conditions* provide the means to do so. These conditions are used in action rules to determine which actions the agent may consider to perform. A mental state condition consists of mental atoms which are conditions on the belief base of the form bel(φ) and conditions on the goal base of the form goal(φ) where φ is a conjunction of literals.

Informally, bel(φ) can be read as "the agent believes that φ". bel(φ) holds whenever φ can be derived from the belief base *in combination with the knowledge base*. Using the same example as above, it follows in the initial state that bel(clear(a)), which expresses that the agent believes that block a is clear. Similarly, goal(φ) can be read as "the agent has a goal that φ". goal(φ) holds whenever φ can be derived from *a single goal* in the goal base *in combination with the knowledge base*.[7] Again using the same example as above, it follows given the goal base of Table 4.2 and the definition of the tower predicate in the **knowledge** section that goal(tower([e,b])) since on(b,table) and on(e,b) are present in the goal base.

---

[7] This reading differs from that provided in [3] where the goal operator is used to denote *achievement goals*, which additionally require that the agent *does not believe that* φ. The goal operator goal introduced here is more basic and, in combination with the belief operator bel, allows to define achievement goals.

A mental state condition is a conjunction of mental atoms of the form bel (φ) and goal (φ), or a negation of a mental state condition ψ of the form not (ψ). For example, the mental state condition

goal(on(b,table)), not(bel(on(b,table))

expresses that the agent has a goal that block b is on the table but does not believe that this is the case (yet). Such goals that have still to be achieved are also called *achievement goals*. As achievement goals are important reasons for choosing actions and are frequently used in GOAL programs to this end, a new operator a-goal (φ) is introduced as an abbreviation for mental state conditions of the form goal (φ), not (bel (φ)).[8]

$$\text{a-goal}(\varphi) \stackrel{df}{=} \text{goal}(\varphi), \ \text{not}(\text{bel}(\varphi))$$

Interestingly, this operator provides what is needed to express that a block is misplaced as a block is misplaced whenever the agent believes that the block's current position is different from the position the agent wants it to be in.[9] As the position of the tower which a block is part of is irrelevant, the fact that a block X is not in position can be represented by a-goal(tower([X|T])) where T is a tower. a-goal(tower([X|T])) expresses that in the goal state block X is on top of the tower T but the agent does not believe that this is already so in the current state. The concept of a misplaced block is important for defining a strategy to resolve a Blocks World problem, since only misplaced blocks have to be moved, and can be expressed easily and elegantly in GOAL using mental state conditions. Another useful mental state condition is goal (φ), bel (φ) which expresses that a (sub)goal has been achieved. Instantiating the template φ with tower([X|T]), this condition expresses that the current position of a block X corresponds with the position it has in the goal state.[10] In this case φ is a (sub)goal that is achieved and we call such a (sub)goal a *goal achieved*. The operator goal-a (φ) is introduced as an abbreviation to denote such goals.

$$\text{goal-a}(\varphi) \stackrel{df}{=} \text{goal}(\varphi), \ \text{bel}(\varphi)$$

The condition a-goal(tower([X,Y|T])), bel(tower([Y|T]) provides another useful example of a mental state condition. It expresses that the achievement goal to construct a tower tower([X,Y|T])) has been realized except for the fact that block X is not yet on top of tower [Y|T]. It is clear that whenever it is possible to move block X on top of block Y the agent would get closer to achiev-

---

[8] See [20] for a discussion of this definition.

[9] Actually, here the difference between *knowledge* and *belief* is important as we normally would say something is misplaced only if we *know* that the block is in a different position. That is, an agent's beliefs about the block's position must also correspond with the actual position of the block. If, in fact, the block is in the desired position, in ordinary language, we would say that the block is *believed to be misplaced* but that in fact it is not.

[10] Note that it would not be possible to express this using an achievement goal operator. In [21] the goal-a operator is used to define the concept of a deadlock [40].

ing (one of) its goals. Such a move, moreover, would be a *constructive move* which means that the block would never have to be moved again. As the possibility to make a move may be verified by checking whether the precondition of the move action holds (see below), in combination with the mental state condition, we are able to verify whether a constructive move can be made. This condition therefore is very useful to define a strategy for solving Blocks World problems, and is used in the first action rule in the **program** section listed in Table 4.2.

Actions

In order to achieve its goals an agent needs to select and perform actions. Unlike other programming languages, but similar to planners, actions that may be performed by a GOAL agent need to be specified by the programmer of that agent. GOAL does provide some special built-in actions but typically most actions that an agent may perform are derived from the environment that the agent acts in. Actions are specified in the **action-spec** section of a GOAL agent. These actions are called *user-defined actions*. Actions are specified by specifying the conditions when an action can be performed and the effects of performing the action. The former are also called *preconditions* and the latter are also called *postconditions*. The **action-spec** section consists of a set of STRIPS-style specifications [27] of the form (cf. Table 4.1):

> *action* {
>   pre {*precondition*}
>   post {*postcondition*}
> }

The *action* specifies the *name* of the action and its *arguments or parameters* and is of the form *id[args]*, where *id* denotes the name of the action and the *[args]* part denotes an optional list of parameters of the form $(p_1, \ldots, p_n)$, where the p_i are Prolog terms. If an agent is connected to an environment, the user-defined actions will be sent to the environment for execution. (In that case it is important that the name of an action corresponds with the name the environment expects to receive when it is requested to perform the action.) The parameters of an action in a GOAL agent may contain free variables which are instantiated at runtime. An action can only be performed if *all free variables in parameters of an action as well as in the postcondition of the action have been completely instantiated*. This is not only true for user-defined actions but also for built-in actions.

The *precondition* in an action specification is a conjunction of literals. Preconditions are used to verify whether it is possible to perform an action. A precondition φ is evaluated by verifying whether (an instantiation of) φ can be derived from the belief base (as always, in combination with knowledge in the knowledge base). Any free variables in a precondition may be instantiated during this process just like executing a Prolog program returns instantiations of variables. An action is said to be *enabled* whenever its precondition is believed to be the case by the agent.

A *postcondition* specifies the effect of an action. A postcondition is a conjunction of literals. In GOAL effects of an action are changes to the mental state of an agent. The effect φ of an action is used to update the beliefs of the agent to ensure the agent believes φ after performing the action. In line with STRIPS terminology, a *postcondition* φ is also called an *add/delete list* (see also [17, 27]). Positive literals φ in a postcondition are said to be part of the add list whereas negative literals not (φ) are said to be part of the delete list. The effect of performing an action is that it updates the belief base by first removing all facts φ present in the delete list and thereafter adding all facts present in the add list. Finally, as an action can only be performed when all free variables in the postcondition have been instantiated, each variable present in a postcondition must also be present in the action parameters or precondition of the action.

In addition, performing an action may affect the goal base of an agent. As a rational agent should not invest resources such as energy or time into achieving a goal that has been realized, such goals are removed from the goal base. That is, goals in the goal base that have been achieved as a result of performing an action are removed. Goals are removed from the goal base, however, only if they have been *completely* achieved. The idea here is that a goal φ in the goal base is achieved only when all of its subgoals are achieved. An agent should not drop any of these subgoals before achieving the overall goal as this would make it impossible for the agent to ensure the overall goal is achieved at a single moment in time (see also the reference to the Sussman anamoly above). The fact that a goal is only removed when it has been achieved implements a so-called *blind commitment strategy* [34]. Agents should be committed to achieving their goals and should not drop goals without reason. The default strategy for dropping a goal in GOAL is rather strict: only do this when the goal has been completely achieved. This default strategy can be adapted by the programmer for particular goals by using the built-in drop action.

In the GOAL agent of Table 4.2 only one action move (X, Y) has been specified. The precondition specifies that in order to be able to perform action move (X, Y) of moving X on top of Y both X and Y have to be clear. In addition, the literal on (X, Z) in the precondition retrieves in variable Z on which particular thing, i.e. block or table, X is currently on, in order to be able to remove this fact after performing the action. The precondition of move (X, Y) in Table 4.2 could have been strengthened by including a condition not (on (X, Y)) to prevent moves which move a block X on top of block Y in case block X already is on top of Y. Clearly, such actions are redundant for solving a Blocks World problem. However, as we will see below, such move options are never generated by the action selection mechanism of GOAL given the action rules in the **program** section. It would be useful to include not (X=Y), however, to prevent moving a misplaced block on the table to another place on the table. The postcondition not (on (X, Z)), on (X, Y) of the action move (X, Y) has the effect of (first) removing the current position on (X, Z) of block X from the belief base and (thereafter) adding the new position on (X, Y) to it. Even though the precondition does not preclude moving a block on top of another block it is already on, observe that in the case that Z=Y the belief base would not change as a result of performing the action.

In addition to the possibility of specifying user-defined actions, GOAL provides several built-in actions for changing the beliefs and goals of an agent, and for communicating with other agents. Here we only briefly discuss the two built-in actions adopt (φ) and drop (φ) which allow for modifying the goal base of an agent. The action adopt (φ) is an action to adopt a new goal φ. The precondition of this action is that the agent does not believe that φ is the case, i.e. in order to execute adopt (φ) we must have not (bel (φ)). The idea is that it would not be rational to adopt a goal that has already been achieved. The effect of the action is the addition of φ as a single, new goal to the goal base. The action drop (φ) is an action to drop goals from the goal base of the agent. The precondition of this action is always true and the action can always be performed. The effect of the action is that any goal in the goal base from which φ can be derived is removed from the goal base. For example, the action drop (on (a, table)) would remove all goals in the goal base that entail on (a, table); in the example agent of Table 4.2 the only goal present in the goal base would be removed by this action.

Action Rules

The **program** section specifies the *strategy* used by the agent to select an action to perform by means of *action rules*. Action rules provide a GOAL agent with the know-how that informs it when it is opportune to perform an action. In line with the fact that GOAL agents derive their choice of action from their beliefs and goals, action rules consist of a mental state condition *msc* and an action *action* and are of the form **if** *msc* **then** *action*. The mental state condition in an action rule determines whether the corresponding action may be considered for execution or not. If (an instantiation of) a mental state condition is true, the corresponding action is said to be *applicable*. Of course, the action may only be executed if it is also *enabled*. If an action is both applicable and enabled we say that it is an *option*. We also say that action rules *generate options*.

The **program** section of Table 4.2 consists of two action rules. These rules specify a simple strategy for solving a Blocks World problem. The rule
if a-goal (tower ([X,Y|T])), bel (tower ([Y|T])) **then** move (X,Y)
specifies that move (X,Y) may be considered for execution whenever move (X,Y) is a constructive move (cf. the discussion about the mental state condition of this rule above). The rule **if** a-goal (tower ([X|T])) **then** move (X, table) specifies that the action move (X, table) of moving block X to the table may be considered for execution if the block is misplaced. As these are all the rules, the agent will only generate options that are constructive moves or move misplaced blocks to the table, and the reader is invited to verify that the agent will never consider moving a block that is in position or making a redundant move that puts a block on top of a block that it already is on. Furthermore,

observe that the mental state condition of the second rule is weaker than the first. In common expert systems terminology, the first rule *subsumes* the second as it is more specific.[11] This implies that whenever a constructive move move(X,Y) is an option the action move(X,table) is also an option. The set of options generated by the action rules thus may consist of more than one action. In that case, GOAL *arbitrarily* selects one action out of the set of all options. As a result, a GOAL agent is nondeterministic and may execute differently each time it is run. A set of action rules may be viewed as specifying a *policy*. There are two differences with standard definitions of a policy in the planning literature, however [17]. First, action rules do not need to generate options for each possible state. Second, action rules may generate *multiple* options in a particular state and do not necessarily define a function from the (mental) state of an agent to an action. A policy for a GOAL agent thus does not need to be *universal*[12] and may *underspecify* the choice of action of an agent.

Execution Traces of The Blocks World Agent

We will trace one particular execution of the Blocks World agent of Table 4.2 in more detail here. As a GOAL agent selects an arbitrary action when there are more options available, there are multiple traces that may be generated by the agent, three of which are listed below.

In the initial state, depicted also in Figure 4.1, the agent can move each of the clear blocks a, d, and f to the table. It is easy to **verify the precondition** of the move action in each of these cases by instantiating the action specification of the move action and inspecting the knowledge and belief bases. For example, instantiating move(X,Y) with block a for variable X and table for variable Y gives the corresponding precondition clear(a), clear(table), on(a,Z). By inspection of the knowledge and belief bases, it immediately follows that clear(table), and we find that by instantiating variable Z with b it follows that on(a,Z). Using the rule for clear it also follows that clear(a) and we conclude that action move(a,table) is enabled. Similar reasoning shows that the actions move(d,table), move(f,table), move(a,d), move(a,f), move(d,a), move(d,f), move(f,d), move(f,a) are enabled as well. The reader is invited to check that no other actions are enabled.

(continued overleaf)

---

[11] Thanks to Jörg Müller for pointing this out.

[12] In the sense of [37], where a "universal plan" or policy specifies the appropriate action for *every* possible situation.

A GOAL agent selects an action using its action rules. In order to verify whether moving the blocks a, d, and f to the table are options we need to **verify applicability** of actions by checking the mental state conditions of action rules that may generate these actions. We will do so for block a here but the other cases are similar. Both rules in the program section of Table 4.2 can be instantiated such that the action of the rule matches with move(a,table). As we know that block a cannot be moved constructively, however, and the mental state condition of the first rule only allows the selection of such constructive moves, this rule is not applicable. The mental state condition of the second rule expresses that a block X is misplaced. As block a clearly is misplaced, this rule is applicable. The reader is invited to verify this by checking that a-goal([a,e,b]) holds in the initial state of the agent.

Assuming that move(a,table) is selected from the set of options, the action is executed by **updating the belief base** with the instantiated postcondition not(on(a,b)), on(a,table). This means that the fact on(a,b) is removed from the belief base and on(a,table) is added. The goal base may need to be updated also when one of the goals has been completely achieved, which is not the case here. As in our example, we have abstracted from perceptions, there is no need to process any and we can repeat the action selection process again to select the next action.

As all blocks except for blocks c and g are misplaced, similar reasoning would result in a possible trace where consecutively move(b,table), move(d,table), move(f,table) are executed. At that point in time, all blocks are on the table, and the first rule of the program can be applied to build the goal configuration, e.g. by executing move(e,b), move(a,e), move(d,c), move(f,d). In this particular trace the goal state would be reached after performing 8 actions.

Additionally, we list the 3 shortest traces - each including 6 actions - that can be generated by the Blocks World agent to reach the goal state:

Trace1 : move(a, table), move(b, table), move(d, c), move(f, d), move(e, b), move(a, e).
Trace2 : move(a, table), move(b, table), move(d, c), move(e, b), move(f, d), move(a, e).
Trace3 : move(a, table), move(b, table), move(d, c), move(e, b), move(a, e), move(f, d).

There are many more possible traces, e.g. by starting with moving block f to the table, all of which consist of more than 6 actions.

To conclude the discussion of the example Blocks World agent, in Figure 4.2 the RSG line shows the average performance of the GOAL agent in number of moves relative to the number of blocks present in a Blocks World problem. This performance is somewhat better than the performance of the simple strategy of first moving all blocks to the table and then restacking the blocks to realize the goal state indicated by the US line[13] as the GOAL agent may perform constructive

---

[13] Observe that this simple strategy never requires more than $2N$ moves if N is the number of blocks. The label "US" stands for "Unstack Strategy" and the label "RSG" stands for "Random Select GOAL", which refers to the default action selection mechanism used by GOAL.

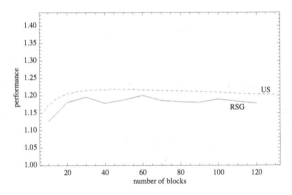

Fig. 4.2 Average Performance of a Blocks World GOAL Agent

moves whenever this is possible and not only after moving all blocks to the table first.

4.2.1.2 Modules and Focus of Attention

Rational agents are assumed to create partial plans for execution and to not over-commit to a particular way of achieving a goal. One important reason for not computing a complete plan is that in a dynamic, uncertain environment an agent typically does not have sufficient knowledge to fill in the details of a plan that is guaranteed to succeed. It therefore is better practice to decide on the action to perform next when the required information is available. As the action selection mechanism in GOAL ensures that agents select their actions by inspection of their current mental state overcommitment is avoided. As a result, the Blocks World agent, for example, provides a robust solution for solving Blocks World problems because it is flexible in its choice of action. It would still perform well even if other agents would interfere, assuming that it is able to perceive what happens in the Blocks World.

Even though action rules provide for a flexible choice of action it is useful to add additional structure to a GOAL agent. As is the case in almost any programming language, it is useful to be able to structure parts of a program in a single unit. In GOAL it is useful to combine related conceptual and domain knowledge, goals, actions and action rules that are relevant for handling particular situations in a single structure. *Modules* provide such a structure in GOAL. Modules provide for reusability and the encapsulation of related knowledge, goals, actions and action rules. They also provide a programmer with a tool to focus on the particular knowledge and skills that an agent needs to handle a situation.

Modules in GOAL also provide for focus in another sense. In many situations it is natural to *focus attention on achieving particular goals* and disregard other goals for the moment. Such focus allows for a more dedicated use of resources and the need for creating plans for a subset of ones goals only. It also allows for sequencing potentially conflicting goals. As an example, consider a truck delivery domain where a truck is supposed to deliver multiple packages to different locations. Given that the load of packages that the truck may carry is limited, it is useful to focus on the delivery of packages to a particular subset of locations and only load packages that need to be delivered to those locations. Modules provide for a mechanism that enables agents to focus attention in this way. In the remainder we will illustrate the use of modules in the Blocks World domain. This example provides a simple illustration of programming with modules which also illustrates how modules can be used to program a different strategy for solving a Blocks World problem.

Syntactically, a module is very similar to a GOAL agent. The main difference with a GOAL agent such as the Blocks World agent discussed in the previous section is that a module has an additional `Context` section, which specifies an *activation condition*. A distinguishing feature of modules in GOAL is that the context of a module is specified *declaratively*. A module's context specifies not only when to activate the module but also for what purpose a module is activated. It thus provides a declarative specification of the intended use of a module. Such specifications are useful for a programmer as a programmer does not have to inspect the implementation details inside a module but can read off the intended use from the context.

Another difference with a GOAL agent is that a module does not have a **beliefs** section and that all sections other than the **program** section are optional. The reason that a module does not have a **beliefs** section is that a module specifies knowledge and skills that are independent of the current state. A module specifies the generic knowledge and know-how to deal with a particular situation but not the specifics of a particular state. The belief base of an agent is used to keep track of the state of the environment and is a "global" component of the agent. This means that the beliefs of an agent are accessible by and may be modified by any module. The **knowledge** and **action-spec** section are optional because the knowledge in the **knowledge** section and all actions specified in the **action-spec** section of the GOAL agent that contains the module are "inherited" by the module and are "globally" accessible as beliefs are. The same does not hold for the goals of an agent, however. The context of a module provides a filter on the set of goals that the agent currently pursues which allows an agent to focus its attention on a subset of these goals.

Table 4.3 presents an example module, which can be used by the Blocks World agent introduced above. In the remainder we assume that the action rules used by the original agent of Table 4.2 are replaced by the module of Table 4.3 and we explain how this change modifies the behaviour of that agent.

The *context* of a module is a mental state condition that serves two functions. The first function is that a context specifies when a module may be activated. For example, the context of the module in Table 4.3 specifies that the module may be activated whenever the agent has an achievement goal to build a tower with block X as the top of that tower. That is, block X should be clear. The context can also be viewed as a (pre)condition for activating a composed activity, or a policy, as a

```
1   module BuildTower
2   { % This module achieves the goal of building a particular tower of blocks.
3     Context{
4        a-goal(clear(X), tower([X|T]))
5     }
6     program{
7        if a-goal(tower([X,Y|T])), bel(tower([Y|T])) then move(X,Y).
8        if bel(tower([X|T]), not(goal(tower([X|T])) then move(X,table).
9     }
10    action-spec{
11       move(X,Y) {
12          pre{ clear(X), clear(Y), on(X,Z) }
13          post{ not(on(X,Z)), on(X,Y) }
14       }
15  }
```

Table 4.3 Module Replacing the **program** Section of the Blocks World Agent

set of action rules in a module specifies such a policy. The second function of a context is that it is used as a filter on the goals that the agent pursues which selects a subset of these goals. The goals currently pursued by an agent are said to be in the agent's *attention set*. After activating a module the attention set of an agent is restricted to those goals in that set that are obtained from a particular instantiation of the context of a module. The goals that are put in the updated attention set are all goals φ that are in the current attention set and correspond with a positive occurence of a mental atom goal (φ) in the instantiated context.[14] This means all other goals in the current attention set of the agent are removed and, that, if a context does not have positive occurrences of such mental atoms all goals in this set are removed.[15] Any goals introduced by the module's **goals** section are added to this updated attention set. For example, upon activation of the module listed in Table 4.3, the context of the module is instantiated such that it becomes true. Assume that the instantiated context is a-goal(clear(g), tower([g])), which is an achievement goal in the initial state of Figure 4.1. As this context is an abbreviation for a mental state condition with a positive occurrence of a mental atom of the form goal(clear(g), tower([g])) the goal clear(g), tower([g]) is included in the attention set of the agent and all other goals are removed from the attention set. As the **goals** section in the module is absent, the resulting attention set would consist of the single goal clear(g), tower([g]).

---

[14] A mental atom goal (φ) occurs positively in a context if it occurs within the scope of an even number of negations not.

[15] Formally, a filter function $filter(c, m)$ with c a context and m a mental state (with a goal base that provides the current attention set) can be defined as follows: $filter(c, m) = \{\varphi \mid m \models_c c\theta \ \& \ goal(\varphi) \in pos(c\theta)\}$ where $pos(c)$ denotes the set of all positive occurrences of mental atoms in c and θ is a substitution for variables that occur in c. For a definition of the entailment relation $\models_c$ see Section 4.2.2.1. The filter function $filter(c, m)$ provides the new attention set after activating a module with context c.

A module provides not only a means to focus on particular goals but also provides a context which restricts the choice of action. When a module is activated the action rules present in the module are the only rules available to generate action options. A module may also introduce action specifications that are only available while the module is executed and specific for handling situations the module has been designed for. Actions specified in the main GOAL agent, but not those specified in other modules, are also accessible from within a module. In the example in Table 4.3 the move action has been moved from the main GOAL agent to the module. As a result, it is only possible to move blocks when the module is activated.

The example module replaces the action rules in the **program** section of the Blocks World agent of Table 4.2. The first action rule of that agent which generates constructive moves is included in the **program** section of the module. The second action rule of this agent which generates moves of misplaced blocks to the table, however, has been replaced by another rule. The reason is that the original rule assumed that each block is part of the goal configuration and, as a consequence, any block is either in position or misplaced. As the attention set of an agent upon activation of a module is restricted we can no longer make this assumption. Instead of being part of a goal condition a block may now be in the way of achieving a goal of the agent, i.e. it may obstruct making moves with a block that is part of such a goal because it is above such a block. Therefore, the second action rule **if** bel(tower([X|T]), not(goal(tower([X|T]))) **then** move(X,table) in Table 4.3 still moves blocks to the table but under a different condition. The mental state condition of this rule expresses that block X is possibly in the way to get to a block needed to achieve a goal of the agent. Here, *possibly in the way* means that the agent does not intend the block to be in the position it believes it to be in.[16] Observe that blocks that are misplaced also satisfy this mental state condition but that blocks that are possibly in the way do not always satisfy the mental statement condition
goal(tower([X|T])), not(bel(tower([X|T]))). The latter condition expresses that block X is misplaced and therefore must be part of the agent's goals whereas a block that is possibly in the way does not need to be part of one of the goals of the agent.[17]

---

[16] We use "does not intend" here instead of the seemingly more natural "does not want" as the agent is supposed to *not* have a goal here. The natural language expression "does not want φ" is more commonly used to express that one wants to be in a state where φ is *not* the case (the effect of which can be strengthed by putting more stress on "not" in the phrase). In other words, this expression is commonly used to express that one has a goal to achieve that φ is not the case. In contrast, the expression "does not intend" is more commonly used to express the lack of an intention or goal. From a more technical point of view, as the knowledge representation used is Prolog, there is no difference between writing not(goal(φ)) or goal(not(φ)) since in Prolog the Closed World Assumption is supported (a similar point can be made for the bel operator). The negation in Prolog is negation as failure and cannot be used to express "explicit" negation which would be needed to make the distinction.

[17] Suppose that block X is misplaced and the agent believes that X is part of a tower [X|T]. In that case, the agent has a goal that the block is part of another tower. That is, we have

The second action rule may generate options that are not needed to realize the achievement goal of the agent as there may be stacks of blocks which do not contain a block needed to build the desired tower and these blocks therefore are not in the way to achieve this goal. The reader is invited to provide a mental state condition that more accurately captures the notion of *a block being in the way*. (Hint: it is useful to introduce a Prolog definition of the concept *above*.) The strategy of building towers in the goal state one by one implemented using the module construct, however, never requires more than $2N$ steps where N is the number of blocks.

Activating a module is making a commitment to achieve the goals in the attention set that is initialised upon activation. A module is terminated only when the attention set, i.e. the set of goals currently pursued by the agent, is empty. The knowledge and skills incorporated in a module need to be sufficient in order to realize the goals in the agent's attention set. In addition, another module may be activated from a module whenever the context of that module is true. In the example, the agent has a goal to achieve clear(g), tower([g]) and after moving block f to the table this goal has been achieved and is removed from the attention set and, as a result, the module is terminated. Upon termination the agent's previous goals except for those that have been *completely* achieved by the module are put back into the attention set and the agent continues execution.[18]

4.2.2 Semantics and Verification

In this section we introduce the formal semantics of GOAL and discuss the verification framework for the language. The semantics of GOAL consists of several more or less independent parts. The first part defines the semantics of the agent's mental state and the mental state conditions that can be used to inspect such states. The second part defines the semantics of actions and the agent's action rules used for choosing an action to perform. The various parts combined together define the *operational semantics* of GOAL.

4.2.2.1 Semantics of Mental States

GOAL is a general-purpose agent programming language. The basic design of the language assumes that beliefs and goals of an agent are specified in a *declarative* way. Beliefs of a GOAL agent thus do not encode procedural knowledge but represent *what is the case* and goals of a GOAL agent do not specify which actions an agent wants to perform but represent *what state an agent wants to achieve*. The

---

not(goal([X|T])). Vice versa, it is not possible to derive from the fact that a block is possibly in the way that the block is part of one of the goals of the agent and we cannot conclude the block is misplaced.

[18] For further details on and explanation of modules the reader is referred to [19].

main benefit of using declarative specifications to represent an agent's beliefs and goals is that it allows an agent to *reason* with its beliefs and goals. GOAL thus aims to facilitate the design of agent programs at the *knowledge level* [31].

An agent's mental state consists of its knowledge, its beliefs and its goals as explained in Section 4.2.1.1. In the current implementation of GOAL these are represented in Prolog [41, 42]. The knowledge and beliefs of an agent in this implementation are stored in two different Prolog databases; the storage of goals in this implementation is slightly more complicated because of the difference in semantics of goals and beliefs. The details are not important here, however, since the main point we want to make is that GOAL does not commit to any particular *knowledge representation technology*. Instead of Prolog an agent might use variants of logic programming such as Answer Set Programming (ASP; [1]), a database language such as Datalog [7], the Planning Domain Definition Language (PDDL; [17]), or other, similar such languages, or possibly even Bayesian Networks [32]. The only assumption that we will make throughout is that an agent uses a *single* knowledge representation technology to represent its knowledge, beliefs and goals. For some preliminary work on lifting this assumption, we refer the reader to [13].

In order to abstract from the details of any specific knowledge representation technology in the presentation of the semantics of GOAL, we first define abstractly what we mean by a knowledge representation technology. The basic capabilities that we need such a technology to provide are the capability to *represent* states of affairs (which is fundamental), the capability to *store* these representations in a storage facility, the capability to *reason* with them and the capability to *change* the representations present in a storage. These capabilities are similar to some of the functions associated with a knowledge technology as discussed in [15].

The first capability to represent states of affairs is realized by means of a *language*. The only assumptions we make about this language is that it defines what a *formula* is and that it contains a special formula $\perp$. In other words, we assume that a language defines the grammar or syntax of *well-formed formulae*. We write $\varphi \in \mathcal{L}$ to denote that φ is a formula of language $\mathcal{L}$; in particular, we have $\perp \in \mathcal{L}$. Intuitively, we think of a formula as a *sentence* that *expresses that a state of affairs is the case (or not)* similar to declarative sentences in natural language. Although the meaning of formulae of a language is not formally defined, informally, we think of a formula as having a *truth value* and of a formula being *true* or *false* (but other possible truth values such as *undefined* are also allowed). The special formula $\perp$ is assumed to always have the truth value false and is introduced to be able to define when a set of formulae is inconsistent.

The second capability to store representations is formalised here by means of the notion of a *set*. We thus abstract from most implementation details typically associated with this capability. A knowledge, belief and goal base each are represented in the semantics as a set of formulae, or, equivalently, as a subset of a language $\mathcal{L}$. Below we use $\mathcal{D} \subseteq \mathcal{L}$ to denote a knowledge base, $\Sigma \subseteq \mathcal{L}$ to denote a belief base, and $\Gamma \subseteq \mathcal{L}$ to denote a goal base.

The third capability is realized by means of a *consequence relation* (also called *entailment*). A consequence relation defines when a formula follows from ("is a consequence of") a set of formulae. We use $\models$ to denote consequence relations and write $T \models \varphi$ for φ follows from a set of formulae T. For example, a formula φ follows from an agent's belief base Σ whenever we have $\Sigma \models \varphi$. When the special formula $\bot$ follows from a set T we say that T is *inconsistent*; the intuition here is that in that case T is contradictory, something we typically want to avoid. For example, we would like an agent's knowledge and belief base to be consistent. A consequence relation is the formal counterpart of the reasoning capability of an agent in the semantics since it allows an agent to derive and reason with its knowledge, beliefs, and goals.

The fourth and final capability we need is the capability to *update* an agent's beliefs.[19] Recall that an agent's knowledge base is assumed to be static and does not change since it is assumed to represent conceptual and domain knowledge that does not change (see also section 4.2.1). In particular we will need to be able to define how an agent's beliefs change when it performs an action. In order to do so an update operator denoted by $\oplus$ is assumed that updates a set of formulae T with a formula φ. That is, $T \oplus \varphi$ denotes the new set of formulae obtained after updating T with φ. This will enable us in the next section to say that the resulting belief base of updating a belief base Σ with the effect φ of an action is $\Sigma \oplus \varphi$. See section 4.2.1.1 for a concrete, informally defined STRIPS-style operator.

Summarizing, a knowledge representation technology is defined here as a triple $\langle \mathcal{L}, \models, \oplus \rangle$ with $\mathcal{L}$ a language to represent states of affairs, $\models$ a consequence relation that defines when a formula follows from a set of formulae, and $\oplus$ defines how a set of formulae is updated with a given formula.[20] Using our definition of a knowledge representation technology, it is now easy to formally define what a *mental state* of an agent is and to formally define the semantics of *mental state conditions*. We first define a mental state, since it is needed to define the semantics of mental state conditions as well, and then proceeed to discuss mental state conditions.

A mental state consists of an agent's knowledge, its beliefs, and its goals. Each of these are represented using a particular knowledge representation language $\mathcal{L}$. The knowledge, beliefs and goals of a *rational* agent should satisfy some additional constraints that we will call *rationality constraints*. First, we assume that an agent's knowledge as well as its beliefs are consistent. This is a reasonable assumption, which may be debated by philosophers, logicians and psychologists, but makes sense in the context of an agent programming language. We also assume that *individual* goals $\gamma \in \Gamma$ in the goal base of an agent are consistent. It is irrational for an agent to pursue inconsisent goals, which by definition it cannot achieve.

---

[19] In the setup we use here, we do not need a special capability to update the goal base when an agent comes to believe it has achieved a goal; in that case we simply remove the goal from the goal base, which is a set-theoretic operation; see the next section.

[20] Technically, we would also need to clarify the notion of a *term* which may be used to instantiate a *variable* in order to specify the use of variables in a GOAL agent, but we abstract from such details here.

The reason that we require single goals in a goal base to be consistent but not conjunctions of multiple goals is that we allow an agent to have conflicting goals in its goal base. For example, an agent may want to achieve a state where the light is on but thereafter may want to achieve a state where the light is off again. Here we assume that the language used to express goals is not capable of expressing such *temporal* dimensions of goals and therefore allow an agent to have multiple goals that when viewed as a single goal would be inconsistent. The main reason for allowing contradictory goals thus is not because we believe that the goals of an agent may be inconsistent but because of the (assumed) lack of expressivity of the knowledge representation language used to represent goals here.[21] Finally, an agent is assumed to only have goals which it does not believe to already have been achieved *completely*. Any rational agent should avoid investing resources into achieving something that is already the case. For that reason it should not have any goals that have already been achieved. Note that an agent is allowed but not required to believe that the opposite of what it wants is the case; for example, it may believe the light is on when it wants to have the light off but does not need to believe so to have the goal.

Definition 4.1. *(Mental State)*
A *mental state* is a triple $\langle \mathcal{D}, \Sigma, \Gamma \rangle$ where $\mathcal{D} \subseteq \mathcal{L}$ is called a *knowledge base*, $\Sigma \subseteq \mathcal{L}$ is a *belief base*, and $\Gamma \subseteq \mathcal{L}$ is a *goal base* that satisfy the following *rationality constraints*:

- An agent's knowledge combined with its beliefs is consistent:

$$\mathcal{D} \cup \Sigma \not\models \bot$$

- Individual goals are consistent with an agent's knowledge:

$$\forall \gamma \in \Gamma : \mathcal{D} \cup \{\gamma\} \not\models \bot$$

- An agent does not have goals it believes to be completely achieved: [22]

$$\forall \gamma \in \Gamma : \mathcal{D} \cup \Sigma \not\models \gamma$$

The next step in defining the semantics of GOAL is to define the semantics of *mental state conditions*. An agent needs to be able to inspect its mental state, and

---

[21] See for work on extending GOAL with temporal logic as a knowledge representation language [20, 23].

[22] The precise formulation of the rationality constraints relating the contents of the goal base to that of the knowledge and/or belief base of an agent may depend on the knowledge representation language. In particular, when the knowledge representation language allows for expressing *temporal conditions*, e.g. allows for expressing that a state of affairs holds at some time in the future, then these constraints and the semantics of the **G** operator below would be in need of reformulation (see [24]). In that case, the third rationality constraint also could be refined and in addition we could require that an agent should not have any goals it believes are impossible to achieve (a condition which can only be properly expressed using temporal operators).

mental state conditions allow an agent to do so. Mental state conditions are conditions on the mental state of an agent, expressing that an agent believes something is the case, has a particular goal, or a combination of the two (see also section 4.2.1). Special operators to inspect the belief base of an agent, we use $\mathbf{B}(\varphi)$ here, and to inspect the goal base of an agent, we use $\mathbf{G}(\varphi)$ here, are introduced to do so. We allow boolean combinations of these basic conditions but do not allow the nesting of operators. Basic conditions may be combined into a conjunction by means of $\land$ and negated by means of $\lnot$. For example, $\mathbf{G}(\varphi) \land \lnot \mathbf{B}(\varphi)$ with $\varphi \in \mathcal{L}$ is a mental state condition, but $\mathbf{B}(\mathbf{G}(\varphi))$ which has nested operators is not. Note that we do not assume the operators $\land$ and $\lnot$ to be present in the $\mathcal{L}$, and if so, a negation operator might still have a different meaning in $\mathcal{L}$.

Definition 4.2. *(Syntax of Mental State Conditions)*
A mental state condition ψ is defined by the following rules:

$$\varphi ::= \text{any element from } \mathcal{L}$$
$$\psi ::= \mathbf{B}(\varphi) \mid \mathbf{G}(\varphi) \mid \psi \land \psi \mid \lnot\psi$$

The meaning of a mental state condition is defined by means of the mental state of an agent. A belief condition $\mathbf{B}(\varphi)$ is true whenever φ follows from the belief base combined with the knowledge stored in the agent's knowledge base (in order to define this the consequence relation of the knowledge representation technology is used). The meaning of a goal condition $\mathbf{G}(\varphi)$ is different from that of a belief condition. Instead of simply defining $\mathbf{G}(\varphi)$ to be true whenever φ follows from *all* of the agent's goals (combined with the knowledge in the knowledge base), we will define $\mathbf{G}(\varphi)$ to be true whenever φ follows from *one* of the agent's goals (and the agent's knowledge). This is in line with the remarks above that a goal base may be inconsistent, i.e. may contain multiple goals that taken together are inconsistent. We do not want an agent to conclude it has the absurd goal $\bot$ (i.e. to achieve the impossible). Since individual goals are assumed to be consistent, we can use these individual goals to infer the goals of an agent.

Definition 4.3. *(Semantics of Mental State Conditions)*
Let $m = \langle \mathcal{D}, \Sigma, \Gamma \rangle$ be a mental state. The semantics of mental state conditions ψ is defined by the following semantic clauses:

$$
\begin{aligned}
m &\models_c \mathbf{B}(\varphi) &&\text{iff } \mathcal{D} \cup \Sigma \models \varphi, \\
m &\models_c \mathbf{G}(\varphi) &&\text{iff } \exists \gamma \in \Gamma : \mathcal{D} \cup \{\gamma\} \models \varphi, \\
m &\models_c \psi_1 \land \psi_2 &&\text{iff } m \models_c \psi_1 \text{ and } m \models_c \psi_2, \\
m &\models_c \lnot\psi &&\text{iff } m \not\models_c \psi.
\end{aligned}
$$

Note that in the definition of the semantics of mental state conditions we have been careful to distinguish between the consequence relation that is defined, denoted by $\models_c$, and the consequence relation $\models$ assumed to be given by the knowledge representation technology and used to define $\models_c$. The definition thus shows how the meaning of a mental state condition can be derived from the semantics of more basic notions defined in an arbitrary knowledge representation technology.[23]

In the remainder of this section, it is useful to assume that the knowledge representation language at least provides the propositional operators for conjunction and negation. Here we will simply use the same notation $\land$ and $\neg$ also used for mental state conditions to refer to these operators in the knowledge representation language $\mathcal{L}$ as well. Given this assumption, note that because of the fact that a goal base may contain multiple goals that are inconsistent when taken together, it follows that we may have that $\mathbf{G}(\varphi)$ as well as $\mathbf{G}(\neg\varphi)$. It should be clear from our previous discussion however that it does not follow from this that $\mathbf{G}(\varphi \land \neg\varphi)$ also holds. To repeat, intuitively, $\mathbf{G}(\varphi)$ should be interpreted as expressing that the agent wants to achieve φ some time in the future. Given this reading of $\mathbf{G}(\varphi)$ it is perfectly consistent for an agent to also have a goal $\neg\varphi$, i.e. $\mathbf{G}(\neg\varphi)$.

P1	if ψ is an instantiation of a classical tautology, then $\models_c \psi$.
P2	if $\models \varphi$, then $\models_c \mathbf{B}\varphi$.
P3	$\models_c \mathbf{B}(\varphi \to \varphi') \to (\mathbf{B}\varphi \to \mathbf{B}\varphi')$.
P4	$\models_c \neg\mathbf{B}\bot$.
P5	$\models_c \neg\mathbf{G}\bot$.
P6	if $\models \varphi \to \varphi'$, then $\models_c \mathbf{G}\varphi \to \mathbf{G}\varphi'$.

Table 4.4 Properties of Beliefs and Goals

Some other properties of the belief and goal modalities and the relation between these operators are listed in Table 4.4. Here, we use $\to$ to denote implication, which can be defined in the usual way by means of the conjunction $\land$ and negation $\neg$. The first property (P1) below states that mental state conditions that instantiate classical tautologies, e.g. $\mathbf{B}\varphi \lor \neg\mathbf{B}\varphi$ and $\mathbf{G}\varphi \to (\mathbf{B}\varphi' \to \mathbf{G}\varphi)$, are valid with respect to $\models_c$. Property (P2) corresponds with the usual necessitation rule of modal logic and states that an agent believes all validities of the base logic. (P3) expresses that the belief modality distributes over implication. This implies that the beliefs of an agent are closed under logical consequence. Finally, (P4) states that the beliefs of an agent are consistent. In essence, the belief operator thus satisfies the properties of the system KD (see e.g. [30]). Although in its current presentation, it is not allowed to nest belief or goal operators in mental state conditions in GOAL, from [30], section 1.7, we conclude that we may assume as if our agent has positive ($\mathbf{B}\varphi \to \mathbf{B}\mathbf{B}\varphi$) and negative ($\neg\mathbf{B}\varphi \to \mathbf{B}\neg\mathbf{B}\varphi$) introspective properties: every formula in the system KD45 (which is KD together with the two mentioned properties) is equivalent to a formula without nestings of operators. Property (P5) states that an agent also does not have inconsistent goals, that is, we have $\models_c \neg\mathbf{G}\bot$. Property (P6) states that the goal operator is closed under implica-

---

[23] This semantics was first introduced in [22]. For a discussion of alternative semantics for goals, see also [35].

tion in the base language. That is, whenever $\varphi \to \varphi'$ is valid in the base language then we also have that $\mathbf{G}\varphi$ implies $\mathbf{G}\varphi'$. This is a difference with the presentation in [3] which is due to the more basic goal modality we have introduced here. For the same reason we also have that $\mathbf{B}\varphi \land \mathbf{G}\varphi$ is not inconsistent.

We may now put our definitions to work and provide some examples of what we can do. First, as discussed in section 4.2.1, we can introduce some useful abbreviations. In particular, we can define the notions of an *achievement goal* $\mathbf{A}\text{-}\mathbf{goal}(\varphi)$ and the notion of a *goal achieved* $\mathbf{goal}\text{-}\mathbf{A}(\varphi)$ as follows:

$$\mathbf{A}\text{-}\mathbf{goal}(\varphi) \stackrel{df}{=} \mathbf{G}(\varphi) \land \neg\mathbf{B}(\varphi),$$
$$\mathbf{goal}\text{-}\mathbf{A}(\varphi) \stackrel{df}{=} \mathbf{G}(\varphi) \land \mathbf{B}(\varphi).$$

For some properties of the **A-goal** operator we refer the reader to [3], Lemma 2.4. Both of these defined operators are useful when writing agent programs. The first is useful to derive whether a part of a goal has not yet been (believed to be) achieved whereas the second is useful to derive whether a part of a goal has already been (believed to be) achieved. For some concrete examples, please refer back to section 4.2.1. It should be noted that an agent is allowed to believe part of one of its goals has been achieved but cannot believe that one of its goals has been *completely* achieved as such goals are removed automatically from the goal base. That is, whenever we have $\gamma \in \Gamma$ we must have both $\mathbf{A}\text{-}\mathbf{goal}(\gamma)$ as well as $\mathbf{G}(\gamma)$ since it is not allowed by the third rationality constraint in Definition 4.1 that an agent believes γ in that case.

Note that in this section we have only used the first two components of a knowledge representation technology, the language $\mathcal{L}$ and consequence relation $\models$, so far. We will use the third component, the update operator $\oplus$, in the next section to formally define the effects of performing an action.

4.2.2.2 Semantics of Actions and Action Selection

GOAL has a formal, operational semantics defined by means of Plotkin-style transition semantics [33]. The details of the semantics of modules and communication are not discussed here.[24]

In order to define the semantics of actions, we need to model both when an action can be performed as well as what the effects of performing an action are. As actions, except for the built-in actions, are user-defined, we introduce some assumptions about what information is available to define the semantics. First, we assume that it is known which actions the agent can perform, i.e. those actions specified by the programmer in the agent program, and that these actions are given by a set $\mathcal{A}$. Second, we assume that two mappings *pre* and *post*

---

[24] The reader is referred to [19] for a detailed semantics of modules. Communication in the current implementation of GOAL implements a simple "mailbox semantics" as in 2APL [12]. In GOAL, messages are stored in an agent's mailbox and may be inspected by querying special, reserved predicates sent and received. See for a discussion also section 4.2.4.

which map actions a from this set of actions $\mathcal{A}$ and mental states m to a formula φ in the knowledge representation language $\mathcal{L}$ are given. The mappings *pre* and *post* are assumed to provide the preconditions respectively postconditions associated with an action in a given state. For example, we would have `pre(move(a,table),`m`)=clear(a), clear(table), on(a,b)` in the initial state mental m of the GOAL agent listed in Table 4.2 and `post(move(a,b),`m`)=not(on(a,b)),on(a,table)`. Finally, we also assume that the postconditions specified by *post* for each action are consistent with the domain knowledge of the agent. As the domain knowledge of an agent is assumed to be static, it would not be possible to perform an action with a postcondition that conflicts with the agent's domain knowledge without violating the rationality constraints introduced earlier.

The precondition of an action is used to represent when an action can be performed, whereas the postcondition is used to represent the effects of an action. An action may affect both the beliefs and goals of an agent. The postcondition expresses how the beliefs of an agent's mental state should be updated. This is where the update operator $\oplus$ of the knowledge representation technology is useful. The new belief base that results from performing an action $a \in \mathcal{A}$ can be obtained by applying this operator. In addition, the goals that have been completely achieved need to be removed from the goal base. This transformation of the mental state is formally defined by means of a mental state transformer function $\mathcal{M}$, which also provides the semantics of the built-in actions **adopt** and **drop** below.

Definition 4.4. *(Mental State Transformer $\mathcal{M}$)*
Let *pre* and *post* be mappings from $\mathcal{A}$ to $\mathcal{L}$. Then the *mental state transformer function* $\mathcal{M}$ is defined as a mapping from user-defined and built-in actions $\mathcal{A} \cup \{\mathbf{adopt}(\varphi), \mathbf{drop}(\varphi) \mid \varphi \in \mathcal{L}\}$ and mental states $m = \langle \mathcal{D}, \Sigma, \Gamma \rangle$ to mental states as follows:

$$\mathcal{M}(a, m) \quad = \begin{cases} \langle \mathcal{D}, \Sigma', \Gamma \setminus Th(\mathcal{D} \cup \Sigma') \rangle & \text{if } \mathcal{D} \cup \Sigma \models pre(a, m) \\ \text{undefined} & \text{otherwise} \end{cases}$$

$$\mathcal{M}(\mathbf{adopt}(\varphi), m) = \begin{cases} \langle \mathcal{D}, \Sigma, \Gamma \cup \{\varphi\} \rangle & \text{if } \not\models \neg\varphi \text{ and } \Sigma \not\models \varphi \\ \text{undefined} & \text{otherwise} \end{cases}$$

$$\mathcal{M}(\mathbf{drop}(\varphi), m) \quad = \langle \Sigma, \Gamma \setminus \{\psi \in \Gamma \mid \psi \models \varphi\} \rangle$$

where $\Sigma' = \Sigma \oplus post(a, m)$ and $Th(T) = \{\varphi \in \mathcal{L} \mid T \models \varphi\}$.

As discussed above, an action rule r is of the form **if** ψ **then** a. An action rule specifies that action a may be performed if the mental state condition ψ and the precondition of a hold. In that case, we say that action a is an *option*. At runtime, a GOAL agent non-deterministically selects an action from the set of options. This is expressed in the following transition rule, describing how an agent gets from one mental state to another.

Definition 4.5. *(Action Semantics)*
Let m be a mental state, and $r =$**if** ψ **then** a be an action rule. The transition relation $\xrightarrow{a}$ is the smallest relation induced by the following transition rule.

$$\frac{m \models_c \psi \quad \mathcal{M}(\mathsf{a}, m) \text{ is defined}}{m \xrightarrow{\mathsf{a}} \mathcal{M}(\mathsf{a}, m)}$$

The execution of a GOAL agent results in a *computation*. We define a computation as a sequence of mental states and actions, such that each mental state can be obtained from the previous by applying the transition rule of Definition 4.5. As GOAL agents are non-deterministic, the semantics of a GOAL agent is defined as the *set* of possible computations of the GOAL agent, where all computations start in the initial mental state of the agent.

Definition 4.6. *(Computation)*
A *computation*, typically denoted by t, is an infinite sequence of mental states $m_0, \mathsf{a}_0, m_1, \mathsf{a}_1, m_2, \mathsf{a}_2, \ldots$ such that for each i we have that $m_i \xrightarrow{\mathsf{a}_i} m_{i+1}$ can be derived using the transition rule of Definition 4.5, or for all $j > i$, $m_j = m_i$ and $m_i \not\xrightarrow{\mathsf{a}} m'$ for any a and m'. The meaning S of a GOAL agent with initial mental state m_0 is the set of all computations starting in that state. We also write t_i^m to denote the ith mental state and t_i^{a} to denote the ith action.

Observe that a computation is infinite by definition, even if the agent is not able to perform any action anymore from some point in time on. Also note that the concept of an agent computation is a general notion in program semantics that is not particular to GOAL. The notion of a computation can be defined for any agent programming language that is provided with a well-defined operational semantics.

4.2.2.3 Verification Framework

A formal verification framework exists to verify properties of GOAL agents [3]. This verification framework allows for compositional verification of GOAL agents and has been related to Intention Logic [20]. The language GOAL thus is firmly rooted in agent theory.
The verification logic for GOAL is based on Linear Temporal Logic extended with modal operators for beliefs and goals. In addition the logic includes a set of Hoare rules to reason about actions [3]. The setup of the verification framework has some similarities with that for Unity [8]. To obtain a verification logic for GOAL agents temporal operators are added on top of mental state conditions to be able to express temporal properties over traces. Additionally an operator **start** is introduced to be able to pinpoint the start of a trace.[25]

Definition 4.7. *(Temporal Language: Syntax)*
The *temporal language* $\mathcal{L}_G$, with typical elements χ, χ', is defined by:

---

[25] Here, only the temporal semantics is presented. The compositional verification of an agent program also requires reasoning about actions. [3] introduces so-called Hoare rules to do so. In [20] an operator $[\mathsf{a}]\chi$ for reasoning about actions is introduced as this makes it easier to relate the verification logic for GOAL to Intention Logic [10].

$$\chi \in \mathcal{L}_G ::= \textbf{start} \mid \psi \in \mathcal{L}_m \mid \neg\chi \mid \chi \wedge \chi \mid \chi \mathcal{U}\chi$$

The semantics of $\mathcal{L}_G$ is defined relative to a trace t and time point i.

Definition 4.8. *(Temporal Language: Semantics)*
The truth conditions of sentences from $\mathcal{L}_G$ given a trace t and time point i are inductively defined by:

$$
\begin{aligned}
t, i &\models \textbf{start} && \text{iff } i = 0, \\
t, i &\models \textbf{B}\phi && \text{iff } t_i^m \models_c \textbf{B}\phi, \\
t, i &\models \textbf{G}\phi && \text{iff } t_i^m \models_c \textbf{G}\phi, \\
t, i &\models \neg\varphi && \text{iff } t, i \not\models \varphi, \\
t, i &\models \varphi \wedge \psi && \text{iff } t, i \models \varphi \text{ and } t, i \models \psi, \\
t, i &\models \bigcirc\psi && \text{iff } t, i + 1 \models \psi, \\
t, i &\models \varphi \mathcal{U}\psi && \text{iff } \exists j \geq i : t, j \models \psi \text{ and } \forall i \leq k < j : t, k \models \varphi
\end{aligned}
$$

Using the $\mathcal{U}$ operator, other temporal operators such as the "sometime in the future operator" $\Diamond$ and the "always in the future operator" $\Box$ can be defined by $\Diamond\psi ::= \texttt{true}\,\mathcal{U}\psi$ and $\Box\psi ::= \neg\Diamond\neg\psi$.

The temporal logic introduced above has provided a basis for a Maude [9] implementation for the GOAL language which facilitates model checking of GOAL agents. Maude has been used to verify the Blocks World agent discussed in this chapter.

4.2.3 Software Engineering Issues

A key step in the development of a GOAL agent is the design of the domain knowledge, the concepts needed to represent the agent's environment in its beliefs and the goals of the agent. As it has been discussed above, GOAL does not commit to any particular knowledge representation language to represent the beliefs and goals of an agent. In section 4.2.2.1 we have abstracted away from any particular knowledge representation language and defined an abstract knowledge representation technology. This abstract knowledge representation has been defined such that it makes clear what the minimal requirements are that a particular knowledge representation language should satisfy in order to facilitate integration into GOAL. Although the current implementation has integrated Prolog as the technology for knowledge representation, in principle, other languages such as Answer Set Programming [1], expert system languages such as CLIPS [26], database languages such as SQL [7], or a language such as PDDL [17] also fit the definition of a knowledge representation technology in section 4.2.2.1 and could have been used as well.

The option to integrate other knowledge representation technologies than Prolog in an agent programming language may facilitate programmers as agent programming per se does not require a programmer to learn a new and specific knowledge representation language but the programmer may choose its own favorite knowledge representation tool instead. In principle this flexibility also allows the integration of, for example, legacy databases. The GOAL interpreter provides an interface that facilitates such integration in Java.

The GOAL interpreter provides other interfaces that facilitate connecting GOAL to an environment or to middleware infrastructure on top of which GOAL agents are run. The interface to an environment is generic and abstracts from the implementation language used to run the environment. At the time of writing, as the GOAL interpreter has been written in Java, Java has been used to connect GOAL agents to an environment. Our view is that this interface can be used and allows the integration of GOAL agents into a larger application, part of which has been written in Java or other languages.

4.2.4 Other features of the language

In this section we briefly discuss some other features of the GOAL language that are important in order to write practical applications. As the main aim of this chapter is to introduce the core concepts that distinguish GOAL from other languages, we only discuss some of the issues that are involved in the development of GOAL agents.

Environments and Sensing

Agents with incomplete information that act in an environment which possibly inhabits other agents need to have sensors for at least two reasons. First, sensors provide an agent with the ability to acquire new information about its environment previously unknown to it and thus to *explore* its environment. Second, sensors provide an agent with the ability to acquire information about changes in its environment that are not caused by the agent itself and thus to *keep track* of the current state of its environment.

In GOAL, sensing is not represented as an explicit act of the agent but a *perceptual interface* is defined between the agent and the environment that specifies which percepts an agent will receive from the environment. A GOAL agent thus does not actively perform sense actions (except for the case where the environment makes such actions available to an agent). Each time after a GOAL agent has performed an action the agent processes any *percepts* it may have received through its perceptual interface. Percepts represent "raw data" received from the environment the agent is operating in. The percept interface is part of the environment interface to connect GOAL agents to an environment.

Multi-Agent Systems

GOAL facilitates the development and execution of multiple GOAL agents. A multi-agent GOAL system needs to be specified by means of a *mas file*. A mas file in GOAL is a recipe for running a multi-agent system. It specifies which agents should be launched when the multi-agent system is launched and which GOAL source files should be used to initialize those agents. GOAL allows for the possibility that multiple agents instantiate a single GOAL agent file. Various features are available to facilitate this. In a mas file one can associate multiple agent names with a single GOAL file. Each agent name additionally can be supplied with a list of optional arguments. These options include the number of instances of an agent, indicated by `#nr`, that should be launched. This option is available to facilitate the launching of large numbers of agents without also having to specify large numbers of different agent names. Other options allow to initialize an agent with a particular set of beliefs specified in a separate file using `#include:filename.bb`. The beliefs in the file `filename.bb` are simply *added* to the belief base specified in the agent file. This option allows for the launching of a multi-agent system with a set of agents that, for example, share the same domain knowledge but have different beliefs about the state of the environment. The `#override:filename.bb` option is provided to completely override and replace the initial beliefs specified in the GOAL agent file. The overriding of a by the `#override:filename.bb` option simply replaces all beliefs in the initial belief base specified in the GOAL file; this is implemented by using the file `filename.bb` to initialize the belief base of the agent instead of loading the beliefs specified in the GOAL file into the agent's belief base. Similar options are available for other sections such as the **goals** and **action-spec** sections of a GOAL agent.

GOAL does not support explicit constructs to enable the mobility of agents. The main concern in the design of the language is to provide appropriate constructs for programming rational agents whereas issues such as mobility are delegated to the middleware infrastructure layer on top of which GOAL agents are run.

Communication at the Knowledge Level

Communication in the current implementation of GOAL is based on a simple "mailbox semantics", very similar to the communication semantics of 2APL [12]. Messages received are stored in an agent's mailbox and may be inspected by the agent by means of queries on special, reserved predicates `sent`(*agent,msg*) and `received`(*agent,msg*) where *agent* denotes the agent the message has been sent to or received from, respectively, and *msg* denotes the content of the message expressed in a knowledge representation language.

Although a "mailbox semantics" can be used to write agents that communicate messages, such a semantics leaves too much to the programmer. We feel that a semantics is needed that facilitates programming with the high-level concepts used to write agents such as beliefs and goals. Agent communication at the knowledge level should facilitate communication between agents about their beliefs and goals. At the time of writing, it seems that there is no commonly agreed approach to incorporate communication into agent programming languages. Various languages take different approaches. The "mailbox semantics" of *2APL* is based on communication primitives `Send(receiver,performative,content)` with the effect of adding `sent(Receiver, Performative, Content)` to the sender's mailbox and `received(Receiver, Performative, Content)` to the receiver's mailbox. A similar construct is available in *Jason* [4]. However, the effect of performing a `.send(Receiver,tell,Content)` where `tell` is a specific instance of a performative is that the receiving agent adds the `Content` of the received message to its belief base instead of the fact that a message has been received.

The semantics of communication in agent programming languages seems rather poor compared to more theoretical frameworks such as FIPA. FIPA introduces many primitive notions of agent communication called *speech acts*. The broad range of speech act types identified, however, may complicate writing agent programs and it makes more sense to us to restrict the set of communication primitives provided by an agent programming language. In this respect we favor the approach taken by *Jason* which limits the set of communication primitives to a core set. We would prefer a set of primitives that allows communication of declarative content only in line with our aim to provide an agent programming language that facilitates declarative programming. We believe this is still an evolving area that requires more research. It would be useful, from a more practical perspective, to gain more experience about what would be useful communication primitives that facilitate the programming of multi-agent systems.

4.3 Platform

4.3.1 Available tools and documentation

The GOAL interpreter can be obtained by downloading the GOAL installer. For the most up to date version as well as information about the GOAL agent programming language the reader may visit

```
http://mmi.tudelft.nl/~koen/goal.html
```

Here also additional references to GOAL-related publications can be found. The language comes with an Integrated Development Environment (IDE) which allows editing and debugging of GOAL agents. The IDE is illustrated in Figures 4.3 and 4.4. Figure 4.3 shows the IDE after loading a mas file into the IDE. Upon loading a mas file, all files related to the same project are loaded and the plain text files (inlcuding GOAL files) are ready for editing. `jar` files related to environments cannot be edited.

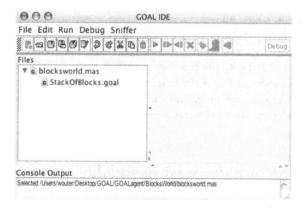

Fig. 4.3 GOAL Integrated Development Environment

Alternatively, a loaded GOAL mas file can be executed from the IDE and the IDE is switched automatically to run environment. Various options are available here to a user to monitor and debug GOAL agents. Figure 4.4 shows the introspector that is associated with each agent that is part of the multi-agent system that has been launched.

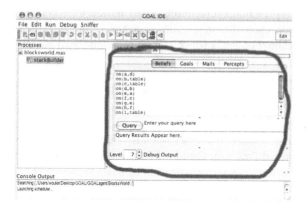

Fig. 4.4 GOAL Agent Introspector

The introspector shows the agent's beliefs and goals, and any percepts and messages received. The knowledge, action rules and action specfications which are static parts of a GOAL agent are not shown here but may be inspected by inspecting the GOAL agent program text. The debugging functionality provided by the IDE can be used to trace the operation of an agent at various levels of granularity, e.g. at the inference level which allows tracing belief and goal inferences as well as at higher levels which allows tracing of action selection only. Additionally, a sniffer is available to monitor message exchanges between agents.

GOAL comes with documentation discussing the language, IDE and some examples that are distributed with the language as well. A manual is provided for GOAL, including a discussion of the main language features, the IDE, installation and some advice on troubleshooting, and can be obtained from the site referenced above. The development of a tutorial is planned.

4.3.2 Standards compliance, interoperability and portability

The implementation of GOAL has been tested and runs on most well-known platforms. The system has been tested on Windows XP, Windows Vista 32bit, OSX Tiger, OSX Leopard (Intel only), and Linux with Ubuntu or Suse 10.1. The GOAL interpreter has been written in Java and needs SUN Java version 1.5 or higher. The design of the interpreter has been structured such that it provides a "plugin framework" that, in principle, can be instantiated with various knowledge representation technologies in line with the discussion in section 4.2.2.1 and various middleware systems that facilitate message passing and distributed computing on multiple machines. This has been achieved by defining a number of *interfaces* that specify what functionality the GOAL interpreter expects to be provided by the knowledge representation technologies or middleware systems. Similarly, an interface has been created that specifies how the GOAL interpreter can be connected to environments, e.g. a robot system or a simulated environment such as the Blocks World.

The requirements on the knowledge representation language used are minimal but the choice may introduce additional dependencies that may have consequences for portability. The current implementation integrates and uses SWI-Prolog [42] as the knowledge representation technology. As SWI-Prolog runs on most well-known operating systems, this does not introduce any severe restrictions, but other choices may do so. The use of SWI-Prolog does have implications for the number of agents that may be run on a single machine, however. Since by default SWI-Prolog reserves 100MB for any instance of a SWI-Prolog engine, in combination with the memory capacity of a machine on which the GOAL interpreter is run, this constrains the number of agents that may be run on that machine. Creating additional GOAL agents that go beyond this limit requires distributing these agents on multiple machines.

Similarly, the GOAL interpreter does not depend on any particular middleware infrastructure. The current implementation uses JADE [2] to facilitate interoperability with other systems that are built on top of JADE, but in principle any other middleware system that provides for message passing and the distributed execution of agents on multiple machines may be chosen. The middleware on top of which GOAL is run may also introduce additional dependencies or constraints on the GOAL interpreter. We did not encounter any severe problems, however, while running GOAL on top of JADE on the platforms listed above.

The GOAL framework does not itself provide support for open systems nor for heterogeneous agents. GOAL agents are particular agents defined by their beliefs, goals and action rules that facilitate decision making. GOAL agents may nevertheless interact with other types of agents whenever these agents run on top of the same middleware infrastructure and exchange messages using the facilities provided by this infrastructure.

4.3.3 Other features of the platform

The current state of the GOAL platform is still a prototype. The core of the GOAL framework is stable and well-defined in several papers [3, 19, 21, 22] and has been implemented in the GOAL interpreter. GOAL will be distributed under the GPL open source license. The GOAL language is aimed at providing a general-purpose programming language for rational agents at the knowledge level. As it does not commit to any particular knowledge representation technology, domain or middleware infrastructure (see also section 4.3.2), users and/or developers of agent systems are provided with the tools to extend the GOAL interpreter with other knowledge representation technologies, and to implement other environments to run agents in.

4.4 Applications supported by the language and/or the platform

The GOAL agent programming language provides a high-level language for programming agents. The language provides high-level concepts such as beliefs, goals and action rules to select actions. GOAL is a general purpose agent programming language, but is most suitable for developing systems of rational agents that derive their choice of action from their beliefs and goals. It is not targeted at any specific application in particular, but may be most beneficially used in domains that are familiar from the traditional planning competitions. The Blocks World example discussed in this chapter provides an example of such a domain, but other domains such as the transportation domain may also provide good examples. GOAL agents provide additional flexibility and robustness as also illustrated by the Blocks World example. This is achieved by a flexible action selection mechanism based on action rules. The GOAL interpreter has been used in education to program agents that operate in a toy world and similarly a multi-agent system for cleaning dirt in a grid world has been written. We are currently looking at more serious applications among which a system of agents that negotiate by exchanging qualitative information besides the traditional bids in an alternating offer protocol

156 Koen V. Hindriks

and a Philips iCat robot with a cognitive control layer that interacts with humans while playing a game.

Acknowledgements I would like to thank everyone who has contributed to the development of GOAL, by helping to implement the language, developing the theoretical foundations, or contributing to extensions of GOAL. The list of people who have been involved one way or the other in the GOAL story so far, all of which I would like to thank are: Lăcrămioaria Aştefănoaei, Frank de Boer, Mehdi Dastani, Wiebe van der Hoek, Catholijn Jonker, John-Jules Ch. Meyer, Peter Novak, M. Birna van Riemsdijk, Tijmen Roberti, Nick Tinnemeier, Wouter de Vries. Special thanks go to Paul Harrenstein, who suggested the acronym GOAL to me, and Wouter Pasman, who did most of the programming of the GOAL interpreter. I would also like to thank Hilko Derde for useful remarks that helped to improve this chapter.

References

1. Baral, C.: Knowledge Representation, Reasoning and Declarative Problem Solving. Cambridge University Pres (2003)
2. Bellifemine, F., Caire, G., Greenwood, D. (eds.): Developing Multi-Agent Systems with JADE. No. 15 in Agent Technology. John Wiley & Sons, Ltd. (2007)
3. de Boer, F., Hindriks, K., van der Hoek, W., Meyer, J.J.: A Verification Framework for Agent Programming with Declarative Goals. Journal of Applied Logic 5(2), 277–302 (2007)
4. Bordini, R.H., Hübner, J.F., Wooldridge, M.: Programming Multi-Agent Systems in AgentSpeak using Jason. John Wiley & Sons (2007)
5. Bratman, M., Israel, D., Pollack, M.: Plans and resource-bounded practical reasoning. In: R. Cummins, J.L. Pollock (eds.) Philosophy and AI: Essays at the Interface, pp. 1–22. The MIT Press (1991)
6. Bratman, M.E.: Intentions, Plans, and Practical Reasoning. Harvard University Press (1987)
7. Ceri, S., Gottlob, G., Tanca, L.: What you always wanted to know about datalog (and never dared to ask). IEEE Trans. of KDE 1(1) (1989)
8. Chandy, K.M., Misra, J.: Parallel Program Design. Addison-Wesley (1988)
9. Clavel, M., Durán, F., Eker, S., Lincoln, P., Martí-Oliet, N., Meseguer, J., Quesada, J.F.: Maude: Specification and programming in rewriting logic. Theoretical Computer Science 285(2), 187–243 (2002)
10. Cohen, P.R., Levesque, H.J.: Intention Is Choice with Commitment. Artificial Intelligence 42, 213–261 (1990)
11. Cook, S., Liu, Y.: A Complete Axiomatization for Blocks World. Journal of Logic and Computation 13(4), 581–594 (2002)
12. Dastani, M.: 2APL: a practical agent programming language. Journal Autonomous Agents and Multi-Agent Systems 16(3), 214–248 (2008)
13. Dastani, M., Hindriks, K.V., Novak, P., Tinnemeier, N.A.: Combining multiple knowledge representation technologies into agent programming languages. In: Proceedings of the International Workshop on Declarative Agent Languages and Theories (DALT'08) (2008). To appear
14. Davidson, D.: Actions, reasons and causes. In: Essays on Actions and Events. Oxford University Press (1980)
15. Davis, R., Shrobe, H.E., Szolovits, P.: What is a knowledge representation? AI 14(1), 17–33 (1993)
16. Dretske, F.: Explaining Behavior: Reasons in a World of Causes. The MIT Press (1995)
17. Ghallab, M., Nau, D., Traverso, P.: Automated Planning: Theory and Practice. Morgan Kaufmann (2004)

18. Gupta, N., Nau, D.S.: On the Complexity of Blocks-World Planning. Artificial Intelligence 56(2-3), 223–254 (1992)
19. Hindriks, K.: Modules as policy-based intentions: Modular agent programming in goal. In: Proceedings of the International Workshop on Programming Multi-Agent Systems (ProMAS'07), vol. 4908 (2008)
20. Hindriks, K., van der Hoek, W.: GOAL agents instantiate intention logic. In: Proceedings of the 11th European Conference on Logics in Artificial Intelligence (JELIA'08), pp. 232–244 (2008)
21. Hindriks, K., Jonker, C., Pasman, W.: Exploring heuristic action selection in agent programming. In: Proceedings of the International Workshop on Programming Multi-Agent Systems (ProMAS'08) (2008)
22. Hindriks, K.V., de Boer, F.S., van der Hoek, W., Meyer, J.J.C.: Agent Programming with Declarative Goals. In: Proceedings of the 7th International Workshop on Agent Theories Architectures and Languages, *LNCS*, vol. 1986, pp. 228–243 (2000)
23. Hindriks, K.V., van Riemsdijk, M.B.: Using temporal logic to integrate goals and qualitative preferences into agent programming. In: Proceedings of the International Workshop on Declarative Agent Languages and Theories, vol. 5397, pp. 215–232 (2008)
24. Hindriks, K.V., van Riemsdijk, M.B., van der Hoek, W.: Agent programming with temporally extended goals. In: Proceedings of the 8th International Conference on Autonomous Agents and Multi-Agent Systems (2009)
25. van der Hoek, W., van Linder, B., Meyer, J.J.: An Integrated Modal Approach to Rational Agents. In: M. Wooldridge (ed.) Foundations of Rational Agency, Applied Logic Series 14, pp. 133–168. Kluwer, Dordrecht (1999)
26. Jackson, P.: Introduction To Expert Systems, 3rd edn. Addison-Wesley (1999)
27. Lifschitz, V.: On the semantics of strips. In: M. Georgeff, A. Lansky (eds.) Reasoning about Actions and Plans, pp. 1–9. Morgan Kaufman (1986)
28. McCarthy, J.: Programs with common sense. In: Proceedings of the Teddington Conference on the Mechanization of Thought Processes, pp. 75–91. Her Majesty's Stationary Office, London (1959)
29. McCarthy, J.: Ascribing mental qualities to machines. Tech. rep., Stanford AI Lab, Stanford, CA (1979)
30. Meyer, J.J.C., van der Hoek, W.: Epistemic Logic for AI and Computer Science. Cambridge: Cambridge University Press (1995)
31. Newell, A.: The Knowledge Level. Artificial Intelligence 18(1), 87–127 (1982)
32. Pearl, J.: Probabilistic Reasoning in Intelligent Systems - Networks of Plausible Inference. Morgan Kaufmann (1988)
33. Plotkin, G.: A Structural Approach to Operational Semantics. Tech. Rep. DAIMI FN-19, University of Aarhus (1981)
34. Rao, A.S., Georgeff, M.P.: Intentions and Rational Commitment. Tech. Rep. 8, Australian Artificial Intelligence Institute (1993)
35. van Riemsdijk, M.B., Dastani, M., Meyer, J.J.C.: Goals in conflict: semantic foundations of goals in agent programming. Autonomous Agents and Multi-Agent Systems (2008). Online
36. Russell, S., Norvig, P.: Artificial Intelligence: A Modern Approach, 2nd edn. Prentice Hall (2003)
37. Schoppers, M.: Universal plans for reactive robots in unpredictable environments. In: Proceedings of the Tenth International Joint Conference on Artificial Intelligence (IJCAI'87) (1987)
38. Scowen, R.S.: Extended BNF - A generic base standard. http://www.cl.cam.ac.uk/~mgk25/iso-14977-paper.pdf (1996)
39. Shoham, Y.: Agent-oriented programming. Artificial Intelligence 60, 51–92 (1993)
40. Slaney, J., Thiébaux, S.: Blocks World revisited. Artificial Intelligence 125, 119–153 (2001)
41. Sterling, L., Shapiro, E.: The Art of Prolog, 2nd edn. MIT Press (1994)
42. http://www.swi-prolog.org/ (2008)

Chapter 5
Merging Agents and Services — the JIAC Agent Platform

Benjamin Hirsch, Thomas Konnerth, and Axel Heßler

Abstract The JIAC V serviceware framework is a Java based agent framework with its emphasis on industrial requirements such as software standards, security, management, and scalability. It has been developed within industry- and government-funded projects during the last two years. JIAC combines agent technology with a service oriented approach. In this chapter we describe the main features of the framework, with a particular focus on the language JADL++ and the service matching capabilities of JIAC V.

5.1 Motivation

The JIAC (Java Intelligent Agents Componentware) agent framework was originally developed in 1998 [1] and has been extended and adapted ever since. Its current incarnation, JIAC V, as well as its predecessor JIAC IV, is based on the premise of service-oriented communication, and the framework as well as its programming language have been geared towards this.

While originally the main application area was telecommunications, JIAC IV has been applied in a number of different projects, ranging from personal information agents [2] and service delivery platforms [22] to simulation environments [5].

The design of JIAC V was guided by the simple paradigm to take the successful features of JIAC IV and rebuild them with modern software-libraries and technologies. However, while the technologies and technical details may have changed, most features of JIAC IV are still present. Nevertheless, we made some deliberate

Benjamin Hirsch
DAI Labor, Technische Universität Berlin, e-mail: Benjamin.Hirsch@dai-labor.de

Thomas Konnerth
DAI Labor, Technische Universität Berlin, e-mail: Thomas.Konnerth@dai-labor.de

Axel Heßler
DAI Labor, Technische Universität Berlin, e-mail: Axel.Hessler@dai-labor.de

R.H. Bordini et al. (eds.), *Multi-Agent Programming,*
DOI 10.1007/978-0-387-89299-3_5, © Springer Science+Business Media, LLC 2009

design changes to the agent architecture. This was mainly aimed at simplifying things for the programmer, as we felt that usability was the aspect that needed the most improvements.

The main objectives of JIACs architecture are:

- Transparent distribution
- Service based interaction
- Semantic Service Descriptions (based on ontologies)
- Generic Security, Management and AAA[1] mechanisms
- Support for flexible and dynamic reconfiguration in distributed environments (component exchange, strong migration, fault tolerance)

JIAC V agents are programmed using JADL++ which is the successor of JADL (JIAC Agent Description Language) [25]. This new language features knowledge or facts based on the ontology language OWL [27] as well as an imperative scripting part that is used for the implementation of plans and protocols. Moreover, it allows to semantically describe services in terms of preconditions and effects, which is used by the architecture to implement features such as semantic service matching and planning from first principles. The architecture implements dynamic service discovery and selection, and thus the programmer does not have to distinguish between remote services and local actions.

The JIAC V agent model is embedded in a flexible component framework that supports component exchange during runtime. Every agent is constructed of a number of components that either perform basic functionalities (such as communication, memory or the execution cycle of an agent) or implement abilities and access to the environment of an agent. These components are bundled into an agent by plugging them into the superstructure of the agent.

During runtime, all parts of an agent, i.e. all components as well as the agent itself, can be monitored and controlled via a generic management framework. This allows either the agent itself or an outside entity such as an administrator to evaluate the performance of an agent. Furthermore, it allows the modification of an agent up to the point where whole components can be exchanged during runtime.

The execution cycle of an agent supports the BDI [4] metaphor and thus realises a goal oriented behaviour for the agents. This behaviour can be extended with agent abilities like planning, monitoring of rules, or components for e.g. handling of security certificates.

Finally, communication between JIAC V agents is based around the service metaphor. This metaphor was already the central point in the design of the JIAC IV architecture. However, JIAC V extends the rather restricted service concept of JIAC IV to include multiple types of services, thereby allowing to integrate all kinds of technologies, ranging from simple Java-methods to semantic service described in OWL-S [3].

---

[1] Authentication, authorisation, and accounting. AAA refers to security protocols and mechanisms used for online transactions and telecommunication. For more information see [29].

5.2 Language

JIAC V features an agent programming language called *JADL++*. While it is possible in JIAC to implement agents using plain Java, JADL++ allows the programmer to implement agents with a high abstraction level and the explicit usage of knowledge based concepts.

JADL++ consists of a scripting and a service description language part. It is designed to support programmers in developing different types of agents, ranging from simple reactive agents to powerful cognitive agents that are able to use reasoning and deliberation. The language is the successor of the JIAC IV Action Description Language *JADL* [25].

In order to understand some of the design choices made, it is useful to compare the main features with JIAC V's predecessor JIAC IV and its agent programming language JADL.

Our experiences with JADL were mixed [20]. On the one hand, using a knowledge oriented scripting language for programming agents worked quite well. With JIAC IV, agents and applications could be programmed very efficiently and on a high abstraction level. Also, the addition of STRIPS style preconditions and effects [13] to action and service descriptions allowed us to enhance agent programs with error correction and planning from first principles, which in turn resulted in more robust and adaptive agents.

However, there were a number of drawbacks that prompted us to change some of the features of JADL++ quite radically. The first of these was the use of a proprietary ontology description language. The use of ontologies to describe data types is a sound principle [6], but the proprietary nature of JIAC IV ontologies defeated the purpose of interoperability. Although we did provide a mapping to OWL ontologies [27], thereby providing some measure of interoperability, it was a clear disadvantage to work with proprietary ontologies, as the whole idea of ontologies is to share knowledge, and to include publicly available knowledge bases. Therefore, we now use OWL for ontology descriptions and OWL-S [3] for service descriptions in JADL++.

Furthermore, JADL allowed exactly one method of agent interaction, namely though service calls. Although a programmer was free to use any FIPA speech acts [14] within that service protocol, the core service protocol itself was always wrapped by a FIPA request protocol [15]. The restriction of communication to services allowed us to implement strong security features which were instrumental in JIAC IV becoming the first security certified agent framework according to common criteria level three [7, 8, 9].

The service approach proved to be quite comfortable for furnishing services with security or quality of service, but it did have some distinct drawbacks with respect to more simple types of communication. For example, it was not possible to send a simple Inform speech act to one or more agents in JADL, unless those agents provided a service that received that speech act. Therefore, JADL++ now features a message based interaction method that allows both, single Inform messages and multicast messages to groups of agents.

Last but not least, we changed the syntax style. JADL++ uses a C-style syntax for most procedural aspects of the language, while JADL used a LISP-like syntax. The reason for this is that the acceptance of JADLs LISP-style syntax among programmers was not very good, and programmers tended to confuse the logical and procedural parts of the language which both had a similar syntax. JADL++ now clearly discerns between the two programming concepts.

5.2.1 Syntactical Aspects

In order to explain the role of JADL++ within an agent, we need to give a brief description of how a JIAC V agent is constructed and how it operates. A more detailed explanation of an agents structure will be given in Section 5.3.

The basic concept of a JIAC V agent is that of an intelligent and autonomously acting entity. Each agent has its own knowledge, its own thread of execution and a set of abilities called actions that it can apply to its knowledge or its environment. Furthermore, agents are able to use abilities provided by other agents, which we then call services.

In order to implement a new agent, a programmer needs to identify the roles the agent is supposed to play. For each of these, relevant goals and actions that are necessary to fulfill the role are specified. Moreover, each action is either marked as private or accessible from other agents. Finally, the programmer needs to implement the actions.

The implementation of the actions can be done in various ways. An action is made available to the agent by the inclusion of a component that executes the actions functionality. Consequently, most basic way to implement an action is to implement it in pure Java, and to include a component that calls the Java code into the agent. Other options include the usage of web services or other existing technologies.

However, while implementing an action with Java and plugging it into an agent is very straightforward, it has some distinct drawbacks. First of all, the composition of multiple actions into a single workflow is complex and error prone. Action invocation in JIAC V is asynchronous and thus the programmer has to take care of the synchronization if he wants to invoke multiple actions. Furthermore, while the agent's memory can be used with simple Java objects, one strong feature of JIAC V is the possibility of using OWL ontologies to represent knowledge. Access to these ontologies is possible from Java, but not very comfortable as most APIs work in a very generic way and require a programmer to know the used ontology by heart.

To alleviate the above issues, we introduce the agent programming language JADL ++. This language does not aim at introducing elaborate language concepts but is merely devised to simplify the implementation of large and complex applications with JIAC V. At the same time, it tries to embed OWL and especially OWL-S and support programmers that do not have a logics background in their usage of both. An action that is implemented in JADL++ can be plugged into an agent via a special component that implements an interpreter for the language and can hold multiple scripts. To the agent, it looks like any other component that provides actions implemented in Java.

JADL++ is fairly easy to learn, as it uses mostly elements from traditional imperative programming languages. The instruction set includes typical elements like assignments, loops, and conditional execution. For the knowledge representation part of the language, JADL++ includes primitive and complex data types, where the notion of complex data types is tightly coupled to OWL-based ontologies. The complex data types are the grounding for the integrated OWL support, and a programmer is free to either use these complex data types like conventional objects or he can use them within their semantic framework, thus creating more powerful services.

```
 1  include de.dailab.ontology.CarOntology;
 2  import de.dailab.service.RegistrationOffice;
 3
 4  service FindAndRegisterCarService
 5    (in $name:string $color:string)
 6    (out $foundCar:CarOntology:Car)
 7    {
 8
 9      if ($name != null) {
10        // create a car template with name and color
11        // and search the memory for it
12
13        $carTemplate = new CarOntology:Car();
14        $carTemplate.owner = $name;
15        $carTemplate.color = $color;
16        $foundCar = read $carTemplate;
17      }
18      else {
19        // if no name is given, any car will do
20
21        $carTemplate = new CarOntology:Car();
22        $carTemplate.color = $color;
23        $foundCar = read $carTemplate;
24      }
25
26      // now call the registration service to register the found car
27      var $result:bool;
28      invoke CarRegistrationService ($foundCar) ($result);
29
30      // and print the results
31      if($result) {
32        log info "Success";
33      } else {
34        log error "Failure";
35      }
36
37      // end of service
38      // the output variable $foundCar is already filled,
39      // so no return is needed.
40    }
```

Fig. 5.1 JADL++ example

A simple example of the language can be seen in Figure 5.1. This example shows the implementation of a service that searches the memory of an agent for a car and then calls a registration service. The service has two input parameters: the name of the owner and the color of the car. Additionally, it has an output parameter that returns the found car. If the name of the owner is left empty, the service will search any car with a matching color.

For the memory search, the script first creates a template (either with the name of the owner or without it). In line 13, new CarOntology:Car is used to create a new object instance from the class Car as described in the ontology CarOntology. Properties of a car are accessed via the . operator. For example, in line 15, $carTemplate.color denotes the color of the car object that is stored in the variable $carTemplate.

Access to the memory is done using a tuple space semantic. That means that the memory is given a template of an object that should be retrieved and then tries to find the object stored in the memory that gives the best match with the template. The match may not have property values that contradict the values of the template. However, if any property values are not set (either for the template or for the matching object) the match is still valid.

During the course of the script, another service is invoked. This service is used to register the car with the registration office. The service is imported via the import statement at the top of the example, so no fully qualified name is necessary. The invoked service has one input and one output parameter and as we have given no further information regarding providers etc., the agent will call the first service it can find that has a matching name and matching parameters.

Figure 5.2 shows a shortened version of the syntax of JADL++ in eBNF notation. We omit production rules for names and identifiers, as well as definitions of constants. The complete syntax with accompanying semantics can be found in [21].

5.2.1.1 Data Types & Ontologies

The primitive data types are an integral part of the language. Internally, data types are mapped to corresponding XSD datatypes[2] [40], as this makes the integration of OWL simpler. Instead of implementing the full range of XSD types only the most important ones, namely bool, int, float, string, and uri, are currently supported.

An important aspect of the language is the integration of *OWL-Ontologies* as a basis for service descriptions and knowledge representation in general. As mentioned already, services are defined using the OWL-S service ontology. OWL provides the semantic grounding for data types, structures, and relations, thus creating a semantical framework for classes and objects that the programmer can use. In contrast to classical objects, however, the programmer does not need to

---

[2] XML Schema, a W3C standard for the definition of XML documents.

```
1  Model :
2     header = (Header)*
3     elements = (Service)*
4  Header :
5     "import" T_YADLImport ";" | "include" T_OWLImport ";"
6  Service :
7     "service" T_BPELConformIdentifier
8        declaration = Declaration
9        body = Seq
10
11 Declaration :
12    "(" "in"  input = (VariableDeclaration)* ")"
13    "(" "out" output = (VariableDeclaration)* ")"
14 VariableDeclaration : "var" Variable ":" AbstractType
15 Variable :  name = T_VariableIdentifier
16             (complex = "." property = Property)?
17 Property :  name = T_BPELConformIdentifier
18
19 Script :
20    Seq | Par | Protect | TryCatch | IfThenElse
21       | Loop | ForEach | Atom
22
23 Seq        : "{" (Script)* "}"
24 Par        : "par" "{" (Script)* "}"
25 Protect    : "protect" "{" (Script)* "}"
26 TryCatch   : "try" "{" (Script)* "}"
27              "catch" "{" (Script)* "}"
28 IfThenElse : "if" "(" Expression ")" Script
29              ("else" Script)?
30 Loop       : "while" "(" Expression ")" Script
31 ForEach    : "foreach" "("
32              element = T_VariableIdentifier "in"
33              list = T_VariableIdentifier ")"
34              Script
35 Atom       : Assign | VariableDeclaration | Invoke
36            | Read | Write | Remove | Query | Send
37
38 Assign      : Variable "=" AssignValue ";"
39 AssignValue : Expression | Read | Remove | Query
40
41 Invoke :  "invoke"
42           name = T_BPELConformIdentifier
43           "(" input = (Term)* ")"
44           "(" output = (T_VariableIdentifier)* ")" ";"
45 Read    : "read" Term ";"
46 Write   : "write" Term ";"
47 Remove  : "remove" Term ";"
48 Query   : "query" "(" subject=Term property=Property object=Term ")"";"
49 Send    : "send" receiver = T_BPELConformIdentifier
50           message = Term ";"
51 Receive : "receive" message Id = BPELConformIdentifier ";";
52
53 Value : "true" | "false" | "null" | URLConst | StringConst
54       | FloatConst | IntConst | HexConst
55       | "new" object = ComplexType "(" ")"
56 Term  : Variable | Value
57
58 Expression      :  (not = "!")? headTerm = ExpressionTerm
59                    tails =(ExpressionTail)*
60 ExpressionTerm  :  Value | Variable | BracketExpression
61 BracketExpression : "(" expression = Expression ")"
62 ExpressionTail  :  operator = Operator term = ExpressionTerm
63
64 Enum Operator :
65    And = "&&" | Or = "||" | NotFac = "!"
66    | Add = "+" | Sub = "-" | Mul = "*" | Div = "/" | Mod = "%"
67    | Lower = "<" | LowerEqual = "<=" | Equal = "=="
68    | NotEqual = "!=" | Grater = ">" | GreaterEqual = ">="
69
70 AbstractType: SimpleType | ComplexType;
71 SimpleType  : datatype = StringType | URLType | BoolType | FloatType
72             | IntType| HexType | DateType | TimeType | AnyType
73 ComplexType : ontology = T_OWLOntology ":"
74             owlClassName = T_BPELConformIdentifier
```

Fig. 5.2 JADL++ syntax

directly and fully instantiate all properties of an object before they are usable, as default-values, inheritance, and reasoning are employed to create properties of an instance that have not been explicitly set.

Currently, we are using ontologies that are compatible to the OWL-Lite standard, as these are still computable and we are interested in the usability of OWL in a programming environment rather than theoretical implications of the ontological framework.

5.2.1.2 Control Flow

These commands control the execution of a script. They are basically the classical control flow operators of a simple *while*-language, consisting only of assignment, choice,and a while loop (see for example [31]), but are extended by commands like *par* and *protect* to allow an optimised execution.

- **Seq**: This is not an actual statement, but rather a structural element. By default, all commands within a script that contains neither a *Par* nor a *Protect*-command, are executed in a sequential order.
- **IfThenElse**: The classical conditional execution.
- **Loop**: A classical while-loop which executes its body while the condition holds.
- **ForEach**: A convenience command that simplifies iterations over a given list of items. The command is mapped to a while-loop.
- **Par**: This command gives the interpreter the freedom to execute the following scripts in a parallel or quasi-parallel fashion, depending on the available resources.
- **Protect**: This command states that the following script should not be interrupted, and thus ensures that all variables and the agents memory are not accessed by any other component while the script is executed. This gives the programmer a tool to actively handle concurrency issues that may occur in parallel execution.

5.2.1.3 Agent Programming Commands

There are a few other commands in the language, namely:

- **read**: Reads data from the agent's memory, without consuming it.
- **remove**: Reads data from the agent's memory and consumes it, thus removing it from the memory.
- **write**: Writes data to the agent's memory.
- **send**: Sends a message to an agent or a group of agents.
- **receive**: Waits for a message.
- **query**: Executes a query and calls the inference engine.
- **invoke**: Tries to invoke another service.

Access to the memory is handled similarly to the language *Linda* [17]. The memory behaves like a tuple space, and all components within an agent, including the interpreter for JADL++, have access to it via the **read, remove** and **write** commands, which correspond to *rd*, *in* and *out* in *Linda*.

The command for messaging (**send**) allow agents to exchange simple messages without the need for a complex service metaphor and thus realise a basic means for communication.

receive allows the agent to wait for a message. It should be noted here though that received messages are by default written in the agent's memory, and a non-blocking receive can thus be implemented by using a **read** statement.

The **query** command is used to trigger the inference engine for reasoning about OWL statements. The queries are encapsulated in order to allow the agents control cycle to keep control over the queries, so the agent can still operate, even if a more complex query is running.

Another important feature of JADL++ is the **invoke**-operation, which calls services of other agents. Catering to industry, we have hidden goal oriented behaviour behind a BPEL[3] [32] like service invocation. Rather than only accepting fully specified service calls, the invoke command accepts abstract and incomplete service descriptions that correspond to goals, and subsequently tries to fulfill the goals. Informally, if the abstract service description only states certain qualities of a service, but does not refer to a concrete service (e.g. it only contains the postcondition of the service, but not its name or provider), the agent maps the operation to an achievement goal and can consequently employ its BDI-cycle to create an appropriate intention and thus find a matching service. However, if the service template can be matched to one and only one service or action, the agent skips its BDI-cycle and directly executes the service. This gives the programmer many options when programming agents, as he can freely decide, when to use classical strict programming techniques, and when to use agent oriented technologies. We describe the matching algorithm in detail in the next section.

5.2.1.4 Communication

JIAC V features two distinct methods for communication, which are mirrored in JADL++. The first is a simple message based method, that works by sending directly addressed messages to an agent or to a group of agents. An agent that receives a message automatically writes the contents of the message into its memory, and from there it is up to the agent to decide what to do with the message. The advantage of this approach is that it makes very little assumptions about the agents involved and thus constitutes a very flexible approach to agent interaction. However, for complex interactions it does not offer much support.

Nowadays, the notion of service has become a very popular approach to software interaction, and JIAC V uses this notion as the predominant means of communi-

---

[3] Business Process Execution Language. BPEL is the de facto standard for web service composition.

cation. The approach in JADL++ for service invocation is based on the premise that in a multi–agent system, a programmer often does not want to care about specific agents or service instances. Rather, agent programming is about functionality and goals. Therefore, JADL++ supports an abstract service invocation, in which a programmer can give an abstract description of the state he wants to achieve, and this template is then used by the agent to find appropriate goals, actions and services to fulfill the request. Based on this template, the agent tries to find an appropriate action within the multi–agent system. A service within JIAC V is merely a special case of an action, namely an action that is executed by another agent and thus has to be invoked remotely. However, this remote invocation is handled by the architecture, thus the programmer can use it as if it were a local action.

5.2.2 Semantic Service Matching and Invocation

In the previous section we have presented the syntax of a JIAC V agent, and the structure of the language JADL++. As mentioned above, JADL++ is based on a *while* language with a number of extensions, but the interpretation is rather straightforward. Therefore, we focus in this section on the service matching part, and refer the reader interested in the formal semantics to [21].

The concept of data structures based on ontologies extends the goal oriented approach of agents. Informally, service matching means to have an expression that describes what the agent want to achieve (its goal), and for each service that may be applicable, to have an expression describing what that service does. To find a matching service, the agent try to find a service with an expression that is semantically equivalent to the goal expression. While other agent programming languages like 3APL [19] or AgentSpeak [36] typically use the underlying semantics of traditional first order logic to identify matching expressions, our approach allows to extend this matching also to the semantic structures of the arguments as they are described in OWL, resulting in a better selection of matching services for a given goal.

Although OWL provides the technical basis for the description of semantic services, it does not offer a structural specification of the semantic services design itself. In order to bridge this gap an OWL-based ontology called OWL-S [3] has been developed that allows the semantic description of web services. The main intention of OWL-S is to offer the discovery, classification and finally invocation of resources. Since the first two attributes are exactly the requirements for the development of matching concepts, OWL-S turns out to be an adequate format.

Therefore, the principal challenge of the JIAC Matcher is to compare the service attributes that are embedded in the OWL-S context. In general, these are input parameters, output parameters, preconditions and effects of a service, often abbreviated as IOPE. Furthermore, user-defined attributes such as Quality-of-Service (QoS), the service's provider, the service name and the category to which the service belongs can represent additional matching information. This information can either be passed on to the JIAC Matcher in OWL-S notation or in a serialized Java class structure.

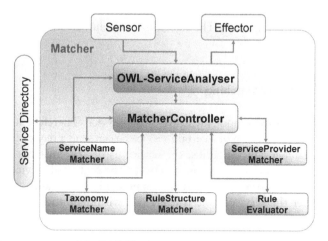

Fig. 5.3 The components of the JIAC Matcher

Figure 5.3 illustrates the internal layout of the JIAC Matcher components. The Sensor entity receives a service query and forwards it to the OWL-ServiceAnalyser module, which parses the OWL-S file for the relevant service attributes (if the service description has not already been passed as a Java object). The ServiceDirectory component in turn provides all existing service descriptions within the platform. It is asked iteratively for available service descriptions, and both the requested service information and the advertised description are being passed to the MatcherController. This entity finally initiates the service matching, which is divided into several categories, which we describe more detail below. The result of the matching process leads to a numerical rating value for each service request/service advertisement pair. After this the service description/value pairs are sorted in a list and returned to the requesting instance via the Effector module. In contrast to most of the other existing OWL-S service matchers [23, 24] the JIAC Matcher[4] implementation is able to compare services not only by input and output parameters but also by precondition and effect as well as by service name and service provider. Depending on the information given by the service request the matching algorithm compares only one, multiple, or all parameters. Furthermore the JIAC Matcher uses a rating-based approach for the classification between a service request and a service advertisement. This means the matching procedure

---

[4] The JIAC Matcher participated at the Semantic Service Selection Contest 2008 in the context of the International Semantic Web Conference (ISWC) in Karlsruhe where it had the name JIAC-OWLSM and achieved good results. For more information see http://www-ags.dfki.uni-sb.de/ klusch/s3/s3c-2008.pdf

is separated into several matching modules, each of them returning a numerical value indicating the matching factor regarding this particular module. All of these values are added to a final result value which indicates the total matching factor of the specific service advertisement in relation to the service request. However, not every module gets the same weighting since some matching aspects are considered as more important than others. The algorithm procedure for each parameter type is explained below.

5.2.2.1 Service Name Matching

The service name is the unique identifier of the service. Therefore if an agent is searching for the description of a certain service he can send a requesting template to the JIAC Matcher containing just the service name. The matching algorithm will then perform a string comparison between the requested service name and all advertised names. Additionally, if the name comparison failed, it is further checked whether the service name is contained within another one, which can indicate that the functionality of the offered service resembles the requested one.

5.2.2.2 Service Provider Matching

The service provider attribute declares which agent offers the respective service. Since agents can vary in their Quality-of-Service characteristics greatly, it is possible to search for services provided by particular agents. Similarly to the service name, the service provider is a unique identifier and the matching also results from a string comparison between requested and advertised service provider.

5.2.2.3 Parameter Taxonomy Matching

Input and output parameters can either be simple data types or more complex concepts defined in ontologies. These concepts are organised hierarchically and therefore the matching algorithm should not only be able to check for the exact equality of requested and advertised input and output parameters but also for some taxonomy dependencies between them. In general the JIAC Matcher distinguishes between four different matching results when comparing two concepts:

- **exact:** the requested concept R and the advertised concept A are equivalent to each other
- **plug-in:**
  - output concept comparison: concept A subsumes concept R
  - input concept comparison: concept R subsumes concept A
- **subsumes:**

- output concept comparison: concept R subsumes concept A
- input concept comparison: concept A subsumes concept R

- **fail:** no equivalence or subsumption between concept R and concept A has been recognized

For instance, if a service request searches a service with input parameter "SMS" and an advertised service expects a parameter "TextMessage" as an input the JIAC Matcher would analyse this as a plug-in matching as far as the ontology describes concept "SMS" as a subclass of concept "TextMessage". Since a SMS is a special form of a text message (consider other text messages like email, etc.) it is reasonable that the proposed service might be suitable for the requester although he has searched for a different parameter. This task of taxonomy matching of input and output parameters is done by the TaxonomyMatcher component within the JIAC Matcher (see Figure 5.3). In contrast to other OWL-S service matchers, the result of a total input/output parameter comparison (a service can require more than one input/output parameter) does not lead to the result of the worst matched parameter pair but to a numerical value. Each of the four different matching levels (exact, plug-in, subsumes, fail) is mapped to a numerical result which is given to each concept pair. The total input/output concept matching result is then computed by the mean value of all concept pair results. This approach has the advantage that the matching quality of services can be differentiated more precisely, since a mean value is more significant then a worst case categorisation. The disadvantage of this procedure however is that a service can be no longer categorised into one of the four levels that easily, because the mean value can lie between two matching level values.

5.2.2.4 Rule Structure Matching (Precondition/Effect Matching)

OWL allows the use of different rule languages for the description of preconditions and effects. One of the most accepted languages is SWRL (Semantic Web Rule Language) [30]. A rule described in SWRL can be structured into several predicate elements which are AND related to each other. The JIAC Matcher breaks up a precondition/effect rule into the predicates for the requesting rule as well as for the advertised rule (processed by RuleStructureMatcher component). This enables the matcher to compare the predicates with each other. If they are exactly the same, an exact matching is recognized. Since predicates are also hierarchically structured, a taxonomy matching has to be done as well. Therefore, if an exact match is not found, the JIAC Matcher tries to find out if either, a plug-in or a subsumes matching, exists. Just like the taxonomy matching of input/output concepts, each result is mapped to a numerical value. This approach applies for preconditions as well as for effects and is done by the PredicateMatcher component. Most of the predicates describe references between subjects and objects, therefore the arguments have to be checked as well. As arguments can be of different types, a type matching between advertised and requested arguments is also necessary. Again, the rule structure matching returns a numerical value which indicates the matching degree between requested effect and advertised effect.

5.2.2.5 Rule Inference Matching

Preconditions contain states that the requesting instance must fulfil in order to use a service. Given an email service for example it is reasonable that the service call of sending an email must not only contain any kind of recipient address as an input parameter, but in particular a valid one (e.g. it is not malformed) . This requirement can be expressed as a precondition. Now the challenge of the Matcher is not only to check if the preconditions of the requester are the same as the advertiser's ones (which rarely might be the case) but to also verify whether the requesting parameter instances really fulfil the advertiser's preconditions. This has been done with the help of a rule engine which is able to derive if an instance fulfils a given rule. Since rules are described in SWRL, a promising rule engine in this aspect is Jess[5] in combination with the OWL API Protégé[6]. The rule engine stores all precondition rules of the advertiser. Then the requested information instance is passed to the Knowledge Base (KB) of the rule engine. If it fulfils the rule's conditions it returns the requesters information instance as a result, which implies that the request corresponds to the advertiser's precondition (in the above example, this would be the recipient address). However, since the updating of the rule engine's KB by inserting all the ontological knowledge of the requesting instance can be very expensive this matching task is only suitable when using the service matcher directly within the requesting agent. Within the JIAC Matcher architecture the rule engine is processed by the RuleEvaluator component.

5.2.3 Other Features of the Language

An interesting aspect of JADL++ and the underlying JIAC V framework is that JADL++ makes no assumptions about an action, other than that the architecture is able to handle it. JIAC V was designed with the primary requirement that it should be able to handle multiple kinds of actions, be it JADL++ scripts, web services, or Java methods. The common denominator is the action– or service description which can come in two variations. There is a simple action descriptions which merely covers input, output and an action name. This is tailored for beginners and allows a programmer to become familiar with JIAC V. The more advanced version utilises OWL-S descriptions for actions and services and thus allows the programmer to use service-matching and the BDI-cycle.

---

[5] http://herzberg.ca.sandia.gov/
[6] http://protege.stanford.edu/

Nevertheless, both action-descriptions are abstract in the sense that they only require some part of the agent to be responsible for the execution. Thus only this component in the agent has to know how to access the underlying technology. For example, the interpreter for JADL++ is the only part that knows about the scripting-part of JADL++. There can be a component dedicated to the invocation of web services. Or there can be multiple components for multiple web services. And so on. This allows us to easily and quickly get access to multiple technologies from JIAC V, and at the same time always use the same programming principles for our agents.

5.3 Platform

JIAC V is aimed at the easy and efficient development of large scale and high performance multi–agent systems. It provides a scalable single-agent model and is built on state-of-the-art standard technologies. The main focus rests on usability, meaning that a developer can use it easily and that the development process is supported by tools.

The framework also incorporates concepts of service oriented architectures such as an explicit notion of service as well as the integration of service interpreters in agents. Interpreters can provide different degrees of intelligence and autonomy, allowing technologies like semantic service matching or service composition. JIAC V supports the user with a built-in administration and management interface, which allows deployment and configuration of agents at runtime.

The JIAC V methodology is based on the JIAC V meta-model and derived from the JIAC IV methodology. JIAC V has explicit notions of rules, actions and services. Composed services are modelled in BPMN and transformed to JADL++. We distinguish between composed services and infrastructure services. The former can be considered a service orchestration with some enhancements (e.g. service matching) whereas the latter describes special services that agents, composed services, or basic actions can use, e.g. user management, communication or directory services. Rules may trigger actions, services or updates of fact base entries. Basic actions are exposed by AgentBeans and constitute agent roles, which are plugged into standard JIAC V agents. The standard JIAC V agent is already capable of finding other JIAC V agents and their services, using infrastructure services, and it provides a number of security and management features.

The core of a JIAC V agent consists of an interpreter that is responsible for executing services (see Figure 5.4).

Our approach is based on a common architecture for single agents in which the agent uses an adaptor concept[7] to interact with the outside world. There exists a local memory for each agent to achieve statefulness, and each agent has dedicated

---

[7] Each of these adaptors may be either a sensor, an effector, or both.

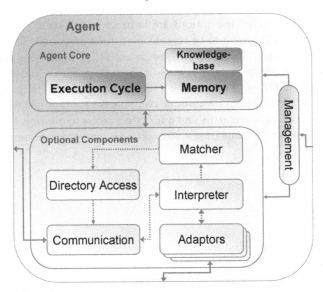

Fig. 5.4 The architecture of a single agent

components (or component groups) that are responsible for decision making and execution.

In JIAC, the adaptor concept is used not only for data transmission, but also for accessing different service technologies that are available today. Thus, any call to a service that is not provided by the agent itself can be pictured as a call to an appropriate effector. Furthermore, the agents' interpreter allows to execute a set of different services. These services' bodies may also contain calls to different services or subprograms. Consequently, an agent is an execution engine for service compositions.

In the following, we will give you a brief explanation of the function of each component:

- **Matcher:** The Matcher is responsible to match the invoke commands against the list of known services, and thus find a list of applicable services for a given invoke. The service templates within the invoke commands may differ in completeness, i.e. a template may contain a specific name of a service together with the appropriate provider, while others may just contain a condition or the set of parameters.

  Once the matcher has identified the list of applicable services, it is up to the interpreter to select a service that is executed. Note that this selection process includes trial&error strategies in the case of failing services.

- **Memory:** The interpreter uses the agent's memory to manage the calls to services as well as the parameters. We use a simple *Linda*-like tuple space [17] for coordination between the components of an agent. Additionally, the current state of the execution can be watched in the memory any time by simply reading the complete contents of the tuple space, allowing for simple solutions for monitoring and debugging.

- **KnowledgeBase:** The knowledge base provides functionalities for reasoning and inferences within an agent. All declarative expressions within either a service description or an action invocation are evaluated against this knowledge base. In contrast to the Memory above, the knowledge base is a semantic memory rather than a simple object store and has a consistent world model.

- **Interpreter:** The interpreter is the core for service execution. It has to be able to interpret and execute services that are written in JADL++. Essentially, all atomic actions that can be used within the language are connected to services from either the interpreter or the effectors of the agent.

- **Adaptor:** The adaptors are the agent's connection to the outside world. This is a sensor/effector concept in which all actions that an agent can execute on an environment (via the appropriate effector) are explicitly represented by an action declaration and optionally a service declaration that is accessible for the matcher. Thus, all actions may have service descriptions that are equivalent to those used for actual services.

5.3.1 Available Tools and Documentation

Our former framework JIAC IV already came with an extensive tool support which has been described in [38]. Consequently, the design of JIAC V was always guided by the requirement to have existing tools be applicable to JIAC V. In the following we will give an overview of these tools and their role in the development process for JIAC applications.

The JIAC agent framework supports the development of multi–agent systems using BDI agents and standard Java technologies. The framework has been implemented using the Java programming language. Two building blocks constitute the basic agent architecture: a Java Spring[8] based component system and the language (JADL++). The basic architecture of a JIAC-based application is summarised in the multi–agent system meta–model, which is shown in Figure 5.5.

In the framework, the following concepts are defined and must be supported by tools:

- Domain Vocabulary

  - *Ontologies* define *classes*, which are used to create the beliefs and the interaction vocabulary of the agents.
  - In addition to classes, ontologies provide *properties* which can describe relationships between class instances.

- Knowledge

---

[8] http://www.springframework.org/

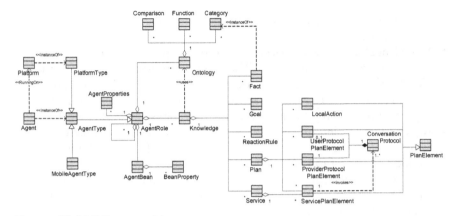

Fig. 5.5 JIAC MAS meta-model

- Initial beliefs (*facts*) using these categories are created before the agent is started.
- *Reaction rules* constitute the reactive behaviour of an agent.
- *Actions* define the behaviour of the agents. They can be deliberatively selected and then become intentions. Actions can be used to aggregate more complex plans by either the developer or a planning component as part of an agent.

- Component

  - *Agent beans* are core components and also used to wrap or connect the non-agent environment via Java APIs or user interfaces. They implement *bean roles* (to allow dynamic bean exchange at runtime) and can communicate with each other using the agent's memory.

- Deployment

  - *Agent roles* are composites of agent functionalities and interaction capabilities (services) from the above concepts.
  - *Agents* are agent roles that have standard components as well as domain specific agent roles and are able to run on an agent platforms.
  - *Agent nodes* are the infrastructure for each computer, which play the role of an Agent Management System (AMS) and Directory Facilitator (DF) [16], i.e. they provide management and white and yellow page services, and constitute the agent environment and infrastructure services.

5.3.1.1 JIAC Methodology

The JIAC methodology is an iterative and incremental process model which supports re–use. It looks very similar to other agent-oriented methodologies, such as PASSI [10] or Prometheus [34], but is, in fact, streamlined to the use of our framework.

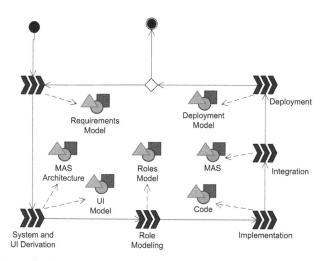

Fig. 5.6 JIAC methodology - iterative and incremental process model in SPEM [33] notation

As shown in Figure 5.6, the development process starts with collecting domain vocabulary and requirements, which then are structured and prioritised. In this step, we also look for ontologies and other artifacts that can be re-used, saving time and effort. Second, we take the requirements with the highest priority and derive a MAS architecture by identifying agents and the platforms where the agents reside on, and create a user interface prototype. The MAS architecture then is detailed by deriving a role model, showing the design concerning functionalities and interactions. Agents and agent roles available can be retrieved from a repository consisting of standard and domain specific configurations. We then implement the agents' behaviour by coding or adapting plans, services and protocols, which are plugged into agents during integration. This phase is accompanied with extensive unit testing. The agents are deployed to one or more agent platforms and the application is ready to be evaluated. Depending on the evaluation, we align and amend requirements and start the cycle again with eliminating bugs and enhancing and adding features until we reach the desired quality of the agent-based application.

We have implemented Toolipse [38], a fully functional prototype of an IDE[9] based on the Eclipse platform, which facilitates the development of agent applications with the JIAC agent framework, increases their quality and shortens the development time. While Toolipse has been developed for the JIAC IV framework, we are currently porting the tools to JIAC V. The aim of the IDE is to hide the language syntax from the developers as much as possible, to allow them to develop

---

[9] Integrated Development Environment

an agent application visually and to assist them where possible. To achieve that, it provides the following main functionalities:

- creating and building projects, managing their resources and providing an internal resource model;
- creating ontologies, manipulating them visually and importing ontologies from other ontology languages;
- developing agent knowledge in a visual environment;
- testing agent behaviours with agent unit tests;
- implementing agent beans in Java;
- configuring and deploying agent roles, agents and nodes visually;
- helping and guiding the developers through the entire development process with documentations, interactive how-to's and interactive tutorials.

Each functionality is realised as an Eclipse feature consisting of one or more plug-ins and typically comprises wizards, editors and views, which are arranged in an own perspective.

In Toolipse, wizards are used for creating projects and skeletal structures of JIAC files; each file type has its own wizard. After creating a file, the agent developers can edit the file with the associated editor, which is in the majority of cases a multi-page editor consisting of a source code editor and of a visual editor. The source code editors support syntax highlighting, warning and error marking, folding, code formatting and code completion which suggests possible completions to incomplete language expressions. In contrast to the source code editors, which require from the developers good knowledge of the language, the visual editors of Toolipse allow to work with abstract models, to create and modify instances of the meta-model graphically. This facilitates the agent development and minimises errors. In order to achieve this, the visual editors model the JIAC concepts with the Eclipse Modeling Framework[10] (EMF), visualise them graphically with the Graphical Editing Framework[11] (GEF) and provide simple graphical layouts such as radial layout, zooming and modifying properties of the visualised elements with the associated dialog windows as well as with the Properties view of Eclipse. This Properties view belongs to one of the so-called workbench part concepts: views. They are typically used to navigate through resources or to assist the editors with extra functionalities. For example, all our editors support the Outline view where the outline of the file which is currently open is displayed. In addition to the Properties and Outline view, which are general views of Eclipse, Toolipse provides its own views that navigate the developers through the JIAC resources, present results of agent unit tests, to help or to guide them through the development process. Figure 5.7 shows the JIAC perspective with an editor and some of these views.

---

[10] http://www.eclipse.org/modeling/emf/

[11] http://www.eclipse.org/gef/

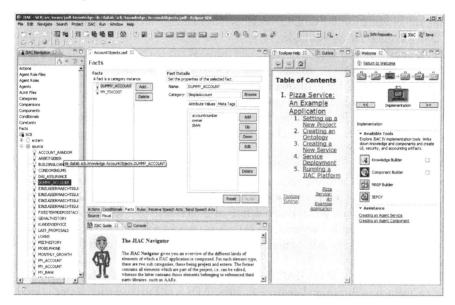

Fig. 5.7 Toolipse with the following components (from left to right): JIAC navigator, knowledge editor (center), JIAC guide (bottom), interactive tutorial and user guide.

5.3.2 Standards Compliance, Interoperability, and Portability

In terms of standards, JIAC V has changed considerably from its predecessors, as we focussed on the use of software standards heavily. However, as of today one important standard, the FIPA speech act, is not explicitly supported. It is of course possible to design messages that comply with the standard but it is not a requirement. However, the underlying technologies are all based on today's industry standards, such as OWL and OWL-S for ontologies, but also JMX[12] [35] for management functionality, JMS[13] [28] for message delivery, and web service integration. For portability to small devices, we have developed a cut-down version of JIAC called MicroJIAC.

5.3.3 MicroJIAC

The MicroJIAC framework is a lightweight agent architecture targeted at devices with different, generally limited, capabilities. It is intended to be scalable and useable on both resource constrained devices (i.e. cell phones and PDAs) and desktop computers. It is implemented in the Java programming language. At the moment a

---

[12] Java Management Extensions
[13] Java Message Service

full implementation for CLDC[14] devices is available, which is the most restricted J2ME[15] configuration available.

The agent definition used here is adapted from [37]. It is a biologically inspired definition where agents are situated in some environment and can modify it through actuators and perceive it through sensors. Thus the framework is also split into environment and agents. The environment is the abstraction layer between the device and agents. It defines life cycle management and communication functionalities. These functionalities include a communication channel through which the agents send their messages.

Agents are created through a combination of different elements. The predefined element types are sensors, actuators, rules, services and components. Actuators and sensors are the interface between the agent and the environment. Rules specify reactive behaviour and services define an interface to provide access to specific functionalities. Finally, components maintain a separate thread and host time consuming computations. All elements are strictly decoupled from each other and are thus exchangeable.

In contrast to JIAC, MicroJIAC does not use an explicit ontology language, goals or an agent programming language such as JADL++. Furthermore, agent migration is restricted to Java configurations which support custom class loaders and reflection. It should be noted here that both architectures, MicroJIAC and JIAC V, are targeted at different fields of application and have different development histories. However, they use a common communication infrastructure to enable information exchange between agents.

5.3.4 Other Features of the Platform

JIAC V aims to easily allow to implement service oriented architectures. In order to support the creation of such systems, JIAC V comes with a workflow editor called VSDT that allows to create diagrams using the Business Process Modeling Notation (BPMN) and compile them into JIAC V [11, 12].

The editor has been developed in the SerCHo project[16] at TU Berlin [26]. While the main intent behind the VSDT was to enable a transformation from BPMN to executable languages it has by now evolved to a mature BPMN modelling tool (Figure 5.8).

Unlike most other BPMN editors, it is not tightly coupled to BPEL, but instead provides a transformation framework that can be extended with transformations to and from any executable language. As the framework provides modules for separate stages of the transformation (Validation, Normalisation, Structure Mapping, Element Mapping, and Clean-Up), parts of it can be reused (or if necessary

---

[14] Connected Limited Device Configuration http://java.sun.com/products/cldc/

[15] Java 2 Platform Micro Edition http://java.sun.com/javame/index.jsp

[16] http://energy.dai-labor.de

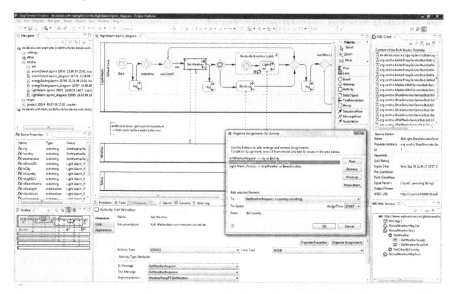

Fig. 5.8 The Visual Service Design Tool. Clockwise: Editor view, RSD client, Web services view, Organize Assignments dialog, property sheet, visual outline, variables inspector, navigator.

refined) for new transformation, which has proven especially useful for the challenging transformation of the process diagram's graph structure to a block structure. Thus, a new transformation feature can easily be implemented and plugged into the tool — in fact, the only stage that *has to* be implemented is the element mapping. Further, the meta model does provide enough information so that a detailed process diagram can be exported to readily executable code, provided that the respective transformation can handle all of these details, too.

5.4 Applications Supported by the Language and/or the Platform

While the DAI-Labor works mainly in the surroundings of telecommunication and network applications, JIAC V is not specifically tailored to that environment. We designed JIAC V to be applicable in a wide range of applications, and are currently evaluating different domains to test the applicability of agents in different fields. While our work with the predecessor platform JIAC IV has already brought some interesting results [20], ranging from personal information agents [2] and service delivery platforms [22] to simulation environments [5], we are currently exploring the context of service composition for small and medium-sized enterprises, office applications, automotive, and energy conservation.

5.4.1 Multi Access, Modular Services

The language JADL++, together with JIAC V, has already been applied and tested in a BMBF[17]-funded project, *Multi Access, Modular Services (MAMS)*[18]. MAMS focused on the development of a new and open service delivery platform, based on Next Generation Networks (NGN). It realises the integration of software development and components, ranging from high level service-orchestration tools over a service-deployment and -execution framework to the integration of the IP-Multimedia Subsystem (IMS).

In the course of the project, JADL++ and its underlying execution framework were used to create the service delivery platform for the execution of newly created service orchestrations. The service creation- and deployment-cycle works as follows:

- A new service orchestration is created by a user with help of a graphical tool and an associated graphical modelling language. Essential for this modelling process is a list of available basic services that can be combined by the user.
- The finished service orchestration is translated into JADL++ and an appropriate agent is instantiated on a running platform.
- Whenever a service is called by a user, the agent starts executing the JADL++-script and calls the appropriate basic services.

So far, the project has realised prototypical scenarios with a very small list of available basic services. However, as we were able to proof our concepts, a follow-up project is currently running, in which a much larger list of services is implemented, and thus we will have a broader base for evaluations.

5.4.2 Agent Contest 2008

The DAI-Labor used JIAC V in the 2008 edition of the ProMAS agent contest, and won the contest. While only some of JIAC's features were actually applicable in the contest, it was still a very good test for our platform's stability and performance. We learned some very interesting lessons. For example the decision to introduce direct messages between agents in addition to the somewhat larger service model allowed for a quick and efficient communication between agents. Furthermore, we were able to reuse a lot of code from our agents of the 2007 competition [18, 39], as the plug-in model of JIAC V allow easy integration of the respective components.

---

[17] *Bundesministerium für Bildung und Forschung (Federal Ministry for Education and Research)*
[18] see http://www.mams-platform.net/

5.4.3 NeSSi

Another project on the basis of JIAC IV is the Network Security Simulator (NeSSi) [5]. In the context of this project, devices within a large telecommunications network and possible threats are simulated. Using the simulator, the behaviour of attackers, threats, and possible counter measures can be evaluated.

The first implementation of this project was done in JIAC IV. However, since JIAC V has reached the required maturity, the simulator was ported to JIAC V agents, resulting in an overall performance increase.

While the initial model used one agent per device for the simulation, the current implementation maps sub-nets onto agents. This change in the design was necessary to allow the system to scale to large networks of thousands of devices. Currently we simulate systems with about 100 sub-nets and about 3500 single devices.

5.4.4 Other Projects

In addition to the projects mentioned above, a number of mostly industry funded projects in the context of energy, automotive, office automation, and self-organising production are carried out where JIAC is used as the underlying technology.

5.5 Final Remarks

JIAC has been around for quite some time now, and has made a number of transitions. This chapter describes the newest incarnation, JIAC V, and while there are still some features missing that the predecessor had, we are continuously improving and bringing it back to have the wealth of features that JIAC IV provided, while at the same time improving performance, interoperability, and stability of the platform.

In contrast to many other agent frameworks, the main focus and driving force of JIAC is the application within industry projects, and the feature set is accordingly different. The service oriented approach, support of management functionalities through JMX, and the inclusion of accounting functionalities are examples of such features. We hope that the focus on these issues allows an easier integration of agent technology in today's software environment of companies, where distributed computing is already a daily reality.

Acknowledgements JIAC V is the work of the Competence Center Agent Core Technologies of the DAI Labor of the TU Berlin, namely Tuguldur Erdene-Ochir, Axel Heßler, Silvan Kaiser, Jan Keiser, Thomas Konnerth, Tobias Küster, Marcel Patzlaff, Alexander Thiele, as well as Michael Burkhardt, Martin Löffelholz, Marco Lützenberger, and Nils Masuch. It has been partially funded by the German Federal Ministry of Education and Research under funding reference number 01BS0813.

References

1. Albayrak, S., Wieczorek, D.: JIAC — an open and scalable agent architecture for telecommunication applications. In: S. Albayrak (ed.) Intelligent Agents in Telecommunications Applications — Basics, Tools, Languages and Applications. IOS Press, Amsterdam (1998)
2. Albayrak, S., Wollny, S., Lommatzsch, A., Milosevic, D.: Agent technology for personalized information filtering: The PIA system. Scientific International Journal for Parallel and Distributed Computing (SCPE) **8 (1)**, 29–40 (2007)
3. Barstow, A., Hendler, J., Skall, M., Pollock, J., Martin, D., Marcatte, V., McGuinness, D.L., Yoshida, H., Roure, D.D.: OWL-S: Semantic markup for web services (2004). URL http://www.w3.org/Submission/OWL-S/
4. Bratman, M.E.: Intentions, Plans, and Practical Reason. Havard University Press, Cambridge, MA (1987)
5. Bye, R., Schmidt, S., Luther, K., Albayrak, S.: Application-level simulation for network security. In: First International Conference on Simulation Tools and Techniques for Communications, Networks and Systems (SimoTools) (2008)
6. Chandrasekaran, B., Josephson, J.R., Benjamins, V.R.: Ontologies: What are they? why do we need them? IEEE Intelligent Systems and Their Applications **14**(1), 20–26 (1999). Special Issue on Ontologies
7. Common Criteria, part 1: Introduction and general model, version 2.1 (1999)
8. Common Criteria, part 2: Security functional requirements, version 2.1 (1999)
9. Common Criteria, part 3: Security assurance requirements, version 2.1 (1999)
10. Cossentino, M., Potts, C.: PASSI: A process for specifying and implementing multi-agent systems using UML. Technical report, University of Palermo (2001)
11. Endert, H., Hirsch, B., Küster, T., Albayrak, S.: Towards a mapping from BPMN to agents. In: J. Huang, R. Kowalczyk, Z. Maamar, D. Martin, I. Müller, S. Stoutenburg, K.P. Sycara (eds.) Service-Oriented Computing: Agents, Semantics, and Engineering, *LNCS*, vol. 4505, pp. 92–106. Springer Berlin / Heidelberg (2007)
12. Endert, H., Küster, T., Hirsch, B., Albayrak, S.: Mapping BPMN to agents: An analysis. In: M. Baldoni, C. Baroglio, V. Mascardi (eds.) Agents, Web-Services, and Ontologies: Integrated Methodologies, pp. 43–58 (2007)
13. Fikes, R., Nilsson, N.: STRIPS: a new approach to the application of theorem proving to problem solving. Artificial Intelligence **2**, 189–208 (1971)
14. Foundation for Intelligent Physical Agents: FIPA agent communication language specifications (2002). URL http://www.fipa.org/repository/aclspecs.html
15. Foundation for Intelligent Physical Agents: Interaction Protocol Specifications (2002). URL http://www.fipa.org/repository/ips.php3
16. Foundation for Intelligent Physical Agents: FIPA agent management specification (2004)
17. Gelernter, D.: Generative communication in linda. ACM Transactions on Programming Languages and Systems **7**(1), 80–112 (1985)
18. Hessler, A., Hirsch, B., Keiser, J.: JIAC IV in Multi-Agent Programming Contest 2007. In: M. Dastani, A.E.F. Segrouchni, A. Ricci, M. Winikoff (eds.) ProMAS 2007 Post-Proceedings, *LNAI*, vol. 4908, pp. 262–266. Springer Berlin / Heidelberg (2008)
19. Hindriks, K.V., Boer, F.S.D., van der Hoek, W., Meyer, J.J.: Agent programming in 3APL. Autonomous Agents and Multi-Agent Systems **2**(4), 357–401 (1999)
20. Hirsch, B., Fricke, S., Kroll-Peters, O.: Agent programming in practise - experiences with the JIAC IV agent framework. In: Proceedings of AT2AI 2008 — Agent Theory to Agent Implementation (2008)

21. Hirsch, B., Konnerth, T., Burkhardt, M.: The JADL++ language — semantics. Technical report, Technische Universität Berlin — DAI Labor (2009)
22. Hirsch, B., Konnerth, T., Hessler, A., Albayrak, S.: A serviceware framework for designing ambient services. In: A. Maña, V. Lotz (eds.) Developing Ambient Intelligence (AmID'06), pp. 124–136. Springer Paris (2006)
23. Jaeger, M.C., Gregor, R.G., Christoph, L., Gero, M., Kurt, G.: Ranked matching for service descriptions using OWL-S. In: Kommunikation in Verteilten Systemen (KiVS) 2005, pp. 91–102. Springer (2005)
24. Klusch, M., Fries, B., Sycara, K.: Automated semantic web service discovery with OWLS-MX. In: H. Nakashima, M.P. Wellman, G. Weiss, P. Stone (eds.) AAMAS, pp. 915–922. ACM (2006)
25. Konnerth, T., Hirsch, B., Albayrak, S.: JADL — an agent description language for smart agents. In: M. Baldoni, U. Endriss (eds.) Declarative Agent Languages and Technologies IV, LNCS, vol. 4327, pp. 141–155. Springer Berlin / Heidelberg (2006)
26. Küster, T., Heßler, A.: Towards transformations from BPMN to heterogeneous systems. In: M. Mecella, J. Yang (eds.) BPM2008 Workshop Proceedings. Springer Berlin (2008)
27. McGuinness, D.L., van Harmelen, F.: OWL web ontology language. W3C recommendation (2004). http://www.w3.org/TR/owl-features/
28. Monson-Haefel, R., Chappell, D.A.: Java Message Service. O'Reilly (2000)
29. Nakhjiri, M., Nakhjiri, M.: AAA and Network Security for Mobile Access: Radius, Diameter, EAP, PKI and IP Mobility. Wiley (2005)
30. Newton, G., Pollock, J., McGuinness, D.L.: Semantic web rule language (SWRL) (2004). http://www.w3.org/Submission/2004/03/
31. Nielson, H.R., Nielson, F.: Semantics with Applications: A Formal Introduction, revised Edition. Wiley (1999)
32. OASIS Committee: Web Services Business Process Execution Language (WS-BPEL) Version 2.0. Specification, OASIS (2007). URL http://docs.oasis-open.org/wsbpel/2.0/Primer/wsbpel-v2.0-Primer.pdf
33. Object Management Group: Software Process Engineering Metamodel (SPEM) Specification. Version 1.1. Object Management Group, Inc. (2005)
34. Padgham, L., Winikoff, M.: Prometheus: A methodology for developing intelligent agents. In: F. Giunchiglia, J. Odell, G. Weiß (eds.) Agent-Oriented Software Engineering III. Revised Papers and Invited Contributions of the Third International Workshop (AOSE 2002), 0558 Lecture Notes in Computer Science, vol. 2585. Springer (2002)
35. Perry, J.S.: Java Management Extensions. O'Reilly (2002)
36. Rao, A.S.: AgentSpeak(L): BDI agents speak out in a logical computable language. In: R. van Hoe (ed.) Agents Breaking Away, 7th European Workshop on Modelling Autonomous Agents in a Multi-Agent World, MAAMAW'96, LNCS, vol. 1038, pp. 42—55. Springer Verlag, Eindhoven, The Netherlands (1996)
37. Russel, S., Norvig, P.: Artificial Intelligence: A Modern Approach, 2nd Edition edn. Prentice Hall (2003)
38. Tuguldur, E.O., Heßler, A., Hirsch, B., Albayrak, S.: Toolipse: An IDE for development of JIAC applications. In: Proceedings of PROMAS08: Programming Multi-Agent Systems (2008)
39. Tuguldur, E.O., Patzlaff, M.: Collecting gold: MicroJIAC agents in multi-agent programming contest. In: M. Dastani, A.E.F. Segrouchni, A. Ricci, M. Winikoff (eds.) ProMAS 2007 Post-Proceedings, LNAI, vol. 4908, pp. 257–261. Springer Berlin / Heidelberg (2008)
40. W3C: XML schema (2004). URL http://www.w3.org/XML/Schema

Chapter 6
Towards Pervasive Intelligence: Reflections on the Evolution of the Agent Factory Framework

Conor Muldoon, Gregory M. P. O'Hare, Rem W. Collier, and Michael J. O'Grady

Abstract Agent Factory is a cohesive framework for the development and deployment of multi-agent systems. Since its inception in the mid 1990s, Agent Factory has gone through a metamorphosis process, whereby several new extensions, revisions, and enhancements have been made. This chapter provides a discussion of the incremental developments in Agent Factory and provides motivations as to why such changes were necessary. Agent Factory distinguishes itself from other intentional agent platforms in several ways. It provides a practical and efficient approach to the development of intentional agent-oriented applications. This is combined with a methodology, integrated development environment support, and a suite of tools that aid the agent fabrication process. A detailed comparison to related work is provided. We include a tutorial on how to use the framework.

6.1 Introduction

A curtsey examination of the research literature will quickly indicate the interest that Multi-Agent Systems (MAS) attract from the Distributed Artificial Intelligence (DAI) community. A number of frameworks, some well-known, others less so, have been documented since the mid 1990s. Agent Factory is an exemplar framework in that it was conceived of and developed at this time, but it has been significantly enhanced over the years in response to ongoing software developments. For example, Wireless Sensor Networks (WSNs) offer a promising solution for many categories of problems, such as real-time environmental monitoring, however, such networks are characterised by limited computational resources. An optimised Agent Factory runtime environment has recently been

C. Muldoon, G. M. P. O' Hare (Corresponding Author), R. W. Collier, and M. J. O'Grady
CLARITY: The Centre for Sensor Web Technologies, School of Computer Science & Informatics, University College Dublin, Belfield, Dublin 4, Ireland, e-mail: conor.muldoon,gregory.ohare,rem.collier,michael.j.ogrady@ucd.ie

R.H. Bordini et al. (eds.), *Multi-Agent Programming*,
DOI 10.1007/978-0-387-89299-3_6, © Springer Science+Business Media, LLC 2009

developed that factors these issues into its design. Thus an Agent Factory MAS can be deployed on a wide range of hardware, extending and increasing the application domains that can harness the MAS paradigm. Today, Agent Factory represents the culmination of over a decadeŠs effort by a number of researchers and has been successfully demonstrated in a wide range of application domains.

This chapter will discuss various facets of Agent Factory and its constituent components. In Section 6.2, a motivation of Agent Factory is presented. This section discusses the chronological enhancements/alterations made to the system over the course of its development. Section 6.3 discusses the Agent Factory Agent Programming Language (AFAPL), AFAPL is an agent-oriented programming language that is based on a logical formalism of belief and commitment. The agent platform is discussed in Section 6.4. At present, Agent Factory is divided, as with many other frameworks, into two editions, one for standard Java, the other for Java Micro Edition (JME) CLDC. We describe some applications of the framework in Section 6.5. Finally, a brief but succinct comparison of Agent Factory with other frameworks is presented in Section 6.6.

6.2 Motivation

In order to motivate the Agent Factory platform and language, the Agent Factory Agent Programming Language (AFAPL), we must put the current system into context; as such, in this section, we provide the history of the system and discuss its evolution into its current form. This provides several motivations as to why certain design decisions were made and reflects the general changing trends in both agent technology and software development in general over the past decade. For instance, when the initial version of the system was developed, the now pervasive Java programming language was only being released and was still a very new and unproven platform. We discuss Agent Factory's development in a chronological narrative that begins in the mid 1990s and progressively introduces the main features of the language and framework, ending with a overview of the system in its current state.

6.2.1 History

Agent Factory was first proposed by O Hare in 1996 [39] and was conceived of as an environment for the prototyping and testing of multi-agent systems. It supported the rapid creation of central agent components and the aggregation of such components into communities, whose model of social interaction would subsequently be described. It differed from other similar frameworks available at the time in its use of an algebraic specification technique (the UMIST Paradox System) that could be directly executed. The system was underpinned by the theory associated with heterogeneous algebras that was developed by Birkhoff and Lispson [5]. The environment drew heavily from Communicating Sequential Processes [23] (CSP) and viewed multi-agent systems as a specific class of complex distributed systems, namely Communicating Intentional Processes (CIP). It built upon and extended pre-existing work to model CIPs effectively [40].

Early work on Agent Factory extended the framework to include an agent classification hierarchy to aid the rapid prototyping of agent designs and a communication infrastructure, based on TCP/IP and Speech Act theory, that enabled the agent communities to be distributed over a network [9]. Due to the difficulties of using the original algebraic approach, this version of the system was implemented using a combination of VDM and Smalltalk-80. The main reason for using Smalltalk-80 was that it was a flexible object-oriented language and thus provided distinct advantages, in terms of rapid prototyping, maintainability, and ease of development, over attempting to directly execute the specifications. At the time, Java was only being released, and was quite a new and unproven platform. C++ was widely used at this time, but it was (and still is) viewed as a bastardised language rather than truly object-oriented. Additionally, Smalltalk contained features, such as reflection, not supported in C++.

Further work redesigned Agent Factory to reflect newer trends in agent development [11]. A generalized agent communication language framework was introduced along with a commitment management system module that could be configured for different commitment models and/or strategies. A mobility feature was subsequently introduced [13]. Up to this point, much work had been done in the field on mobility, but it primarily focused on the actual mechanism for agent transfer; the intelligent component and decision making process in migration was largely ignored. Agent Factory merged the notion of intentional decision making with mobility.

At the start of the millennium, work began to focus on the possibility of using Agent Factory for the creation of mobile context sensitive applications, such as Guilliver's Gennie [38]. A new Java version of the system was developed. The reason for this development was that, at the time, there were no Smalltalk-80 interpreters or byte code compilers/translators for the Microsoft Pocket PC operating system. There was, however, a (rather slow) Esermertec Jeode Java interpreter that was based on PersonalJava, the forerunner to what is now known as the JME CDC Java configuration augmented with Personal Profile. At this time, there were two versions of Agent Factory in operation. The Smalltalk-80 version was intended for desktop environments, whereas the Java version was intended for mobile devices. This motivated the development of the Agent Factory Agent Programming Language (AFAPL), which drew heavily from Shoham's AGENT0 [44] language and Agent Oriented Programming. AFAPL was an abstract declarative language that enabled agents to be created that were based upon a theory of rational agency. It enabled the creation of agent designs that were independent of the underlying imperative environment in which they were to operate. The idea was that different interpreters, written in different languages, could be developed for AFAPL, but the specification of the agent design would remain consistent regardless of the environment in which it would subsequently be executed. Additionally, AFAPL supported the notion of agent design inheritance. This enabled the creation of generic agent designs that could be reused and augmented with application specific functionality. This version of the Agent Factory laid the foundation for Collier's thesis [10], which provided a cohesive framework for mobile distributed multi-agent application development, and was based upon a logical formalism of belief and commitment. The thesis introduced an agent development methodology that drew from early work by O Hare and Wooldridge [41] on Agent-Oriented Software Engineering.

Due to the differences in the languages and the need to duplicate new features of the system, it was decided to drop the Smalltalk-80 version of the system. It had to be the Smalltalk version of the system that was dropped because, as noted earlier, there was no Smalltalk-80 interpreter for Pocket PC. PersonalJava was, more or less, a full Java platform for embedded devices, almost identical to standard Java less the Swing graphical interfacing capabilities. It was therefore possible to have a single Agent Factory platform for mobile and desktop applications. The Smalltalk-80 version of the system didn't add enough to justify its continued maintenance.

At this time, the primary general purpose programmable mobile devices being used were Personal Digital Assistants (PDAs). This market, however, never really took off in the mainstream. Much of the functionality of the PDA was beginning to be incorporated in to mobile phones. In contrast to the PDA market, the mobile phone market was in the billions. The problem, however, was that the standard Java environment for phones was the J2ME Constrained Limited Device Configuration (CLDC) augmented with the Mobile Information Device Profile (MIDP). Agent Factory was developed for use with the CDC Java environment augmented with Personal Profile. This environment, although classified as J2ME, is closer to standard Java than it is to CLDC, which is highly constrained and limited. Therefore, it was not possible to use Agent Factory, in its current form, for the development of mobile phone applications.

In 2005, Muldoon developed a minimised footprint version of Agent Factory that facilitated the development and deployment of intentional agents for highly constrained mobile and ubiquitous devices [35, 34, 33]. This version of Agent Factory was referred to as Agent Factory Micro Edition (AFME). Initially, AFME targeted cellular digital mobile phones. It soon became clear, however, that AFME could be deployed on a much broader array of devices, since it was based on CLDC, which is the de factor standard Java environment for constrained environments. In 2007, Sun launched the SunSPOT mote in Europe, which was based on CLDC. AFME was subsequently deployed on the SunSPOT , making it the first intentional agent platform to be used to control the leaf nodes of a Wireless Sensor Network (WSN). AFAPL was developed to provide a common high-level language that would be consistent between Smalltalk-80 and Java. Although Smalltalk-80 was no longer supported, this approach proved useful again, but in a different context, to ensure that an agent could be represented consistently among different Java environments.

In parallel to the development of AFME, a new concept of a role was introduced to AFAPL [8]. This version of AFAPL became known as AFAPL2. The notion of a role improved the efficiency of the platform. The idea was that, at various stages throughout execution, triggers would cause commitment rules to be added to the rule set of the agent. That is, an agent would adopt various behaviours, referred to collectively as a role, if some trigger condition was true. The trigger condition was evaluated by checking the agent's beliefs. If an agent had a particular belief and that belief matched the trigger condition, the role would be adopted. If the role was no longer relevant or the objectives associated with the role were achieved, the role would be retracted by an actuator. In this way, the overhead for evaluating the role would only be incurred at times when the role was active. The trigger did not represent a maintenance condition for the role. The execution of the retraction actuator would be evaluated in the usual manner i.e. either directly though the evaluation of the commitment rules or through the execution of a plan. The version of Agent Factory represents its current form.

6.3 Language

Agent Factory is an open framework for building agent-based systems (see Section 6.4), and as such, does not enforce a single flavour of agent upon the developer. Instead, the developer is free to either use a pre-existing agent interpreter / architecture, or develop a custom solution that is more suited to their specific needs.

That said, as was highlighted in Section 6.2, Agent Factory has a long tradition of promoting the use of intentional agents to construct multi-agent applications. Support for this style of agent has been realized through the Agent Factory Agent Programming Language (AFAPL), which is now in its second incarnation, and is known as AFAPL2. AFAPL2 is an agent programming language that supports the development of agents that use a mental state architecture to reason about how best to act. The remainder of this section will provide a brief summary of AFAPL.

The AFAPL2 language supports the fabrication of agents whose mental state is comprised of beliefs, goals, and commitments. Beliefs describe - possibly incorrectly - the state of the environment in which the agent is situated, goals describe future states of the environment that the agent would like to bring about, and commitments describe the activity that the agent is committed to realising. The behaviour of the agent is realised primarily through a purpose-built execution algorithm that is centred about the notion of commitment management.

Commitments are viewed as the mental equivalent of a contract; they define a course of action/activity that the agent has agreed to, when it must realise that activity, to whom the commitment was made, and fnally, what conditions, if any, would lead to it not having to fulfil the commitment. Commitment management is then a meta-level process that AFAPL2 agents employ to manipulate their commitments based upon some underlying strategy known as a commitment management strategy. This strategy specifies a set of sub-strategies that:

- define how an agent adopts new commitments; maintains its existing commitments.
- refines commitments to plans into additional commitments.
- realises commitments to primitive actions; and handles failed commitments.

The principal sub-strategy that underpins the behaviour of AFAPL2 agents is commitment adoption. Commitments are adopted either as a result of a decision to realise some activity, or through the refinement of an existing activity. The former type of commitment is known as a primary commitment and the latter as a secondary commitment. The adoption of a primary commitment occurs as a result of one of two processes: (1) in response to a decision to attempt to achieve a goal using a plan of action, or (2) as a result of the triggering of a commitment rule. Commitment rules define situations (a conjunction of positive and negative belief atoms) in which the agent should adopt a primary commitment.

6.3.1 Syntactical Aspects

The first step in understanding how to program AFAPL2 agents is to understand how beliefs are used to construct models of the current state of the environment. Without this model, the agents will not be aware of what is happening in the environment, and consequently, will not be able to act in a meaningful way.

The key step underpinning the generation of an agents' belief model is perception. This is the process by which an agent converts raw environment data (sensor readings, ACL messages, address books, etc.) into various beliefs that provide a higher-level representation of this data (and consequently, the state of the environment). Perception is an integral part of the belief update phase of the AFAPL2 interpreter cycle.

The principle building block of the perception process is the perceptor unit. This is a Java class that collates any relevant raw data and generates a corresponding set of beliefs. Perceptors are associated with agents via the PERCEPTOR construct. This construct generates a mapping between specific perceptor units and a given AFAPL2 agent program. For example, when developing a robot soccer agent, a ball perceptor unit may be created that uses visual information to decide whether or not the robot has the ball. In the AFAPL2 program, this perceptor would be declared through the following statement:

```
PERCEPTOR BallWatcher  CLASS perceptor.BallPerceptor;
```

Where perceptor.BallPerceptor is the Java class that implements the perceptor unit. This unit would then be responsible for generating a corresponding belief about the presence of the ball (e.g. BELIEF(hasBall) or BELIEF(noBall)).

AFAPL2 has been designed to support the fabrication of agents that exist within highly dynamic environments. As such, agents may adopt beliefs that quickly become invalid. For example, consider a robot soccer agent that has a perceptor which generates a belief about whether the agent can see the ball or not. If the ball passes quickly in front of the agent, then it may see the ball only for one or two iterations of the interpreter cycle.

Rather than implement a complex belief revision algorithm that tries to under-stand when a belief has become invalid, the approach adopted in AFAPL2 is to assume that, by default, all beliefs become invalid at the end of a given iteration of the AFAPL2 interpreter cycle. In this way, perception becomes the process by which the agent generates a snapshot of the current state of the environment. This snapshot is then thrown away immediately before the next snapshot is generated. While this approach helps to simplify the maintenance of an agentŠs beliefs, it is not always appropriate (sometimes we need beliefs that persist for longer). To handle this requirement, AFAPL2 also provides a number of temporal operators, which can be used to define beliefs that persist for more than one iteration.

This first example illustrates how to create an Agent Factory perceptor. To implement a perceptor, we create a Java class that is a subclass of the class com.agentfactory.logic.agent.Perceptor, and implement the perceive() method:

```
import com.agentfactory.logic.agent.Perceptor;

public class AlivePerceptor extends Perceptor {
    public void perceive() {
        adoptBelief( "BELIEF(alive)" );
    }
}
```

The above perceptor generates a single belief that represents the fact that the agent is "alive". This belief is added to the agent's belief set at the start of each iteration of the interpreter cycle. The name of the Java class is specified within the agent design file.

The next example illustrates how to specify an action (and the corresponding ac-tuator) in AFAPL2. Actions are used to enable agents to affect their environment. To implement an action, we must do two things: first, we need to create an actua-tor that contains the implementation of the action. After this, we need to specify our action in an AFAPL2 file, using the ACTION construct.

Actuators are Java classes that subclass the com.agentfactory.logic.agent. Actuator class and implement the act(..) method. Upon creation, the agent creates on in-stance of each specified actuator. Thus, the same instance is used even when the action is being performed concurrently. Consequently, actuators must be implemented as thread-safe classes.

To illustrate how to create an actuator, we will develop a "helloWorld" action that prints the string "Hello World" to the console.

```
import com.agentfactory.logic.agent.Actuator;
import com.agentfactory.logic.lang.FOS;

public class HelloWorldActuator extends Actuator {
        public boolean act( FOS action ) {
                System.out.println( "Hello World" );
                return true;
        }
}
```

What the above actuator implementation does is fairly obvious. The only "issue" is the return value of an actuator. This is used to define whether the commitment to the corresponding action failed or succeeded. This is useful in situations where it is possible for the actuator to complete unsuccessfully, for example, updating a table in a database. In such cases, the actuator can indicate its failure by returning false instead of true.

For an actuator to be used by an agent, an action definition for the actuator must be specified in the agent design. The action definition below specifies an action called "helloWorld" and links the action to the HelloWorldActuator. In addition, this definition requires that any pre and post conditions that apply to the action be specified.

Pre-conditions are used to ensure that the action is only performed when it is possible. For example, a robot soccer agent program may include a "kick" action. The pre-condition for this action would be that the agent has the ball (i.e. BELIEF(hasBall)). Conversely, post-conditions are used to identify which actions can be used to achieve the goals of the agent. For this example, we will declare both the pre- and post- condition of our action to be true (this is a default that means "no precondition or postcondition").

> ACTION helloWorld PRECONDITION BELIEF(true); POSTCONDITION BELIEF(true);
>   CLASS helloworld.HelloWorldActuator;

Many scenarios require that an agent act in response to some change in its environment (for example the receipt of a message from another agent, the triggering of a sensor, the location of additional resources for processing, and so on). In such cases, we require a mechanism that allows the developer to define situations in which the agent must commit to some activity (i.e. some action or plan). Agent Factory supports this through the use of commitment rules. Commitment rules specify situations (defined as a belief sentence) in which the agent should adopt a commitment.

The following example illustrates the situation in which we want to program our robot soccer agent to move towards the ball whenever it sees it. This is achieved through a rule of the following form:

```
BELIEF(seesBall)    =>    COMMIT(?self,    ?now,    BELIEF(seesBall),
moveTo(ball));
```

This rule states that, if the robot soccer agent sees the ball, then it should commit to the action of moving to that ball. Two key points to take from the above example are:

- The introduction of two pre-defined variables, ?self and ?now, which are bound to constants representing the agents name and the current time respectively.
- The use of a maintenance condition to constrain the persistence of the commitment when adopted. The agent maintains the commitment to move to the ball until either the moveTo(ball) action completes or the agent no longer believes that it sees the ball.

Should the robot soccer agent ever come to believe that it sees the ball (i.e. it has the belief BELIEF(seesBall)), then the commitment rule would be fired. This would cause the agent to adopt the corresponding commitment. So, if the agent was called striker, and it saw the ball at 11:46am, then it would adopt a commitment of the form:

```
COMMIT(striker, 11:46, BELIEF(seesBall), moveTo(ball))
```

The above commitment rule specifies a behaviour that is realised through the adoption of a single commitment. Commitment rules can also be used to drive the adoption of multiple commitments simultaneously. This can be achieved by introducing variables into the situation definition.

For example, consider an agent-based security system that includes a monitoring agent that is responsible for monitoring what Radio Frequency IDentification (RFID) tags that enter or leave a specified region (which is monitored by one or more RFID antenna). This agent may be designed to handle beliefs of the form BELIEF(newTag(?tagID)) where ?tagID is a unique code that is assigned to every RFID tag, and the belief itself is used to represent the fact that an new RFID tag has entered the monitored region.

The expected behaviour of this agent is that it will perform a security check whenever a tag enters the monitored region. The agent uses the result of the security check to determine whether or not it should raise an alarm.

To implement this behaviour within AFAPL2, a commitment rule of the form is added:

BELIEF(newTag(?tagID)) => COMMIT(?self, ?now, BELIEF(true), check-Tag(?tagID));

Informally, this rule states that, if the agent detects that a new RFID tag has entered the monitored region, then it should perform a check to see whether that tag is allowed to be in the monitored region. What the agent does when the tag has been checked can be specified through the introduction of additional commitment rules. For example:

BELIEF(illegalTagMovement(?tagID))   &   BE-LIEF(tagAuthority(?agentName, ?agentAddress)) => COMMIT(?self, ?now, BELIEF(true), inform(agentID(?agentName, ?agentAddress), illegal-TagMovement(?tagID)));

This second rule states that if the agent believes that a tag is not allowed to be in the monitored region (this is the first of the beliefs on the left hand side of the belief rule) and it knows a tag authority agent (this is the second of the beliefs on the left hand side of the belief rule), then it informs the tag authority agent that it has detected an illegal tag movement (this happens through the adoption of the commitment on the right hand side of the commitment rule).

Agent Factory uses resolution-based reasoning to evaluate the truth of the belief sentence part of a commitment rule. To illustrate this point, let us consider the RFID scenario in more detail. The agent is responsible for monitoring the movement of objects in a physical space of a building using RFID tags. In such systems, the actual monitoring of the space is carried out by an one or more RFID antenna. The corresponding agent is then linked to that antenna (or set of antenna) via some form of interface that generates events when RFID tags enter or leave the monitored space. To make the agent aware of these events, we introduce an event perceptor that generates beliefs based on the events that are produced by the interface. For events where an object that has an RFID tag enters the monitored space, the perceptor generates beliefs of the form BELIEF(newTag(?tagID)), which corresponds to the belief on the left hand side of the second commitment rule.

As an example, consider the case where a single tagged object (with a unique identifier of 101 - for simplicity) enters the region that is monitored by an agent with identifier "lobby". The entry of this tag is detected by the antenna and passed to the agent's perceptor via the interface. This causes the perceptor to generate the belief BELIEF(newTag(101)). The adoption of this belief causes the second commitment rule to be triggered. That is, the belief sentence on the left hand side of this commitment rule is evaluated to true when the variable binding ?tagID / 101 is applied. This results in the adoption of a single commitment of the form:

COMMIT(lobby, 9:28, BELIEF(true), checkTag(101))

If, at the same time, a second tag, with identifier 320, also entered the monitored region, then the agent would have a second belief of the form BELIEF(newTag(320)). This would cause the query process to generate two variable bindings for the second commitment rule: tagID / 101 and ?tagID / 320 . Based on these bindings, two commitments would now be adopted by the agent: the commitment above, and a second commitment of the form:

COMMIT(lobby, 9:28, BELIEF(true), checkTag(320))

So, what this example highlights is that the interpreter generates every possible variable binding for the belief sentence component of each commitment rule. These bindings are then applied to the commitment component of each commitment rule and the resultant commitments are adopted.

To summarise some of the main features of the language:

- The language is deliberative and is based on a logical formalism of beliefs and commitments. Reactive behaviour within the framework is encoded imperatively within Java (more recently, some work has been done to put structure around the reactive behaviour within the SoSAA architecture [18]).
- The language provides high level speech act primitives for communication. It facilitates the broadcast of messages through the use of wild card pattern matching.
- The language is relatively easy to understand for developers that have experience of declarative or logic-based programming. For developers without such experience, the learning curve is steeper.

6.3.2 Semantics and Verification

The language has a clear and precise semantics. The original version of AFAPL was formalised in Collier's Thesis [10]. Work is underway to provide a formal operational semantics of the language in its current form for a future paper. The a language is suitable for the creation of a wide variety of agent-oriented applications (see Section 6.5).

6.3.3 Software Engineering Issues

The Agent Factory system, in general, has been designed with Software Engineering concerns at its core. Developing a system and methodology that had a sound software engineering basis was one of the contributions of Collier's thesis [10]. The Agent Factory system is modular and can be extended with functionality for a number of different agent architectures. The design of AFME has been strongly influenced by good objected oriented precepts, such as the 'Law of Demeter' (LoD) [30]. The LoD, which was popularised by Grady Booch and James Rumbaugh [6, 43] in the 1990s, greatly improves the maintainability of the software. As with many researchers in the Software Engineering and Object-Oriented community, we view the overuse of inheritance as a bad thing and tend to favour composition.

The language is integrated with Java. At present, no support is provided for integrating the language with other classical (imperative) languages, but there is no reason why such support could not be provided in the future.

6.3.4 Other features of the language

The platform supports the construction and deployment of mobile agents. Truly strong migration is not possible in Java because much of the system state is controlled by the JVM and cannot be directly accessed (see Section 6.4). Within Agent Factory support is provided for the migration of both code (application classes) and the agents' mental state. Within AFME, support is only provided for the transferral of state. The language does not facilitate the definition of new language components from basic constructs.

6.4 Platform

As with many other agent frameworks (see Section 6.6), Agent Factory has been divided into two editions, one for standard Java, the other for JME CLDC. In this section, we initially discuss the standard platform, then AFME.

Agent Factory is an open source framework that has been developed to support the deployment of multi-agent systems [12]. It is broadly compliant with the current FIPA standards and is implemented in the Java programming language. In its latest incarnation, the framework has been restructured to facilitate the deployment of applications that consist of multiple agents that employ a diverse range of agent architectures. As such, the framework has become an enabling middleware layer that can easily be extended and adapted for different application domains.

The Agent Factory framework can be broken down into three parts:

- a distributed Run-Time Environment (RTE) that consists of a FIPA-compliant agent platform together with a number of prefabricated agent system architectures that have been built to provide infrastructure services for applications;
- a set of Development Kits (DK) that contain agent interpreter / architecture implementations together with relevant tool support; and
- a Deployment Process that provides a structured approach to the deployment of multi-agent systems using the framework.

The critical components used in the deployment of a multi-agent system are the agent platforms and the development kits. Agent platforms deliver the machinery necessary to create and support agents that are developed using one or more of the development kits. These development kits include:

- an agent container that holds the agents currently resident on the agent platform;
- a platform service manager that supports the deployment of a set of platform services that implement shared resources that are available to some or all of the resident agents;
- a security module that controls what platform services each agent has access to;
- an architecture factory module that manages the instantiation of the various agent interpreters / architectures that can be deployed on the platform; and
- a module that creates and deploys any run-time tools that are required to provide necessary support for the visualization, management, profiling, and debugging of the resident agents.

Conversely, each development kit provides some form of template agent interpreter / architecture that can be used to create application agents. The most common support tools that a development kit provides are: a customized agent inspector that allows the visualization of the internal state of that architecture; and code templates for an appropriate IDE. However, other support tools may be added if deemed appropriate. Currently, Agent Factory provides two basic development kits: the AFAPL2 Development Kit, which supports the creation of intentional agents; and the Reactive Message Agent (RMA) development kit, which provides a simple reactive agent architecture that combines message handlers, event handlers, and an internal memory.

The configuration of the agent platform and the specification of the initial agent community are supported via two deployment files: the platform configuration file is used to specify a configuration for each agent platform and the agent platform script is used to specify the initial community of agents that are to be deployed on that platform.

The platform configuration file aids developers in defining what platform services, agent architectures, and run-time tools should be deployed on each agent platform. It is also used to assign a default name to each agent platform. Perhaps the most common use of this configuration file is to specify what message transport services will be made available to agents residing on the platform. They are deployed as platform services, and currently, implementations exist for local message passing, HTTP, UDP and XMPP.

Conversely, the agent platform script is used to declare the initial agent community that will be deployed on an agent platform at start-up. This file allows developers to define what agents will be created, to initialize the state of those agents, and when to start their execution. The script allows the creation of two kinds of agents: system agents and application agents. System agents are those agents that make up the system architecture, while application agents are those agents that contain the application logic. The main practical differences between system agents and application agents are that system agents are created first and have the chance to carry out initial configuration before the application agents are created, and system agents start executing by default, while application agents do not.

In summary, Agent Factory provides a modular and extensible framework for constructing and deploying multi-agent systems. It offers a set of APIs that can be used to implement and integrate agents that employ different architectures and can support multiple interpreters that realise high-level AOP languages via the creation of development kits. One such language, which is described in the next section, is the Agent Factory Agent Programming Language (AFAPL).

6.4.1 Agent Factory Micro Edition

Agent Factory Micro Edition (AFME) is a minimized footprint version of the Agent Factory platform designed specifically for use with resource constrained devices. AFME was originally used for the development of applications for cellular digital mobile phones, but has since been ported to the leaf nodes of a WSN and specifically Sun SPOT motes. In deploying agents on sensor nodes, developers are faced with a number of problems; perhaps the most obvious is the limited spatiotemporal computational and power resources available. It is for this reason that initial agent frameworks developed for WSNs were based on a weak notion of agency, whereby agents did not possess reasoning capabilities, the canonical example being Agilla. Other more recent approaches focus on particular algorithms for agent interaction [46], but the agents would not be considered strong in the traditional sense of the word.

This chapter advocates the use of AFME agents, which are loosely based on the BDI notion of agency. The BDI model is an appropriate paradigm for devices such as WSN motes in that it acknowledges that agents are resource constrained and will be unable to achieve all of their desires even if their desires are consistent. An agent must fix upon a subset of desires within its intention selection process and commit resources to achieving them.

Traditionally, the BDI model of agency would be considered too computationally intensive for small devices, such as WSN motes. In this paper, we agree with this argument, in so far as that we are not proposing to deploy BDI agents on extremely low specification nesC type devices, such as the Berkeley or Tyndall motes. Nonetheless, there are now several devices on the market, such as the Sun SPOT or Imote2, that have considerably more resources available than early motes. On such devices, it is quite feasible to deploy minimized footprint BDI agents. For this to be practical, however, it is still essential to ensure that resources are not squandered and are used in an intelligent and prudent manner. BDI languages are, for the most part, declarative although in practice most of them are used in conjunction with imperative components. In general, the declarative components specify a theory of the problem to be solved, whereas as the imperative components specify the low level coding procedures. The imperative components are usually written in object languages, such as Java or C++. The agent languages represent a logical abstraction. Various interpreters can be built for them so that they can be used in different environments. There are no failsafe development methodologies that ensure a good agent design. The design decisions made are of significant importance in the WSN domain where resources are extremely scarce. There is an inherent cost in controlling a system and in performing computations. The complexity of algorithms puts certain constraints on the time in which we may obtain the results of the computation; therefore there is a limit to the amount of knowledge or information we can attain at a particular time point. Either we accept errors due to the lack of information and allow the system to be responsive or we allow the system to carry on operating in a suboptimal manner as we are performing computations or obtaining information so as to make better decisions. That is, the fact that performing a computation has a spatiotemporal and energy usage overhead prevents us from controlling a large system perfectly [3]. In developing software systems in practice, this ultimately comes down to a granularity problem.

In AFME, we provide the developer with functionality to encode the deliberative behaviour of agents yet they may also encode functionality at an imperative level directly within Java. The decision as to whether a particular task should be declarative or imperative is not clear cut and ultimately comes down to the experience and knowledge of the developer. It often depends on whether the developer believes something should be a task or a goal. Tasks are less expensive in that they use fewer resources and the result may be obtained faster, but they are also less flexible and reduce the possibilities for recovery from failure.

In developing BDI agents for sensor networks, the developer could be tempted to develop everything as a task, but this would be little better than using the weak approach to agency. At the other extreme if the agent does too much reasoning, resources will be wasted and the system will be unresponsive. The development framework discussed in this article supports both approaches. It is our belief that it is no longer the case that the BDI model of agency is too computationally intensive for resource constrained devices. With developments in computing technology, improvements in the efficiency of algorithms, and the dissemination of good design practices and the knowledge of algorithms to developers, the traditional arguments no longer hold. It is for this reason that a number of agent-based ambient systems have begun to emerge. To the best of our knowledge, AFME was the first BDI framework to be deployed on the leaf nodes of a wireless sensor network.

Each agent in AFME consists of a set of roles, which are adopted at various points throughout execution. Each role consists of a trigger condition and a set of commitment rules. Once an agent adopts a belief that matches the trigger, the role is adopted and the set of commitment rules are added to the agent's mental state. Subsequently, on each iteration of the agent's control process, the commitment rules are evaluated until either the role is retracted or the agent is terminated. The set of commitment rules adopted when a role is triggered specify the conditions under which commitments are adopted for the role. Originally, these conditions only included the agent's beliefs, but more recently, in AFME, support has been added for equalities, inequalities, and rudimentary mathematic operations. This is useful because it allows developers to specify, at a declarative level, relationships among beliefs. For instance, if an agent had beliefs about the cost of bread and butter, the developer could encode conditions such as if bread costs more than butter or if bread costs less than butter minus 10. With the original approach, this is not possible without writing imperative code to compare the beliefs or belief arguments. Once commitments have been adopted, the agent commences the commitment management process. Various arguments are passed to the commitment when it is adopted, such as the time at which it should commence, to whom the commitment is made, and the maintenance condition of the commitment. An identifier is specified which acts as a trigger for the plan or primitive action to be performed. In subsequent iterations of the control algorithm, the commitment is invoked subject to the arguments specified.

6.4.1.1 AFME Platform and Life Cycle

An AFME platform comprises a scheduler, several platform services, and a collection of agents. The scheduler is responsible for the scheduling of agents to execute at periodic intervals. Rather than each agent creating a new thread when they begin operating, agents share a thread pool. Platform services are a shared information space amongst agents. Platform services, such as the local message transport service, are required in situations where agents must gain access to a shared object instance so as to act upon the object or perceive its state.

AFME delivers support for the creation of agents that follow a sense-deliberate-act cycle. The control algorithm performs four functions (see Figure 6.1). First, preceptors are fired and beliefs are updated. Second, the agent's desired states are identified. A subset of desires (new intentions) is chosen, and added to the agent's commitment set. It should be noted that if the agent has older commitments, which are of lower importance, they will be dropped if there is not enough resources available to execute all commitments. This is handled through the knapsack procedure. Fourth, depending on the nature of the agent's commitments, various actuators are fired.

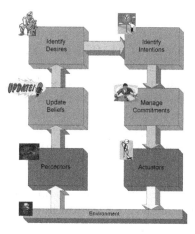

Fig. 6.1 The AFME Control Process

6.4.2 Available tools and documentation

Both Agent Factory and AFME are well documented and provide tool based support for the development and debugging of applications:

- The platform has extensive documentation available from the Agent Factory website (http://www.agentfactory.com). This includes tutorials on how to use the framework and technical documentation, such as Javadoc.
- An agent logger and visual debugging tool, which enables the developer to examine the agent's mental state, is available.
- On-line help is available from the website along with information on how to download and install the system.
- Tools for the administration, management, and configuration of the platform are integrated into the Netbeans IDE.

6.4.3 Agent Factory/AFME Integration

Agent Factory and AFME are integrated through the message transport and migration services. Both platforms are FIPA compliant therefore and message transfer and communication is consistent. In terms of migration, it is necessary for agents to change their form when migrating from a standard desktop environment to a constrained device and vice versa. The remainder of this section will discuss how the message transport and migration services of AFME have been developed to integrate with Agent Factory.

6.4.3.1 Message Transport Service

The Message Transport Service of AFME had to be changed considerably from the original design. This was because the local GPRS and 3G service providers have a firewall operating to prevent incoming socket connections and also because MIDP and J2SE support different APIs for networking. Rather than having a server operating on the mobile device, the message transport service periodically polls a mailbox server operating outside the firewall domain. Incoming messages are stored in the mailbox until a connection is made from the client devices, at which point all stored messages are transferred. This increases the latency of message passing but is necessary to pierce the firewall.

The message transport service has two modes of operation, namely synchronous and asynchronous. These modes are related to how outgoing messages are processed. Incoming messages are handled generically. When operating in synchronous mode, all outgoing messages are buffered within the service. When a connection is made to the mailbox server and all incoming messages have been received, the same socket connection is kept open and used to transfer outgoing messages. When the mailbox server receives the outgoing messages, they are forwarded on to their destination. When operating in asynchronous mode, outgoing messages are sent directly within their own individual sockets. This is possible because the firewall only blocks incoming sockets not outgoing. The choice made of which mode to use when developing an application depends on whether the developer wishes to minimize latency or maximize performance. When operating within synchronous mode, there will be less socket connections made, whereas in asynchronous mode the latency of outgoing messages will be lower.

When the mailbox server receives an outgoing connection from an embedded device, it is in the form of a direct binary connection over TCP. The use of a direct binary connection improves the performance of message transfer. This binary information is converted to an XML format and subsequently forwarded over HTTP in compliance with the FIPA specifications. When receiving incoming messages for an embedded device from other platforms, this process is reversed, thus the HTTP is converted into a binary format. In this respect, the AFME message transport service supports transparent communication between agents operating on embedded devices and those operating on the standard version of the system or other FIPA compliant platforms. Agents are unaware of whether the cohort they are communicating with is behind a firewall or not. They correspond with the mailbox server in the same manner as if they were communicating with a platform directly.

6.4.3.2 Migration

Agent migration is often classified as either strong or weak. This classification is related to the amount of information transferred when an agent moves from one platform to another. Truly strong migration is not possible in Java. Within

AFME support is only provided for the transfer of the agent's mental state (see Figure 6.2). Any classes required by the agent must already be present at the destination. This is because CLDC does not contain an API for introspection and is thus prevented from dynamically loading foreign objects. The reason CLDC applications do not contain security managers or class loaders that would enable the dynamic execution of foreign code is that the JVM specification does not contain a class verifier. The verifier forms one of the most important security aspects of the original J2SE JVM architecture. It ensures the integrity of a sequence of byte codes by performing a data-flow analysis on them at runtime. Conversely, within CLDC the code must be pre-verified in order to execute. This improves the performance of the system in that the code does not have to be continuously checked while executing. It prevents the system however from dynamically downloading and executing foreign objects because the system cannot verify that the objects' code is safe to use. Malicious developers could simply alter the structure of a class, for example by changing the operand of a jump opcode such as goto, to crash the JVM and potentially the operating system of the mobile device. Thus no support for introspection is provided.

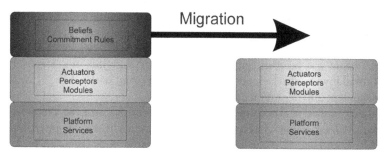

Fig. 6.2 AFME Migration

To facilitate the migration process within AFME a similar approach is taken to that of the message transport service. This is because agents must also be capable of penetrating the service provider firewall. Thus, agents first migrate to a migration server where they wait for a connection from their destination platform. When a connection is received they are transferred accordingly. When migrating back the agents also go through the migration server.

As agents move to and from embedded devices the BDI commitment rules that govern the agents' behaviour are altered to enable the agents to adapt to their environments. The agents' designs are decoupled into the core behaviours that operate on all platforms and platform specific behaviours that contain dependencies on a particular framework. The core behaviours represent the lowest common denominator or the essence of an agent's functionality that will execute on all devices. The platform specific behaviour represents the commitment rules that need to be altered when an agent moves from one type of environment to another. The essence of the agent is always contained within the agent design, whereas agents maintain beliefs about where the platform specific commitment rules may be obtained. These beliefs are in the form of URLs and represent the location at which the rules may be downloaded. These URLs are used within the mailbox server in the creation of agent designs that combine the essence of the agents with their platform specific functionality.

6.4.4 Standards compliance, interoperability and portability

Although the AFAPL is a general language, at the moment the interpreters and all of the tools for both Agent Factory and AFME are based on Java. Communication in the system is consistent with the FIPA specifications.

- At present, the platform requires Java to operate. The desktop version of the system will work with either standard Java or the JME CDC platform; it cannot work with CLDC. AFME has been specifically designed for the JME CLDC Java platform, but it can also work with standard Java.
- The message transport service and architecture of the system is consistent with the FIPA specifications. We discuss the message transport service in greater detail in the previous subsection. Additionally, support for yellow and white page services is provided.
- The System has been integrated with Java Servlets, JSP, and Struts. Future work will investigate the incorporation of the system with OSGi [2] for service management and deployment.
- Standard Java is required for the current framework and the Netbeans IDE is required for some of the tools to operate. In theory, an interpreter for AFAPL could be written in any imperative programming language. In the past, a Smalltalk-80 AFAPL interpreter was maintained, but at present, however, Java is necessary.
- The platform supports open multi-agent systems and heterogeneous agents.

6.4.5 Other features of the platform

Agent Factory is a modular open source platform. It supports the development and deployment of different types of agent architectures. Nevertheless, the platform is generally used for the development of intentional agents. The AFAPL interpreter is quite efficient when compared to other work in this area, but it is acknowledged that AFAPL does not conform to the same semantics as other systems. The footprint of the software has been reduced with the development of AFME. We discuss this in greater detail in Section 6.6.

- Agent Factory is a modular system and has been specifically designed to enable its core functionality to be extended with new features. It is open source and is freely available from SourceForge.
- The overhead of Agent Factory depends on the type of agents that are developed using the framework. AFAPL is quite practical and efficient when considered in the context of intentional agent platforms.
- The platform is currently a stable open source distribution.
- The structure of the agent community developed using Agent Factory is dependent on the design of the individual agents. As such, centralised, distributed, or hierarchical control can be catered for, but it does not provide libraries for interaction protocols or group templates.
- The platform enables the reuse of agent designs through the use of inheritance and dynamic role adoption.

6.5 Applications supported by the language and/or the platform

Over the years, the Agent Factory Framework has been used for the development of several research projects. The results and requirements of these projects have influenced the design of the system and have motivated the introduction of new features and functionality.

- At present, the majority of applications Agent Factory has been used for have been research projects that reflect the requirements of real world applications.
- Agent Factory does not target a specific domain and has been deployed in an array of diverse application domains. These have included E-Commerce [26], Ubiquitous Computing [36], Mobile Computing [38], Robotics [19], Wireless Sensor Networks [37], and Mixed Reality [17].

6.6 Comparison to Related Work

Agent Factory distinguishes itself from other intelligent agent frameworks [25, 32, 45, 1] in several ways. It is founded upon a logical formalism of belief and commitment [10] and enables agents to be programmed directly in terms of their commitments (see Section 6.3 for a discussion of the commitment management process). Additionally, it was one of the earliest frameworks to consider software engineering issues at its core, drawing from, and building upon, early work on Agent Oriented Software Engineering [41]. The framework comprises a four layer architecture that includes a development methodology, integrated development environment support, an agent-oriented programming language, and a runtime environment.

There currently a trend in the development of programming languages that use an XML syntax [7, 21, 48, 14, 47, 29, 16]. Although these systems have made many significant and innovative contributions to the field, the use of XML has to be called to account. This approach has not been adopted in Agent Factory/AFME. XML is useful as a mechanism for data exchange between computer programs, but not as a language to be used by humans. It's a sophisticated data format nothing more (see Terence Parr's soapbox [42] for more details). The correct approach is to write a parser and lexical analyzer, lest pay a heavy price in productivity due to the cumbersome nature of XML. Even if XML were to be used, the data must still be interpreted. That is, even though XML has an extensible syntax, the developer must still write code to "make sense" of, or use, the information obtained from the parser when additional functionality or requirements are added. The semantics must still be encoded in the application or agent, regardless of the manner in which the agent design is represented. James Davidson, the creator of the well known Apache Ant, one of the most widely used XML-based tools, notes about the XML syntax of Ant in [15]:

> "If I knew then what I know now, I would have tried using a real scripting language, such as JavaScript via the Rhino component or Python via JPython, with bindings to Java objects that implemented the functionality expressed in today's tasks. Then, there would be a first-class way to express logic, and we wouldn't be stuck with XML as a format that is too bulky for the way that people really want to use the tool."

XML is overly verbose and is far from ideal as the syntax of a programming language, specification language, or for configuration files to be used by people. As noted by Parr [42]:

> "Humans have an innate ability to apply structure to a stream of characters (sentences), therefore, adding mark-up symbols can only make it harder for us to read and more laborious to type. The problem is that most programmers have very little experience designing and parsing computer languages. Rather than spending the time to design and parse a human-friendly language, programmers are using the fastest path to providing a specification language and implementation: "Oh, use XML. Done." And that's OK, but I want programmers to recognize that they are providing an inferior interface when they take that easy route."

Several agent frameworks have been developed for the fabrication of agents for desktop environments. With the explosive growth of the mobile phone market, there has been a drive to develop similar frameworks for constrained environments and in particular JME CLDC. Typically, these systems have two versions of the agent platform, one for the desktop environment and one for the CLDC environment. This is the case with Agent Factory/AFME. Other examples include Jade/Jade LEAP [4], 3APL/3APL-M [28], SAGE/SAGE-Lite [27], and Cougaar/-CourgaarME [49]. Agent Factory/AFME distinguishes themselves from these other frameworks in a number of ways. JADE-LEAP, CougaarME, MicroFIPA-OS, and SAGE-Lite are frameworks for the development of agent technology, but they are not reflective and do not use an abstract agent programming language that is based on a theory of rational agency[1]. 3APL-M is similar to AFME/Agent Factory in that it does contain reasoning capabilities, but it does not contain a networking component. If the developer wishes an agent to communicate over the network, they must write the code from scratch. Agent Factory/AFME provides support for networking through the message transport service.

At present, most of these frameworks target mobile phones and PDAs. Agilla [20] is an agent platform that has been developed for WSNs, but it also does not contain reasoning capabilities and therefore does not conform to the same definition of agency as Agent Factory/AFME.

The design of AFME has been strongly influenced by the 'Law of Demeter' [30], which specifies the coding guideline "only talk to your immediate friends". The 'Law of Demeter', or Principle of Least Knowledge, leads to the creation of loosely coupled classes that improve the maintainability of the software [6, 43]. Using the Law as a general principle, tends to favour composition over inheritance and avoids the use of accessor (get/set) methods[2]. Rather than a callee obtaining data from an object to perform some operation through the use of an accessor method, the callee directs the object to perform the operation on its behalf [24]. That is, objects are designed in terms of their capabilities and their state is not exposed through the use of accessors. This is often referred to as 'delegation' by object-oriented developers. It leads to a more declarative approach to object development and also tends to reduce the footprint of the software by minimising code duplication.

The footprint of AFME is quite low. For instance, the core infrastructure has a Jar size of 77k, an NCSS value [22] of 2601, and a McCabe cyclomatic complexity [31] (not to be confused with algorithmic complexity) of 2.91. If just the core reasoning capabilities of the platform are considered and the Jar file is obfuscated, the Jar size can be reduced to 17k. When considering the footprint, we must also take into account the overhead and resource requirements of the software necessary to run the platform. With AFME, the JME CLDC Java platform is required. CLDC is considerably less resource intensive than standard Java. As noted earlier, there have been a number of platforms developed for CLDC. 3APL-M is the closest framework to AFME in that it is based on a theory for rational agency and contains reasoning capabilities. Through our experience and experimentation [33], it has been found that AFME is considerably faster than 3APL-M in terms of execution time. Nevertheless, it is acknowledged that 3APL-M contains features not supported by AFME. To the best of our knowledge, AFME is the smallest footprint reflective agent-oriented platform. Nevertheless, it is accepted that AFME does not conform to the same semantics as other reflective platforms. For instance, 3APL-M has been incorporated with a complete Prolog engine, AFME has not.

---

[1] Intelligent extensions built for JADE will not work with the CLDC version of LEAP without making modifications to the code due to the different APIs supported by standard Java and CLDC.

[2] It should be noted that the LoD does not only apply to accessors (see [30] for more details).

6.7 Conclusion

Agent Factory is a flexible FIPA compliant open source Java-based platform for the development, visualisation, and deployment of multi-agent systems. It is an evolving project and over the years has gone through a metamorphosis process, producing sibling frameworks such as AFME. Agent Factory has been designed with Software Engineering principles at its core and represents a modular framework that supports the development of a diverse variety of agent-oriented applications. The footprint of the system has been further reduced with the development of AFME. This chapter discussed the various modifications and enhancements that were made to the framework together with the motivations for such. As new technologies emerge, it is envisaged that Agent Factory will be further augmented to reflect new threads and developments. In the short term, we are investigating the potential to further enhance and optimise performance for embedded and resource constrained devices. In the longer term, as the number of heterogeneous devices and platforms increases, we are looking at the potential of using technologies, such as OSGi [2], for service management and deployment.

Acknowledgements The authors gratefully acknowledge the kind support of Science Foundation Ireland (SFI) under grant no. 07/CE/I1147 and the Irish Research Council for Science, Engineering, and Technology (IRCSET).

References

1. Albuquerque, R., Hübner, F., de Paula, G., Sichman, J., Ramalho, G.: Ksaci: A handheld device infrastructure for agents communicaiton. Pre-proceedings of the Workshop on Agent Theories, Architectures, and Languages, (ATAL) (2001)
2. Alliance, O.: OSGi Service Platform, Release 3. IOS Press, Inc. (2003)
3. Bellman, R.E.: Some Vistas of Modern Mathematics. University of Kentucky Press (1968)
4. Berger, M., Rusitschka, S., Toropov, D., Watzke, M., Schlichte, M.: The Development of the Lightweight Extensible Agent Platform. EXP in Search of Innovation 3(3), 32–41 (2003)
5. Birkhoff, G., Lipson, J.: Heterogeneous algebras. Journal of Combinatorial Theory 8(1), 15–133 (1970)
6. Booch, G.: Object-oriented Analysis and Design, 2nd edition. Addison Wesley (1994)
7. Braubach, L., Pokahr, A., Lamersdorf, W.: Jadex: A BDI agent system combining middleware and reasoning. In: M.K. R. Unland M. Calisti (ed.) Software Agent-Based Applications, Platforms and Development Kits, pp. 143–168. Birkhäuser-Verlag, Basel-Boston-Berlin (2005). Book chapter
8. Collier, R., Ross, R., O Hare, G.M.P.: A role-based approach to reuse in agent-oriented programming. AAAI Fall Symposium on Roles, an interdisciplinary perspective (Roles 2005) (2005)
9. Collier, R.W.: The realisation of Agent Factory: An environment for the rapid prototyping of intelligent agents. M. Phil., Univ. of Manchester (1996)
10. Collier, R.W.: Agent Factory: A Framework for the Engineering of Agent-Oriented Applications. Ph.D. Thesis (2001)
11. Collier, R.W., O Hare, G.M.P.: Agent Factory: A Revised Agent Prototyping Environment. In: 10th Irish Conference on Artificial Intelligence & Cognitive Science, pp. 1–3 (1999)

12. Collier, R.W., O Hare, G.M.P., Lowen, T., Rooney, C.: Beyond prototyping in the factory of the agents. 3rd Central and Eastern European Conference on Multi-Agent Systems (CEEMAS'03), Lecture Notes in Computer Science (LNCS) **2691** (2003)
13. Collier, R.W., Rooney, C.F.B., Donoghue, R.P.S., O'Hare, G.M.P.: Mobile BDI agents. In Proceedings of the 11th Irish Conference on Artificial Intelligence and Cognitive Science (2000). URL citeseer.ist.psu.edu/collier00mobile.html
14. Cossentino, M., Burrafato, P., Lombardo, S., Sabatucci, L.: Introducing Pattern Reuse in the Design of Multi-agent Systems. Lecture Notes in Computer Science pp. 107–120 (2003)
15. Davidson, J.D.: The Creator of Ant Exorcizes One of His Demons. Pragmatic Project Automation: How to Build, Deploy, and Monitor Java Apps by M. Clark. The Pragmatic Programmers (2004)
16. De Meo, P., Garro, A., Terracina, G., Ursino, D.: X-Learn: An XML-Based, Multi-agent System for Supporting "User-Device" Adaptive E-learning. Lecture Notes in Computer Science pp. 739–756 (2003)
17. Dragone, M., Holz, T., Duffy, B.R., O Hare, G.M.P.: Ubiquitous Realities through Situated Social Agents. In: Proc. of the 5th Intl. Working Conference of Computer Animation and Social Agents (CASAŠ05) (2005)
18. Dragone, M., Lillis, D., Collier, R.W., O Hare, G.M.P.: Sosaa: A framework for integrating agents and components. In: 24th Annual Symposium on Applied Computing (ACM SAC 2009), Special Track on Agent-Oriented Programming, Systems, Languages, and Applications. Honolulu, Hawaii, USA (2009)
19. Duffy, B.R., Collier, R.W., O Hare, G.M.P., Rooney, C.F.B., O'Donoghue, R.P.S.: Social Robotics: Reality and Virtuality in Agent-Based Robotics. In: Bar-Ilan Symposium on the Foundations of Artificial Intelligence: Bridging Theory and Practice (BISFAI) (1999)
20. Fok, C.L., Roman, G.C., Lu, C.: Rapid development and flexible deployment of adaptive wireless sensor network applications. In: Proceedings of the 24th International Conference on Distributed Computing Systems (ICDCS'05), pp. 653–662. IEEE (2005)
21. Garro, A., Palopoli, L.: An XML Multi-agent System for E-learning and Skill Management. Lecture Notes in Computer Science pp. 283–294 (2003)
22. Grady, R.B.: Successfully applying software metrics. Computer **27**(9), 18–25 (1994). DOI http://dx.doi.org/10.1109/2.312034
23. Hoare, C.A.R.: Communicating sequential processes. Communications of the ACM **21**(8), 666–677 (1978)
24. Holub, A.: Holub on Patterns: Learning Design Patterns by Looking at Code. APress (2004)
25. Howden, N., Ronnquist, R., Hodgson, A., Lucas, A.: JACK Intelligent Agents-Summary of an Agent Infrastructure. In: 5th International Conference on Autonomous Agents (2001)
26. Keegan, S., O'Hare, G.M.P., O'Grady, M.J.: Easishop: Ambient intelligence assists everyday shopping. Information Sciences **178**(3), 588–611 (2008)
27. Khalique, S., Farooq, S., Ahmad, H.F., Suguri, H., Ali, A.: Sage-lite: An architecture and implementation of light weight multiagent system. ISADS **0**, 239–244 (2007). DOI http://doi.ieeecomputersociety.org/10.1109/ISADS.2007.68
28. Koch, F., Meyer, J.J., Dignum, F., Rahwan, I.: Programming Deliberative Agents for Mobile Services: the 3APL-M Platform. AAMAS'05 Workshop on Programming Multi-Agent Systems (ProMAS05) (2005)
29. Konnerth, T., Endert, H., HeSSler, A.: JIAC IV Programmers guide (2007)
30. Lieberherr, K., Holland, I., Riel, A.: Object-oriented programming: An objective sense of style. in Object Oriented Programming Systems, Languages and Applications Conference, in special issue of SIGPLAN notices pp. 323–334 (1988)
31. McCabe, T.J.: A software complexity measure. IEEE Transactions on Software Engineering **2**(4), 308–320 (1976)
32. Morley, D., Myers, K.: The spark agent framework. In: AAMAS '04: Proceedings of the Third International Joint Conference on Autonomous Agents and Multiagent Systems, pp. 714–721. IEEE Computer Society, Washington, DC, USA (2004). DOI http://dx.doi.org/10.1109/AAMAS.2004.267

33. Muldoon, C.: An Agent Framework for Ubiquitous Services. Ph.D. thesis, School of Computer Science and Informatics, Dublin, Ireland (2007)
34. Muldoon, C., O Hare, G.M.P., Bradley, J.F.: Towards Reflective Mobile Agents for Resource Constrained Mobile Devices. In: AAMAS 07: Proceedings of the Sixth International Joint conference on Autonomous Agents and Multiagent Systems. ACM, Honolulu, Hawai'i (2007)
35. Muldoon, C., O Hare, G.M.P., Collier, R.W., O Grady, M.J.: Agent Factory Micro Edition: A Framework for Ambient Applications. In: Intelligent Agents in Computing Systems, *Lecture Notes in Computer Science*, vol. 3993, pp. 727–734. Springer, Reading, UK (2006)
36. Muldoon, C., O Hare, G.M.P., Phelan, D., Strahan, R., Collier, R.W.: ACCESS: An Agent Architecture for Ubiquitous Service Delivery. In: Proceedings Seventh International Workshop on Cooperative Information Agents (CIA), *Lecture Notes in Computer Science*, vol. 2782, pp. 1–15. Springer, Helsinki (2003)
37. Muldoon, C., Tynan, R., O Grady, M.J., O Hare, G.M.P.: Realising an agent-oriented middleware for heterogeneous sensor networks. In: ACM/IFIP/USENIX 9th International Middleware Conference, pp. 82–83. ACM Press (2008)
38. O Grady, M.J., O Hare, G.M.P.: Gulliver's genie: agency, mobility, adaptivity. Computers & Graphics 28(5), 677–689 (2004)
39. O Hare, G.M.P.: Agent Factory: An Environment for the Fabrication of Distributed Artificial Systems. O Hare, Gregory M. P. and Jennings, N. R.(Eds.), Foundations of Distributed Artificial Intelligence, Sixth Generation Computer Series, Wiley Interscience Pubs pp. 449–484 (1996)
40. O Hare, G.M.P., Abbas, S.: Agent Oriented Programming: Communicating Intentional Processes (1994)
41. O Hare, G.M.P., Wooldridge, M.J.: A software engineering perspective on multi-agent system design: experience in the development of MADE. Kluwer Computer And Information Science Series pp. 109–127 (1992)
42. Parr,   T.:   Soapbox: Humans   should   not   have   to   grok   XML. http://www.ibm.com/developerworks/xml/library/x-sbxml.html (2001)
43. Rumbaugh, J., Blaha, M., Premerlani, W., Eddy, F., Lorensen, W.: Object Oriented Modeling and Design. Prentice Hall (1991)
44. Shoham, Y.: AGENT0: A simple agent language and its interpreter. In: Proceedings of the Ninth National Conference on Artificial Intelligence, vol. 2, pp. 704–709 (1991)
45. Sierhuis, M.: Brahms: A Multi-Agent Modeling and Simulation Language for Work System Analysis and Design. Ph.D. thesis (2001)
46. Teacy, W., Farinelli, A., Grabham, N., Padhy, P., Rogers, A., Jennings, N.: Max-sum decentralised coordination for sensor systems. In: Proceedings of the 7th international joint conference on Autonomous agents and multiagent systems: demo papers, pp. 1697–1698. International Foundation for Autonomous Agents and Multiagent Systems Richland, SC (2008)
47. Tuguldur, E., Patzlaff, M.: Collecting Gold: MicroJIAC Agents in Multi-Agent Programming Contest. Lecture Notes in Computer Science 4908, 251 (2008)
48. Weiliang, M., Sheng, H.: An XML-Based Language for Coordination Protocol Description in Multi-agent System. In: Proceedings of the 14th International conference on Industrial and engineering applications of artificial intelligence and expert systems: engineering of intelligent systems, pp. 708–717. Springer-Verlag London, UK (2001)
49. Wright, W., Moore, D.: Design considerations for multiagent systems on very small platforms. In: AAMAS '03: Proceedings of the second international joint conference on Autonomous agents and multiagent systems, pp. 1160–1161. ACM Press, New York, NY, USA (2003). DOI http://doi.acm.org/10.1145/860575.860845

Part II
Tools

Chapter 7
Debugging and Testing of Multi-Agent Systems using Design Artefacts

David Poutakidis*, Michael Winikoff†, Lin Padgham, and Zhiyong Zhang

Abstract Agents are a promising technology for dealing with increasingly complex system development. An agent may have many ways of achieving a given task, and it selects the most appropriate way of dealing with a given task based on the context. Although this makes agents flexible and robust, it makes testing and debugging of agent systems challenging. This chapter presents two tools: one for generating test cases for unit testing agent systems, and one for debugging agent systems by monitoring a running system. Both tools are based on the thesis that *design artefacts can be valuable resources in testing and debugging*. An empirical evaluation that was performed with the debugging tool showed that the debugging tool was useful to developers, providing a significant improvement in the number of bugs that were fixed, and in the amount of time taken.

David Poutakidis
Adaptive Intelligent Systems, Melbourne, Australia
School of Computer Science & IT, RMIT University, Melbourne, Australia, e-mail: davpout@cs.rmit.edu.au

Michael Winikoff
School of Computer Science & IT, RMIT University, Melbourne, Australia
University of Otago, Dunedin, New Zealand, e-mail: michael.winikoff@otago.ac.nz

Lin Padgham
School of Computer Science & IT, RMIT University, Melbourne, Australia, e-mail: lin.padgham@cs.rmit.edu.au

Zhiyong Zhang
School of Computer Science & IT, RMIT University, Melbourne, Australia, e-mail: zhzhang@cs.rmit.edu.au

* The work described here was done while Poutakidis was a PhD candidate at RMIT University

† The work described here was done while Winikoff was at RMIT University

R.H. Bordini et al. (eds.), *Multi-Agent Programming*,
DOI 10.1007/978-0-387-89299-3_7, © Springer Science+Business Media, LLC 2009

7.1 Introduction

> *"As soon as we started programming, we found to our surprise that it wasn't as easy to get programs right as we had thought. Debugging had to be discovered. I can remember the exact instant when I realized that a large part of my life from then on was going to be spent in finding mistakes in my own programs."* — Maurice Wilkes

Agents are seen as a promising technology for dealing with increasingly complex system development, with a range of agent-based solutions having now been developed in a range of domains [4, 44]. Agents provide a flexible and robust approach to task achievement making them ideal for deployment in challenging environments. Agents can be equipped with multiple ways of achieving tasks, and depending on the task and the context in which the task should be completed, can select the most appropriate way for dealing with it.

To support the development of agent systems a new field of software engineering, commonly referred to as agent-oriented software engineering, has emerged, in which the agent is proposed as the central design metaphor. A vital and time consuming part of any software engineering process is testing and debugging. However, the autonomous and distributed nature of agent systems, while modular and powerful, is notoriously difficult to test and debug [27].

It has been argued that multi-agent systems merely represent a specific form of distributed systems [51]. Several methods have been developed to assist in the debugging of distributed systems: recording a history of execution for analysis or replay [36]; animating the execution of a system at run-time by providing a visual representation of the program [8], and race detection algorithms to facilitate the detection of simultaneous access to shared resources [65, 47]. However, although debugging techniques developed for distributed systems can be used to facilitate the debugging of multi-agent systems to some extent, there are characteristics of agent systems that require specific attention. Traditional distributed systems support distributed information and algorithms whereas multi-agent systems address distributed tasks achieved by coarse grained agents. The individual agents within a multi-agent system are autonomous and they can act in complicated and sophisticated ways. Furthermore, the interactions between agents are complex and often unexpected. These issues and others need to be addressed for a multi-agent debugging approach.

During testing and debugging the aim is to reconcile any differences between the actual program behaviour and the expected behaviour in order to uncover and resolve bugs. Current techniques fail to take advantage of the underlying design of systems to support the debugging task. This problem is best summed up by Hailpern & Santhanam [29]:

> There is a clear need for a stronger (automatic) link between the software design (what the code is intended to do) ... and test execution (what is actually tested) in order to minimize the difficulty in identifying the offending code...

Our central thesis is that the design documents and system models developed when following an agent based software engineering methodology will be valuable resources during the testing and debugging process and should facilitate the automatic or semi-automatic detection of errors.

This chapter describes two tools that follow this central thesis and use design artefacts to assist in the testing and debugging process:

1. A testing tool [71] that uses design artefacts to generate test cases; and
2. A debugging tool [55, 59, 60, 61] that uses artefacts to monitor a system, and alerts the developer should the system deviate from the behaviour specified by the design artefacts.

Although both tools use design artefacts, and focus on detecting errors, there are significant differences between them. Firstly, the testing tool does *unit* testing of entities within a single agent (e.g. plans, events, beliefs), whereas the debugging tool detects errors in a complete running system. Secondly, the testing tool detects certain domain-independent error conditions such as a plan never being used, whereas the debugging tool detects domain-specific error conditions relating to interaction protocols not being followed correctly[1]. Thirdly, the debugging tool observes the system in action, leaving it up to the user to adequately exercise the system's functionality. By contrast, the testing tool systematically generates a wide range of test cases.

Thus the two tools are complementary: we envision that the testing tool would be used initially to do unit testing, and then, once the system is integrated, the debugging tool would be used to monitor the whole system.

Both tools have been implemented, and the implementations were used for evaluation. The debugging tool is not yet integrated and documented in a manner suitable for public release, but is available from David Poutakidis on request. The testing tool is under further development and is not yet available.

The remainder of this chapter is structured as follows. Section 7.2 reviews relevant background material, including previous work on testing and on debugging, and a review of the design artefacts that we use. Sections 7.3 and 7.4 respectively describe the testing and the debugging tools. We have chosen to have two "tool" sections, since we are describing two separate tools. Our evaluation is covered in section 7.5, and we conclude in section 7.6.

7.2 Background

This section begins by reviewing model based testing (section 7.2.1), then briefly reviews related work on testing and on debugging (sections 7.2.2 and 7.2.3). We then (section 7.2.4) introduce the design artefacts that we use in the remainder of the chapter.

---

[1] However, there is some overlap in functionality, in that both tools detect errors relating to coverage and overlap (see section 7.2.4.3).

7.2.1 *Model Based Testing*

Model Based Testing ([1, 25]) proposes that testing be in some way based on models of the system, which are abstractions of the actual system, and can be used for automated generation of test cases. Automated test case generation is attractive because it has the potential to reduce the time required for testing, but perhaps more importantly it is likely to lead to far more testing being done, and hopefully therefore more robust systems.

Design models which are developed as part of the process of developing the system are one kind of model which can readily be used for model based testing. They specify aspects of expected/designed system behaviour which can be systematically checked under a broad range of situations. Different approaches to model based testing have focussed on different kinds of models, which are then used to generate certain kinds of test cases. For example Apfelbaum and Doyle [1] describe model based testing focussing on use scenarios defined by sequences of actions and paths through the code, which are then used to generate the test cases. This kind of testing is similar to integration testing or acceptance testing. Others (e.g. [17]) focus on models that specify correct input and output data, but these are not so appropriate for testing of complex behaviour models.

In current software development, some level of design modelling is almost always used. These design models specify certain aspects of the system, and can therefore be used as a basis against which to check runtime behaviour under a range of conditions. Substantial work has been done using UML models as the basis for model based testing approaches. Binder [5] summarised the elements of UML diagrams, exploring how these elements can be used for test design and how to develop UML models with sufficient information to produce test cases. He developed a range of testability extensions for each kind of UML diagram where such is needed for test generation.

There are a number of agent system development methodologies, such as Tropos [46], Prometheus [53], MaSE [18] and others, which have well developed structured models that are potentially suitable as a basis for model based testing, in a similar way to the use of UML. The design artefacts representing aspects of these models are potentially well suited to use in guiding testing.

7.2.2 *Testing Agent Systems*

There has been increasing work on testing of agent systems in recent years, with several systems using design models for some level of assistance in generation of test cases.

One approach is to use existing design models to derive test cases. For instance, the eCAT system associated with Tropos [49] uses the goal hierarchy created during system specification in order to generate test suite skeletons, which must be completed by the developer/tester, and which are then run automatically. There has also been work on generating test cases based on application domain ontologies [50]. The eCAT system also uses continuous testing of the system under development, an approach that could be used with our own testing tool as well.

Another instance of deriving test cases from existing information is the work of Low *et al.* [38] which derives test cases for BDI systems based on the structure of plans. Their work investigates a range of criteria for test-case generation, and assesses the relationships between the different criteria, specifically which criteria subsume which other criteria.

Another approach is to introduce new design artefacts that contain additional details which are used in testing. For instance, the work of Caire *et al.* [11] derives test cases from (additional) detailed design artefacts called "Multi-Agent Zoomable Behaviour Descriptions" (MAZBDs), which are based on UML activity diagrams. However, user intervention is required to derive test cases from the MAZBDs.

A number of other agent development systems also have testing support subsystems, such as SUNIT [24] for SEAGENT, the JAT testing framework [13], and the testing framework of INGENIAS [28]. Testing is also discussed by Knublauch [35] and by Rouff [64]. However, all of these approaches require manual development of test cases, which may then be run automatically.

To our knowledge, our testing tool is the only agent testing system which (a) focusses on unit testing, and (b) fully automates the generation of test cases as well as the running of them.

7.2.3 Debugging

Although there is some speculation as to where the term *bug* was first used [14, 33] it is widely accepted that the term is used to describe a mistake, malfunction or error associated with a computer program. Most commonly we are able to identify that such a *bug* exists because some observed execution of a program (or observation of the recorded output of a program) does not conform with what is expected. From this we can define debugging in the following way: Debugging is the process of locating, analysing and correcting suspected errors [42].

To aid the debugging process debugging tools have been developed to help with all three of these activities. Fault localisation, which is defined by Hall *et al.* as tracing a bug to its cause [30], is seen by some as the most difficult part in debugging [34, 23, 68]. Indeed, most of the debugging support provided by debugging tools focusses on the process of localising a discovered fault. Such tools are typically tailored to a specific target programming language for which they have been designed. However, there are a number of features that one may come to expect from a debugging tool. Namely, tracing the execution of a program, defining breakpoints, and variable or memory display and manipulation. In the context of agents, a number of platforms (e.g. [48, 10, 58]) provide traditional debugging support, i.e. breakpoints, stepping through code, and an ability to display agent specific properties, such as goals and tasks.

Program tracing allows one to follow the executable program as lines in the source code are executed. This can be useful for understanding the flow of control within a program. Although, in a large search space or when long iteration sequences are being followed this can become difficult. Breakpoints are a special instruction that can be inserted into a program such that the program will halt when the instruction is reached. This is an efficient way of allowing a program to run to a specific location and then halt to allow some other debugging activity to occur from that point, for example, tracing from the breakpoint onwards, or inspecting the state of a variable and possibly changing it before continuing execution.

For effective debugging sufficient understanding and comprehension of both the implemented system and the design that the system is based on are required. It is necessary to gain sufficient understanding of these two closely related parts of system development for the purposes of identifying and resolving behaviour that is not consistent with the design specification. Developing the necessary understanding of the implemented system can, to some degree, be accomplished by performing code walkthroughs, or more formally code inspections [26]. Code inspections are incrementally applied to parts of the source code to develop the necessary understanding of the system to uncover code defects. The utility of this process has also been shown to be effective [22, 40]. However, observing the behaviour of the system as it executes is still an extremely useful and common exercise that is employed by developers to obtain a more complete understanding of the behaviour of the implemented system. One issue is that, often, there is too much information available, and it can be hard for a developer to know what to focus on when debugging.

An interesting approach to helping users understand the complex behaviours and interdependencies in applications is proposed in the Whyline framework where users are able to ask 'why?' or 'why not?' questions about observations they make while interacting with a system [45]. These questions, which are automatically derived, are typically of the form "why does property p of object o have value v?". The Whyline system recursively traverses through the operations that cause properties to take on their values and provides an answer to the question. In a user study the Whyline approach was found to be very effective in improving understanding in computer programs. However, it is not clear how generally applicable the approach is.

Another attempt at focusing the debugging task takes the approach of abstractions over the target program. This is especially important in domains such as distributed programming where the data, especially event data, can be overwhelming. By using the abstractions appropriate to developing distributed software Bates [2] has shown that a debugging system, consisting of a model builder, event models and an event recogniser can greatly reduce the amount of event information being propagated to the developer. Primitive event instances need to be defined such that they can be automatically identified in a program. Once identified the program needs to be modified to announce the event to an external component (such as the event recogniser). Models are built using an Event Description Language (EDL), as defined in [2]. With such a language one can build expressions and further abstractions over the primitive events. Instead of being informed of the primitive event data, the developer is instead alerted to the meta events defined in the models. The benefit of such an approach is a greatly reduced amount of event information. One of the major limitations of this approach is that one needs to learn the EDL and also manually define the models used for comparison. The model is built on the users' interpretation of how the system should behave, based on such things as their interpretation of potentially informal design documents. This leads to another concern that the abstractions that have been applied should not filter out any information required for a particular diagnosis. In addition the diagnosis can only be successful if the model developed is a correct representation of expected behaviour.

Other noteworthy approaches to debugging include techniques such as program slicing [69, 6], algorithmic debugging [66] and model based diagnosis [12, 41, 70] which each provide support for automating, or partially automating, the debugging process.

7.2.4 Design Artefacts

Both tools follow our central thesis, using design artefacts to assist in testing and debugging. This section briefly introduces the specific design artefacts that the tools use.

The testing tool is a generic framework that can be applied to any agent based system with appropriate models available. The models against which it analyses test output are primarily design artefacts that describe the detailed *structure* within each agent: how plans, events, and data are connected. In the context of Prometheus this information can be found in Agent and Capability Overview Diagrams (see section 7.2.4.2), as well as information regarding coverage and overlap, extracted from message descriptors (section 7.2.4.3), which is also used by the debugging tool.

In addition important information is extracted from the descriptor forms of beliefs, events and plans, regarding variables relevant to the entity, their types and value ranges, as well as potential relationships between them. For example a design descriptor of a plan to make a savings deposit, may state that there are two relevant variables: income and expenses. The relationship is that income > expenses (this is the context condition for this plan, which deposits the surplus to a savings account). Each are of type money with value range 0 to ∞.

In addition to the information obtained from design descriptors, some additional information is added specifically for the purpose of testing. This includes links between design variables and their implementation counterparts, or some other method to allow assignment of values for the different test cases. It can also include application initialisation processes necessary before testing can commence, as well as such things as stubs for other system agents necessary for testing a particular unit.

The debugging *framework* we present is generic, and can be applied to a wide range of design artefacts. However, the *tool* that we have developed (and evaluated) exploits two particular design artefact types: interaction protocols (see section 7.2.4.1), and the coverage and overlap information mentioned above.

Note that although our work has been done in the context of the Prometheus methodology [53], the approach is generic. Furthermore, the artefacts that we have chosen are ones that are common to many methodologies. Interaction protocols are used in many methodologies, and indeed, due to the adoption of Agent UML [3] by a number of methodologies, the same notation is widely used. Some form of structural diagram is used in all of the major methodologies, including Prometheus [53], MaSE [20], and Tropos [7]. On the other hand, coverage and overlap are specific details about the intent of event handling (in BDI^2 systems) that are specified in the Prometheus methodology.

In this chapter we are concerned more with using design artefacts, and less with how they are developed. We do note that methodological guidance is important, and that good tool support is invaluable in creating and, more importantly, maintaining designs. Fortunately, many methodologies provide mature tool support (e.g. [19, 43, 52]).

We now discuss each of these design artefacts in turn.

7.2.4.1 Interaction Protocols

Interaction protocols can be defined in a number of ways: as state machines [21, page 110], in which the states might express the concept of waiting for a message, and the transitions express the concept of sending/receiving a message [67]; as statecharts backed by a program logic with formal semantics [57]; as Petri nets where Petri net places specify protocol state and Petri net transitions encode message types [16, 62]; as standard UML [37], or more commonly with an extension to UML in the form of the Agent UML (AUML) notation [3].

In this chapter we focus on Petri nets: since they are simple and precisely defined they serve well as a *lingua franca* for other notations. Indeed, we have defined translations from the older version of AUML [3] into Petri nets [60], and also from the more recent version of AUML [32] into Petri nets [59, Chapter 4]. Additionally, we classify places as either *message* places, which correspond to a message in the protocol and do not have incoming transitions, or *state* places.

Petri nets are a model of procedures that support the flow of information, in particular the concurrent flow of information. A Petri net (named after Carl Adam Petri) consists of places (depicted graphically as circles) and transitions (depicted graphically as rectangles). Places and transitions are linked by arcs which indicate the relation between the elements in the net. This relation is called the *flow-relation*, and the flow-relation may only connect places to transitions and transitions to places [63].

---

^{2} Belief-Desire-Intention

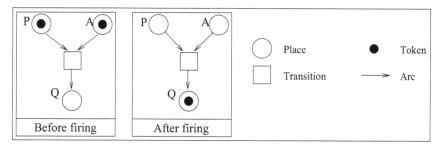

Fig. 7.1 Example of a Petri net firing

Additionally, places may contain tokens. The placement of tokens on a net is its *marking*, and executing ("firing") a Petri net consists of moving tokens around according to a simple rule; the places, transitions, and the links between them remain unchanged. A transition in a Petri net is *enabled* if each incoming place (i.e. a place with an arrow going to the transition) has at least one token. An enabled transition can be *fired* by removing a token from each incoming place and placing a token on each outgoing place (i.e. each place with an arrow from the transition to it). For example, figure 7.1 shows a very simple Petri net, the transition in this Petri net is enabled because both state P and state A are marked. The transition fires by removing a token from state A and from state P and placing a token on state Q.

In this chapter we present most of our discussions on Petri nets using this graphical notation. A formal definition is not required for this chapter, and can be found elsewhere [59].

7.2.4.2 Overview Diagrams

Prometheus captures the static structure of the system being designed using a range of overview diagrams. Specifically, there is a single System Overview Diagram which captures the overall structure of the whole system; there is an Agent Overview Diagram for each agent type in the system; and there is a Capability Overview Diagram for each capability.

These overview diagrams use a common notation where nodes represent entities in the design — with a different icon being used to distinguish between different entity type (e.g. agent, plan, protocol) — and relationships between entities are depicted using arrows between entities (optionally labelled with the nature of the relationship, where this isn't clear from context) [54]. Figure 7.2 shows the notation used, and figure 7.3 depicts an example System Overview Diagram for a conference management system.

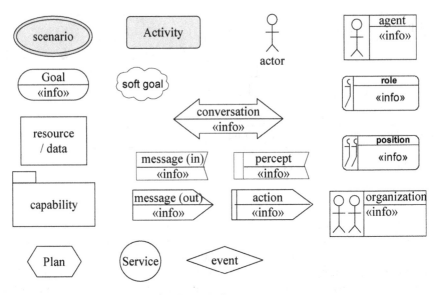

Fig. 7.2 Overview Diagram Notation (From [54])

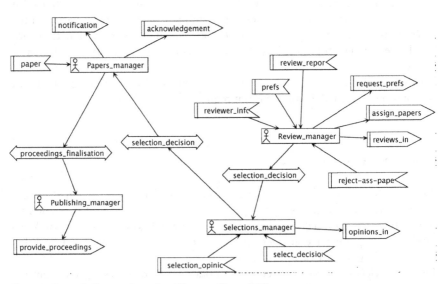

Fig. 7.3 Example System Overview Diagram (From [54])

7.2.4.3 Descriptors

The overview diagrams (system, agent, and capability) provide a graphical visualisation of the static structure of the system. As their names suggest, they are well-suited to giving a high-level overview, but they are not intended for capturing the details of entities. Instead, in Prometheus, the details of entities are captured using *descriptors*.

Each entity type has its own descriptor form, which is filled out for each instance of that type. For example, each agent (type) has its own agent descriptor form, which captures such information as how many instances of the agent type will exist at run-time, when these agent instances are created and destroyed, and what needs to be done to initialise an agent instance. For the unit testing currently covered by the testing tool, belief, plan and event descriptors are used. Much of the information from the overview diagrams is also available in the descriptor as it is automatically propagated.

Both the debugging and testing tool use information relating to coverage and overlap (defined below) which is extracted from message[3] descriptor forms.

In BDI agent systems such as JACK [10], JAM [31], and Jadex [58] in which agents select an appropriate pre-defined plan from a plan library, one common cause of errors is incorrectly specifying when a plan should be selected by the agent for execution. This often results in one of two situations: either there is no plan suitable to respond to a given goal or event, resulting in the goal not being attempted or the event not being reacted to; or alternatively there may be multiple suitable plans, and the one chosen is not the one intended[4].

The Prometheus methodology prompts the developer to consider how many plans are expected to be suitable for each event type in all possible situations. For each event the developer is asked to specify whether it is ever expected that either multiple plans will be applicable[5], or that no plans will be applicable. Two concepts are introduced within Prometheus in order to facilitate this consideration. They are *coverage* and *overlap*. Having full coverage specifies that the event is expected to have at least one applicable plan found under all circumstances. Overlap specifies that it is possible, although not required, that multiple plans are applicable at the time the event occurs.

Full coverage means that the context conditions of the plans that are relevant for the event must not have any "holes". An example of an unintended hole that can occur is if two plans are specified for an event, one with context $temperature < 0°$ and the other with context $temperature > 0°$. $Temperature = 0°$ is then a "hole" and if that is the situation when the event occurs, no plan will be applicable. If at design time the developer specifies that an event type has full coverage, and yet at run-time a situation occurs when there is no applicable plan for an event of that type, then an error can be reported.

---

[3] Prometheus views events as being "internal messages".

[4] Both these situations may occur legitimately, however, they are sometimes an indication of a problem.

[5] A plan is *applicable* if its context condition is true at the current time.

For an event to have *no overlap* requires that the context conditions of plans relevant for that event are mutually exclusive. If overlap is intended, the developer is prompted to specify whether plans should be tried in a particular order, and if so how that will be accomplished. Overlap can occur when multiple plan types are applicable or when a single plan can result in multiple versions of itself based on the variable assignments that may occur during plan initialisation. For example, in JACK if there is more than one way to satisfy a context method's logical expression, there will be multiple instances of the plan that are applicable. One applicable instance will be generated for each set of bindings that satisfy the context condition. The developer is also prompted at design time to specify which of these situations is expected if overlap is possible.

7.3 Testing Tool Description

The testing tool that we have developed does automated generation and execution of test cases. Test cases cover the internals of agents. In order to do so we need to make some assumptions about how the agents are structured internally, and we assume that agents are designed and implemented in terms of the BDI architecture, that is that agents consist internally of event-triggered plans and beliefs (as well as capabilities [9], a modularisation construct introduced by JACK). In terms of design artefacts, we use the Prometheus structural overview diagrams and descriptor forms, but the information that we require could also be extracted from the sorts of information provided by other methodologies, or from the code itself.

The approach followed aims to support a "test as you go" approach to unit testing of the building blocks within an individual agent, as the developer moves from design to code. There are of necessity some constraints in that it does not make sense to test units which have dependencies on other units, before those units themselves have been tested. Consequently ordering of testing of units is an important part of the tool, and units which are depended on must be tested (and therefore developed) before those depending on them, or at least, they must be appropriately stubbed.

As was indicated in section 7.2.4 the basic units being tested are beliefs, plans and events. There are some nuances, as discussed in [71], but the dependencies are essentially that:

- a plan is dependent on beliefs that it accesses, on subgoals/events/messages that it posts, and on anything on which these subgoals/events/messages are dependent;
- an event/subgoal/message is dependent on plans that it triggers and all that these plans are dependent on;
- beliefs are independent of other units;
- cycles must be treated as a unit, as described in [71].

If testing all units within something such as a capability, or an agent (or any collection of units), an initial step is to generate the appropriate testing order for these units. Following this each unit is tested individually, by running a suite of automatically generated (or user defined) test cases. If a sufficiently serious error is encountered, no further testing will be attempted for units which depend on the unit for which an error was detected.

The focus of the testing tool is to *automatically* generate and run a sufficiently comprehensive set of tests for each unit. However, there are cases where developers want, or need, to specify specific test cases, and this is also supported. User defined test cases are stored, and combined with system generated test cases each time testing is done.

The overview of the testing process, using our tool, is as follows:

1. The user selects a set of units for test (often all units within a particular capability or agent).
2. Using the information available in the capability and agent overview models, the testing tool determines test case order.
3. Following the testing order, each unit is augmented with code to provide appropriate information to the testing system, and placed within the *subsystem under test*.
4. Units on which the *unit under test* is dependent are placed into the subsystem under test, with code augmented if needed.
5. Appropriate combinations of variable values are generated to adequately test the unit, using heuristics to reduce the number of cases as appropriate (see [71] for details).
6. The environment is initialised and a test cases for the unit is run for each set of variable values identified.
7. The data collected is analysed, and errors and warnings are recorded for the report.
8. Following completion of all tests on all units, a report is generated, providing both an overview and details. Problems are classified as either errors, or warnings.

Figure 7.4 shows an abstract view of the testing framework for a plan unit. It has two distinct components, the *test-driver* and the *subsystem under test*. The test-driver component contains the test-agent, testing specific message-events that are sent to and from the test-agent, and a plan (test-driver plan) that initiates the testing process, and also sends certain results back to the testing agent. This plan is embedded into the subsystem under test as part of the code augmenting process. The *subsystem under test* is the portion of the system that is needed for testing of the *unit under test* and includes the units on which it depends.

Figure 7.4 illustrates the steps in the testing process for a plan: the *test-agent* generates the test cases, and runs each test case by sending an activation message to the *test-driver plan*; the *test-driver plan* sets up the input and activates the subsystem under test that executes and sends information (via specially inserted code)

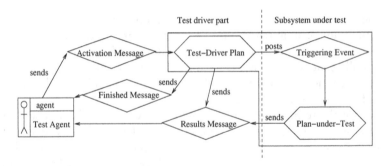

Fig. 7.4 Abstract Testing Framework for a Plan

back to the *test-agent*; when testing is complete the *test-agent* generates an HTML report providing both a summary and details of the testing results.

7.3.1 Errors detected

As described earlier, our testing tool tests each belief, plan, and event, to ascertain whether, across a range of testing values, they behave as expected, based on the agent paradigm used, and on the specific application models, as exemplified in the relevant agent and capability overviews, as well as the descriptors. We list here the kind of errors that we are able to detect in the testing tool.

Plan errors

- **Plan is never executed.** If a plan is included in a system as one option for responding to an event/goal, one would expect to observe that it is used in some situations, if there is sufficient sampling of the state space. If when testing an event, some plan that is specified as triggered by that event never executes, then this is reported as a warning. This error is often caused by an incorrectly specified context condition of this plan, or another plan handling the same event. This can cause both to evaluate to true, unintentionally, and due to declaration order the other plan is always selected.

  This is however a warning only, as it is possible that the plan is developed only for use as a backup, if the intended plan (perhaps non-deterministically) fails. Also it is possible that despite an effort to cover the state space, a variable combination that would cause the context condition to evaluate to True was not selected. In this case, on reading the test report the developer/tester should add a test case which will ensure that the plan is chosen.

- **Context condition is never valid.** If a context condition never evaluates to True, this is an indication that there is a problem. However, it is reported only as a warning, as it may be the case that (as above) the system, despite its efforts, did not choose the correct set of variable values. As above, an appropriate test case should then be manually added.

- **Missing subtasks or messages.** If there are events specified in the design to be generated from a plan, but these are not seen in any test case run, then this is likely to be an error. As above it is however possible that suitable values have not been chosen, in which case a test case should be manually added.
- **Plan does not complete.** While it is difficult to determine whether a plan completes successfully or not, we can at least determine whether the plan executed to completion. If the plan does not complete then there is an error.[6]

Event errors

- **Failure to handle the event.** If there is a test case for an event where the event has no applicable plan, then this indicates that there are gaps in what we call *coverage*. That is, there are some situations where there is no applicable plan to handle this event. This may be intended, but is in fact a very common cause of errors in agent programs. In the design descriptors for events in the Prometheus Design Tool (PDT), the developer notes whether coverage is intended. If it is, then this is a definite error. If not a warning is still generated to allow the developer to check that the lack of coverage was intended.
- **Multiple applicable plans.** It is common that there are multiple applicable plans for handling an event. At design time this needs to be considered to ensure correct precedence in selection (if this matters). If the developer has indicated that *overlap* (the existence of multiple applicable plans in some situations) is not intended, then this is an error. A warning is always generated to allow easy checking of whether the overlap was intended, as this is a common cause of problems in practice. Unintended overlap easily results in a different plan being selected than that intended.

Belief errors

- **Failure of basic operations.** Basic operations of *insert, update, delete* and *modify* should work as expected. The testing framework attempts each of these operations on the beliefset and checks that the expected result holds using a beliefset query.
- **Failure to post specified events.** Beliefsets can be specified to generate automatic events based on the basic behaviours of insert, modify, delete and update. If an event is not posted as expected, this is an error.
- **Posting of an event even if the corresponding beliefset operation fails.** If for some reason a particular beliefset operation fails (e.g. insert may fail if the belief to be inserted already exists), then an automated event based on this operation should not be generated. If it is, then this is an error.

The testing system currently only deals with testing of beliefs that are part of the agent's explicit beliefset structure. In fact any arbitrary data can represent aspects

---

[6] When deployed, a plan may well fail due to some change in the environment after the time it was selected. However, in the controlled testing situation where there are no external changes, a plan that does not complete properly (due to failure at some step) should not have been selected.

of the agent's beliefs, but these are not currently tested, other than as they are used by plans.

Faults identified (or possible faults) are categorised into different levels in order to specify the effect that they should have with regard to running an entire test suite. If a definite error is identified within a particular unit, there is no point testing other units dependent on it, and all such scheduled tests should be aborted until the problem is fixed. However if a warning is identified, this may be simply because suitable test cases have not been identified. The user can specify whether they wish the testing to continue or to abort in such situations, with regard to dependent units.

7.3.2 Test case input

An aim of testing is to generate a range of test cases that adequately covers the entire space of situations that can be encountered. Specifying a comprehensive set of test cases for each unit is tedious and time consuming, and so we have automated this in an attempt to obtain good coverage. However, we also allow for specification of specific test cases by the developer/tester. Once specified these are stored and always used when the unit is tested, in addition to those automatically generated.

The test cases are comprised of combinations of relevant variable values, which must then be initialised within the environment of the unit to be tested, or must be part of the input to the test. Relevant variables include those within an event, those referenced in a plan's context condition or body, and those within a beliefset. We require the design documentation for a particular unit to identify the variables that affect that unit, as well as a mapping to enable values to be assigned to these variables during the testing process.

In order to generate the value combinations that define the different test cases, we employ the following steps:

1. Variable extraction from the design documents.
2. Generation of equivalence classes within the input range of each variable.
3. Generation of combinations of the equivalence classes using a heuristic to reduce the number of different combinations.
4. Generation of specific input values.

Values that are within the specified range for a particular variable we call *valid* values, while ones outside the specified range we call *invalid*. We test using both valid and invalid values, under the assumption that the system should gracefully degrade in the presence of invalid input, rather than crash.

Partitioning into equivalence classes [56, p.67] [5, p.401] allows us to obtain groupings of values where it is assumed that any value in the group will be processed similarly. We use standard techniques to create equivalence class structures with five fields:[7]

---

[7] More complete details are available in [71].

1. *var-name*: The name of the variable.
2. *index*: A unique identifier.
3. *domain*: An open interval or a concrete value.
4. *validity*: Whether the domain is valid or invalid.
5. *sample*: A sample value from the domain: if the domain is an open interval (e.g. (0.0, $+\infty$)), it is a random value in this interval (e.g 778); if the domain is a concrete value (x = 3), it is this value.

As the number of all possible combinations of equivalence classes can be very large, we use combinatorial design [15]. to generate a reduced set of value combinations that cover all n-wise (n$\geq$2) interactions among the test parameters and their values. We use the CTS (Combinational Testing Service) software library of Hartman and Raskin[8] which implements this approach. Where viable, we do however ensure that all combinations of valid data are used to increase the likelihood that all options through the code are exercised.

7.3.3 *The testing report*

Once a suite of test cases have been run an HTML report is generated to allow the developer/tester to view the test results. The overview lists the agent that the units tested belong to, the number of units tested for that agent, the number of faults found and whether they were warnings or errors. The summaries for each unit can then be accessed via a link, and figure 7.5 shows an example of such a summary for the plan "Book_Query". As shown in figure 7.5 it is then possible to review the specific values for the problematic test cases, in order to assess modifications needed. In some cases, as for the second fault in "Book_Query", there is not a specific test case which causes the problem, but rather the fault arises from an analysis across the range of test cases. In this example "Book_Query" is specified to post the message "Check_Category". This means that in some situation such a message would be posted by this plan. If in the set of test cases generated to cover the range of values of variables, the message is never posted, it is an indication either that there is an error, or that a suitable test case has not been generated to exercise this posting. Sometimes, by providing an appropriate test case, such faults can be eliminated.

7.3.4 *Evaluation*

An initial validation of the testing tool has been done using the case study of the *Electronic Bookstore* system as described in [53]. The *Stock Manager* agent was implemented according to the design specified, and then deliberately seeded with a range of faults, such as failing to post an expected message. Examples of each

---

[8] http://www.alphaworks.ibm.com/tech/cts

AGENT TEST REPORT

Agent Description:

> Agent under test : Stock_Manager
>
> # of Units: 4
>
> Log Dir: (link)

Test Overview: (click a unit name to review its unit test report)

List of units in which errors occur: (#:1)

#	Unit	Unit Type	# of test cases	# of faults	comment
3	Query_Book	plan	27	2	Error: The plan fails in following test cases: Case.4, Case.8, Case.12, Case.16, Case.25, Case.27 *Click on cases to obtain details*
					Warning: No message is posted at run-time! (Outgoing messages specified in design: Check_Category)

UNIT TEST REPORT

Test Case.4---- (back to: cases list, test summary, top)
   Input:

#	variable name	type	sample value	is legal	domain	index of Equivalence class
1	Keyword	string	null	false	null	1
2	BookCate	BookCategory	"history"	true	"history"	1
3	Price	int	200	true	200.0	4

The value of Context Condition: true

The Plan FAILS

Test Case.27---- (back to: cases list, test summary, top)
   Input:

#	variable name	type	sample value	is legal	domain	index of Equivalence class
1	Keyword	string	"math"	true	"math"	2
2	BookCate	BookCategory	"science"	true	"science"	2
3	Price	int	200	true	200.0	4

The value of Context Condition: true

The Plan FAILS

Fig. 7.5 Example of portions of testing report

of the kinds of faults discussed above, were introduced into the *Stock Manager* agent; for instance, the *Stock Manager* agent is designed with the plan *Out of stock response*, which posts the subtask *Decide supplier*, if the default supplier is out of stock and the number of books ordered is not greater than 100. The code was modified so that the condition check never returned true, resulting in the *Decide supplier* subtask never being posted. The testing framework generator automatically generated the testing framework for the testable units of the *Stock Manager*, and then executed the testing process for each unit following the sequence determined by the testing-order algorithm. For each unit, the testing framework ran one test suite, which was composed of a set of test cases, with each case having as input one of the value combinations determined. Further details and examples are described in [71]. All faults were successfully found by the tool, which generated a total of 252 test cases.

We are currently in the process of doing a more thorough evaluation, using a number of programs with design models, developed as part of a class on Agent Programming and Design. Once this is completed we will be able to comment on the kind of faults identified and the relationship of these to errors identified during marking the assignments. We have also evaluated the testing system on a demonstration program developed for teaching purposes. In this program 22 units were tested with 208 automatically generated test cases. This uncovered 2 errors where messages were not posted as specified in the design (apparently due to unfinished coding), and one error where certain data caused an exception to be thrown, due to a certain input data type that can not currently be handled by the testing tool (the tool is under improvement to solve this issue). This program had been tested by its developer, so the results of this testing process would seem to indicate that the generation and execution of automated test cases were effective in uncovering bugs in the system.

However the testing tool is limited in what it tests for. It does not currently test for any higher level functionality, such as agent interaction according to specified processes, or the satisfactory following of scenarios as specified during requirements. We plan to add these aspects of testing in future work. Our debugging tool (described in the next section) should be able to be combined with automated generation of variable values and a test harness, to realise focussed interaction testing.

7.4 Debugging Tool Description

In this section we describe the debugging tool. We begin (section 7.4.1) by describing the debugging framework which the tool instantiates. We then discuss the types of bugs that can occur in interactions (section 7.4.2) before proceeding to discuss how interactions are monitored (section 7.4.3) and how erroneous interactions can be identified (section 7.4.4) and reported (section 7.4.5).

7.4.1 Architecture of the Debugging Framework

The debugging framework that we have developed uses the design artefacts, applying to them a process to produce debugging components to facilitate the automatic debugging of agent systems. The debugging framework is based on the premise that we can utilise the system design artefacts as a partial specification of correct system behaviour. We describe this framework in terms of the processes that are applied as well as the underlying debugging infrastructure required to support the observation of the system, comparison of the system against the developed debugging artefacts, and the reporting of the system to the user.

Figure 7.6 provides an overview of our debugging framework. This consists of a set of debugging components, framed with a solid line and annotated with C1, C2, and so on, that together represent the run-time debugging environment. In addition to the debugging components are a set of processes, framed with a broken line and annotated with P1, P2, and so on, that represent the processes that need to be applied to generate the debugging components.

The run-time system (C1) in the center of the figure depicts the agent system that is the focus of the debugging exercise. It is developed using the system design artefacts (P1). During execution the run-time system sends information to one or more monitoring components (C3). The monitoring components are supplied by a library of debugging artefacts that specify correct system behaviour (C2). The debugging artefacts represent a partial model of correct behaviour that is generated by following processes P1 through P3.

The processes in the debugging framework specify how to develop a suitable debugging component from a system design artefact. Each of the design artefacts from the set of system design artefacts (P1) are considered. From these we identify and select suitable design artefacts that could be used as debugging components (P2). From the identified artefacts we develop a partial model of correct system behaviour. This requires that we develop a machine interpretable format for the design artefacts (P3). Each of the developed debugging artefacts feed into the library of debugging artefacts that is used in the monitoring component for run-time debugging.

The monitoring components are where the comparison between actual system behaviour and expected system behaviour is carried out. Before such a comparison can be carried out we must determine a method for extracting the relevant run-time information from the run-time system that should be sent to the monitoring components. The necessary information is identified and the source code is instrumented (P4) so that when certain events of interest occur in the system they are forwarded onto the monitoring components for consideration. Once the system has been modified to send the relevant information it can be compared to the debugging artefact and then a report can be sent to the user via the user interface in (C4).

In this chapter we focus our attention on two important design artefacts, *Interaction Protocols* for detecting interaction related bugs and *Event Descriptors* for detecting incorrect interactions between events and plans (as discussed in section 7.2.4.3).

The debugging *framework* is generic: it does not make any assumptions about agent architectures or implementation platforms. However, when instantiating the framework in a tool, we must select design artefacts, and the choice may result in assumptions about the agent architecture. For example, debugging incorrect interactions between events and plans assumes that agents are implemented in terms of these concepts, i.e. that a BDI-like platform is used. On the other hand, no as-

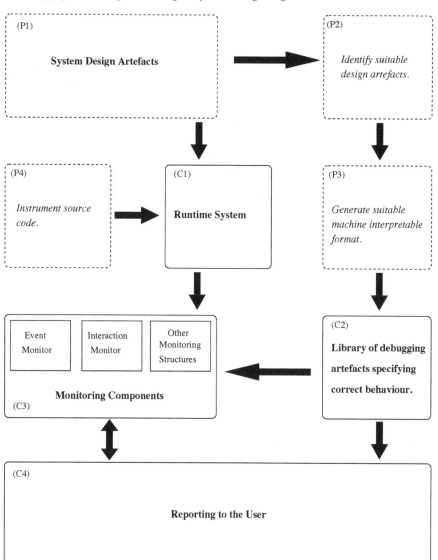

Fig. 7.6 Debugging Framework

sumptions about the agent architecture are required in order to debug interaction related bugs.

This framework forms the foundations of our approach to debugging multi-agent system. Before we move forward and discuss the generation of the different debugging artefacts we will first provide a review of the types of bugs that we will expect to resolve.

7.4.2 Types of Bugs

Interaction related bugs, where agents at run-time do not interact with each other as expected, are a common source of problems in multi-agent systems. Following is a discussion of several types of interaction related bugs that we have identified as being characteristic in multi-agent systems.

- **Sending the wrong message:**
  We define the sending the wrong message bug as the act of an agent sending a message that is not appropriate given the current expectations as defined by the protocol.
  This bug represents the case where the protocol requires an agent to send message $m1$ but instead some other message, $m2$, is sent. Typically $m2$ is a message that is valid at some other point in the protocol, but it may also be a message that is never valid in the protocol that the agents are meant to be following.

- **Failure to send a message:**
  We define failure to send a message as the act of an agent failing to send a message when the protocol required that one be sent.
  Failing to send a message when one is expected is often symptomatic of a failure in some part of the agent system. When developing the agent goals and plans the requirements of the protocols are considered. Failure to respond according to the protocol can be an indication that the agent or some part of the agent has stopped functioning correctly.

- **Sending a message to the wrong recipient:**
  We define sending a message to the wrong recipient as the act of sending a message to an agent that is not the intended recipient as specified by the protocol design.
  When sending a message to another agent the receiver is chosen and explicitly referenced in the message header. If at run-time the message is sent to a different agent than that specified in the design this is incorrect. The wrong recipient may be wrong based on the agent role that received the message, or could be wrong based on the agent bindings that may have already occurred in a conversation.

- **Sending the same message multiple times:**
  We define sending the same message multiple times as the act of an agent incorrectly sending the same message multiple times when only one message should have been sent.
  When an agent wishes to send a message to another agent it should do so only once, unless the interaction protocol or some other logic dictates otherwise.

If the same message is sent multiple times it is possible that the message will be processed by the receiving agent multiple times. Doing so could result in incorrect or unexpected behaviour. For instance if a customer agent sends a message to purchase goods from a merchant multiple times, it is likely that the merchant will also process the order multiple times, sending more than one order.

Although sending a message more than once may seem to be unlikely, it is, in fact, behaviour that can arise due to the failure handling mechanism used by a range of BDI systems. In such systems it is common to have a number of different ways of achieving the goals that the agent adopts. The choice of plan is made at run-time and it is inside these plans that the messages are created and transmitted to other agents. The plan failure mechanism within these systems enables the agent to select alternative plans if a plan fails to achieve the goal for which it is selected. If the same plan can be retried after a message is sent but before the goal is achieved, or if alternative plans can be tried that send the same message upon failure then unless care is taken it is possible that the agent is unaware that it might have sent the same message multiple times.

7.4.3 Monitoring Interactions

We now discuss how we use derived Petri net protocols to monitor and provide useful information about the interactions occurring between agents to support the debugging of multi-agent systems. We present the *Interaction Monitor*: an instance of the abstract Monitoring component discussed in section 7.4.1. The Interaction Monitor is responsible for processing messages that are exchanged within the system by modelling the messages as conversations within the Petri net protocols. In addition to the mechanics of the Petri nets, the Interaction Monitor utilises a number of other processes and algorithms to determine the correctness of the messages exchanged in the monitored system.

Following this, we describe how the Interaction Monitor detects the bug types which we have identified. Each of the bug types that were introduced in section 7.4.2 are discussed. Reporting the results of the Interaction Monitor is carried out by a reporting interface that we have developed as part of our Debugging Toolkit. The reporting interface is a basic prototype tool that we use to convey the results of the Interaction Monitor to the developer.

Modelling and processing conversations occurs within the debugging framework introduced in section 7.4.1. Figure 7.7 shows an abstract view of the Interaction Monitor which is responsible for debugging agent interactions in a deployed multi-agent system. The Interaction Monitor is responsible for processing messages within the Petri net protocols for the purpose of detecting erroneous interactions. It is composed of a message queue that is used to store the incoming messages while an existing message is being processed, and a Conversation List which contains the set of active conversations. Messages are removed from the

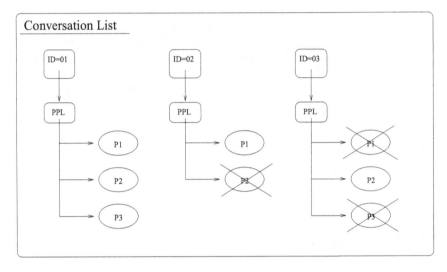

Fig. 7.7 Overview of the Interaction Monitor.

message queue and partitioned into conversations based on the conversation id
that is included with each message[9].

When a message is removed from the queue the conversation id is inspected. The
first step in processing the message is to determine which conversation it belongs
to. If the conversation id matches any active conversations then the message is
directed to the respective conversation. If, however, the conversation id is not
matched to a conversation a new conversation is initialised.

We construct a conversation list which is used to hold all of the active conversations occurring in the multi-agent system. Each conversation is comprised of
a conversation id, a Possible Protocol List (PPL), and a role map (not shown in
figure 7.7) which is used to map agent instances with role types and is used to
reason about role related bugs. The PPL contains an instantiation of each of the
protocols that *could* be the protocol that the agents are using to direct their conversation. We need the PPL because we do not require that the agents include the
name of the protocol when sending messages to one another, and take the view
that each protocol in the PPL is potentially the protocol that the agents are fol-

---

[9] The agents are required to create new conversation ids for new conversations, and then to
include the relevant conversation id with each message.

lowing. When a message sequence violates a protocol we mark it as in error and continue to process any other remaining possible protocols.

Initially the conversation list is empty. Upon removing a message from the message queue a conversation is created and the message is modelled in the conversation. If a conversation already exists, because the currently dequeued message shares the same conversation id as a previously received message, then the message is added to that conversation. Adding a message to a conversation is done by adding it to each of the protocols in the PPL. The message is simulated as a token in the Petri nets and the Petri nets are fired to enable any valid transitions. The protocols are then checked for errors and if necessary the user is alerted.

The following summarises the monitoring procedure that we use to detect protocol related errors. Below we discuss the details for steps 1, 2, 6, and 8. Steps 3, 4, 5, 7 and 11 are trivial and do not require further discussion. Step 9 is covered in section 7.4.4 and step 10 is discussed in section 7.4.5.

```
 1  intercept a message;
 2  add message to queue;
 3  while message queue is not empty do
 4  |   remove message from head of queue;
 5  |   if message does not belong to an existing conversation then
 6  |   |   initialise a new conversation;
 7  |   end
 8  |   add message to each protocol in the PPL for the relevant conversation
    |   and fire Petri nets;
 9  |   check for errors;
10  |   report errors if necessary;
11  end
```

7.4.3.1 Intercepting Messages (steps 1 and 2)

The Interaction Monitor needs to receive a copy of every message that is transmitted in the system that it monitors. The mechanism for sending a copy of the message to the Interaction Monitor will be platform dependent. However, the technique of overloading which we use in our JACK prototype should be generally applicable. We overload the JACK send method so that each time it is invoked a message is also sent to the Interaction Monitor. This approach does not intrude on the developer, nor does it complicate the source code that the developer works with.

The overhead in relation to the number of messages transmitted in the system is for every message sent, a copy of the message is also sent to the Interaction Monitor. If the target system is highly timing dependent then the additional messages being transmitted and the additional time taken to transmit a carbon copy of messages may affect the system's behaviour. This is a standard concern with adding debugging support to timing dependent systems. The benefit of the debugging support will need to be considered in terms of the possibility of adversely affecting the execution of the system. However, given that multi-agent systems are designed to function with often unknown numbers of agents, and hence unknown numbers of messages, this overhead should not prove a problem in any but the most sensitive systems.

7.4.3.2 Initialising a Conversation (step 6)

Initialising a new conversation is primarily concerned with identifying and setting up the Petri net protocols so that the conversation can be modelled. A given message may require the initialisation of multiple interaction protocols, depending on the number of protocols for which the start message matches. Further, the starting message of a protocol is not guaranteed to be unique: for example, both the *Contract Net* protocol and the *Iterated Contract Net* protocol have a *cfp* message as their starting message.

The process for creating a new conversation involves searching the Protocol Library for all correct protocols that could possibly be used to model the conversation. The protocols that will be used to model the conversation will be the protocols that have an initial message that matches the message type of the sent message m. We define an initial message as any message in a protocol from the Protocol Library where the message place in the Petri net has an outgoing transition that is also an outgoing transition of the start state (recall that the start state is the only non-message state that has no incoming transitions). For example, in figure 7.8, *request* is an initial message because it shares an outgoing transition (T1) with the start place (A). Note that identifying the initial messages for each protocol can be computed in advance.

The Interaction Monitor creates a copy of each matching protocol (i.e. one with an initial message that matches the dequeued message) initialises the protocol by placing a token on its start place, and adds the protocol to the PPL of the conversation.

7.4.3.3 Add Message and Fire Petri Nets (step 8)

After a conversation has been initialised, and the PPL contains at least one protocol, the currently dequeued message is added to each of the Petri nets in the PPL. The message place matching the dequeued message is identified and a token is created and deposited onto the place. The Petri net is *fired* to allow for any enabled transition to fire and the tokens are removed and deposited in the standard method for Petri nets.

Messages will be processed inside the Petri net in this manner until either an error is detected or the Petri net protocol terminates successfully. A conversation is said to have successfully terminated if all tokens in the net reside on a final state place. A final state place is any state place that is not an input to any transition. When one of the valid protocols terminates successfully the conversation is marked as successfully terminating, indicating that no errors were detected in the protocol. Given that the PPL may contain other currently valid protocols, it is possible that after one protocol terminates successfully there are other protocols that are not in error but also are not complete. Any further messages received in a conversation that has an already terminated protocol will still be processed inside the other relevant protocols, and in the event that one of these protocols results in an error this will be indicated to the user.

7.4.4 Identifying Erroneous Interactions

The reason for processing messages inside Petri nets is to identify erroneous situations. For example, if a wrong message is sent we would want to identify this and report it accordingly. Identifying information such as this is precisely how we use the Petri net models of agent interactions to assist in debugging interactions. We can determine the state of a Petri net protocol by considering the distribution of tokens over places. Inspection of the Petri net can indicate, among other things, the current state of the conversation and the next valid message. This is an important property that we leverage to help identify errors, and provide useful debugging information. The various methods that we employ to identify errors will be the subject of this section.

We now discuss the following three cases:

1. Observing a wrong message (which includes sending a message multiple times)
2. Failure to observe a message
3. Role-related errors (including situations where the message is correct, but the recipient or sender is the wrong agent)

7.4.4.1 Observing a Wrong Message

Sending the wrong message is characterised by an agent sending a message that is not valid. There are two main cases that we focus on: (A) the message not being valid in the protocol at all, and (B) the message not being valid at the current time (because of the previous messages that have been sent). Case (A) is detected by identifying that the message does not match any messages in any of the protocols in the PPL. Case (B) is identified when the message does not successfully fire any transitions in any protocol.

We now consider case (B), where the message is valid in the protocol but is not valid given the current state of the protocol. We begin this discussion starting from the protocol state represented by figure 7.8. At this point the *participant* agent has agreed to perform the required task. Consider what happens if the next message sent and subsequently received into the Petri net is a *refuse* message. A token will be generated and the *refuse* message place will be located and a token deposited onto it. When the Petri net fires no transition is enabled. For a transition to fire there would need to be a token on state place *B*, which would enable transition *T2*. The conversation has already transitioned beyond this state, hence, the addition of the message does not trigger any transitions.

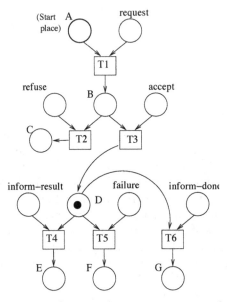

Fig. 7.8 Modelling a conversation following the FIPA request protocol.

We use the following logic to determine that this behaviour indicates an error in the conversation: when a token is deposited onto a message place the token represents the receipt of a message. If the message is valid, based on the current state of the conversation, a transition should be enabled to advance the protocol into a subsequent valid state. If no transition is enabled the message must not have been valid. Therefore, if after adding the message token and checking for enabled transitions (firing the net), a token still resides on a message place it can be concluded that the message was sent at the wrong time. As discussed previously the protocol is marked as in error but the conversation only reports an error if no error-free protocols remain in the PPL.

In addition to identifying the error we can also identify the set of valid messages based on the current marking of the Petri net. We identify the valid messages by locating any message place that shares an outgoing transition with any state place that contains a token. For example, in figure 7.8 both *failure* and *inform-result* share an outgoing transition with state place D, and hence are valid messages.

7.4.4.2 Failure to Observe a Message

Thus far, we have described error detection based on receipt of messages. The Interaction Monitor receives a message and determines if it is valid based on the current state of the conversation. This process will not identify conditions in which an agent has failed to act, rather than acted in the wrong way. In terms of interaction modelling, this problem is characterised by an agent not sending a message that it was expected to send.

In a framework based on observations, we need to consider the issue of observing something that does *not* happen. To enable this we need to redefine our semantics of observation, from those in which the observer waits forever for an event to occur, to one in which the observer waits for an event to occur over a specific time period. Under such conditions an observer can make assertions such as over time period t, event e has not been observed to have occurred.

When developing an interaction protocol there is an expectation that if an agent receives a message it will reply with an appropriate message. Yet, although protocols can be specified with deadlines for message transmission this feature is often not used[10]. The reason that time limits are not imposed on the replying agent is that there is an expectation that the agent will reply as soon as is practicable. Given that agents can engage in multiple dialogues, waiting for a reply in one conversation does not have an impact on executing another. There is, however, an expectation that the reply will be made in a *reasonable* time.

Identifying when a failure has occurred requires that we both determine a time frame for each message and devise a method for determining when the time frame has been exceeded. The first problem is one that should be considered by the developers of the system. If one wishes to have support for identifying when a message is not sent, then, effort must be expended to determine the timing constraints on the interactions. Each protocol, or if desired, each protocol state, must have a duration added. The time limit will indicate the duration that the Interaction Monitor will use to determine if a message has been received.

To support the detection of a failure to send a message we add timer support to the Interaction Monitor. The state places of the Petri net protocols (representing the state the conversation is in) have a timer added such that whenever a token is deposited the timer is triggered. When a valid message for the current state of the conversation is received a transition is enabled and the token that was marking the state is removed and a new token is generated on another state place. The removal of the token from the state place stops the timer indicating that the message has advanced the state of the conversation. If a timer expires it is inferred that a mes-

---

[10] Auction protocols are a notable exception, however only the initial *propose* message has a deadline.

sage that should have been sent has not been sent, hence the error: failure to send a message.

In the event that a timer does expire the Interaction Monitor is able to report the current state of the conversation and can indicate the next valid messages. However, instead of reporting an error, a warning is reported. We view the failure to send a message as a warning rather than an error because it is possible that too short a timer has been set. In the early stages of development the timing characteristics of the system may not be well understood and may require refinement. By reporting a warning we are able to alert the developers to possible problems for investigation.

In terms of processing messages into the protocols stored in the Possible Protocols List, those protocols that have been marked as a warning are handled differently to a protocol that has been marked as an error. When a conversation is considered to be in error no more messages are delivered to the Petri net. In the case of a warning, messages are still delivered and processed by the Petri net. If a message that was previously marked as not being received subsequently arrives then the status of the Petri net will be changed to reflect that the conversation has returned to an active, valid state. Or in the case that the message was invalid, the protocol can then be marked with an error.

7.4.4.3 Role-related Errors

During the initialisation phase we also assign agent instances to roles for each of the protocols in the PPL. The protocols are specified with role types and each role type is associated with a set of messages that it can send and a set of messages that it can receive. By mapping agent instances to roles in this way we are then in a position to identify certain role related errors.

Roles are assigned to agent instances based on the contents of the header of the initial message that triggered the creation of a new conversation. The sending agent, whose name appears in the sender field of the message header, is mapped to the role that triggers the conversation. The recipient of the message, whose name appears in the recipient field, is mapped to the role that receives the message in the protocol. Once roles have been mapped to agent instances any message that appears in the conversation will only be considered valid if it first matches the role mapping. We consider the information relating to both the sender and the recipient of a message when performing the role checks. In the event that there are more than two roles in a protocol the role map will not be completely assigned after the first message is sent. Subsequent messages will be used to assign any unmapped roles.

To illustrate the role mapping consider the situation where the Interaction Monitor receives a *propose* message that was sent from agent A to agent B. In this example there is only one protocol that matches the *propose* message. The messages that are valid for the initiator are:

$\langle$ *initiator* $\Rightarrow$ *propose* $\rangle$

The messages that are valid for the participant are:

⟨ *participant* ⇒ *accept, refuse, failure , inform-done, inform-result* ⟩

Since we are in the initialisation phase we simply map the agents to the roles for this protocol. Agent *A* is mapped to the *initiator* role and agent *B* is mapped to the *participant* role. For all subsequent messages that are exchanged in this conversation the role map is queried to verify that the sender and receiver fields in the message header match those that have been defined in the role mapping. Or if roles are appearing for the first time the agent instances are mapped and added to the role map.

The role mapping procedure supports the mapping of agent instances to multiple roles within the same conversation. This is achieved by allowing a one to many association in the mapping procedure which allows agent instances to play multiple roles. Since role mappings are done at the conversation level there is no restriction placed on which roles an agent plays in different conversations. For example, an agent can play an initiator in one conversation and a participant in another.

Having developed a procedure for mapping agent instances to roles we are in a position to identify certain errors to do with the sending and receiving of messages. We had previously stated that the rule for depositing a token into the net was to locate the message place that matched the received message and generate a token on that place. However, once the message place has been located a further check is performed to ensure that the agent that sent the message was permitted to send it, and that the recipient is permitted to receive it. This is the verification of the role assignments.

Using the role map we can identify two different errors. Sending a message to the wrong agent, and the wrong agent sending a message. Both are identified in the same manner. After the first message from each role has been sent any further messages must conform to the (possibly partial) mapping established. When a message is received the sender and receiver are extracted from the message and compared against the role map. If either of the two fields conflict with what is stored in the mapping no token is generated for the Petri net. Instead, the Petri net is marked as being in error for either sending a message to the wrong recipient, or the wrong agent sending a message.

7.4.5 Reporting Errors

When an interaction is found to be in error it is necessary to communicate this fact to the developer. In reporting errors (or warnings) we include a range of information such as which protocol was being followed, which agent instances were mapped to which roles, and the point at which a conversation diverged from the allowed behaviour. This information can assist in locating the underlying error in the agent code that is the cause of a bug.

The examples in this section are from the meeting scheduler application which was used for evaluation (see section 7.5.1 for details).

We have developed a simple prototype interface to display information about the status of active and completed conversations that occur in the deployed multi-agent system. The prototype interface also reports coverage and overlap errors. The user interface provides a collection of tabbed text areas, one for each conversation. Each of the conversation panels displays the status of the conversation by both a text description of the status and the icon on the conversation tab. The text area is responsible for displaying the messages received for each conversation. While a conversation is progressing correctly the text area in the tool will simply output each of the messages in the form[11]:

```
AddTaskEv(Lenny -> Carl)
Possible Protocols:
AddTask, AddTaskMoveTask
```

When a conversation is known to be in error, i.e. there are no remaining possible protocols that are not in error, the relevant conversation's tab has a red cross added, and the text area provides details of the error, with a message of the form:

```
*** ERROR TaskAddedByDP (Lenny -> Carl)
    Message is not a valid start message
```

In this example the conversation is in error because the message that was sent as the first message in the conversation is not a start message in any of the protocols within the system, hence an error is immediately reported.

The Interaction Monitor keeps track of the time elapsed since the last message is received in a conversation. If the time exceeds the developer defined duration then a warning can be reported by changing the conversation's tab label to include a warning icon and giving a warning message which indicates what messages were expected based on the current state of each protocol in the PPL:

```
*** WARNING. Expected a message by now.
Expected:
        AddTaskToDPEv from AddTaskProtocol.
        AddTaskToDPEv from AddTaskMoveTask protocol.
```

---

[11] In the interests of brevity and readability we have simply provided the output text, rather than given screenshots.

Since this is only a warning, if a correct message is received after the conversation has been set to a warning then normal operation can continue. The conversation is switched back to active and the warning icon is removed.

When a conversation completes successfully the icon on the tab will change to a green tick and a message will be displayed indicating that the conversation has completed successfully:

```
TaskAddedEv (TodoList@John -> GUIProxy)
Conversation finished successfully
```

If any further messages are received with the conversation id of an already completed conversation they will cause the conversation to be in error.

In the current version of the reporting interface all previous conversation panels are retained. If the number of conversations becomes large it would not be practical to keep the successfully completed panels on the main interface. A first step would be to move the completed conversation panels to a secondary location.

From the user's perspective using the debugging tool is non-intrusive: the application being developed is run and tested as normal, and the debugging tool monitors its behaviour and reports errors/warnings.

7.5 Evaluation of the Debugging Tool

We wish to evaluate the degree to which such debugging support translates to an improvement in debugging performance. In the background section we discussed the three main stages that a user will proceed through during a debugging task. These are, firstly, *identifying the bug* by identifying that the program is not acting as expected. Secondly, *locating the cause of the bug*, by locating the part (or parts) of the source code that are responsible for the bug. And finally, *fixing the bug* by providing the necessary source code modifications to remove the bug.

For each of these — identification, location and fixing — we investigate to what extent our tool assists. We measure both overall success, i.e. the *number* of programmers who were able to identify/locate/fix a given bug, and also the *time* that they took to do so.

7.5.1 Experimental Process

The multi-agent test application that we developed for the experiment is a multi-user personal organiser (called "MAPO") with support for managing a user's daily activities. A user can add tasks and meetings with properties such as duration, priority and deadlines. MAPO automatically schedules (and re-schedules) tasks and meetings. The application was designed using the Prometheus methodology [53] and was implemented using the JACK Intelligent Agents programming platform [10]. Each user is support by an instance of the MAPO system, which contains 5 agent types which use 55 plans to handle 63 event types. For our experiments we used three instances of MAPO (corresponding to three hypothetical users).

Four variants of MAPO were developed, each seeded with a different bug. Bugs one and two were of the plan selection type as discussed in section 7.2.4.3, and Bugs three and four were of the interaction type as described in section 7.4.2.

Since MAPO was developed using JACK, participants in the experiment had to be familiar with the JACK platform. We contacted members of the local agent community in Melbourne, Australia, an email was also sent to an international JACK programming mailing list, and finally the developers of the JACK programming platform were contacted for participation. In total 20 subjects completed the experiment with the majority (17) being from Melbourne, Australia.

To ensure comparable levels of ability between groups. we administered a pre-experiment survey to measure the experience and ability of each participant with regard to programming generally and specifically programming on an agent platform such as JACK. The surveys were evaluated and the participants were assigned to one of three categories: beginner, intermediate and advanced. We then randomly allocated equal numbers of each category to the two groups. Group A used the debugging tool for bugs 1 and 2 but not for bugs 3 and 4, whereas Group B used the debugging tool for bugs 3 and 4 but not for bugs 1 and 2. By having each participant work both with and without our tool, we were able to compare the performance of individuals against themselves (see section 7.5.2.4, for more details see [59, Section 6.2.4]).

Participants were provided with documentation for MAPO, consisting of approximately 40 pages of functional specifications and design documentation, including the design artefacts used as inputs to the debugging tool. These design artefacts included a number of Agent UML (AUML) interaction protocols, which were converted to Petri nets (using the translation rules of [59, Chapter 4]) and added to the debugging tool for use in the experiments.

Each participant was also provided with instructions that included a set of steps to be followed. Each set of steps comprised the minimum test data that would ensure the system would encounter the planted bug. We chose to direct the testing activities of the participants rather than leave them to define their own test cases as there was a concern that if we did not direct the test input the participants may be unlikely to encounter the bugs in the limited time available. However, this approach inevitably results in the participants quickly identifying the bugs. Consequently we were unable to fully evaluate our first hypothesis, that the debugging tool would help to identify bugs more easily. This is a limitation of the evaluation procedure but seemed necessary.

A maximum of 1 hour per bug was permitted to limit the experiment to approximately half a day per participant. This seemed to be the maximum length of time that many of the participants would be willing to spend on such an experiment.

For each bug we collected information on what the participants thought the bug was (i.e. identification), what they saw as the cause of the bug (i.e. location), and how they fixed the bug (i.e. fixing). For each participant and each bug we assessed whether they had successfully identified, located and fixed the bug. That is, a participant's description of the bug's existence, cause and its fix, was assessed as being either correct or incorrect[12]. To limit the possibility of bias, grading was carried out without knowledge of which participant used the debugging tool for which debugging task. Only after the forms had been graded were the results added to the appropriate group.

The bug data collection form also included a field for recording the time when each of the three debugging sub tasks was completed. Given that we asked participants to record the actual time we end up with a cumulative time for each of the debugging phases. This means that the time to fix a bug includes the time taken to locate the cause of the bug and to identify that the bug exists in the first place. Statistical analysis of how many participants were able to identify/locate/fix a given bug used a chi-square test, whereas statistical analysis of the time taken used a Wilcoxon rank sum test (see [59, Section 6.1.7] for a discussion of these tests and the rationale for their selection).

7.5.2 Results

In this section we present the results of the debugging experiments We compare the results over each of the sub problems that occur during debugging: identify, locate and fix. For each of these problems we consider if the participant was successful as well as the time taken to resolve the bug (bug resolution speed). We analyse the difference between the two groups with respect to our hypothesis to identify the effect that our debugging tool has on debugging the test application.

7.5.2.1 Identifying the Bug

Since participants were provided with instructions that guided them to identify the bug, we did not find significant differences in identifying bugs between debugging with and without the tool. Bug 1 was identified by all participants, and bugs 2-4 were identified by all ten participants with the debugger, and by 9 of the participants who did not use the debugger for that bug (this difference is not significant, $p = 0.3049$).

Similarly, there is little difference between the time taken for the two groups ($p = 0.4638$ for bug 1, 0.898 for bug 2, 0.79 for bug 3). Bug 4 is interesting in that the median time for participants who used the debugger was *higher* (14 minutes, compared with 9), but this difference was was not quite significant ($p = 0.06317$).

---

[12] In fact, we originally used a three point scale.

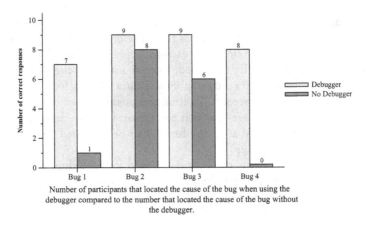

Number of participants that located the cause of the bug when using the debugger compared to the number that located the cause of the bug without the debugger.

Fig. 7.9 Number of participants able to locate bug

7.5.2.2 Locating the Cause of the Bug

Figure 7.9 shows the number of participants that successfully located the cause of the bug for each of the bug revisions. There is a very clear and significant difference between the proportions for both bug 1 (p = 0.0062) and bug 4 (p = 0.0003). For instance, for bug 4, only participants who used the debugger were able to locate the cause of the bug within an hour. The proportion data for bug 2 and bug 3 also show differences, but these do not appear to be significant (p = 0.5312 for bug 2, p = 0.1213 for bug 3).

Figure 7.10 shows the box plots for each of the 4 bug revisions concerning the time spent trying to locate the cause of the bug. As previously mentioned, it should be noted that the time recorded here is *cumulative* from the time the experiment was started for the bug revision, i.e. it includes the time taken to identify the presence of the bug. Furthermore, since there was a one hour time limit imposed on the bug version the y-axis is marked from 0 to 61 minutes. We extend the axis by 1 minute to differentiate between participants that finished in exactly 1 hour and those that did not finish. The latter case is presented as taking 61 minutes to complete the task.

Using the debugging tool clearly shows an improvement in performance for bugs 1 and 4. This difference is significant (p = 0.0027 for bug 1, and p = 0.0003 for bug 4). From these results we can conclude that the difference between the median time to locate bug 1 was at least 22 minutes (38 minutes vs. 60(+1) minutes). For bug 4 it was at least 19 minutes. This is quite a substantial amount and we can speculate that if the one hour time limit was not imposed the real difference could be greater. The results for bug 2 reveal less of a difference between the two groups. The group that used the debugging tool had a median time of 23 minutes compared with 37.5 minutes for the group that did not use the tool. However, this difference is not quite significant (p = 0.0683). For bug 3 there was a greater

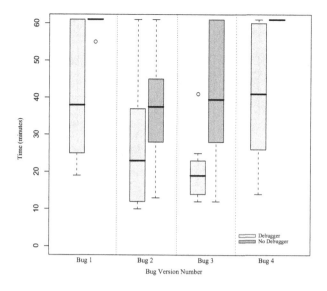

Fig. 7.10 Time taken to locate bug

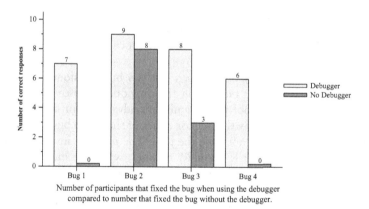

Fig. 7.11 Number of participants able to fix bug

(and significant, $p = 0.0059$) difference: more than a 20 minute increase in time for the group that did not use the debugging tool.

7.5.2.3 Fixing the Bug

Figure 7.11 shows the proportion of participants that were able to successfully fix the bug within what time was left of the 1 hour time limit. There is a clear

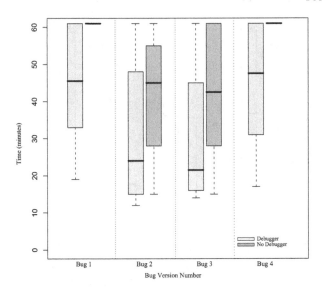

Fig. 7.12 Time taken to fix bug

difference between the two groups for bug 1 (p = 0.001), bug 3 (p = 0.0246) and bug 4 (p = 0.0034). However, the results for bug 2 do not show a significant difference between the two groups (p = 0.5312).

Figure 7.12 shows the box plots for each of the 4 bug revisions concerning the time spent trying to fix the bug. As in the previous phase there is strong evidence that the debugging tool was a significant advantage for bug 1 and bug 4. No participant was able to fix the bug for either of these two bug versions if they were in the group that did not have the tool. The median time for completing the task is therefore artificially set at 61 minutes, while the median time taken for the group that used the tool was 45.5 minutes for bug 1 and 47.5 minutes for bug 4. These differences are statistically significant with both recording a p-value of 0.0015. For bug 2 there is a large difference between the median times to provide the fix (24 minutes for one group versus 45 for the other), but there is also a large variation in the recorded times, and the difference between the groups is not significant (p = 0.1192). Bug 3 shows a similar trend. The difference between the median time to provide a fix for the bug is the same as for bug 2, 21 minutes. There are, however, slight differences in the distribution of times that make this bug version more statistically significant than the previous one (p = 0.0497).

7.5.2.4 Within Subject Analysis

It is likely that a certain amount of variability exists because of the varying abilities of each of the participants. A within subject analysis is an effective method

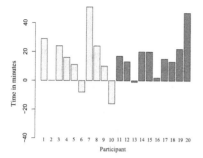
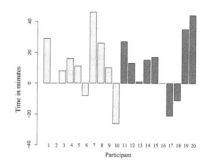

Fig. 7.13 Difference in time to locate the bugs (left) and fix the bugs (right)

for handling the variability between subjects and can shed some further light on the effect of the debugging tool on an individual's performance. The general process of evaluation is to have each participant complete a task under two different circumstances (typically described as a control task and a treatment task). Scores are recorded for each task and the difference between the scores for the two tasks is obtained. If the difference is close to zero then we can conclude that the treatment variable (the debugging tool) had no effect on the outcome. However, if a large difference is measured then there is evidence that the treatment condition did effect the outcome.

For this analysis we will concentrate on bug 2 and bug 3, and on the second two phases (locating and fixing the bug). We do this because we have already noted a statistically significant advantage for using the debugging tool for bugs 1 and 4, and we see no advantage to using the debugging tool for the first phase. Group A comprises participants 1 though 10, who used the debugging tool for bug 2 but not for bug 3. Group B comprises participants 11 through 20 who used the tool for bug 3 but not for bug 2.

Figure 7.13 (left) is a graphical representation of the differences in the time taken for each participant to *locate* the cause of bugs 2 and 3. Group A is represented by the light shading of grey and group B by the dark shading of grey. This graph shows how much quicker each participant was able to locate each of the bugs. For example, participant 1 was observed to have a 30 minute speed increase in locating bug 2 (using the tool) over Bug 3 (not using the tool). The graph shows an increase in performance for most subjects when the debugging tool was used to locate the bug. However, there are three exceptions. Participant 6, 10 and 13 had a performance decrease of approximately 7, 16 and 1 minutes respectively. However, overall the debugging tool results in bugs being located more quickly (p = 0.00987).

Figure 7.13 (right) shows the difference that the debugging tool had for each participant in *fixing* the bugs. Again this graph clearly shows that the majority of the participants were able to fix the bug more quickly when using the tool than without (p = 0.00987).

7.6 Conclusion

In this chapter we explored the problems associated with testing and debugging multi-agent systems and have provided a framework for testing and debugging based on using design documents to automatically identify errors in developed systems. We have demonstrated two proof of concept tools: one that uses design documents to generate extensive test cases for unit testing, and another that uses design documents (specifically protocol specifications and parts of event descriptors) to help in debugging.

The debugging tool was used to assess the effectiveness of our debugging technique via an empirical evaluation. The results that we obtained clearly demonstrate that using the debugging tool translates to an improvement in debugging performance. We gathered data from twenty participants over four debugging tasks. Each debugging task was measured over the three aspects of debugging; identifying, locating and fixing a bug. In terms of overall successes in locating the cause and fixing the bugs we identified that using the debugging tool afforded the participant a considerable advantage.

One advantage of using design artefacts in testing and debugging is that it provides continued checking that the design and code are consistent, thus helping to avoid the typical accumulation of differences, leading to out-of-date design documents. There are a number of areas for future work including:

- Improving the user interface of the debugging tool, and looking at possibly integrating it into an agent-based design tool, such as the Prometheus Design Tool (PDT).
- Developing a distributed debugging environment, with multiple debugging agents. This would be needed to debug large agent systems that comprise hundreds or even thousands of agents. A key challenge is managing the interactions between debugging agents and determining how to group agents.
- Extending testing to focus on higher level aspects such as scenarios and goals.
- Thorough evaluation of the testing approach including common types of errors **not** able to be identified.

Although much interesting work remains to be done, this chapter has established the viability and effectiveness of the approach to using design artefacts in the testing and debugging of multi-agent systems.

Acknowledgements We would like to thank John Thangarajah for discussions relating to the testing tool, and co-supervision of the PhD work on this topic. We would like to acknowledge the support of of Agent Oriented Software Pty. Ltd. and of the Australian Research Council (ARC) under grant LP0453486.

References

1. Apfelbaum, L., Doyle, J.: Model Based Testing. In: the 10th International Software Quality Week Conference. CA, USA (1997)
2. Bates, P.: EBBA Modelling Tool a.k.a Event Definition Language. Tech. rep., Department of Computer Science University of Massachusetts, Amherst, MA, USA (1987)
3. Bauer, B., Müller, J.P., Odell, J.: Agent UML: A Formalism for Specifying Multiagent Interaction. In: P. Ciancarini, M. Wooldridge (eds.) Agent-Oriented Software Engineering, pp. 91–103. Springer-Verlag, Berlin (2001)
4. Benfield, S.S., Hendrickson, J., Galanti, D.: Making a strong business case for multiagent technology. In: P. Stone, G. Weiss (eds.) Autonomous Agents and Multi-Agent Systems (AAMAS), pp. 10–15. ACM Press (2006)
5. Binder, R.V.: Testing Object-Oriented Systems: Models, Patterns, and Tools. Addison-Wesley Longman Publishing Co., Inc., Boston, MA, USA (1999)
6. Binkley, D., Gold, N., Harman, M.: An empirical study of static program slice size. ACM Transactions on Software Engineering and Methodology 16(2), 8 (2007). DOI http://doi.acm.org/10.1145/1217295.1217297
7. Bresciani, P., Giorgini, P., Giunchiglia, F., Mylopoulos, J., Perini, A.: Tropos: An agent-oriented software development methodology. Journal of Autonomous Agents and Multi-Agent Systems 8, 203–236 (2004)
8. Bruegge, B., Gottschalk, T., Luo, B.: A framework for dynamic program analyzers. In: Object-Oriented Programming Systems, Languages, and Applications. OOPSLA, pp. 65–82. ACM Press, Washington (1993)
9. Busetta, P., Howden, N., Rönnquist, R., Hodgson, A.: Structuring BDI agents in functional clusters. In: Agent Theories, Architectures, and Languages (ATAL-99), pp. 277–289. Springer-Verlag (2000). LNCS 1757
10. Busetta, P., Rönnquist, R., Hodgson, A., Lucas, A.: JACK Intelligent Agents - Components for Intelligent Agents in Java. Tech. rep., Agent Oriented Software Pty. Ltd, Melbourne, Australia (1998)
11. Caire, G., Cossentino, M., Negri, A., Poggi, A., Turci, P.: Multi-Agent Systems Implementation and Testing. In: the Fourth International Symposium: From Agent Theory to Agent Implementation. Vienna, Austria (EU) (2004)
12. Clarke, E.M., Grumberg, O., Long, D.E.: Model checking and abstraction. ACM Transactions on Programming Languages and Systems 16(5), 1512–1542 (1994). URL citeseer.ist.psu.edu/clarke92model.html
13. Coelho, R., Kulesza, U., von Staa, A., Lucena, C.: Unit Testing in Multi-Agent Systems using Mock Agents and Aspects. In: Proceedings of the 2006 International Workshop on Software Engineering for Large-Scale Multi-Agent Systems, pp. 83–90 (2006)
14. Cohen, B.: The use of bug in computing. IEEE Annals of the History of Computing 16, No 2 (1994)
15. Cohen, D.M., Dalal, S.R., Fredman, M.L., Patton, G.C.: The AETG system: An Approach to Testing Based on Combinatorial Design. Software Engineering 23(7), 437–444 (1997). URL citeseer.ist.psu.edu/cohen97aetg.html
16. Cost, R.S., Chen, Y., Finin, T., Labrou, Y., Peng, Y.: Using colored petri nets for conversation modeling. In: F. Dignum, M. Greaves (eds.) Issues in Agent Communication, pp. 178–192. Springer-Verlag: Heidelberg, Germany (2000). URL citeseer.ist.psu.edu/article/cost99using.html
17. Dalal, S.R., Jain, A., Karunanithi, N., Leaton, J.M., Lott, C.M., Patton, G.C., Horowitz, B.M.: Model-based testing in practice. In: International Conference on Software Engineering (1999)
18. DeLoach, S.A.: Analysis and design using MaSE and agentTool. In: Proceedings of the 12th Midwest Artificial Intelligence and Cognitive Science Conference (MAICS 2001) (2001)
19. DeLoach, S.A.: Developing a multiagent conference management system using the O-MaSE process framework. In: Luck and Padgham [39], pp. 168–181

20. DeLoach, S.A., Wood, M.F., Sparkman, C.H.: Multiagent systems engineering. International Journal of Software Engineering and Knowledge Engineering 11(3), 231–258 (2001)
21. Dignum, F., Sierra, C. (eds.): Agent Mediated Electronic Commerce: The European Agentlink Perspective. Lecture Notes in Artificial Intelligence. Springer-Verlag, London, UK (1991)
22. Doolan, E.P.: Experience with Fagan's inspection method. Software Practice and Experience 22(2), 173–182 (1992)
23. Ducassé, M.: A pragmatic survey of automated debugging. In: Automated and Algorithmic Debugging, *LNCS*, vol. 749, pp. 1–15. Springer Berlin / Heidelberg (1993). URL citeseer.ist.psu.edu/367030.html
24. Ekinci, E.E., Tiryaki, A.M., Çetin, Ö.: Goal-oriented agent testing revisited. In: J.J. Gomez-Sanz, M. Luck (eds.) Ninth International Workshop on Agent-Oriented Software Engineering, pp. 85–96 (2008)
25. El-Far, I.K., Whittaker, J.A.: Model-Based Software Testing, pp. 825–837. Wiley (2001)
26. Fagan, M.E.: Advances in software inspections. IEEE Transactions on Software Engineering SE-12(7), 744–751 (1986)
27. Flater, D.: Debugging agent interactions: a case study. In: Proceedings of the 16th ACM Symposium on Applied Computing (SAC2001), pp. 107–114. ACM Press (2001)
28. Gomez-Sanz, J.J., Botía, J., Serrano, E., Pavón, J.: Testing and debugging of MAS interactions with INGENIAS. In: J.J. Gomez-Sanz, M. Luck (eds.) Ninth International Workshop on Agent-Oriented Software Engineering, pp. 133–144 (2008)
29. Hailpern, B., Santhanam, P.: Software debugging, testing, and verification. IBM Systems Journal 41(1), 1–12 (2002)
30. Hall, C., Hammond, K., O'Donnell, J.: An algorithmic and semantic approach to debugging. In: Proceedings of the 1990 Glasgow Workshop on Functional Programming, pp. 44–53 (1990)
31. Huber, M.J.: JAM: A BDI-theoretic mobile agent architecture. In: Proceedings of the Third International Conference on Autonomous Agents (Agents'99), pp. 236–243 (1999)
32. Huget, M.P., Odell, J., Haugen, Ø., Nodine, M.M., Cranefield, S., Levy, R., Padgham., L.: Fipa modeling: Interaction diagrams. On *www.auml.org* under "Working Documents" (2003). FIPA Working Draft (version 2003-07-02)
33. Johnson, M.S.: A software debugging glossary. ACM SIGPLAN Notices 17(2), 53–70 (1982)
34. Jones, J.A.: Fault localization using visualization of test information. In: Proceedings of the 26th International Conference on Software Engineering, pp. 54–56. IEEE Computer Society, Washington, DC, USA (2004)
35. Knublauch, H.: Extreme programming of multi-agent systems. In: Proceedings of the First International Joint Conference on Autonomous Agents and Multi-Agent Systems (AAMAS) (2002). URL citeseer.ist.psu.edu/knublauch02extreme.html
36. LeBlanc, T., Mellor-Crummey, J., Fowler, R.: Analyzing parallel program executions using multiple views. Parallel and Distributed Computing 9(2), 203–217 (1990)
37. Lind, J.: Specifying agent interaction protocols with standard UML. In: Agent-Oriented Software Engineering II: Second International Workshop, Montreal Canada, *LNCS*, vol. 2222, pp. 136–147 (2001). URL citeseer.ist.psu.edu/lind01specifying.html
38. Low, C.K., Chen, T.Y., Rönnquist, R.: Automated Test Case Generation for BDI agents. Autonomous Agents and Multi-Agent Systems 2(4), 311–332 (1999)
39. Luck, M., Padgham, L. (eds.): Agent-Oriented Software Engineering VIII, 8th International Workshop, AOSE 2007, Honolulu, HI, USA, May 14, 2007, Revised Selected Papers, *Lecture Notes in Computer Science*, vol. 4951. Springer (2008)
40. Madachy, R.: Process improvement analysis of a corporate inspection program. In: Seventh Software Engineering Process Group Conference, Boston, MA (1995)
41. Mayer, W., Stumptner, M.: Model-based debugging - state of the art and future challenges. Electronic Notes in Theoretical Computer Science 174(4), 61–82 (2007). DOI http://dx.doi.org/10.1016/j.entcs.2006.12.030
42. McDowell, C., Helmbold, D.: Debugging concurrent programs. ACM Computing Surveys 21(4), 593–622 (1989)

43. Morandini, M., Nguyen, D.C., Perini, A., Siena, A., Susi, A.: Tool-supported development with Tropos: The conference management system case study. In: Luck and Padgham [39], pp. 182–196
44. Munroe, S., Miller, T., Belecheanu, R., Pechoucek, M., McBurney, P., Luck, M.: Crossing the agent technology chasm: Experiences and challenges in commercial applications of agents. Knowledge Engineering Review **21**(4), 345–392 (2006)
45. Myers, B.A., Weitzman, D.A., Ko, A.J., Chau, D.H.: Answering why and why not questions in user interfaces. In: Proceedings of the SIGCHI conference on Human Factors in computing systems, pp. 397–406. ACM, New York, NY, USA (2006)
46. Mylopoulos, J., Castro, J., Kolp, M.: Tropos: Toward agent-oriented information systems engineering. In: Second International Bi-Conference Workshop on Agent-Oriented Information Systems (AOIS2000) (2000)
47. Naish, L.: A declarative debugging scheme. Journal of Functional and Logic Programming **1997**(3), 1–27 (1997)
48. Ndumu, D.T., Nwana, H.S., Lee, L.C., Collis, J.C.: Visualising and debugging distributed multi-agent systems. In: Proceedings of the third annual conference on Autonomous Agents, pp. 326–333. ACM Press (1999). DOI http://doi.acm.org/10.1145/301136.301220
49. Nguyen, C.D., Perini, A., Tonella, P.: eCAT: A tool for automating test cases generation and execution in testing multi-agent systems (demo paper). In: 7th International Conference on Autonomous Agents and Multiagent Systems (AAMAS 2008). Estoril, Portugal (2008)
50. Nguyen, C.D., Perini, A., Tonella, P.: Ontology-based test generation for multi agent systems (short paper). In: 7th International Conference on Autonomous Agents and Multiagent Systems (AAMAS 2008). Estoril, Portugal (2008)
51. O'Hare, G.M.P., Wooldridge, M.J.: A software engineering perspective on multi-agent system design: experience in the development of MADE. In: Distributed artificial intelligence: theory and praxis, pp. 109–127. Kluwer Academic Publishers (1992)
52. Padgham, L., Thangarajah, J., Winikoff, M.: The prometheus design tool - a conference management system case study. In: Luck and Padgham [39], pp. 197–211
53. Padgham, L., Winikoff, M.: Developing Intelligent Agent Systems: A Practical Guide. John Wiley and Sons (2004). ISBN 0-470-86120-7
54. Padgham, L., Winikoff, M., DeLoach, S., Cossentino, M.: A unified graphical notation for AOSE. In: Ninth International Workshop on Agent Oriented Software Engineering (AOSE) (2008)
55. Padgham, L., Winikoff, M., Poutakidis, D.: Adding debugging support to the prometheus methodology. Engineering Applications of Artificial Intelligence, special issue on Agent-oriented Software Development **18**(2), 173–190 (2005)
56. Patton, R.: Software Testing (Second Edition). Sams, Indianapolis, IN, USA (2005)
57. Paurobally, S., Cunningham, J., Jennings, N.R.: Developing agent interaction protocols graphically and logically. In: Programming Multi-Agent Systems, *Lecture Notes in Artificial Intelligence*, vol. 3067, pp. 149–168 (2004)
58. Pokahr, A., Braubach, L., Lamersdorf, W.: Jadex: Implementing a BDI-Infrastructure for JADE Agents. EXP - In Search of Innovation (Special Issue on JADE) **3**(3), 76–85 (2003)
59. Poutakidis, D.: Debugging multi-agent systems with design documents. Ph.D. thesis, RMIT University, School of Computer Science and IT (2008)
60. Poutakidis, D., Padgham, L., Winikoff, M.: Debugging multi-agent systems using design artifacts: The case of interaction protocols. In: Proceedings of the First International Joint Conference on Autonomous Agents and Multi Agent Systems (AAMAS'02) (2002)
61. Poutakidis, D., Padgham, L., Winikoff, M.: An exploration of bugs and debugging in multi-agent systems. In: Proceedings of the 14th International Symposium on Methodologies for Intelligent Systems (ISMIS), pp. 628–632. Maebashi City, Japan (2003)
62. Purvis, M., Cranefield, S., Nowostawski, M., Purvis, M.: Multi-agent system interaction protocols in a dynamically changing environment. In: T. Wagner (ed.) An Application Science for Multi-Agent Systems, pp. 95–112. Kluwer Academic (2004)
63. Reisig, W.: Petri Nets: An Introduction. EATCS Monographs on Theoretical Computer Science. Springer-Verlag (1985). ISBN 0-387-13723-8

64. Rouff, C.: A Test Agent for Testing Agents and their Communities. Aerospace Conference Proceedings, 2002. IEEE 5, 2638 (2002)
65. Schwarz, R., Mattern, F.: Detecting causal relationships in distributed computations: In search of the holy grail. Distributed Computing 7(3), 149–174 (1994). URL citeseer.nj.nec.com/schwarz94detecting.html
66. Shapiro, E.Y.: Algorithmic Program Debugging. MIT Press, Cambridge, MA, USA (1983)
67. Sprinkle, J., van Buskirk, C.P., Karsai, G.: Modeling agent negotiation. In: Proceedings of the 2000 IEEE International Conference on Systems, Man, and Cybernetics, Nashville, TN, vol. 1, pp. 454–459 (2000)
68. Vessey, I.: Expertise in debugging computer programs: A process analysis. International Journal of Man-Machine Studies 23(5), 459–494 (1985)
69. Weiser, M.: Programmers use slices when debugging. Communications of the ACM 25(7), 446–452 (1982). DOI http://doi.acm.org/10.1145/358557.358577
70. Yilmaz, C., Williams, C.: An automated model-based debugging approach. In: Proceedings of the twenty-second IEEE/ACM international conference on Automated software engineering, pp. 174–183. ACM, New York, NY, USA (2007). DOI http://doi.acm.org/10.1145/1321631.1321659
71. Zhang, Z., Thangarajah, J., Padgham, L.: Automated unit testing for agent systems. In: Second International Working Conference on Evaluation of Novel Approaches to Software Engineering (ENASE), pp. 10–18 (2007)

Chapter 8
Environment Programming in **CArtAgO**

Alessandro Ricci, Michele Piunti, Mirko Viroli, and Andrea Omicini

Abstract **CArtAgO** is a platform and infrastructure providing a general-purpose programming model for building shared computational worlds – referred here as *work environments* – that agents, possibly belonging to heterogeneous agent platforms, can exploit to work together inside a Multi-Agent System. Being based on the A&A (Agents and Artifacts) conceptual model, **CArtAgO** work environments are modelled and engineered in terms of set of *artifacts* programmed by MAS designers, collected in *workspaces*. From the agent viewpoint, artifacts are first-class entities representing resources and tools that agents can dynamically instantiate, share and use to support their individual and collective activities. After describing the basic motivations behind the approach, the chapter provides an overview of the programming model promoted by **CArtAgO** for the definition of artifacts (MAS designer's viewpoint) and for the use of artifacts (agent's viewpoint), using *Jason* as reference platform for MAS programming.

8.1 Introduction

The notion of *environment* is a primary concept in the agent literature, as the place – either virtual or physical – where agents are situated, which agents are capable of *sensing* through some kind of sensors, and of *modifying* through a reper-

Alessandro Ricci
DEIS, Università di Bologna, Italy, e-mail: a.ricci@unibo.it

Michele Piunti
Istituto di Scienze e Tecnologie della Cognizione (ISTC-CNR), Roma, Italy
DEIS, Università di Bologna, Italy, e-mail: michele.piunti@unibo.it

Mirko Viroli
DEIS, Università di Bologna, Italy, e-mail: mirko.viroli@unibo.it

Andrea Omicini
DEIS, Università di Bologna, Italy, e-mail: andrea.omicini@unibo.it

R.H. Bordini et al. (eds.), *Multi-Agent Programming*,
DOI 10.1007/978-0-387-89299-3_8, © Springer Science+Business Media, LLC 2009

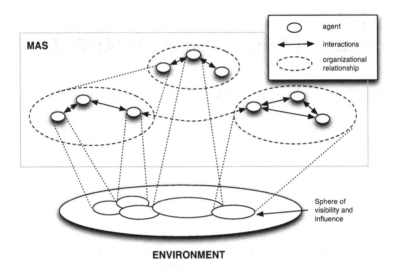

Fig. 8.1 The canonical view of MAS as defined in [10].

toire of actions provided by some kind of effectors. A canonical representation of a Multi-Agent Systems (MAS) including the environment is shown in Fig. 8.1 (adapted from [10]). There, the environment is depicted as the context shared by multiple agents, each one having some kind of *sphere of influence* on it, i.e. that portion that they are able to (partially) control, and that could overlap with other agent's sphere of influence—meaning that the environment is shared and could be jointly controlled.

This perspective is reflected by existing agent programming languages and platforms for programming MAS, which typically provide some kind of API to define agent actions and perceptions implementing the interaction with some kind of external system. Quite frequently, the API also includes some kind of support for defining the structure and behaviour of the environment – besides the interface – so as to set up simulations of the overall system.

So, in this canonical view the environment is basically conceived as a black box, defining the set of the possible agent moves and generating perceptions accordingly. Besides this perspective, which is rooted mainly in the Artificial Intelligence view [27], recent works pointed out the important role that the environment can play in MAS engineering [30]: essentially, by being the enabler and mediator of agent interactions, MAS environment can be the right place where to encapsulate functionalities that concern the management of such interactions, making it possible to define and enact strategies for MAS coordination, organisation, security. The interested reader can find in [31] a survey of these works, summing up the the results of three years of the E4MAS (Environment for Multi-Agent Systems) workshop, held at the AAMAS (Autonomous Agents and Multi-Agent Systems) conference from 2004 to 2006.

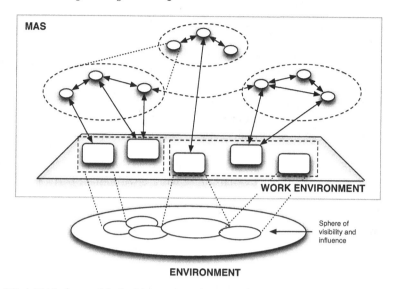

Fig. 8.2 A MAS view enriched with a work environment layer.

By generalising this view, in this chapter we envision a novel perspective on the environment concept: rather than from merely a target of agent actions and generator of agent perceptions, the environment should be conceived as something that can be (partially) designed to be a good place for agents to live and work in. In other words, the idea is to *design worlds in the agent world aimed at the agents' use*. We refer to such a kind of world as *work environment*, as that part of the MAS which, on the one side, is explicitly designed and programmed by MAS engineers, and, on the other side, is perceived and used by agents as a first-class entity of their world, aimed at easing their activities, in particular those involving interaction, coordination, cooperation. By referring to the MAS representation previously seen, work environments could be represented as an extra computational layer within the MAS, conceptually placed between agents and the external environment, and mediating agent activities and agent interaction with the external environment (see Fig. 8.2).

Then, by taking the MAS programming perspective, which is the focus of this volume, an important issue concerns what kind of (general-purpose) programming and computational models can be adopted in order to design and program work environments. Desiderata, quite common in computer programming and software engineering, include:

Abstraction | The programming model adopted should preserve the agent abstraction level, i.e. the main concepts used to define work environments structure and dynamics (including interaction with agents) should be consistent with agent main concepts and semantics. Moreover, such concepts should be effective and general enough to capture main properties of work environments (such as being observable and controllable).

Modularity | The programming model should introduce concepts to modularise work environments, away from the monolithic and centralised view which is typically adopted for MAS environment in general.

Orthogonality | The programming model should be as much orthogonal as possible with respect to the models, architectures, languages adopted for agent programming, so as to naturally support the engineering of heterogeneous systems.

(Dynamic) Extensibility | The programming model should support the dynamic construction, replacement, extension of work environment parts, in the *open system* perspective.

Reusability | The programming model should promote the reuse of work environment parts in different application contexts/domains.

To this end, **CArtAgO** is a platform/infrastructure providing a programming model and a runtime environment for creating work environments based on the notions of artifact and workspace, as defined by the A&A (Agents and Artifact) model [18, 25]. The basic idea of work environment provided by A&A and **CArtAgO** is metaphorically depicted in Fig. 8.3 (representing a kind of bakery): the work environment of a MAS is composed by a set of resources and tools that we refer generally as *artifacts* that agents share and cooperatively use to perform their activities inside some workspace. Some artifacts are used to mediate the interaction between agents and the external environment (such as the communication channel), some other as just instruments to help their work (such as the blackboard or the task scheduler), and some other else as resources target of the agent work (such as the cake).

Before discussing in more detail the feature of **CArtAgO** as a platform for programming artifact-based environments and its integration with main existing agent programming platforms (Section 8.3), next section will provide a background discussion about the A&A conceptual model, focussing in particular on the features of the artifact abstraction and its computational model.

8.2 The A&A Model

8.2.1 Artifacts and Workspaces in Multi-Agent Systems

Agents & Artifacts (A&A) is a conceptual (or meta) model introducing the notion of *artifact*, along with agents, as a first-class abstraction for modelling and engineering of Multi-Agent Systems [18, 25]. The main inspiration of A&A comes from Activity Theory [15]—a psycho-sociological conceptual approach started in the Soviet Union at the beginning of the 20th century, further developed in northern Europe in particular—today, a main reference for HCI (Human Computer

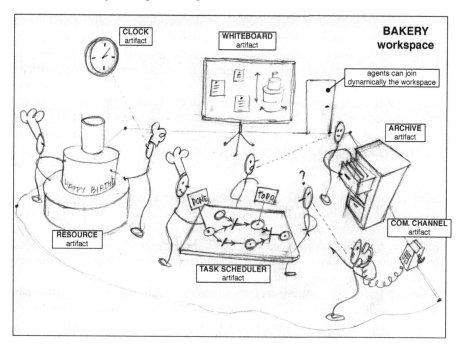

Fig. 8.3 A metaphorical representation of a MAS according to the A&A meta-model.

Interaction) and CSCW (Computer Supported Cooperative Work) contexts. One of the main concepts put forward by Activity Theory – along with Distributed Cognition and other movements within cognitive science – is that, in human societies, properly designed artifacts and tools play a fundamental (mediation) role in coping with the scaling up of complexity in human activities, in particular when social activities are concerned, by simplifying the execution of tasks, improving problem-solving capabilities, and enabling the efficient coordination and cooperation in social contexts [16]. In Activity Theory, the concept of tool is broad enough to embrace both technical tools, intended to manipulate physical objects (e.g., a hammer), and psychological tools, used by humans to influence other people or even themselves (e.g., the multiplication table or a calendar).

The A&A conceptual framework brings these ideas in the context of multi-agent systems, in particular for designing and programming complex software systems based on MAS [18]. According to this, a MAS is conceived, designed and developed in terms of an ensemble of agents that play together within a common environment not only by communicating through some high-level agent communication language (ACL), but also co-constructing and co-using using different kinds of *artifacts* organised in *workspaces*.

At the core of the A&A model, the artifact[1] abstraction is introduced as a unit to structure and organise work environments. From the MAS designer's viewpoint, artifacts are the basic building blocks – or rather the *first-class abstraction* – to design and engineer agent work environments; from the agent view point, artifacts are first-class entities of their world that they can instantiate, discover, share, and finally use and observe to perform their activities and achieve their goals. If agents are the basic bricks to design the autonomous and goal/task-oriented part of the MAS, artifacts are the basic entities to organise the *non-autonomous, function-oriented*[2] (from the agent point view) part of it.

Artifacts are then a natural abstraction to model and implement existing computational entities and mechanisms that are frequently introduced in the engineering of MAS representing shared resources, such as shared data stores, or coordination media, such as blackboards, tuple spaces, event managers. Besides this, analogously to the human context [16], artifacts can be specifically designed to change (improve) the way tasks get done by agents, by distributing actions across time (*precomputation*) and agents (*distributed cognition*), and also by changing the way in which individuals perform the activity.

Besides artifacts, A&A introduces the notion of *workspace* to structure and organise the overall set of artifacts (and agents) in a MAS from a topological point of view (see Fig. 8.4, left). A workspace is a logic container of agents and artifacts, providing a logical notion of locality and situatedness for agents, by defining a scope for the interactions and observability of events, as well as for the set of related activities carried by a group of agents using some set of artifacts. A complex MAS can then be organised as a set of workspaces, distributed among multiple nodes of the network, with agents possibly joining multiple workspaces at the same time.

8.2.2 A Computational Model for Artifacts

The development model introduced with A&A and adopted in CArtAgO aims at both capturing the *function-oriented* nature of artifacts, as computational entities that are *used* (observed, controlled) by agents, and being sufficiently general-purpose to be used in programming any type of artifact that might be useful in MAS applications.

An abstract view of the computational model is shown in Fig. 8.4 (on the right). Artifact functionalities are defined in terms of *operations*, which can be triggered by agents via artifact *usage interface*. Analogously to usage interface of artifacts in the real world, an artifact usage interface is composed by a set of *usage interface controls* that agents can trigger to start and control the execution of an operation, and more generally the artifact behaviour. Each usage interface control is

---

[1] The term *artifact* has been explicitly taken from Activity Theory and Distributed Cognition, to recall the properties that such a notion have in the context of human environments.

[2] The term *function* is used here with the meaning of "intended purpose".

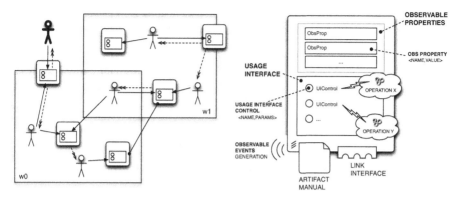

Fig. 8.4 *(left)* An abstract representation of a MAS involving both agents (represented by stick figures) and artifacts (squares with a sketch of an interface inside), collected in workspaces (w0 and w1). Main interaction types are represented: use interaction (solid arrows from agents to artifacts), observation (dotted arrows from artifacts to agents), artifact link (solid lines among artifacts). Among the artifacts, some are used as interfaces to interact with the environment outside the MAS (artifacts on the workspace border), including GUIs for interacting with human users (thick stick figure). Direct communications among agents are not represented. *(right)* An abstract representation of an artifact, showing the main features of the model as defined in A&A.

identified by a label (typically equals to the operation name) and a list of input parameters.

Operations are the basic units for structuring artifact functionalities, and can be either atomic or processes involving a sequence of atomic computational steps. Executing an artifact operation can result both in changes in the artifact inner (non-observable) state, and in the generation of a stream of *observable events* that can be perceived by the agents using or observing the artifact.

Besides observable events generated with operation execution, an artifact may expose a set of *observable properties*, i.e. properties whose dynamic values can be observed by agents without necessarily interacting with it, i.e. without going through the usage interface. Differently from events, which are non-persistent signals carrying some kind of information, observable properties are persistent – typically dynamic – attributes of an artifact.

Analogously to artifacts in the human case, in A&A each artifact is meant to be equipped with a *manual* describing the artifact function (i.e., its intended purpose), the artifact usage interface (i.e., the observable "shape" of the artifact), and the artifact *operating instructions* (i.e., usage protocols or simply how to correctly use the artifact so as to take advantage of all its functionalities). Artifact manuals are meant to be inspected and used at runtime, in particular intelligent agents, for reasoning about how to select and use artifacts so as to best achieve their goals. This is a fundamental feature for developing open systems, where agents cannot have *a priori* knowledge of all the artifacts available in their workspaces since new instances and types of artifacts can be created dynamically, at runtime. Currently, no commitments towards specific models, ontologies, and technologies to

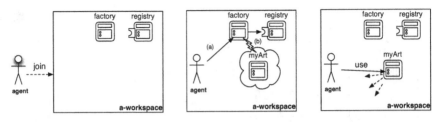

Fig. 8.5 Workspace dynamics: an agent joining a workspace called **a-workspace** and creating an artifact called **myArg**. Artifact creation is not a primitive action: it is a functionality provided by a predefined artifact available in each workspace called **factory**. Besides **factory**, also a **registry** is available, which keeps tracks of all the artifacts currently available in the workspace.

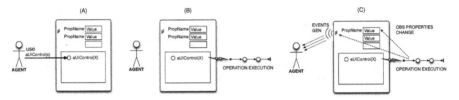

Fig. 8.6 Using an artifact: by selecting the **myOpControl** control belonging to the usage interface, a new operation instance starts its execution inside the artifact. The execution of the operation will eventually generate events observable to the user agents – and to all the agents observing the artifact – and possibly update artifact observable properties.

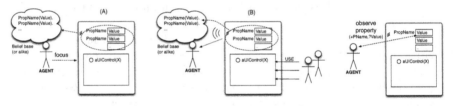

Fig. 8.7 Observing an artifact: by focussing an artifact, an agent is (1) continuously made aware of observable properties value as percepts typically mapped into agent belief base, and (2) receives all the observable events generated by the artifact in executing operations possibly triggered by other user agents.

be adopted for manual description have as yet been made, as this is part of ongoing work.

Finally, as a principle of composition, artifacts can be linked together, to enable inter-artifact interaction. This is realised through *link interfaces*, which are analogous to interfaces of artifacts in the real world (e.g., linking/connecting/plugging the earphones into an MP3 player, or using a remote control for the TV). Linking is supported also for artifacts belonging to distinct workspaces, possibly residing on different network nodes.

8.2.2.1 Agent-Artifact Interaction Model: Use and Observation

The interaction between agents and artifacts mimics the way in which humans use their artifacts. As a simple but effective analogy, we adopt here a coffee machine artifact. The set of buttons of the coffee machine represents the usage interface, while the displays used to show the state of the machine represent artifact observable properties. The signals emitted by the coffee machine during its usage represent observable events generated by the artifact.

The interaction takes place by means of a use action (see Fig. 8.6), which agents can perform to select (i.e. act upon) a control of the usage interface, specifying the parameters possibly required by the control. If the use action succeeds, then a new instance of the operation linked to the usage interface control starts its execution inside the artifact. The execution of the operation eventually generates a stream of observable events that may be perceived both by the agent which is responsible of the operation execution and by all the agents that are *observing* the artifact—we will come back on the notion of observation later in this chapter. Some basic types of events are meant to be generated by default by artifacts, independently of their specific type, in correspondence to situations such as the completion or failure of an operation, the update of an observable property, or rather the disposal of an artifact.

To perceive the observable events generated by the artifact, two basic modalities are possible, called here *active* and *passive*. In the active modality, the agent performing a use action explicitly specifies a *sensor*, where artifact observable events are collected as percepts as soon as they are generated; then, a further sense action is available to the agent so as to actively fetch the percept from the sensor *as soon as it needs it*, possibly specifying some filters and eventually blocking the course of the activity until a matching percept is found. In this case, sensors play the role of *perceptual memory* explicitly manageable by the agent, who can use them to organise in a flexible way the processing of the events, possibly generated by multiple different artifacts that an agent can be using for different, even concurrent, activities.

In the passive modality, events generated by an artifact are made observable to the agent directly as internal event or new beliefs about the occurrence of the event (depending on the specific agent model and architecture), without the explicit mediation of sensors. Compared to the previous one, this modality promotes a *reactive* approach in managing interaction with artifacts.

Some notes here are useful to clarify the features of the use action and interaction. First, the execution of a use action on a usage interface control involves a *synchronous* interaction between the agent and the artifact (analogous to pressing a button on the usage interface of the coffee machine): action success means that the operation linked to the control has started its execution. This should be contrasted with inter-agent communication, which is based, instead, on fully asynchronous communication. Second, the execution of operations is completely *asynchronous to the agent activity*. So, the use action does not involve any transfer of control as it happens in the case of remote procedure call or method invocation in procedure-based or object-oriented systems.

Besides use, *observation* is the other main aspect concerning agent-artifact interaction, that account for perceiving observable properties and events of an artifact *without necessarily using it*, i.e. without acting on its usage interface. To this end, two basic actions are provided, observeProperty and focus. The observeProperty action simply makes it possible to read the current value of a specific observable property, which is returned directly as feedback of the action. The focus action is more complex (see Fig. 8.7): by executing a focus on a specific artifact, an agent starts continuously perceiving the state of artifact observable properties and is notified of all the observable events that the artifact will generate from that moment on, even though it is not actually using it. Observable properties are directly mapped onto agent percepts, that is, for cognitive agent architecture in particular, on beliefs about the state of the artifact. For observable events, the two perceiving modalities are available also for focus, either specifying or not a sensor. The semantics is the same as the use case: by specifying a sensor all the observable events generated by the artifact are detected by the sensor and fetched by the agent through a sense internal action whenever it decides to do it.

Some more notes concerning observation: first, focus and observeProperty actions do not have any effect on artifact structure and behaviour, and then no real interaction actually takes place between the observer agent(s) and the observed artifacts. So, conceptually and practically, observation is radically different from analogous scenarios purely based on agents, such as request-response interactions between information requester and information provider agents. Second, continuous observation of properties – on the one hand – and of events – on the other hand – have deeply different characteristics (and then purposes, from the designer point of view). In particular, observable properties represent the *state* of the world – structured in this case as a set of artifacts – which, as such, could change with a frequency that could be beyond agent perceiving capabilities. Instead, observable events, representing *changes* in the world, are conceptually all buffered and processed, in some kind of order that depends on event priorities.

After this overview of the computational model of artifacts and the agent-artifact interaction model, in next section we describe how this is concretely supported by the CArtAgO platform.

8.3 The **CArtAgO** Platform

8.3.1 Overview

CArtAgO (Common Artifact infrastructure for Agent Open environment) is a platform and infrastructure for programming and executing artifact-based work environments for MAS, implementing the A&A conceptual model [25]. In detail, the platform includes:

- a Java-based API for programming artifacts, for defining (programming) new types of artifacts following the A&A programming model (a general overview with examples will be given in Subsection 8.3.2);
- an agent API on the agent side to play within CArtAgO work environments, composed by a basic set of actions for creating and interacting with artifacts, and managing and joining workspace (an overview will be given in Subsection 8.3.1.2);
- a runtime environment and related tools, supporting the distribution and execution of work environments, managing workspace and artifact lifecycle.

CArtAgO technology is open-source[3] and is implemented on top of the Java platform.

8.3.1.1 The Application Model

A work environment in CArtAgO is conceived as collection of workspaces possibly distributed on different nodes where the infrastructure has been installed (referred in the following as CArtAgO nodes). Agents – possibly in execution on multiple and heterogeneous agent platforms – can dynamically join and quit the workspaces, possibly working in multiple/distributed workspaces at the same time.

A Role-Based Access Control (RBAC) model is adopted for specifying and managing security aspects at workspace level, ruling agent entrance and exit, and agent access and interaction with artifacts. In particular, for each workspace a (dynamic) set of roles can be defined, and for each role policies can be specified to constrain the overall set of actions permitted to agents playing that role, including agent entrance/exit from the workspace and agent use/observation of artifacts. The set of roles and of the policies associated to roles can be inspected and changed dynamically, both by human administrators and by agents themselves.

By default, each workspace contains a set of pre-defined artifacts, created at the workspace creation time, which provides some fundamental functionalities and facilities for agents working inside the workspace and for workspaces management. Such a set currently includes:

- factory artifact – used to instantiate artifacts, specifying the artifact template and a name. The artifact provides functionalities also to manage the set of artifact template that can be created inside the workspace.
- registry artifact – used to keep track of the set of artifacts actually available in the workspace.
- security-registry artifact – used to manage the set of roles and role policies defined in the workspace.

---

[3] Available at http://cartago.sourceforge.org.

- **console** artifact – used as standard output, to print messages that can be read by human users.

So the **CArtAgO** background idea here is to *reify* in terms of a suitably-designed artifact every infrastructure part and functionality so as to make it observable, controllable, adaptable by agents themselves (for agents that have the permission to do that according to their role), besides human administrators.

8.3.1.2 Integration with Agent Platforms

As mentioned before, **CArtAgO** is orthogonal to the specific model(s) and technology adopted for the agents playing within work environments. Actually, it has been conceived and designed to be integrated and exploited in principle by *any* agent programming platform, enabling agents from heterogeneous platforms (with heterogeneous models and architectures) to interact and interoperate as part of the MAS, sharing common artifact-based environments [24].

In order to realise such an integration, both from a conceptual and an engineering point of view, the notion of *agent body* has been introduced, as that part of an agent which is – on the one hand – situated in a workspace, containing effectors to act upon workspace artifacts and sensors to perceive workspace observable events, and – on the other hand – governed by the *agent mind* which is in execution externally, on the agent platform side (see Fig. 8.8).

From an architectural point of view, platform-specific *bridges* are introduced to connect mind and body(ies), functioning as wrappers on the agent mind side to control the body and perceive stimuli collected by body sensors. Currently, bridges exist for *Jason*[4] platform [3], an interpreter for an extended version of AgentSpeak, Jadex[5] [22], a BDI agent platform based on Java and XML as mainstream language/technologies to develop intelligent software agent systems, and **simpA**[6] [26], a Java-based agent-oriented framework based on the A&A conceptual model[7].

The integration extends the repertoire of agent actions natively provided by the agent platform with a new set of actions for playing inside an artifact-based environment. The concrete realisation of all such actions can vary, depending on the specific agent programming platform [24]. Four main action groups can be identified (see Table 8.1):

- join and leave workspaces;
- create, lookup, dispose artifacts;
- use artifacts;

---

[4] http://jason.sourceforge.net)

[5] http://vsis-www.informatik.uni-hamburg.de/projects/jadex/

[6] http://simpa.sourceforge.net

[7] At the time of writing, ongoing work is on the integrations with 2APL [6] and JADE platform [1].

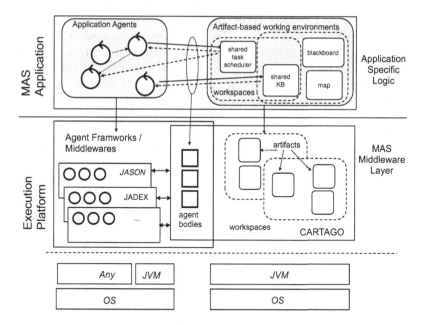

Fig. 8.8 A layered representation of a MAS in execution on top of CArtAgO, with in evidence *agent bodies* functioning as mediators with external agent platforms.

(1) `joinWorkspace(+Workspace[,Node])`
(2) `quitWorkspace`
(3) `makeArtifact(+Artifact,+ArtifactType[,ArtifactConfig])`
(4) `lookupArtifact(+ArtifactDesc,?Artifact)`
(5) `disposeArtifact(+Artifact)`
(6) `use(+Artifact,+UIControl([Params])[,Sensor][,Timeout][,Filter])`
(7) `sense(+Sensor,?PerceivedEvent[,Filter][,Timeout])`
(8) `focus(+Artifact[,Sensor] [,Filter])`
(9) `stopFocussing(+Artifact)`
(10) `observeProperty(+Artifact,+Property,?PropertyValue)`

Table 8.1 Actions for agents' interaction with the working environment: managing workspaces (1–2), creating, disposing and looking up artifacts (3–5), using artifacts (6–7), and observing artifacts (8–10). Syntax is expressed in a logic-like notation, where italicised items in square brackets are optional.

- observe artifacts without directly using them.

Actions in the first group (1–2 in Table 8.1) are used to manage a working session inside a workspace, joining or quitting a given workspace. The address of the CArtAgO node hosting the workspace can be specified, if the workspace is not on the local node.

In the second group (3–5), makeArtifact is used to create a new artifact (instance) specifying the artifact name and the artifact type. The type corresponds to the full name of the Java class implementing the artifact structure and behaviour (this point will be clairified in next section). Then, disposeArtifact is used to dispose of an existing artifact, and lookupArtifact to locate an artifact given its description. Actually, actions in this group are not primitive: they are built on top of the basic use and sense actions described in next group, and operate on some basic artifacts available by default in each workspace—in particular, the factory and registry artifacts.

Actions in the third group (6–7) are the core part of the API, described in Subsection 8.2.2.1: use selects (or acts on) a control of the artifact usage-interface to trigger the execution of an operation, while sense actively retrieves the percepts collected by a sensor. If a sensor is specified, it is used to collect any observable event subsequently generated by the artifact as an effect of the operation execution. If, instead, no sensor is specified, observable events are made observable to the agent directly as internal events to which the agent can react directly. Then, the action sense, in its turn, suspends the current agent's activity until a percept is available: optional parameters include a timeout (after which the action is considered failed), and a filter to select the percepts of interest.

Finally, actions in the fourth group (8–10) concern the capability of continuously observing artifacts' events (focus/stopFocussing) and properties (observeProperty) without directly using the operation controls, following the semantics informally described in Subsection 8.2.2.1. By executing focus on a specific artifact, all the observable events generated by such an artifact from that time on are made observable to the agent, despite the cause that originated them (such as the execution of an operation by some agent or an update of their observable properties). As in the case of use, a sensor may or may not be specified, according to the desired perception modality. It is worth noting that observeProperty does not involve sensors nor events: the value of the property is returned as an action feedback.

8.3.2 Programming and Using Artifacts: Basic Examples

In this section we briefly describe the main features of the API for programming artifacts and of the agent API to play within work environment by using some simple examples of artifacts and related agents working with them. The complexity of the type of artifacts used in the example is gradual, starting from a simple counter artifact, which is almost the simplest possible example useful to show the basics about artifact structure/behaviour and and artifact usage/observation. Then, more advanced features of artifact computational model are discussed in two further examples, showing the implementation of a bounded inventory artifact and and of a synchronizer artifact, along with the agents exploiting them. Other main features of the artifact computational model – linkability among the others – are not discussed here: the interested reader can find examples in CArtAgO documentation.

On the agent side *Jason* is adopted here as reference agent programming language, being general enough to make it straightforward for the reader to figure out how the same examples could be implemented different agent languages, in particular BDI-based such as Jadex and 2APL. The bridge integrating *Jason* with CArtAgO is called C4Jason, and is available on CArtAgO Web Site—along with the documentation describing how to set up a *Jason* MAS using CArtAgO and the concrete set of actions made available to agents to work within the CArtAgO environment.

8.3.2.1 First Step: A Counter

An artifact template (or type) is programmed directly by defining a Java class extending a pre-existing class – `alice.cartago.Artifact`, part of the API – and using a basic set of Java annotations[8] and existing methods to define the elements of artifact structure and behaviour. As a first example, we consider here a simple *counter* artifact, as an artifact displaying a count and providing the means to increment it (see Fig. 8.9, left): to this end, the artifact has a single observable property called count, displaying the current value of the count, and a single usage interface control called inc, used to increment the count. An example of the counter usage could be keeping track of the number of hits found by a team of agents searching for Web pages containing some information.

The implementation of the artifact using the Java-based CArtAgO API is shown in Fig. 8.9 (right side). The Counter artifact template is implemented by the Java class with the same name, extending the `alice.cartago.Artifact` class. The usage interface is implemented as a set of methods annotated with @OPERATION whose signatures coincide with the usage interface controls triggering operations and whose bodies represent the computational behaviour of the operation triggered by the control. Counter has a single inc usage interface control. For simple operations, like in this case, the operation is composed by a single atomic step, so the body of inc method represents the computational behaviour of the full operation. The init operation is executed by default when the artifact is instantiated, similarly to a constructor in the case of objects.

Observable properties are defined, typically during artifact initialisation, by means of the `defineObsProperty` primitive, specifying the property name and initial value. The counter has a single count observable property, which is read and updated by the execution of the inc operation by means of available primitives (`getObsProperty`, `updateObsProperty`). In this case, the artifact has no inner state variables, which would be implemented as directly instance fields of the object.

---

[8] A feature introduced with Java 5.0 that makes it possible to tag some elements of a class description on the source code – including methods, fields, and the class definition itself – with some descriptors possibly containing attributes that can be accessed at runtime by the program itself, through the reflection API. Annotations are represented by symbols of the kind @ANNOT_NAME, possibly containing also attributes @ANNOT_NAME(attrib=value,...).

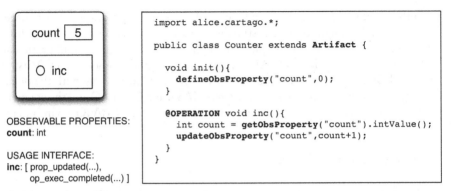

```
import alice.cartago.*;

public class Counter extends Artifact {

    void init(){
        defineObsProperty("count",0);
    }

    @OPERATION void inc(){
        int count = getObsProperty("count").intValue();
        updateObsProperty("count",count+1);
    }
}
```

OBSERVABLE PROPERTIES:
count: int

USAGE INTERFACE:
inc: [prop_updated(...),
    op_exec_completed(...)]

Fig. 8.9 A simple *counter* artifact example: on the left an abstract description of the counter observable properties and usage interface; on the right, an implementation in CArtAgO. The usage interface control (`inc`) includes also the list of the possible observable events generated by the operation execution. In this case the operation does not explicitly generate any observable event: `prop_updated` and `op_exec_completed` are generated by default when respectively an observable property is updated (`count` in this case) and when the operation execution has completed.

```
import alice.cartago.*;

public class Counter2 extends Artifact {
    int count;

    void init(){
        count = 0;
    }

    @OPERATION void inc(){
        count++;
        signal("count_incremented",count);
    }
}
```

OBSERVABLE PROPERTIES:
none

USAGE INTERFACE:
inc: [count_incremented(C),
    op_exec_completed(...)]

Fig. 8.10 An alternative version of the counter without observable properties, generating observable events only. Note that in this case the specification of the observable properties for the inc operation control includes also `count_incremented`, which is explicitly generated with the `signal` primitive.

In this minimal example, no observable events are explicitly generated by artifact operation: however, some observable events are generated by default, in particular `op_exec_completed(OpName)` is generated as soon as the operation has completed its execution and `prop_updated(PropName,NewValue,OldValue)` is generated as soon as the count observable property is updated. A variant of the counter without observable properties, purely based on observable events, is shown in Fig. 8.10. In this case, an observable event `count_incremented(C)` is explicitly generated by the `signal` primitive in the inc operation.

Then, two Jason agents interacting with an artifact counter follow. The first one simply creates a `Counter` artifact called `mycount` and interacts with it by selecting twice the `inc` operation and finally printing on the `console` artifact the value of the observable property `count`, retrieved by means of the `observeProperty` action:

```
!create_and_use.
+!create_and_use : true <-
  cartago.makeArtifact("mycount","Counter",C);
  cartago.use(C,inc);
  cartago.use(C,inc,s0);
  cartago.sense(s0,op_exec_completed(_),1000);
  cartago.observeProperty(C,count(V));
  cartago.use(console,println("Final count value: ", V)).
```

Brief explanation of the *Jason* code: `!create_and_use` defines agen's initial goal, i.e. `create_and_use`. Then it follows a plan to achieve the goal, which is triggered by the `+!create_and_use` goal addition event. Among the actions in the plan, those starting with "`cartago.`" are provided by the **CArtAgO** bridge.

The first occurrence of `use` action just triggers the operation without caring about events generated, the second one instead specifes the `s0` sensor and by means of the `sense` action executed on it the agent suspends its intention (for a maximum of 1000 milliseconds) until a perception matching `op_exec_completed(Op)` is found in the sensor or a timeout occurs. In the case of timeout, the action and then the plan fail.

The second agent – showed in the following – acts as a purely observer, first locating the `mycount` artifact and then starting to observe it and printing on the console a message as soon as it has a new percept about the value of the observable property:

```
!discover_and_observe.
+!discover_and_observe : true <-
  !locateCount(C);
  cartago.focus(C).

+count(V) : true <-
  cartago.use(
    console,println("Current observed count is ",V)
    ).

+!locateCount(C) : true <-
  cartago.lookupArtifact("mycount",C).
-!locateCount(C) : true <-
  .wait(10);
  !locateCount(C).
```

The *Jason* construct `!locateCount(C)` in the plan body specifies an achievement goal (`locateCount(C)`) which must be achieved before the execution of the rest of the plan. The `locateCount` block deserves some explanation. It is the plan to locate in the workspace the mycount artifact: first the agent tries to locate it by the lookupArtifact action. If the action fails, because the artifact has not been instantiated yet, then the locateCount plan fails and -!locateCount handles this event, specifying a contingency plan which suspends the activity for 10 milliseconds and after that retries to achieve the goal.

A main difference with respect to the previous agent is that in this case the agent reacts on the addition of the belief that concerns the count observable property, not on the detection of observable events.

A slightly different example involving observable events follows, in which the agent observes a Count2 artifact (see Fig. 8.10), which has no observable properties but generates the count_incremented(C) event with the inc operation execution:

```
!discover_and_observe.
+! discover_and_observe : true <-
  !locateCount(C);
  cartago.focus(C).

+count_incremented(V) [source("mycount2")]: true <-
  cartago.use(
    console,println("Current observed count is ",V)
    ).
...
```

Here the agent reacts to +count_incremented(V) which does not refer to the addition or change of a belief about the world, like in the case of count(C) percept in the previous case, but to the occurrence of an observable event, generated by mycount2 artifact. The snipped of code shows how *Jason* annotations are exploited for managing additional information brought by a CArtAgO event, such as the artifact source of the event (shown in the example), the name of the operation that generated the event, the artifact time in which the event has been generated, and so on.

8.3.2.2 Second Step: Usage Interface Controls with Guards

For each usage interface control a *guard* can be specified, as a condition over artifact state specifying if (when) the operation control is either *enabled* or *disabled*. Therefore, an operation control can change dynamically its status, from enabled to disabled and vice-versa, according to the state of the artifact. On the agent side, the behaviour of the use action depends on the usage interface control status: if it is enabled, the action succeeds and operation is triggered; if it is disabled, the use action is suspended until either the usage interface control becomes enabled or the timeout possibly specified as parameter of the use action occurs. Multiple use actions, typically executed by different agents, can be suspended on the same con-

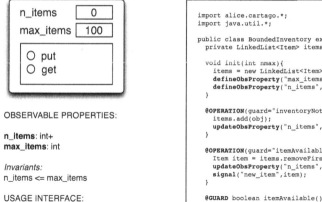

```
n_items     [  0  ]
max_items   [ 100 ]

O put
O get
```

OBSERVABLE PROPERTIES:

n_items: int+
max_items: int

Invariants:
n_items <= max_items

USAGE INTERFACE:

put(item:Item) / (n_items < max_items):
[prop_updated(...), op_exec_completed(...)]

get / (n_items >= 0) :
[prop_updated(...), new_item(item:Item),
op_exec_completed(...)]

```java
import alice.cartago.*;
import java.util.*;

public class BoundedInventory extends Artifact {
    private LinkedList<Item> items;

    void init(int nmax){
        items = new LinkedList<Item>();
        defineObsProperty("max_items",nmax);
        defineObsProperty("n_items",0);
    }

    @OPERATION(guard="inventoryNotFull") void put(Item obj){
        items.add(obj);
        updateObsProperty("n_items",items.size()+1);
    }

    @OPERATION(guard="itemAvailable") void get(){
        Item item = items.removeFirst();
        updateObsProperty("n_items",items.size()-1);
        signal("new_item",item);
    }

    @GUARD boolean itemAvailable(){ return items.size() > 0; }

    @GUARD boolean inventoryNotFull(Item obj){
        int maxItems = getObsProperty("max_items").intValue();
        return items.size() < maxItems;
    }
}
```

Fig. 8.11 A simple bounded-inventory artifact, exploiting guards in usage interface controls to synchronize agent use of the inventory.

trol: when (if) the control becomes active, one is selected non deterministically for being served and the other ones keep being suspended.

This feature is useful in general for realising quite easily basic forms of synchronization among multiple agents using an artifact. As a simple yet quite effective example, Fig. 8.11 shows the description and implementation of a *bounded-inventory* artifact, that is an artifact designed to function as a shared inventory mediating the exchange of some kind of *items* between a possibly dynamic number of *producer* agents and *consumer* agents. The producers-consumers architecture is quite common in concurrent systems, and requires some kind of effective coordination mechanism in order to coordinate the cyclic production of items by producer agents and its consumption by available consumer agents. The coordination strategy must be effective both for the performance (time) and the memory consumed. The introduction of a bounded-inventory is typically adopted as a mechanism to uncouple the interaction of producers and consumers and, at the same time, synchronize their activities, providing a locus of design (the size of the inventory) for tuning the performance of the system [13].

Fig. 8.11 shows an implementation of a bounder inventory artifact. The usage interface includes two guarded usage interface controls to respectively insert (put) e consume (get) items. Two observable properties are defined: max_nitems, showing the maximum capacity of the inventory, and n_items, showing the current number of items stored in the inventory. Internally, a simple linked list is used to store items.

Guards are implemented as boolean methods annotated with @GUARD, associated to operation controls by the guard attribute inside @OPERATION. In the example, the put control is enabled only when the inventory is not full (inventoryNotFull guard), and get is enabled when the inventory is not empty (itemAvailable guard). Then, for instance, if an agent selects the put operation control and the inventory is full, the action is suspended.

It follows a generic producer agent, which cyclically produce a new item object and tries to insert it into a myInventory artifact.

```
!produce.

+!produce: true <-
  +count(0);
  !produceItems.

+!produceItems : true <-
  ?nextItemToProduce(Item);
  cartago.use(myInventory,put(Item),5000);
  !produceItems.

-!produceItems: true <-
  cartago.use(console,println("Inventory timeout.")).

+?nextItemToProduce(Item) : true <-
  ?count(N);
  -+count(N+1);
  cartago.newObj("Item", [N],Item).
```

A count(N) belief, with N initially set to zero and then increment at each cycle, is used to represent the information content of the items to be inserted in the buffer. The *Jason* construct ?count(N) (and ?nextItemToProduce) is a test goal, used to retrieve information (the belief count(N)) from the belief base.

Differently from previous examples, here the agent selects the put usage interface control specifying a five seconds timeout, after which the use action and the overall plan fail and a message is printed on the console by the goal deletion plan -!produceItems.

An important issue concerning the integration of **CArtAgO** with agent platforms concerns the data structures exchanged with agent-artifact interaction, in particular as usage interface control parameters and observable events/properties arguments. To this end, object-oriented data structures are exploited – Java objects in particular – and the **CArtAgO** bridges provide specific API to create, manipulate, access from the agent platforms. In the example a new Item object is instantiated by the newObj internal action, which is part of the **CArtAgO** bridge API to work with objects; the Item class, not reported here, has a constructor accepting an integer value. An XML-based approach could be adopted as an alternative solution: Java objects are currently used for convenience, being **CArtAgO** currently implemented on Java. However it's worth remarking that, conceptually, the choice of the language to represent data objects is independent from the artifact computational model.

A generic consumer agent follows, cyclically interacting with the inventory to consume items:

```
!consume.

+!consume: true <-
  cartago.use(myInventory,get,s0,10000);
  cartago.sense(s0,new_item(Item));
  !consumeItem(Item);
  !consume.

+!consumeItem(Item) : true <- ...
```

In this case sensors are explicitly used to detect and manage the observable events of type new_item(Item) generated by the artifact executing the get operation. Note that here, differently from the counter user seen previously, the timeout is not specified for the sense action (so by default the sense timeout is infinite in this case) but for the use action selecting get.

8.3.2.3 Third Step: Composed Operations and Coordination Artifacts

In the previous examples, artifact operations were *atomic*, composed by a single step. In the most general case, which we will see is particularly useful to design coordination artifacts, operations can be conceived as controllable processes composed by the execution of multiple guarded computational steps, each one executed atomically. In that way multiple operations can be simultaneously in execution inside an artifact, by interleaving the steps. In CArtAgO operation steps are implemented by methods annotated with @OPSTEP, and a primitive called nextStep is provided to specify the chain of steps constituting an operation. In particular nextStep makes it possible to specify (from the computational body of an operation/step) the name and parameters of the next step to be triggered. Also for steps a guard can be specified, so a triggered step is executed actually only when (if) its guard is satisfied. The execution of an operation is considered completed only when no operation steps are pending.

Composed operations are useful to implement: *(i)* long-term operations inside artifacts, which need to provide some control points to their execution; *(ii)* coordination artifacts, which typically accounts for some structured operations interleaving their guarded steps. Here we consider one of the simplest cases of coordination artifact: a *synchronizer*, shown in Fig. 8.12. More complex cases, such as artifact implementing blackboards, tuple spaces, schedulers, have a similar design, based on structured operations with guarded operation steps.

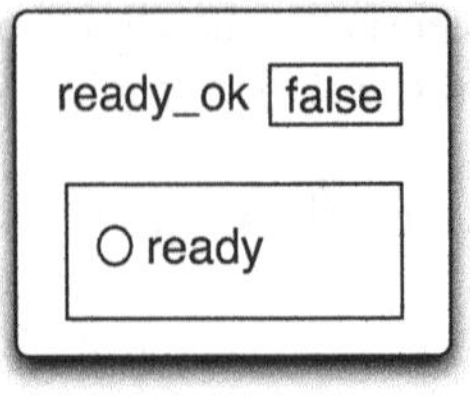

```
ready_ok  false

O ready
```

```
OBSERVABLE PROPERTIES:
ready_ok: {true,false}

USAGE INTERFACE:
ready: [ op_exec_completed(...),
         prop_updated(...) ]
reset: [ op_exec_completed(...),
         prop_updated(...)]
```

```java
import alice.cartago.*;

public class Syncroniser extends Artifact {
  int nReady, nParticipants;

  void init(int nParticipants){
    defineObsProperty("ready_ok",false);
    nReady = 0;
    this.nParticipants = nParticipants;
  }

  @OPERATION void ready(){
    nReady++;
    nextStep("setReadyOK");
  }

  @OPSTEP(guard="allReady") void setReadyOK(Item obj){
    updateObsProperty("ready_ok",true);
  }

  @GUARD boolean allReady(){ return nReady == nParticipants; }
```

Fig. 8.12 A synchronizer artifact, with a composed operation (ready).

The synchronizer is meant to be useful for a team of agents performing independent activities that need, at a certain point, to synchronize before proceeding. The usage interface of the artifact includes two operation controls: ready, which must be selected by each agent of the group as soon as it is ready to synchronize with the rest of the team, and reset, used to reset the synchronizer. Finally, the artifact has a ready_ok observable boolean property, which is set to true as soon as *all* the agents have achieved the synchronization point. The ready operation is structured in two steps: the first one is executed as soon as the operation control is selected, and it updates the inner state variable (nReady) which is used to keep track of the number of agents that have already reached the synchronization point. The second step called setReadyOK, triggered by the first one, is executed as soon as such a number of agents achieve the total number of agents to be synchronized (allReady guard), and its execution accounts for switching the ready_ok observable property to true.

A snipped of the code of a generic agent using the synchronizer follows, in two different versions:

```
!work.                             !work.

+!work: true <-                    +!work: true <-
   ...                                ...
   // synchronize                     // synchronize
   cartago.focus(mySynch);            cartago.use(mySynch,ready,s1);
   cartago.use(mySynch,ready).        cartago.sense(s1,
                                          op_exec_completed(ready));
+ready_ok(true) : true <-             // synchronized: go on
   // synchronized: go on              // working
   // working                         ...
   ...
```

In the first one, on the left, continuous observation is exploited and the agent proceeds its work as soon as it perceive the observable property `ready_ok` set to true. In the second one, on the right, a sensor is used and the agent proceeds its work as soon as it perceives the completion of the `ready` operation (the execution of an operation is considered completed only when there are no pending computational steps). The example does not include the creation of the `mySynch` artifact, which must be initialised with the number of agents participating to the synchronization.

8.4 Evaluation

From the agent programming languages/platforms perspective, CArtAgO can be conceived as a general-purpose tool to be exploited in all such application domains or problems in which the introduction of a suitably designed work environment could be useful and effective for designing and programming the MAS. In particular, the CArtAgO model provides a direct support for programming MAS featuring some degree of:

- *Distribution*: agents can join and work simultaneously in multiple workspaces possibly (not necessarily) hosted in different network nodes (i.e. CArtAgO nodes). Artifacts cannot be distributed across workspaces: however, distributed artifacts can be realised by linking together artifacts belonging to different workspaces (in different nodes).
- *Openness*: referring to the structure of the MAS, agents can dynamically join and quit from workspaces, and can dynamically change the set of artifacts in workspaces by creating and disposing them. The RBAC model makes it possible to constrain such openness according to policies that can be changed dynamically either by humans or by agents, since the functionality is encapsulated in proper system artifacts.
- *Heterogeneity*: being orthogonal to the specific model and architecture adopted to define agents, CArtAgO in principle supports the development of fully heterogenous MAS, in which different types of agents – either goal-oriented or reactive, in execution on different agent platforms – work together inside a common work environment. This feature could be a first step towards a novel form of *interoperability* in open MAS, besides the traditional one based on ACL-based communication, based in this case on working in the same workspace(s) and sharing and using the same artifacts with a common understanding of such a use—possibly using artifact manuals if necessary.

Besides these general features, in the following we describe some specific MAS programming contexts and problems where artifacts and CArtAgO have been already exploited with some results.

Coordination

Artifacts are a natural abstraction to encapsulate coordination mechanisms and make it available to agents as first-class entities to be controlled and managed by agents themselves [19]. By working as interaction enablers and mediators, coordination artifacts are particularly useful in all such contexts or problems which require a loosely-coupled interaction (in particular from a temporal and spatial point of view) among agents, and where it is useful to adopt an *objective* approach to coordination [17], i.e. encapsulating the state and the rules defining the coordination policy in some proper controllable medium, out of the interacting agents. Objective coordination is particularly useful when *(i)* the coordination laws are stable and the objective is to automate the coordination process as much as possible, without the need of negotiation among the participants which are even not required to know or understand to the overall coordination strategy; *(ii)* the coordination rules must be enforced besides the individual behaviour of the participants (prescriptive coordination), but without violating their autonomy (i.e. control of their behaviour). In our case all this is achieved by designing proper coordination tools that agents create, share and use at runtime.

Agents' capability to replace artifacts at runtime or to inspect and possibly change/adapt artifact functioning dynamically make the approach interesting for those contexts in which the overall coordination policies need to be changed at runtime, possibly without requiring changes in participant agents.

Organisation-Oriented Programming

Organisation Oriented Programming (OOP) in MAS is concerned with the introduction of proper organisation modelling languages and corresponding organisation-oriented middleware for supporting both organisations and their members [2]. One of the challenges there is to conceive and design proper infrastructures (i.e. middleware) for enacting the organisational rules and processed defined by organisational models without violating agent autonomy, and, at the same time, supporting *open* organisations. To this end, in the ORA4MAS proposal [11] artifact-based work environments are used to embody the functional side of MAS organisation—modelled in that case with MOISE+ organisation modelling language [9]. In ORA4MAS organisational infrastructure the functional part of the organisation is represented (and enacted) by some *organisational artifacts* used, on the one side, by organisation members to access to organisation services and, on the other side, controlled by organisational agents, reifying in that way part of the organisation as a set of distributed first-class entities populating the agent world.

System and Technology Integration

The integration and interaction with existing systems and technologies is a very common issue in building real applications with MAS. An example among the others is the integration of agent-based systems with Web based technologies (used as case study in many agent books, such as [20, 3]), including Web Services [8]. Typical solution to this problem accounts for either extending the set of agent actions with ad hoc new actions, which enable the interaction with external systems, or introducing wrapper agents that play the role of mediators (for instance the WSIG gateway agent proposed in the FIPA platform for mediating the interaction with Web Services [8]), encapsulating the machinery required to interact with the external system. An alternative solution is to introduce properly designed artifacts to be exploited by agents as tools providing functionalities to interact with external systems, and configured and adapted by agents according to their need. An example is described in [23], in which a basic set of artifacts is introduced to interact with Web Services and to implement Web Services in the Service-Oriented Architecture (SOA) context. This solution is more effective than the previous one in particular when the mediation function does not require autonomy, but, instead, controllability and (dynamic) configurability.

More generally, artifacts provide a principled way to reuse in agent languages existing technologies and libraries, typically developed in general-purpose non-agent languages such as Java or C, suitably wrapped in artifacts and represented as first-class entities in the agent world. As a simple yet common example, consider the need to create, access and manage a database from an agent-based application. A quite natural way to solve the problem using CArtAgO is to design a DBase artifact, providing a usage interface to make the SQL queries, mapping the information generated by the database (such as the answer to queries) as observable events or properties, and encapsulating in the artifact implementation the use of the standard JDBC Java library for database access. It is worth noting that in this case, by adopting this design, the artifact does not represent just a library of actions to access databases, but a specific instance of a database: multiple instances of the same artifact can be used to work with different databases.

Graphical User Interfaces are another quite explicative and useful example in this context. By adopting CArtAgO, a GUI can be easily implemented as an artifact used and observed by human users on the one side and by agents on the other side, wrapping and hiding the use of object-oriented GUI frameworks (such as Java Swing). As a concrete example, Fig. 8.13 shows the artifact implementation of a simple GUI frame (window) providing a button (get) and a text field functioning as a display. The usage interface provides the setValue) interface control to set the value of the display. Then, the artifact is programmed to generate two observable events: get_selected whenever the button is pressed and closed whenever the window is closing. Actually, the artifact in the example extends GUIArtifact which is an existing type of artifact included in CArtAgO libraries encapsulating the implementation of the mechanisms related to Java Swing event management. Such mechanisms are hidden inside the *mapXXXEvent* methods (ex-

```
!manage_gui.

+!manage_gui : true <-
  cartago.makeArtifact(myGUI,
            "MyGUIArtifact",GUI);
  cartago.focus(GUI).

+get_selected(Ev)[source(myGUI)]: true <-
  .random(R);
  cartago.use(myGUI,setValue(R)).

+closed(Ev)[source(myGUI)] : true <-
  .my_name(Me);
  .kill_agent(Me).
```

```
import javax.swing.*;
import alice.cartago.*;

public class MyGUIArtifact extends GUIArtifact {
  private MyFrame frame;

  void init() throws CartagoException {
    frame = new MyFrame();
    frame.setVisible(true);
    mapActionEvent(frame.getButton,"actionPerformed","get_selected");
    mapWindowEvent(frame, "windowClosing", "closed");
  }

  @OPERATION void setValue(double value){
    frame.text.setText(""+value);
  }

  class MyFrame extends JFrame {
    public JTextField text;

    public MyFrame(){
      setTitle("Simple GUI Artifact");
      setSize(200,100);
      JPanel panel = new JPanel();
      setContentPane(panel);
      JButton button = new JButton("get");
      button.setSize(80,50);
      panel.add(button);
      text = new JTextField(10);
      text.setEditable(false);
      panel.add(text);
    }
  }
}
```

Fig. 8.13 An example of simple GUI artifact implementation (right) used by a *Jason* agent (top-left).

amples are `mapActionEvent` and `mapWindowEvent` used in in Fig. 8.13), which make it possible to specify which observable events must be generated when a specific GUI events occur. In the example, an observable event `get_selected` is generated whenever an `actionPerformed` is triggered on the `frame.getButton` button, and `closed` when the frame is closed by the human user. The *Jason* agent shown in Fig. 8.13 observes the artifact and whenever a `get_selected` event is detected, it changes the value of the display with a random number by acting on the `setValue` control. If a `closed` event is detected, the agent terminates.

Goal-directed Use of Artifacts

An important research theme concerning A&A and **CArtAgO** is how artifacts could be effectively exploited in the context of intelligent agents to improve agents' ability to execute individual as well as social tasks. Questions related to this theme are: which reasoning models could be adopted by agents to use artifacts in the best way, simplifying their job; how could the manual be used in agent reasoning processes, in order to help them using artifacts and finally achieving their goal(s); how could an agent reason to select which artifacts to use; how could artifact function description be exploited for this purpose; how could agents reason to construct or adapt artifacts behaviour in order to be useful for their goals. Actually all these questions are strictly related to some of the main *foci* in the research in MAS applied to service-oriented architectures [14].

On the one side, the simplest case concerns agents directly programmed to use specific artifacts, like the examples shown in this chapter, with usage protocols directly defined by the programmer as part of the procedural knowledge/plans of the agents. In spite of its simplicity, this case can bring several advantages for MAS engineers, exploiting separation of concerns when programming agents on the one hand and work environments on the other hand. On the other side, in the case of fully *open* systems, the intuition is that artifact *manual* can be the key for building MAS where intelligent agents dynamically look for and select which artifacts to use, and then exploit them accordingly, simplifying the reasoning required to achieve the goals with respect to the case in which artifacts are not available. We refer to this as *goal-directed use of artifacts*.

Actually, it is useful to frame such abilities progressively, scaling with the openness and complexity of the domain context. Some levels can be identified, involving different kinds of artifact aspects and agents' abilities:

- *unaware use* – at this level, agents exploit artifacts without being aware of them. In other words, agents' actions never refer explicitly to the execution of operations on some kinds of artifacts.

- *programmed use* – at this level agents use some artifacts according to what has been explicitly programmed by the agent designer. In the case of cognitive agents, for instance, agent programmers can specify usage protocols directly as part of the agent plan. For the agent point of view, there is no need to understand explicitly artifacts' operating instructions or function: the only requirement is that the agent model adopted could be expressive enough to model in some way the execution of external actions and the perception of external events.

- *cognitive use* – at this level, the agent programmer directly specifies in the agent program some knowledge about what artifacts to use. However, how to exploit the artifacts is dynamically discovered by the agent, by reading the operating instructions inside the manual. So, generally speaking the agent must be able to embed the procedural knowledge given by the operating instructions in the procedural knowledge defined in its plans. First investigations on this level can be found in [29]. In this case the adoption of shared ontologies for operating instructions description/goal description is necessary.

- *cognitive selection and use* – this case extends the previous one by conceiving agents that autonomously select artifacts to use, get operating instructions and use them. With respect to the previous case, agents must be able both to understand and embed the operating instructions, and also understand artifacts function description, in order to possibly decide to use the artifacts for their own goal(s). It is worth noting that such a selection process can concern also set of cooperative agents, interested in using a coordination artifact for their social activities. As in the previous case, shared ontologies are necessary, in this case both for operating instructions and function description. Besides ontologies, from a cognitive point of view this level requires that both the artifact representational and operational contents are mapped into reasoning processes, in particular artifact representational contents (both static, such as the manuals, and dynamic, such as observable properties) has to be grounded with agents epistemic (beliefs) and motivational (goals) states. First investigation on this level can be found [21], which focuses goal-directed interaction in Jadex agents using artifacts, and in the notion of *extrospective agent* developed in [12].

- *construction and manipulation* – in this case the point of view is changed, considering agents playing the role of *designers* of the artifacts. At this level agents are supposed to understand how artifacts work, and to adapt their behaviour (or build new ones from scratch) in order to make it more effective or efficient for other agents' goals. For its complexity, this level generally concerns humans. However, agents can e.g. be adopted to change artifact behaviour according to schema explicitly defined by the agent programmer.

Future work is planned in particular for the last two levels, which are the core of the goal-directed use of work environments.

8.5 Conclusion and Future Developments

CArtAgO provides agent programming platforms with a principled and uniform approach to construct and use work environments in MAS, useful for both engineering the integration with the real external (physical or computational) environments and, in particular, for designing computational worlds inside the MAS that agents can exploit to perform their work.

Among the planned future works, the definition of a formal model and semantics for CArtAgO aligned with existing models defined for agent languages (such as [7]) will be important for both easing the integration of further agent platforms, and investigating the formal verification of MAS which include artifacts, along the line of the work suggested in [4].

Then, currently CArtAgO lacks a reference model and ontologies for defining the machine-readable content of artifact manuals, and this partially limits the level of inter-operability and openness that can be achieved. Accordingly, some planned future work is in this direction: towards the definition of a common model for manuals, with a shared semantics of the description of artifact purpose and usage. For this purpose, existing work on related research domains, such as the Semantic Web [28] and Functional Reasoning [5], will be an important reference. This step is particularly important for the investigations about the intelligent use, construction and adaptation of work environments by cognitive agents, as discussed in Section 8.4.

Besides open systems and interoperability, the integration with heterogeneous cognitive agent platforms makes it possible to easily create testbeds for benchmarking and comparing different agents and MAS models and their design solutions. Then, future work will also account for exploring how the different cognitive models may differ in their performances given their different reasoning processes and problem-solving styles.

References

1. Bellifemine, F.L., Caire, G., Greenwood, D.: Developing Multi-Agent Systems with JADE. Wiley (2007)
2. Boissier, O., Hübner, J.F., Sichman, J.S.: Organization oriented programming: from closed to open organizations. In: G. O'Hare, O. Dikenelli, A. Ricci (eds.) Engineering Societies in the Agents World VII (ESAW 06). Selected and Revised papers., *LNCS*, vol. 4457, pp. 86–105. Springer-Verlag (2007)
3. Bordini, R., Hübner, J., Wooldridge, M.: Programming Multi-Agent Systems in AgentSpeak Using Jason. John Wiley & Sons, Ltd (2007)
4. Bordini, R.H., Fisher, M., Visser, W., Wooldridge, M.: Verifying multi-agent programs by model checking. Autonomous Agents and Multi-Agent Systems **12**(2), 239–256 (2006)
5. Chandrasekaran, B.: Functional representation: a brief historical perspective. Applied Artificial Intelligence **8**, 173–197 (1994)
6. Dastani, M., Meyer, J.J.: A practical agent programming language. In: Proceedings of the 5th International Workshop on Programming Multi-agent Systems (ProMAS'07) (2007)
7. Dennis, L.A., Farwer, B., Bordini, H.R., Fisher, M., Wooldridge, M.: A common semantic basis for BDI languages. In: Programming Multi-Agent Systems, no. 4908 in Lecture Notes in Computer Science. Springer Berlin / Heidelberg (2007)
8. Greenwood, D., Lyell, M., Mallya, A., Suguri, H.: The IEEE FIPA approach to integrating software agents and web services. In: AAMAS '07: Proceedings of the 6th international joint conference on Autonomous agents and multiagent systems, pp. 1–7. ACM, New York, NY, USA (2007). DOI http://doi.acm.org/10.1145/1329125.1329458
9. Hübner, J.F., , Sichman, J.S., Boissier, O.: Developing organised multi-agent systems using the MOISE+ model: Programming issues at the system and agent levels. International Journal of Agent-Oriented Software Engineering **1**(3/4), 370–395 (2007)
10. Jennings, N.R.: An agent-based approach for building complex software systems. Commun. ACM **44**(4), 35–41 (2001)
11. Kitio, R., Boissier, O., Hübner, J.F., Ricci, A.: Organisational artifacts and agents for open multi-agent organisations: "Giving the power back to the agents". In: J.S. Sichman, P. Noriega, J. Padget, S. Ossowski (eds.) Coordination, Organizations, Institutions, and Norms in Agent Systems III. Selected and revised papers., *LNCS*, vol. 4870, pp. 171–186. Springer-Verlag (2008)
12. L. Acay, D., Sonenberg, L., Ricci, A., Pasquier, P.: How situated is your agent? a cognitive perspective. In: Post-proceedings of the 6th International Workshop "Programming Multi-Agent Systems" (PROMAS 2008) (2008)
13. Malone, T., Crowston, K.: The interdisciplinary study of coordination. ACM Computing Surveys **26**(1), 87–119 (1994)
14. N. Huhns, M., Singh, M.P., Burstein, M., et al.: Research directions for service-oriented multiagent systems. IEEE Internet Computing **9**(6), 69–70 (2005)
15. Nardi, B. (ed.): Context and Consciousness: Activity Theory and Human-Computer Interaction. MIT Press (1996)
16. Norman, D.: Cognitive artifacts. In: J. Carroll (ed.) Designing interaction: Psychology at the human–computer interface, pp. 17–38. Cambridge University Press, New York (1991)
17. Omicini, A., Ossowski, S.: Objective versus subjective coordination in the engineering of agent systems. In: M. Klusch, S. Bergamaschi, P. Edwards, P. Petta (eds.) Intelligent Information Agents: An AgentLink Perspective, *LNAI: State-of-the-Art Survey*, vol. 2586, pp. 179–202. Springer-Verlag (2003). DOI 10.1007/3-540-36561-3
18. Omicini, A., Ricci, A., Viroli, M.: Artifacts in the A&A meta-model for multi-agent systems. Autonomous Agents and Multi-Agent Systems **17** (3) (2008)
19. Omicini, A., Ricci, A., Viroli, M., Castelfranchi, C., Tummolini, L.: Coordination artifacts: Environment-based coordination for intelligent agents. In: AAMAS'04, vol. 1, pp. 286–293. ACM, New York, USA (2004)

20. Padgham, L., Wiknikoff, M.: Developing Intelligent Agent Systems: A Practical Guide. Wiley (2004)
21. Piunti, M., Ricci, A., Braubach, L., Pokahr, A.: Goal-directed interactions in artifact-based mas: Jadex agents playing in CARTAGO environments. In: Proc. of IAT (Intelligent Agent Technology) '08 Conference (2008)
22. Pokahr, A., Braubach, L., Lamersdorf, W.: Jadex: A BDI reasoning engine. In: R. Bordini, M. Dastani, J. Dix, A.E.F. Seghrouchni (eds.) Multi-Agent Programming. Kluwer (2005)
23. Ricci, A., Denti, E., Piunti, M.: A platform for developing SOA/WS applications as open and heterogeneous multi-agent systems. Accepted for publication in the Multiagent and Grid Systems International Journal (MAGS), Special Issue about "Agents, Web Services and Ontologies: Integrated Methodologies" (2009)
24. Ricci, A., Piunti, M., Acay, L.D., Bordini, R., Hubner, J., Dastani, M.: Integrating artifact-based environments with heterogeneous agent-programming platforms. In: Proceedings of 7th International Conference on Agents and Multi Agents Systems (AAMAS08) (2008)
25. Ricci, A., Viroli, M., Omicini, A.: The A&A programming model & technology for developing agent environments in MAS. In: M. Dastani, A. El Fallah Seghrouchni, A. Ricci, M. Winikoff (eds.) Post-proceedings of the 5th International Workshop "Programming Multi-Agent Systems" (PROMAS 2007), LNAI, vol. 4908, pp. 91–109. Springer (2007)
26. Ricci, A., Viroli, M., Piancastelli, G.: simpA: A simple agent-oriented Java extension for developing concurrent applications. In: M. Dastani, A.E.F. Seghrouchni, J. Leite, P. Torroni (eds.) Languages, Methodologies and Development Tools for Multi-Agent Systems (LADS 2007). Selected and Revised Papers., LNAI, vol. 5118, pp. 176–191. Springer-Verlag: Heidelberg, Germany, Durham, UK (2007)
27. Russell, S., Norvig, P.: Artificial Intelligence, A Modern Approach (second edition). Prentice Hall (2003)
28. Shadbolt, N., Berners-Lee, T., Hall, W.: The semantic web revisited. IEEE Intelligent Systems 21(3), 96–101 (2006)
29. Viroli, M., Ricci, A., Omicini, A.: Operating instructions for intelligent agent coordination. The Knowledge Engineering Review 21(1), 49–69 (2006). DOI 10.1017/S0269888906000774
30. Weyns, D., Omicini, A., Odell, J.J.: Environment as a first-class abstraction in multi-agent systems. Autonomous Agents and Multi-Agent Systems 14(1), 5–30 (2007). DOI 10.1007/s10458-006-0012-0. Special Issue on Environments for Multi-agent Systems
31. Weyns, D., Parunak, H.V.D. (eds.): Journal of Autonomous Agents and Multi-Agent Systems. Special Issue: Environment for Multi-Agent Systems, vol. 14(1). Springer Netherlands (2007)

Chapter 9
A Survey of Agent-oriented Development Tools

Alexander Pokahr and Lars Braubach

Abstract Development tools represent an important additive for the practical realization of software applications, mainly because they help automating development activities and are able to hide complexity from developers. In this chapter,
the requirements for tools are generically analyzed by the various tasks that need
to be performed in the different development phases. These requirements are the
foundation for a detailed investigation of the landscape of available agent-oriented
development tools. In order to assess the variety of tools systematically, existing
surveys and evaluations have been used to isolate three important categories of
tools, which are treated separately: modeling tools, IDEs and phase-specific tools.
For each of these categories specific requirements are elaborated, an overview of
existing tools is given and one representative tool is presented in more detail.

9.1 Introduction

The term *tool* is defined in dictionaries as a means used in performing an operation
or task. In computing, a (software) tool is therefore a software for developing
software or hardware.[1] As the product that is developed with a software tool is

Alexander Pokahr
Distributed Systems and Information Systems Group,
Computer Science Department, University of Hamburg,
Vogt-Kölln-Str. 30, D-22527 Hamburg, Germany
e-mail: pokahr@informatik.uni-hamburg.de

Lars Braubach
Distributed Systems and Information Systems Group,
Computer Science Department, University of Hamburg,
Vogt-Kölln-Str. 30, D-22527 Hamburg, Germany
e-mail: braubach@informatik.uni-hamburg.de

[1] Wiktionary.com: "tool" (5 October 2008),
http://en.wiktionary.org/w/index.php?title=tool&oldid=5262373

R.H. Bordini et al. (eds.), *Multi-Agent Programming*,
DOI 10.1007/978-0-387-89299-3_9, © Springer Science+Business Media, LLC 2009

itself again a piece of software, we further want to restrict our discussions on tools to so called *development tools* . A development tool is a software that is used by a software developer to produce some result (e.g. a text editor used for editing a source file). Unlike other kinds of software (e.g. libraries or agent platforms), a development tool is only used during the development of a system and not part of the final software product.

The results presented in this chapter are part of a larger survey on agent-oriented development artifacts. Specifically, agent architectures, languages, methodologies, platforms and tools have been researched. For the evaluation of the surveyed representatives, a criteria catalog has been developed, which covers besides functional criteria also non-functional issues such as usability, operating ability and pragmatics. Details of the criteria catalog as well as condensed and summarized survey results can be found in [14]. The criteria catalog will be used in this chapter as a guiding principle for discussing requirements with respect to tool support. More information on the survey is available in [11], covering architectures, methodologies and platforms, and in [47], dealing with languages and tools.

In the next section, the background on software development tools will be presented, thereby highlighting general requirements and providing a model for assessing tool support for the different phases in the software development process. Section 9.3 deals with agent-oriented tools. In this section, a survey about existing agent-oriented software development tools will be given. Thereafter, in Sections 9.4 and 9.5, two important categories of tools – namely modeling tools and integrated development environments (IDEs) – are discussed in detail. In Section 9.6, tools for individual phases of the development process are presented. A short evaluation of the presented state-of-the-art is given in Section 9.7. The chapter closes with a summary and conclusion.

9.2 Background

The following sections discuss which kinds of tools are employed in the different phases of the software development process. For generality and simplicity, a basic and well-known five phase model [6] is used as a foundation instead of a concrete and detailed agent-oriented methodology such as Gaia [73] or Prometheus [45]. The five phase model distinguishes between 1) requirements, 2) design, 3) implementation, 4) testing, and 5) deployment.

First, an overview of common development tasks in each of the phases will be given (Section 9.2.1). For a structured and systematic discussion, these tasks are then unified according to a generalized classification scheme (Section 9.2.2). Further, kinds of tools for supporting the tasks as well as criteria for assessing the quality of tool support are presented in Section 9.2.3. The following discussions are intentionally kept general (i.e. not specific to agent-oriented software development) to avoid an isolated "agents only" view and for facilitating a comparison of the state of the art of agent tools with respect to the state of the art in software engineering in general.

9.2.1 Development Tasks During the Software Engineering Process

This section describes the tasks, a developer has to perform during the different phases of the software development process. Usually, these tasks correspond to single steps, which have to be conducted more than once during iterative refinements.

The *requirements* phase is necessary to elaborate the requirements of the software to be. This phase involves talking to end users and customers to identify the needs and wishes. These have to be analyzed for being able to write them down in a precisely defined and unambiguous form. The elaborated requirements also have to be checked for consistency to each other and the requirements specifications have to be validated with the aid of the customers and end users.

After the requirements have been fixed, the *design* of the system can start. The design phase has the goal to develop a blueprint of a system that captures all identified requirements. During the continuous refinements of the design it should be checked for consistency of the design artifacts to each other. Moreover, the design should be validated with respect to the identified requirements, such that problems in the development process can be detected early.

Tasks during the *implementation* phase mainly consist in editing the source code. This includes, besides creating new code fragments, also the task of refactoring, which is a systematic restructuring of the source with the aim of preserving the existing functionality but at the same time e.g. better supporting the integration of planned future functionality. Depending on the level of detail in the design, code generation can be used to produce initial code fragments automatically based on the design information. For iterative development processes it is in this case necessary that changes to the code are also reflected in the original design artifacts, e.g. by using reverse engineering technologies. Another important task during the implementation phase is producing documentation to keep the code base maintainable and understandable. Therefore, decisions should be documented, which are necessary because of a higher abstraction of design artifacts compared to the concrete code. Especially, the concrete interfaces between modules of the system should be described, as in larger projects these modules are often developed by independent developer teams.

In accordance with the V-model [22, 52], the steps of system *testing* mirror the steps of system design in the opposite direction. System design moves from abstract requirements to detailed design-specification and finally concrete code. To validate an implementation, these steps should be taken backwards. Therefore one starts validating concrete implementations of partial functionalities (e.g. by so called unit testing). Validation errors occurring in this step usually can be cor-

rected directly in the code. When the functionality of single components is verified, the correct interplay between these components can be validated (integration
testing). This shows, if design specification (e.g. interface definitions) are sufficient
to ensure the smooth integration of components. If validation errors occur at this
stage, often design decisions have to be revised and implementations adapted accordingly. Finally, a validation of the system as a whole is performed with respect
to the initially identified requirements. In so called system tests, the developers
can play through the defined use cases. During acceptance tests, the system is evaluated by the real end users and customers. Problems, which are identified in these
tests, form the requirements that are used in the next iteration of the development
process.

The *deployment* of a software system follows a sequence of several steps (cf. [40]).
Because systems are usually not developed from scratch, the first step is to ob-
tain/provide the required additional components. Thereafter, the obtained and
newly developed components have to be configured according to the intended
usage contexts resulting in a set of application configuration specifications. For
each application configuration, a deployment plan needs to be devised. In the
preparation step, the code of the application components will be placed at the required target locations. When all components are installed, the application can be
started, meaning that for a complex distributed application several components
on potentially different network nodes need to be started. Once the application is
running, the maintenance phase starts, during which e.g. changes to the application configurations can be made. Such changes may not require performing a new
iteration of the development process, if they have been already considered in the
system design. Depending on the runtime infrastructure may be possible while
the application runs or may require the application to be restarted. For unforeseen
changes, the development process has to start again for designing, implementing,
testing and deploying changed components according to the new requirements.

Besides these tasks corresponding to the five development process phase, there are
other cross-cutting tasks, which have to be conducted during the whole development process. Among such tasks are the provision, management and usage of a
repository for holding and providing consistent access to the different versions
of the produced specifications and code. Also the coordination among software
developers is a task that is required in all phases.

9.2.2 Classification of Software Engineering Tasks

The aim of the last section was to give an overview of the different tasks and
activities that have to be performed during the software development process.
This section investigates how these tasks can be supported by software tools. To
keep the discussion general it is abstracted away from concrete tools and specific
tasks. Instead it is tried to identify the commonalities for tasks that recur in similar
forms in different phases. This investigation helps to identify the kind of tool

support that is required in general and also sheds some light on the relations between different kinds of tools.

A unification and categorization of the tasks from the last section is illustrated graphically in Figure 9.1. The five phases of the software development process (*requirements, design, implementation, testing, deployment*) are shown from the left to the right. From top to bottom, you can find a classification according to *primary tasks, ancillary tasks,* and *cross-cutting tasks* (see left hand side legend).

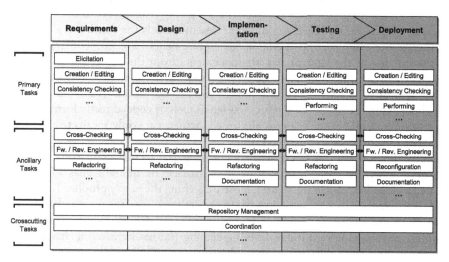

Fig. 9.1 Tasks in the software engineering process

Primary tasks are those tasks, that form the major part of a phase. Therefore, such tasks should if possible be supported by a single integrated tool to avoid having to switch often between different work environments. This means that, e.g., a design tool should support all tasks of the design phase in an integrated and consistent way.

Supporting tasks, which are optional or required less often compared to primary tasks are termed ancillary tasks. Because these tasks make up only a low portion of the overall development effort, requirements for tool support for these tasks are somewhat reduced. E.g. support for some of these tasks need not be part of an integrated tool but can also be realized in several independent tools, without causing too much interruption in the workflow of the developer. Nevertheless, an integration of such tools would be beneficial, e.g. in the form of plug-in mechanisms that allow to invoke external tools from an integrated development environment. Finally, cross-cutting tasks are not associated only to a single phase of the development process. Therefore, tool support for these tasks should be realized separately from any tool that is only intended for a specific phase so as not to require the use of tools from different phases. E.g., repository management support should not be realized solely as part of a design tool, otherwise developers would be required to always have the design tool at hand even in the later development phases. Nevertheless, some integration of the functionality (e.g. using plug-ins) into phase specific tools can be beneficial as long as it does not hinder the consistent usage across all phases.

In the following, the concretely identified generalized tasks as shown inside the Figure 9.1 will be explained in more detail. In the figure, similar tasks are subsumed under a common name. Therefore, a common primary task for all phases is the *creation and editing* of artifacts, where artifacts depend on the phase (e.g. requirements specifications, design models, application code, test cases, or deployment descriptors). Also, the *consistency checking* refers to the artifacts of the respective phases, e.g. checking different design models for consistency to each other. Some tasks such as *elicitation* of requirements have no counterpart on other phases, as the later phases, the documents from the earlier phases are directly used as input. Similarly, the *performing* of artifacts such as test cases and deployment plans only happens in the last two phases respectively, because in the earlier phases, the produced artifacts (design models or code) directly form the desired result, while in the last two phases, the artifacts are only means to the final goal of a validated resp. installed system.

Unlike the primary task of consistency checking, the ancillary *cross-checking* task refers to checking the consistency between artifacts of different phases (as indicated by small arrows in the figure), mostly checking the newly produced artifacts of the current phase for consistency with the artifacts from the earlier phase(s) to verify that, e.g., design models capture all previously defined requirements. In a similar way, also forward and reverse engineering (*fw. rev. engineering*) has to consider artifacts from different phases. The aim is to automatically create artifacts for one phase out of the information available in artifacts in an earlier (forward engineering) or later phase (reverse engineering). A common form of this task is code generation, which produces an implementation phase artifact (code) based on some design phase artifacts (design models). *Refactoring* is the task of systematically changing a set of artifacts with respect to a common restructuring goal. Systematic means that changes apply to many artifacts at once and special care has to be taken to ensure the consistency of the artifacts.[2] These tasks are termed ancillary because they are partially optional (fw./rev. engineering and refactoring) or are only require limited amount of effort (cross-checking) compared to the primary tasks. Another ancillary task that requires limited amount of effort is producing *documentation* for the specific phase. Because the major artifacts of the requirements and design phase have documentary character themselves, a separate documentation task is not considered for these phases, in other words, (creating/editing of) documentation is a primary task in these phases.

Cross-cutting tasks are also associated to the artifacts of the different phases. E.g. the aim of *repository management* is to store the artifacts and their changes and to provide access to them, when needed. Besides the artifacts itself, meta-information such as the user, version and time of a change needs to be stored. Also the *coordi-*

---

[2] Although refactoring is often referred to in the context of code refactoring only, it is also possible to generalize the refactoring idea to other kinds of artifacts. For example, [61, 7] propose refactoring mechanism for UML design models.

nation is usually tightly coupled to the creation and editing of artifacts. E.g. it has to be coordination who is allowed to edit which artifact (access management) and who is responsible for creating which artifact (task allocation).

The dots in the categories indicate that the figure is not claimed to be complete with respect to all possible kinds of software development tasks. For example the list of tasks could easily be extended to tasks, which are less focused to direct development tasks, such as e.g. project management or quality assurance.

9.2.3 Tool Support for Development Tasks

For an effective and efficient software development it is essential that preferably all tasks and activities during the development process are adequately supported by tools. Nowadays, a huge amount of vastly different tools has been developed in research and industry. Grundy and Hosking [30] have given a broad overview over the state of the art in the area of software tools. Their overview considers tools in general (i.e. not specifically focused on agent-oriented application development). Grundy and Hosking identify 18 different kinds of tools (e.g. design tools, IDEs, as well as testing and debugging tools) and describe the phases in the development process, where these tools are used. The considered tools usually support more than a single activity or task inside a phase like, e.g. design tools, which besides the creation and editing of design models also often support consistency checking and/or code generation. Moreover, some tools can be used across different development phases. For example, many IDEs not only address the implementation phase, but also offer support for testing and debugging as well as sometimes aspects of deployment.

The quality of any tool support can be assessed by considering the degree of support for the different phases and tasks. The support for all tasks and activities in the sense of a complete tool-support for the software development process can be achieved on the one hand by combining a multitude of specialized tools for single tasks or on the other hand by a few powerful tools, each of which addresses a large portion of software development tasks. Besides this functional quality aspects, also non-functional quality criteria, such as usability, operating ability and pragmatic aspects (cf. [14]) should be considered when evaluating or designing tool support. For these criteria, the continuity of the tool support is of primal importance (cf. [51]). In this respect, continuity refers to the seamless working with the same artifacts across different interrelated tasks. This continuity can easily be obtained, if support for related tasks is combined in a larger tool (e.g. design tool or IDE). When related tasks are supported by separate tools, the continuity needs to be achieved by an integration of these tools. A fully integrated tool support also directly improves usability, because it provides a unified view of the development process reducing the learning effort and the potential for errors. According to Figure 9.1, integration can be pursued across two axes. On the one hand, integration can consider two tasks from different phases (horizontal integration). For example design and implementation tools, which are both responsible for creating and editing artifacts could be integrated by providing an interface for data interchange. On the other hand, tasks from the same phases can be integrated (vertical integration), like combining support for these tasks inside a common usage interface, e.g. using a plug-in mechanism. Grundy and Hosking [30], differentiate four basic ways of integration: *data integration, control integration, presentation integration* and *process integration*. Data integration is achieved by the already mentioned data interchange interfaces and can be based on standardized as well as proprietary data formats. Data interchange is essential to allow consistency checking among artifacts created with different tools (especially for cross-checking artifacts from different phases). Control integration allows redirecting commands issued in one tool to another tools. As an example consider a debugger and a source code editor, where the debugger has to tell the editor, which line to show, when the developer issues a program step. Presentation integration has the goal to combine the functionality of different tools in a unified user interface, e.g. simply by invoking the command line tools such as CVS/SVN and present their output or by using sophisticated plug-in facilities that allow to extend also the user interfaces, e.g. of integrated development environments. Finally, process integration focuses on integrating subsequent activities or steps. Therefore, process integration has to combine data, control, and presentation integration and adds knowledge about the development process and the interdependencies of process steps, i.e. process integration automatically presents to the developer the right tool with the right data for the next required working task.

To summarize the preceding analysis of tools and tool support it is noted that, according to Section 9.2.2, the quality of tool support and integration is more important for the primary tasks than for ancillary tasks. With respect to the goal of achieving a complete and continuous tool supported development process this means that modeling or design tools as well as IDEs are the most important class of tools, as these tools aim to combine and integrate most of the primary tasks and also many ancillary tasks from the requirements and design as well as implementation testing and deployment phases. Moreover, cross-cutting tasks should be supported by separate tools, which are not bound to a specific development phase. In the following, it will be investigated, how these requirements for design tools, IDEs, and tools for cross-cutting tasks can be met by existing agent-oriented software tools.

9.3 Agent-oriented Development Tools

The previous sections of this chapter have taken a general viewpoint towards tools. This section investigates, which kind of tools exist in the specific area of agent-oriented software engineering. For this investigation, existing surveys and online resources on agent software are used as a starting point. As some of these surveys have a quite specific focus, the results of them cannot be easily compared to each other. Particularly, some surveys consider quite different kinds of agent software, not limited to pure development tools as defined in the introduction, but often also agent platforms and execution environments. Moreover, it should be distinguished between generic software and software that is targeted to a specific application domain or category. Such category-specific software e.g. supports the creation of virtual characters or the building and execution of simulation experiments. In addition, some of the surveys also include built agent-oriented applications. To give a coherent view of existing agent software, the following analysis presents not only development tools, but also runtime-relevant software like agent platforms and support libraries. Further categories of software are introduced as needed, when they are present in some survey or online resource. Nevertheless, in the subsequent discussions the scope will again be reduced to development tools.

9.3.1 Analysis of Existing Surveys and Online Resources

The examined surveys differ in the selection of tools as well as in the definition of the investigated categories. Some investigations only define a single category and only study representatives of this category. Other surveys have the aim to be broader and therefore examine different representatives of categories, which are defined in advance or afterwards.

Among the surveys focused on a single category, Eiter and Mascardi [23] and Bitting et al. [5] only consider environments for developing agent applications. The term multi-agent system development kit (MASDK) is introduced to denote integrated development environments with functionalities similar to object-oriented IDEs, such as eclipse[3] or IntelliJ IDEA[4]. Considering the examined development environments such as AgentBuilder [53], IMPACT [21], JACK [71], and Zeus [39], it can be noted that each of them introduces a new proprietary programming language for agent specification. In contrast, object-oriented IDEs usually support existing languages like C++ and Java. This difference is probably due to the fact, that in the area of agent technology no broad consensus exists about how to implement the agent specific concepts leading to quite different approaches with their own respective advantages and drawbacks. The use of proprietary concepts and languages forces these development environments to also include runtime components such as an agent platform for supporting the execution of the developed agents. Runtime environments resp. platforms for executing agents are the focus of Serenko and Detlor [56], Fonseca et al. [24] as well as Pokahr and Braubach [48, 13]. These surveys consider in addition to platforms as part of a development environment also pure execution environments like JADE [3] and ADK

---

[3] http://www.eclipse.org
[4] http://www.jetbrains.com/idea/

[64]. These platforms do not introduce new proprietary programming languages, but instead rely on existing object-oriented languages such as Java.

The respective aims of the broader surveys are sometimes quite difficult to define. E.g. Mangina [36] considers agent software in general, based on the entries of the AgentLink agent software directory at that time. The survey includes 36 representatives, but partitions them in quite vaguely defined categories such as "development environment" or "support software". Newer reviews of Bordini et al. [9, 8] and Unland et al. [65] consider current software from the area of agent-oriented software engineering categorized, e.g., in languages, platforms, and applications [9].

9.3.1.1 Agent Software in the AgentLink Software Directory

The most current and comprehensive overview over agent software is the publicly available AgentLink agent software directory.[5] It was initiated in the context of a series of EU-funded research networks. Although AgentLink ended in 2005, the list has still been updated since then.[6] With a total of 125 entries[7] it is therefore much more up-to-date than other online resources, which seem to be no longer maintained, such as the UMBC Agent Web software directory (149 entries until 2003)[8] or the even no longer available Université Laval Agents Portal (40 entries until 2006) or MultiAgent.com (35 entries until 2007).

An in-depth analysis of the representatives listed in the AgentLink directory results in the chart shown in Figure 9.2. For the chart, each of the entries has first been assigned to one of the major groups introduced in the beginning of this section, namely *tools* (left hand side), *runtime* software (middle) and software for a *specific application category* (right). The tools group is subdivided into *IDEs*, *design* tools, as well as *other* tools. In the runtime software group it is further distinguished between complete *platforms* and additional supporting *libraries*, which do not form a platform in their own respect. Category-specific software comprises runtime environments for simulation (*sim.*), applications (*app.*) and miscellaneous agent software (*misc.*), which does not fit into any other category, such as libraries for developing virtual characters.

For valid conclusions about the current state of the art, it has also been investigated, which of the representatives are still actively developed. A representative is termed inactive, if there has not been a software update or a publication about the software in the last two years. The number in braces give the exact number of representatives, whereas the first number is only the active representatives, while the second number is the total number (i.e. active and inactive) representatives.

---

[5] http://eprints.agentlink.org/view/type/software.html

[6] Last entry was added on September 10th, 2007.

[7] Of the actually 128 entries, three have been identified as duplicates.

[8] http://agents.umbc.edu/Applications_and_Software/Software/index.shtml

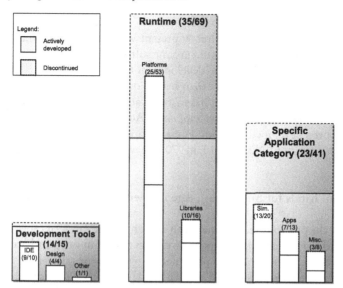

Fig. 9.2 Analysis based on AgentLink tool directory

Considering the distribution of entries into the three major groups, it can be observed, that runtime software is by far the most common group (69 of 125, i.e 55%). The smallest part is tools with only 15 of 125 entries (12%). The reason for this distribution could be that agent programming is still young compared to e.g. object-oriented programming and therefore the main focus of research and development has initially been on the basic infrastructure for execution, and somewhat less on abstract and easy to use development tools. When considering only actively developed representatives, the picture changes in favor of the tools, which now make up 20% (14 of 72) compared to now only 48% for runtime software, while the third category stays around the same level of 32%. This result could be an indication that the available runtime infrastructure has matured in the recent years as now the focus has shifted towards higher level tools.

Concerning the subdivisions in the major groups, it can be noted that platforms are by far the most commonly developed kind of agent software (53 of 125 entries, i.e. 42%). A reason for this might be the already mentioned lack of consensus among agent researchers forcing many research teams to develop a platform on their own instead of reusing existing software. Also, simulation software makes up a considerable portion (16%), which is even higher than the tools group in total and indicates that agent technology is already quite well accepted in the area of simulation. Another noticeable fact is that IDEs are developed twice as much compared to design tools. A possible reason for this could be that the proprietary programming languages often require developing new IDEs while for modeling techniques, which are not specifically agent-oriented, existing tools (e.g. UML tools) can partially be used.

Finally, the reduction of the subcategories to only active representatives is explained. It confirms the picture already present with regard to the major groups, namely, that fewer representatives of runtime software like platforms and libraries remain compared to, e.g. IDEs and development tools. The biggest reduction is in the area of platforms, where more than half of the platforms (54%) are no longer developed. This indicates this area has matured and a convergence to a few widely used platforms, such as JADE, has happened. Additionally, only few of the platforms have been developed in a commercial setting (ca. 10 of 53, i.e. less than 20%) while the majority of IDEs (7 of 10, i.e. 70%) have a commercial background.[9]

9.3.1.2 Tool Kinds for Supporting Agent-oriented Software Development

The goal of the previous sections has been to identify the kinds of tools, which are required and already used for supporting the development of agent-based applications. Therefore, Section 9.2.1 has presented an overview of software development tasks, which have been generalized and classified in Section 9.2.2, according to process phases, as well as primary, ancillary and cross-cutting tasks. Moreover, Section 9.2.3 has discussed how these single tasks should be addressed by integrated (sets of) tools. Finally, Section 9.3.1.1 has given an overview of tools and other development supporting software in the area of agent technology. This overview identifies the important classes of IDEs and design tools and therefore fits well with the generic analysis from Section 9.2.3, which identifies modeling tools and IDEs as the basis of a continuous tools support, augmented by additional tools for project management, coordination and special purpose tasks. This leads to the question, for which tasks specific agent-oriented tools are necessary and for which other tasks existing tools e.g. from the object-oriented world would be sufficient. An important criterion for this decision is the kind of artifact, that is manipulated by a tool, i.e. for working with agent-specific artifacts like design models or program code specific agent tools would be advantageous. Cross-cutting tasks (cf. Figure 9.1) like project or repository management abstract away from concrete artifact types and therefore can be adequately supported by existing tools, such as Microsoft Project[10] or CVS[11].

Therefore the identified modeling tools and IDEs form the most important aspect of a tool-supported agent-oriented software development process to adequately support the requirements and design, as well as implementation, testing and deployment phases. In the following two sections, these two tool kinds will be analyzed in more detail, by discussing the common properties and giving an overview of typical representatives.

---

[9] This is also due to the fact that many commercial agent platforms like JACK include IDE support and have therefore been assigned to the IDE category.

[10] http://microsoft.com/office/project

[11] http://www.nongnu.org/cvs/

9.4 Modeling Tools

Agent-oriented graphical modeling tools are developed to support the software engineer during modeling tasks and to simplify the transition from an abstract specification to an implemented multi-agent system. Replacing or augmenting existing object-oriented modeling techniques as e.g. available in UML [41], new agent-oriented diagram types are introduced, which allow to specify e.g. interaction protocols or describe internal agent properties at the abstraction level of graphical modeling. A modeling tool realizes the corresponding user interface for working with these diagram types. The graphical representation of system properties allows visualizing interdependencies between the elements and improves the developer's understanding of the structure of single agents as well as the system as a whole.

Graphical agent-oriented modeling techniques usually are not self-contained (with the exception of AUML [42] for specifying agent interactions), but rather are embedded into complete software engineering methodologies (see, e.g., [58] or [31] for an overview). Methodologies provide besides modeling techniques also a development process, in which the single techniques are embedded. The development process defines a sequence of steps, which have to be passed through during the realization of a system, and the techniques to be employed in each of the steps [59]. Regarding this aspect, some methodologies are more strict than others, i.e., some restrict single techniques to be only used in some of the steps, while others propagate an iterative refinement of specifications in subsequent steps using the same modeling technique. This strictness can be supported by a tool by offering only those modeling techniques, which correspond to the current process step.

9.4.1 Requirements for Modeling Tools

This section discusses the specific requirements for modeling tools by referring to the general discussions from Sections 9.2.2 and 9.2.3. With respect to development tasks (cf. Figure 9.1), modeling tools address the design phase as well as (sometimes) the requirements phase. Artifacts of these phases are graphical models and text-based specifications, which can be written in natural language or follow a predefined (formal) scheme (e.g. role schema definitions in GAIA [73]). The main function of a modeling tool is to enable the developer to create and edit these models and specifications. Depending on how strict or formal the models and specifications of the employed technique or methodology are, a tool can also check the consistency of created artifacts and suggest changes for improving the specification (so called design critics [55]).

Among the further tasks in the requirements and design phases is validating specifications or modeling artifacts from different phases with respect to each other. E.g., it can be checked that design documents adequately reflect the scenarios, which have been identified in the requirements phase [2]. Moreover, it is advantageous, if a tool provides the developer with an option to transform artifacts from one phase into artifacts of another phase. For instance, a tool might be able to generate code fragments based on design information (forward engineering) or extract design information out of existing application code (reverse engineering). A drawback of forward or reverse engineering techniques is that after a once generated artifact has been changed manually, forward or reverse engineering cannot be reapplied without loosing the changes, i.e. the so called "post editing problem" [62]. The combined support of forward and reverse engineering, such that changes in one artifact can always be merged into the other without compromising consistency or loosing changes, is called round-trip engineering. Round-trip engineering allows employing forward or reverse engineering techniques also in iterated and agile development processes, where existing implementations are used as a basis for the design of the next iteration. Refactoring techniques are also most useful in agile development processes. Initially only applied to the implementation phase, refactoring ideas have recently also been transferred to graphical modeling [61, 7]. Among the non-functional criteria, especially the group of usability criteria (cf. [14]) requires a specific treatment. To evaluate the usability of graphical modeling tools, the ergonomics of the user interface is of primary importance. In general, this covers properties, such as the suitability for the intended task and controllability (cf. ISO 9241-110 "Ergonomics of human-system interaction - Dialogue principles" [32]). In the specific context of modeling tools, these properties can be refined to concrete requirements. For instance, a tool should relieve the developer by automating tedious tasks like the uniform and clearly arranged placement of diagram elements, but without posing unnecessary restrictions on the user. Moreover, it should be possible to take back actions in case of undesired effects (undo), and often used functionality should be easily accessible without forcing the developer to repeatedly change between mouse and keyboard (e.g. by enabling commands to be issued through hot keys as well as dialog elements).

9.4.2 Existing Agent-oriented Modeling Tools

The analysis of existing agent-oriented tools from Section 9.3.1.1 has shown that the choice of tools in the area of agent technology is somewhat limited. Most tools evolved in the context of a specific project or product. Hence, for each specific approach, such as a concrete agent-oriented programming language or development methodology, usually only a single tool (if any) is available, which is highly tailored for this specific approach.

Due to this situation, it seems appropriate to examine tools not in isolation, but to also consider the project or product context. Figure 9.3 shows current agent-oriented design tools and highlights their interdependencies to other agent-oriented development artifacts. In the figure, design tools are depicted in the highlighted column in the middle. To the left hand side of the design tools, their conceptual foundations are given in the form of development *methodolo-*

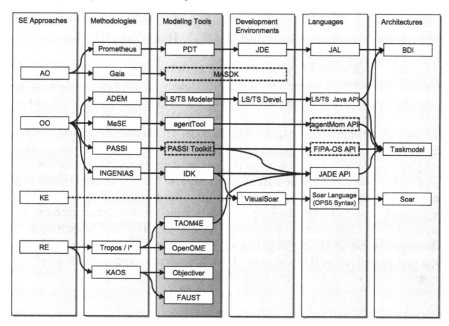

Fig. 9.3 Modeling tools and relations to other artifacts

gies. Methodologies in turn are related to their originating software engineering (*SE*) *approaches*, which, according to [14], are given as agent orientation (*AO*), object orientation (*OO*), knowledge engineering (*KE*), and requirements engineering (*RE*). To the right of the design tool column, interdependencies to implementation aspects of the modeled agents can be seen. Those interdependencies go through the *development environments* (i.e. IDEs), which are also covered in this chapter, and programming languages to the behavioral agent architectures, which in turn form the conceptual foundation of the programming languages. For reasons of clarity, artifacts without relations to modeling tools are not shown in this figure, even if they will be covered later with regard to IDEs (e.g. 2APL or AOP languages and associated tools).

All modeling tools shown in the figure have been developed to support a concrete methodology, but not all of them are related to some agent-oriented IDE. The relation to an IDE follows from the fact that a tool is able to generate code of a specific agent programming language or platform, supported by this IDE. For example this is the case for the Prometheus Design Tool (PDT)[12] [63] and the LS/TS Modeler, which are developed for the Prometheus methodology [72] resp. the Agent DEvelopment Methodology (ADEM, [67]), are able to generate code for the language JAL of the JACK agent platform [71] resp. the Java API of the Living Systems Technology Suite LS/TS [54]. The INGENIAS Development Kit

---

[12] http://www.cs.rmit.edu.au/agents/pdt/

(IDK)[13] [27] supports the INGENIAS Development Process IDP [46] and generates code for two languages/platforms (JADE [3, 4] and Soar [34]), one of which (Soar) is supported by a specific IDE.

Other tools, such as the PASSI Toolkit[14] and agentTool[15], which have been developed for the PASSI [16] resp. the MaSE methodology [20], are able to create code from the models, but no specific IDEs exist for the target languages. Especially tools related to requirements engineering (OpenOME[16], Objectiver[17], FAUST[18]) are not capable of generating agent-oriented code. This is probably due to the fact that the supported methodologies KAOS [35] and i* [74] as a foundation of Tropos [26] consider agents merely as an abstract modeling concepts and do not target an agent-oriented implementation. The TAOM4e tool[19] is an exception to this case, because unlike OpenOME supporting i*, it supports the Tropos methodology directly and therefore explicitly considers using agent-oriented concepts for the implementation (here by generating JADE code). The Multi Agent System Development Kit MASDK, [28], deserves a special presentation covering the design tool as well as the IDE column. MASDK realizes an approach for graphical programming, which is inspired by the Gaia methodology [73].

9.4.3 Example Modeling Tool: Prometheus Design Tool (PDT)

The Prometheus Design Tool (PDT) is developed at the RMIT University in Melbourne [44, 43]. It has the objective to support the agent-oriented development according to the Prometheus methodology [72]. The Prometheus methodology consists of three subsequent stages: system specification, architectural design, and detailed design. In each of these stages a developer specifies design artifacts, which is supported by the PDT. In Figure 9.4 a screenshot of the PDT user interface is shown. The basic working area is split into four main regions. At the upper left pane the three mentioned development stages and the associated design diagrams are listed. This area can be used to select a specific diagram, which is then shown at the right hand side and can be edited there. Each element of a design is also contained in an entity list at the lower left region. For each design element the editor for the type-dependent textual descriptor can be activated and used for adding further details (bottom right area of main window).

In the system specification phase an analysis of the problem domain is pursued. Main goal in this phase is the specification and elaboration of the analysis

---

[13] http://ingenias.sourceforge.net/

[14] http://sourceforge.net/projects/ptk

[15] http://macr.cis.ksu.edu/projects/agentTool/agentool.htm

[16] http://www.cs.toronto.edu/km/openome/

[17] http://www.objectiver.com/

[18] http://faust.cetic.be

[19] http://sra.itc.it/tools/taom4e/

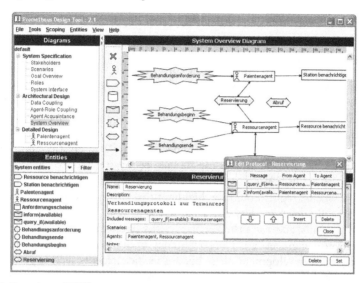

Fig. 9.4 Overview of PDT

overview diagram, which has the purpose to highlight the main use cases and the stakeholders participating in these use cases. This diagram can be further refined to include also the interface of the system described by percepts as inputs and actions as outputs of scenarios. In addition to this analysis overview, a system goal hierarchy can be modeled. As starting point, it is assumed that for each scenario one top-level goal exists, which can be used for a subsequent refinement into lower-level goals.

The next phase is the architectural design, where the internal composition of the system is specified. In this phase it needs to be decided which agent types make up the system and additionally in which way these agent types communicate via protocols. An agent type here is seen as a composition of one or more roles and is guided by data coupling and acquaintance considerations. Once the agent types have been identified, the agent overview diagram can be composed. This diagram is similar to an object-oriented class diagram, because it mainly highlights the agent types and their communication relationships. Also similar to class diagrams, the system overview diagram plays a central role in Prometheus and represents one of the most important artifacts produced by the methodology.

Finally, in the detailed design phase the agent internals are specified in order to equip the agents with the means to achieve their goals and handle their interactions appropriately. For each agent type, represented in an agent overview diagram, a functional decomposition is performed in order to identify its required functionalities. These functionalities are grouped according to their coherence and consistency into so called capabilities (agent modules). For each capability a capability overview diagram is developed, which shows how a functionality can be realized in terms of belief-desire-intention concepts. For these concepts individual textual descriptors can be devised. Using the detailed design artifacts, the code generation facility of the PDT can be employed for automatically producing JACK agent language code.

PDT provides all standard functionalities of a modeling tool. It allows design diagrams being created and refined and also exported in a graphical format for documentation purposes. In addition, the consistency of the design artifacts is ensured to some degree based on constraints derived from the Prometheus metamodel. According to [44], the tool inter alia avoids references to non-existing entities, giving the same name to two elements, connecting unrelated entities and breaking interface rules. Semantical aspects can be further investigated by the tool, which generates a report indicating possible weaknesses and inconsistencies in the current design. Such a report could e.g. highlight that the model contains a message, which is actually never send by any agent in the design.

PDT also partially addresses the ancillary tasks (cross-checking, refactoring and forward/reverse engineering). The consistency of different artifacts is mainly ensured within one development phase but as specific elements such as percepts and actions are used throughout all phases, also cross-stage consistency is respected. Additionally, the automatic propagation of elements to diagrams of later phases increases the consistency further. Refactoring is not supported by the PDT so far, even though the persistent usage of elements throughout different diagrams helps to make simple operations like renaming of elements work without consistency problems. The PDT offers a code generation module for producing code skeletons directly from the models (forward engineering). If changes in the design are done only within the tool, it will preserve hand-made code changes and hence mitigate the post-editing problem [62]. A reverse engineering for producing design artifacts out of existing code is not yet available and hence no round-trip engineering is possible.

The PDT aims at supporting all relevant modeling activities of a system. A vertical integration, i.e. the integration of further tools for enabling a richer modeling experience, is currently not provided. Concerning the horizontal integration, the PDT has the already mentioned code generation mechanism, which represents a weak form of data integration. The data integration is weak, because it works in one direction only (from PDT -> Code). Furthermore, a PDT eclipse plugin is available, which allows using PDT from eclipse and realizes a control integration. For the future several extensions are planned. One aspect is the achievement of a complete data integration between the design and code layer. Moreover, the functionalities of the PDT eclipse plugin shall be extended substantially to provide further integration facilities. In this respect, it is aimed at supporting code generation also for other target agent platforms and allow other modeling tools (e.g. UML) to be used directly from PDT, e.g. to model non-agent related system aspects such as the underlying data model. The horizontal integration shall be further extended in direction of including the test and deployment phases as part of Prometheus and PDT.

9.5 Integrated Development Environments (IDEs)

IDEs are software applications, which combine different development tools under a unified user interface. The main focus of IDEs are the programming tasks that appear primarily in the implementation phase, but also in the testing and (partially) deployment phases (cf. Sections 9.2.1 and 9.2.3). Therefore most IDEs are restricted to these phases. Yet, some IDEs offer graphical modeling features, but these are usually not focused on providing a fully fledged design phase support, but instead target an abstract visual way of programming (e.g. MASDK [28]).

In the area of object-oriented software engineering there are numerous IDEs of different levels of maturity. E.g., among mature IDEs focusing on Java programming, the most widely used ones are eclipse[20], IntelliJ IDEA[21] and NetBeans[22] (cf. Methods & Tools[23] and ComputerWire[24]). IDEA is a commercial product of the company JetBrains, whereas eclipse and NetBeans are freely available Open Source solutions, which are nevertheless initiated and pushed forward by commercial companies (Sun Microsystems in case of NetBeans and a consortium of IBM, Borland, QNX, RedHat, SuSE and others for eclipse).

The following section will discuss desired features of IDEs in general, backed by the analysis from Section 9.2.2 and the available features of the aforementioned state-of-the art object-oriented IDEs.

9.5.1 Requirements for IDEs

A simple IDE at least combines an editor for working on source code with a compiler or interpreter, which translates code to a runnable program or directly executes it. Additional important functionalities of an IDE are a debugger, which allows monitoring and control a running program in order to find programming errors, as well as a repository management functionality for dealing with the files associated to a development project.

The central component of an IDE from the viewpoint of the developer is the editor, which is used primarily to create and edit source code but sometimes also other kinds of artifacts, such as deployment descriptors. The editor should offer integrated consistency checks, validating the code while it is typed. To improve the productivity of a developer, many IDEs additionally offer so called auto-completion, i.e. the IDE makes useful suggestions to the developer, how the partial code pieces can be expanded (e.g. variable or method names). These sugges-

---

[20] http://www.eclipse.org/

[21] http://www.jetbrains.com/idea/

[22] http://www.netbeans.org/

[23] http://www.methodsandtools.com/facts/facts.php?nov03

[24] http://www.computerwire.com/industries/research/?pid=8885533F-BE8C-4760-881C-0BBBFECF534E

tions bear on the one hand on a syntactical understanding of the programming language and on the other hand on the current context, i.e. knowledge of the classes, variables, methods, etc. of the current project, which are accessible from the given code location. Similar knowledge is required for refactoring functionalities, which in the implementation phase also belong to the duties of an editor (e.g. the consistent renaming of methods). Besides text-based source code editors, some IDEs offer other (e.g. visual) description means for specific aspects of a system, such as graphical user interfaces, and transform these descriptions to source code automatically.

To verify progress during programming, the developer continuously has to execute and test those parts of the system, she is working on. Therefore, the IDE on the one hand has to transform source code into an executable program. For larger projects this can include, besides compiling single source files, also additional steps, such as pre- and post-processing as well as creating and assembling complex subcomponents (e.g. libraries). The IDE should enable the developer to specify/alter project specific guidelines for the build process and define all the required steps for constructing the application. Capabilities of an IDE related to the build process therefore also address tasks from the deployment phase. On the other hand, the IDE has to provide a runtime environment, in which partially completed versions of an application can be executed. Using different execution configurations, a developer can select different parts of the application for execution, based on her current situation.

A common task during the programming activity is the process of localizing bugs in a running system. For this purpose, IDEs offer so called debuggers, which allow executing a program in a step-wise manner, while observing the position in the source code as well as current variable values. A central concept of a debugger are breakpoints, i.e. positions that a developer has marked in the source code and at which executing should be interrupted. For compiled programs the debugger therefore has to be enabled to map the internal machine representation of the running program back to the source code. To support this process, program binaries usually are enriched with debugging information during the compilation process. Modern IDEs support in addition to simple breakpoints also semantic breakpoints, which are activated only, when certain conditions or events are detected (e.g. the occurrence of a specific exception type).

Besides phase-specific activities in the area of implementation, testing and deployment, many IDEs also support cross-cutting tasks. Especially the repository management or an integration of an existing repository management or versioning system is among the standard features of today's IDEs. The first goal of repository management is grouping all files belonging to a project into a common (e.g. directory) structure, such that the developer can easily grasp the current state of the project. Moreover, versioning features allow retrieving different (earlier) states of single files or the project as a whole, when needed. The integration with an external repository management system like CVS further facilitates a parallel and distributed development in larger project teams.

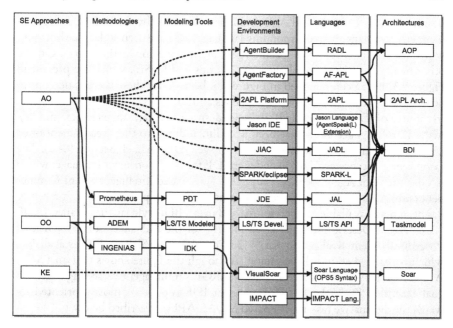

Fig. 9.5 Agent-oriented IDEs and relations to other artifacts

9.5.2 Existing Agent-oriented IDEs

For a systematic overview of existing agent-oriented IDEs , the approach from Section 9.4.2 is picked up. Therefore Figure 9.5 shows in the style of Figure 9.3 the interdependencies of existing agent-oriented IDEs with other development artifacts. E.g. the Visual Soar IDE[25] supports the Soar Language, for which the IDK modeling tool can generate code as also already shown in Figure 9.3.

Extending Figure 9.3, the AOP and 3APL/2APL architectures have now been included in the figure (see top right), because corresponding IDEs are available. The current 2APL platform[26] [19] supporting the 2APL language provides an IDE-like tool, that offers code editing as well as debugging capabilities. AgentBuilder[27] is a commercial agent platform and toolkit supporting the Reticular Agent Definition Language (RADL), while Agent Factory[28] (see Chapter 6) is an IDE supported framework for the Agent Factory Agent Programming language (AF-APL) and its variations. Both RADL and AF-APL are inspired by the seminal work of Shoham [57] on Agent-oriented Programming (AOP).

---

[25] http://www.eecs.umich.edu/ soar/sitemaker/projects/visualsoar/

[26] http://www.cs.uu.nl/2apl/

[27] http://www.agentbuilder.com/

[28] http://www.agentfactory.com/

Besides the 3APL/2APL and AOP branches, additionally, the IMPACT development environment and corresponding language [21] have been added (see bottom), which are not inspired by a specific agent architecture or methodology. On the other hand, several methodologies (e.g. Tropos and MaSE), which are present in Figure 9.3, have been removed in Figure 9.5, because for these there is no continuous tool support available, which includes an IDE.

In the area of IDEs supporting BDI (belief-desire-intention) languages (cf. middle), many IDE/language pairs have been added in addition to the already mentioned JACK development environment and language (JDE, JAL, cf. Section 9.4.2). The Jason agent interpreter[29] [10] includes an IDE for the Jason agent language, which is a derivative of AgentSpeak(L) [50]. JIAC (Java-based Intelligent Agent Componentware)[30] [25] is a sophisticated tool suite and agent platform, which recently has been made available as open source and uses a BDI-style language called JADL (JIAC Agent Description Language). Finally, for the PRS successor SPARK (SRI Procedural Agent Realization Kit)[31] [38], developed at SRI, an IDE is available, which is realized as an eclipse plugin. Although the figure shows that an LS/TS API for BDI-style agents is available (MARGE - multi-agent reasoning based on goal execution [70]), the LS/TS Developer IDE support is mostly oriented towards the alternative task-model based MDAL API as described below.

9.5.3 Example IDE: LS/TS Developer

The LS/TS Developer is part of the Living Systems Technology Suite (LS/TS) of Whitestein Technologies.[32] As already mentioned in the last section, instead of a new agent language, LS/TS provides several APIs that allow implementing agent applications in Java. The agent concepts and behavioral architecture are realized in the existing framework classes, while the programmer can provide new implementations of API classes that are called by the framework at relevant time points (inversion of control principle). One example of such a class is a user defined message handling component to be executed, when a matching message is received. The basic API of LS/TS is CAL (core agent layer) [68] on top of which the other APIs are built. CAL only provides a very basic autonomous agent that reacts on incoming messages or the passage of time. Besides the autonomous agent, CAL also provides so called Servants, representing passive service, and DAOs (data access objects) for managing potentially persistent data. The MDAL (message dispatching agent logic) [69] extends CAL and introduces mechanisms for selecting specific components (so called message handlers) based on properties of incoming messages. Each message handler is responsible for a sequence of messages (e.g. a

---

[29] http://jason.sourceforge.net/

[30] http://www.jiac.de/

[31] http://www.ai.sri.com/ spark/

[32] http://www.whitestein.com/

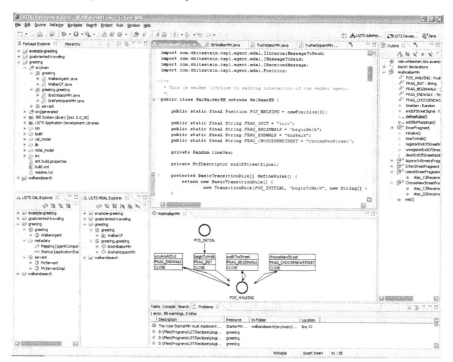

Fig. 9.6 Developer perspective of the LS/TS Development Suite in eclipse

negotiation with another agent) and is composed of so called fragments for each single step of the interaction. A so called context factory is responsible for instantiating new message handlers for messages that cannot be assigned to an existing message handler.

The LS/TS Development Suite includes on the one hand the already mentioned LS/TS Modeler (cf. Section 9.4.2) and on the other hand a set of development tools, which provide views and editors for working with CAL and MDAL elements, carrying handy names such as Developer, Debugger, Tester, and Administrator. Despite this naming, these are not separate tools, but integrated into the eclipse IDE, therefore offering an agent developer an accustomed environment allowing flexible access to the additional agent-oriented development features. The features are grouped into two perspectives that offer a useful predefined layout of the available views that can also be adapted if necessary. In the developer perspective, the agent-specific code of an application can be edited. The administrator perspective contains tools for monitoring and manipulating a running agent application.

Figure 9.6 shows some features of the developer perspective. In the upper half, there are existing eclipse views for Java programming (package explorer left, Java source editor middle, Java source outline right), which are useful also for editing CAL and MDAL artifacts. The lower area shows extensions like the CAL explorer and MDAL explorer (both left) or message handler diagrams (middle). In the following, the tool support available in the LS/TS Developer will be discussed with respect to the phases implementation, testing, and deployment as well as the corresponding tasks.

Relevant implementation artifacts of LS/TS applications are Java files as well as (mostly XML-based) configuration files. Elements of the CAL and MDAL APIs are represented as Java classes that can be created and edited using existing eclipse mechanisms. Additionally, the LS/TS Developer introduces new wizards that simplify the creation of such elements based on predefined templates and can be activated from the CAL/MDAL explorer and partially also directly from the Java code editor. Syntactical consistency of Java classes can also be checked using existing eclipse mechanisms. Dependencies between MDAL elements (e.g. message handlers and contained fragments) are not considered by eclipse, because these are stored in string-based mapping tables in Java code. Besides editing Java code directly, two graphical views are provided. The first (agent diagram) allows observing and manipulating the aforementioned dependencies between context factories, message handlers, and fragments. The agent diagram is extracted from the Java sources and changes to the graphical view, such as adding/removing elements, are written back to the corresponding Java files after the changes have been reviewed and accepted/rejected by the developer in a preview window (roundtrip engineering). The second view (message handler diagram, cf. Figure 9.6 middle) is also extracted from the Java code and shows the execution flow of a message handler as a Petri-net. Editing of this diagram is not possible. Refactoring for Java source files is already supported in eclipse and can also be applied to the Java-based CAL and MDAL elements, but may lead to inconsistencies, because references to elements in the aforementioned mapping tables and e.g. in XML-base deployment descriptors will not be considered by eclipse. Similarly, automatic cross-checking between different phases (e.g. implementation classes and deployment descriptors) is currently not supported and therefore has to be performed by hand. No additional support is offered for documentation tasks (e.g. it is not directly possible to export message handler and agent diagrams or include these automatically in generated Javadoc documentation).

For testing and debugging, existing Java mechanisms of eclipse can be reused. Additionally, LS/TS extends Java breakpoints in terms of agent concepts, allowing the developer to focus on specific agent instances or message types. The administrator perspective allows to record messages that are passed between agents and, for the purpose of debugging, display these messages in a sequence diagram like view as well as in a topological view. Creating test cases is supported by a test framework based on the open source jUnit[33] framework. It allows testing parts of agents (e.g. message handlers) and is supported in the IDE through wizards that enable the creation of test cases based on templates. Consistency checking and refactoring, is supported by existing eclipse mechanisms, but, as in the implementation phase, does not respect all dependencies.

---

[33] http://www.junit.org/

Application configurations for deployment are stored in XML files. A mapping file declares available agent types and relates them to the implementing Java classes. A startup file defines the required agent instances for a concrete application configuration by specifying for each agent instance the name, type and optionally parameters. Both descriptors can be edited in XML directly as well as in a specific form based editor that abstracts away from XML syntax and provides all settings in an intuitive manner. To create an application from a specified configuration, a build process can be initiated, that is based on a predefined Ant[34] build file. Using a dialog, settings can be made that specify which configuration files are to be used and if the application should be directly deployed into an existing runtime environment. Once specified, such deployment configurations can then be executed as needed.

Cross-cutting tasks like project and repository management are already supported in part by existing eclipse features or separately available eclipse plugins for e.g. repository management with CVS. For project management, eclipse offers e.g. management of to-do entries and various search features. LS/TS additionally offers access to project files through the CAL and MDAL explorers. Moreover, the MDAL explorer offers special search functionality that simplifies the navigation in the project.

9.6 Phase-specific Tools

Besides the already discussed modeling tools and IDEs, which generally span several development phases, in this section phase-specific tools will be discussed. Phase-specific tools can substantially support selected development tasks. Nonetheless, these tools are intentionally not meant to be a universal solution for building software. In order to build software the whole development process consisting of all mentioned phases need to be homogeneously tool supported. In this respect, it is of crucial importance that the tools can be integrated with each other and therefore allow a smooth transition forward and back along the different development phases, meaning that artifacts produced in one phase can be also used or refined in another phase. This integration is rather difficult to achieve and requires agreed upon conceptual models as well as standards or at least published specifications. In the area of multi-agent systems, a high heterogeneity on all layers exists rendering a desired fully-integrated tool-support across all development even harder to achieve than for the standard object-oriented paradigm. The following sections will introduce the specific requirements each phase poses towards the possible tool support, name important tool representatives and discuss one of these representatives in detail.

---

[34] http://ant.apache.org/

9.6.1 Requirements Analysis Phase

The artifacts of the requirements analysis phase are graphical models and/or textual specifications of an initially abstract problem. These artifacts represent concretized requirements for the system to be built. At this point in the development process, normally no decision is made about the usage of agent or an alternative technology for the realization of the system. Therefore, the produced artifacts in this stage are generally not agent-specific, which makes it possible to employ existing techniques for the communication between the customers and users on the one side and developers on the other side. Among such techniques, use cases [33] are a widespread approach that allow for capturing the main interaction possibilities of users with the system at a high abstraction level and thus facilitate the customer-developer communication. Another well-known technique is rapid prototyping, which aims at developing software demonstrators with limited functionality very early to be able to get feedback from the customers as soon as possible. As an alternative, also agent-related requirements engineering techniques can be used. Examples especially include the goal-driven approaches i* [74] and KAOS [35], which do not prescribe an agent-oriented implementation of the system, even though the transition to agent systems is conceptually more straight-forward than to traditional approaches.

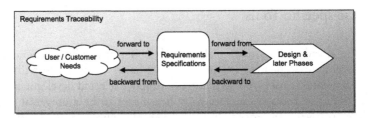

Fig. 9.7 Requirements traceability (from [47])

One important requisite for tools from this phase consist in the traceability of the produced application requirements, which means that the state of a requirement can be described and can be traced from all development phases. This traceability includes two different aspects (cf. Figure 9.7). From the viewpoint of a developer, traceability mainly refers to the later development phases, whereby the components responsible for implementing requirements should be locatable (forward tracing) and also the other way around the contribution of components to the requirements should be determinable (backward tracing). Taking up the customer's perspective, it is of importance that changed requirements are adequately communicated to the developers (forward tracing) and also that user groups can be identified, which are responsible for specific requirements (backward tracing). Requirements traceability can be realized utilizing different strategies (cf. [29]). One example are cross-references between requirements and other artifacts, which need to be explicitly specified.

As tools in this phase need not to be agent-oriented, among many different traditional and agent-related tools can be chosen. Overviews of the different tools available in this phase can be e.g. found at the web.[35] If use cases shall be utilized, it is also possible to resort to standard UML case tools.[36] As agent-related requirement tools facilitate an agent-oriented design and implementation, in the following the Objectiver tool for KAOS will be shortly presented.

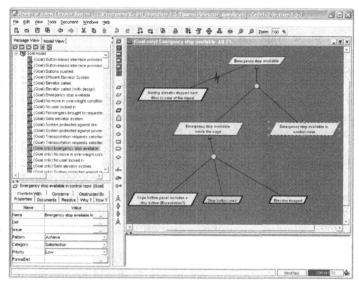

Fig. 9.8 Objectiver tool

The commercial Objectiver tool is developed by company Respect-IT.[37] It supports a KAOS-based goal-driven requirements specification, whereby a goal is meant to describe what the system needs to achieve. Goals are described in terms of so called patterns, which define their behavior in temporal logic. In many cases, standard patterns such as "achieve", for making true a specific world state ($\Diamond P$) or "maintain" for permanently preserving a state ($\Box P$). The initial system goal definitions will subsequently be refined to a goal hierarchy using "why" and "how" questions until the point is reached that the subgoals on the lowest level can be clearly assigned to one of the actors. In a second step, besides the goal view, also system responsibilities, data objects and operations are considered and integrated to a holistic system requirements specification. In Figure 9.8 a screenshot of the Objectiver tool is depicted. In the main area a goal hierarchy is shown, which decomposes the top-level goal "emergency stop available" into several subgoals.

---

[35] http://easyweb.easynet.co.uk/ iany/other/vendors.htm
http://www.volere.co.uk/tools.htm

[36] http://www.objectsbydesign.com/tools/umltools_byCompany.html

[37] http://www.objectiver.com/ http://www.objectiver.com/

Using the form at the bottom left, various entity properties can be edited. An overview of all different diagrams is given via the tree structure above. The tool automatically ensures consistency between different diagrams and can also test the specifications for plausibility and completeness.

9.6.2 Design Phase

In the design phase graphical and textual specifications for different aspects of the system to be realized are described. In contrast to the requirements analysis phase, agent concepts play an essential role in this stage of the development process. Considering the system as a whole, organizational concepts play an important role and can be used to describe the high-level structures of the system. In this respect, e.g. the AGR-model has been conceived for defining a system in terms of agents, groups, and roles. For the design of concrete system functionalities on the agent level, the internal agent architecture concepts are of primary interest. For example, if intentional agents shall be designed, BDI concepts such as beliefs, goals and plans could be utilized. Besides these agent related concepts, for the description of specific aspects the agent-based views can be complemented by standard modeling concepts. One prominent area is the description of data model or conversation relationships, which can e.g. be done by using standard UML class and sequence diagrams.

The most important requirement for design tools relates to their integration ability with earlier and later development phases. It should be possible to systematically deal with already defined requirements and connect them to the newly specified design artifacts. Furthermore, the connection from the typically graphical design phase to the following code-centric implementation phase is of vital importance. This connection is difficult to achieve, because the often existing conceptual gap and additionally, the different representation media (diagrams vs. code) have to be bridged adequately.

Existing tools for the design of agent systems mainly have two different origins. First, many agent-oriented tools exist that aim at supporting a specific agent-oriented methodology such as PDT, TAOM4e or agentTool. These kinds of tools have already been discussed in the context of modeling tools (cf. Section 9.4) and will not be considered further here. Second, a few dedicated agent-oriented modeling tools have been developed to support the agent-oriented design approaches such as AUML and AML (agent modeling notation)[66]. The main contribution of AUML consists in the definition of a standard interaction diagram notation, which has influenced the UML 2.0 standard. Hence, traditional UML case tools can readily be used for modeling agent interactions. AML is already conceived as an agent-specific extension to UML 2.0 and extends it with agent concepts to also support the design of such kinds of software systems. An overview of the new AML diagram is given in Figure 9.9. In the following the LS/TS modeler, which can be used for creating AML designs, will be presented in more detail.

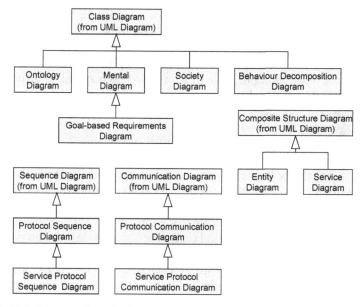

Fig. 9.9 AML Diagrams (from [66])

The LS/TS Modeler is part of the commercial Living Systems Technology Suite, which is distributed by Whitestein technologies. All new diagram types of AML have been introduced as refinements of existing diagram types using the standardized UML extension mechanisms. This allows normal UML case tools to be used for AML modeling when an AML UML profile for the tool exists. So far, Whitestein has developed an UML profile for the Enterprise Architect UML tool. The modeler supports all new kinds of AML diagrams, which can be categorized into architectural, behavioral and communication diagrams. Architecture diagrams are intended to describe a multi-agent system as a whole, whereas behavioral diagrams relate to the internal agent architecture and finally communication diagrams refine protocol specification facilities. As the tool is based on a standard UML tool it exhibits all necessary modeling features. In addition, the modeler add-in mainly provides code generation mechanism that can be used to create agent skeleton code for the LS/TS platform.

9.6.3 Implementation Phase

The focus of the implementation phase is on code and corresponding editing tasks. A major concern therefore is the agent-specific code, which depends on the chosen agent architecture and platform. E.g. for a BDI-based platform, the developer will have to write textual specifications of beliefs, goals, and plans in the provided agent language, while for a platform supporting the task model, the activities of an agent and their interrelations have to be coded (e.g. in Java). Regardless of the internal agent architecture, also communication and integration aspects have to be implemented. This includes e.g. Java classes or XML-Schema definitions for representing message content as well as mapping information for persistent data. Often, for the communication and integration issues, traditional implementation means (e.g. XML, JDBC) can be used alternatively to possibly available agent-specific solutions.

Most important requirement for agent-oriented implementation tools is the ability to deal with agent-specific code. In this respect, agent-oriented tools should strive to offer the same level of support that developers are used to in the prevailing object-oriented world. Besides the primary tasks such as creation and editing, therefore also the ancillary tasks should be adequately supported. E.g. in object orientation, code metrics are available that allow to check code consistency not only on the basis of a strict syntactical check, but also provide indications in terms of good or bad design. Moreover, given that some communication and integration issues can be realized using existing techniques, there should be tools, which provide the necessary "glue" to seamlessly operate on the different specification means.

Primary tasks are captured by IDEs for specific agent languages. Adaptable editors, such as jEdit[38] or extensible IDEs like eclipse can be used as a basis for building such IDEs to support features like syntax checks and syntax highlighting. For consistency checks, separately developed tools, such as [60], can be implemented. Moreover, some existing object-oriented metrics or style check programs allow additional metrics or inspections being added (e.g. Eclipse Checkstyle[39]), which allows adding agent-specific consistency checks. To provide the necessary glue between different technologies, often plugins or code generation templates can be used. E.g. the database mapping framework Apache Cayenne[40] supports custom code templates being used and therefore can be adapted to agent-specific requirements and for the ontology editor Protégé several plugins exist that aim at integrating ontology-based knowledge representation with an agent platform. As one example of such a tool, the Beanynizer plugin, which is part of the Jadex BDI agent framework [49], will be shortly described.

The Beanynizer is a plugin to Protégé and allows generating Java classes from an ontology modeled in Protégé. The output format is defined using templates written in the Apache Velocity[41] template language. Besides using custom templates, the Beanynizer includes two ready to use template sets – one for JADE ontology code and one for JavaBeans compliant code. For the JADE template set, the modeled ontology has to be based on a standard FIPA ontology, which includes common agent-related concepts like actions and agent identifiers. Gener-

---

[38] http://www.jedit.org/

[39] http://eclipse-cs.sourceforge.net/

[40] http://cayenne.apache.org/

[41] http://velocity.apache.org/

ated classes can be used for developing JADE-based agents communicating, e.g., via the FIPA-SL content representation language. The JavaBeans templates generate platform independent pure Java code, which can e.g. be processed by the Java XML de- and encoding facilities.

9.6.4 Testing Phase

The aim of the testing phase is to find and correct conceptual as well as technical implementation errors. As these errors are also called "bugs" a common name for this activity in the development process is debugging. According to Dassen and Sprinkhuizen-Kuyper [18] debugging mainly consists of three subsequent steps: noticing the bug, localizing the bug and finally fixing the bug. To find possible bugs in a systematic way, often a testing approach is chosen, which requires that important aspects are captured in test cases. These test cases represent requirements that can be verified against the current implementation. The localization of bugs is still a manual skill that requires considerable effort, experience and creativity. It mainly requires the programmer to inspect the source code in detail and possibly use a debugger tool execute the program stepwise resp. stop it at specific breakpoints. As errors may manifest themselves in unpredictable behavior their identification can be a very hard and complex task. Fixing the bug is not directly part of the testing phase but requires a developer to step back to the implementation phase or in case of conceptual problems even to the design phase and correct the identified artifacts. As can be seen from this description, additional artifacts in this phase are only constructed for specifying test cases. The other activities fully operate on existing artifacts, especially on the code level.

Main requirements for tools of this phase consist in a conceptual and technical support for the detection and localization of bugs. For the systematic detection of bugs tools should facilitate the implementation and automated execution of test cases. This should include test cases for different layers such as unit tests for single functionalities, integration tests for larger components and system tests for the validation of system requirements. In addition, it is helpful if the test coverage, i.e. which system aspects are tested to what degree, can be automatically calculated and presented to the developer. An indication of possible bugs can also be produced by software metrics that try to capture the quality of source code.

Tools supporting the testing phase have mainly been developed in the context of object-oriented languages and are often directly integrated into IDEs. In the area of multi-agent systems, only recently the testing topic has gained some attention. Conceptually, multi-agent systems increase the complexity of all activities in this phase, so that a direct transfer of existing solutions is not easily possible. Testing and debugging on the level of the whole multi-agent system entails all the difficulties involved in testing and debugging distributed system (e.g. concurrency and lack of global state). Tools in this area focus on the interactions, i.e. the messages passed between agents and allow monitoring messages (e.g. JADE Sniffer) or testing compliance to specified protocols (e.g. [1]). To address the issues of debugging under consideration of the whole development process, it is also researched how design artifacts can support this phase (see Chapter 7). Support for unit testing at the level of single agents has been devised in the context of tool suites for agent platforms such as JADE , Jadex and LS/TS . Furthermore, nearly all existing agent platforms offer (at least simple) debugging tools, which allow the stepwise execution of agents. In the following Jadex TestCenter tool will be shortly described.

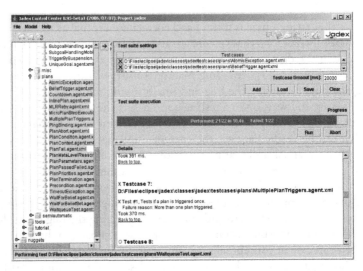

Fig. 9.10 Jadex TestCenter

A screenshot of the Jadex TestCenter is shown in Figure 9.10. Its underlying concepts are based on JUnit, i.e. it is possible to define a set of test cases as test suite (in form of a list at the top right area) and then execute this suite automatically (control area below the list). Here, test agents containing an arbitrary number of test cases can be directly added from the file system view (left area) to the list. The results of the test suite execution are summarized as a colored bar, which is green in case all test cases have been successful and red in case at least one test failed. The detailed test results are displayed in a form of a textual report (right bottom), which explains what the individual test cases do, which ones have failed and a possible reason for that failure.

9.6.5 Deployment Phase

For object-oriented systems the tasks of the deployment phase are clearly specified and also well tool-supported. In this context, the Object Management Group (OMG) has defined deployment as the activity between obtaining and operating a software product. More concretely, in [40] the OMG has specified a general deployment process consisting of five subsequent steps. In the first, so called *installation step*, the software is obtained and stored in a local repository, which must not necessarily be the same location as the destined execution location. In the following *configuration step*, the software is parametrized according to the intended use cases. Hereafter, a deployment plan is devised in the *planning step*. This plan is then used in the *preparation step* to install the desired components on the target platforms. In the final *launching step* the application is started and hence put into operation, which might require further configuring activities at runtime.

Regarding agent-based systems this process is usually more flexible, because the constituents are not passive components, but active autonomous entities [12]. Nonetheless, the aforementioned steps remain important for multi-agent systems as well. In the installation step the execution infrastructure for the agents, i.e. the agent platform and also the application specific components, e.g. consisting of agent code as well as standard libraries, have to be available. This may not necessarily mean that the application code has to be obtained completely in beforehand. Possibly agent code could also be downloaded on demand at runtime. The functional configuration of the application can be done by defining the number and kinds of agents that should be initially started and by setting their initial parameters to appropriate values. The planning and preparation steps mainly need to take into account at which hosts which infrastructure should be accessible and which agents should be located. In case of mobile agents, the distribution of agents at the different nodes could also be adjusted at runtime, e.g. with respect to non-functional aspects like load balancing. Starting an agent application is quite different from launching a component-based software, because there is no single centralized starting point. Instead a set of (possibly independent or interrelated) actors need to be created in a meaningful way. Hence, in order to specify agent applications it should be abstracted away from single agents and some form of application descriptors should be made available.

Artifacts of the deployment phase are therefore mainly these application and agent descriptors. Tools of this phase have the tasks of supporting the creation and processing of such descriptors, whereby the creation can be associated with the configuration and the processing with the launching step. In addition, deployment tools can also be extended in direction of runtime monitoring facilities.

Tool-based deployment support for agent applications is rather limited today. It has mainly been considered technically in the context of agent platforms and several similar ad-hoc solutions have been provided so far. E.g. in Agent Academy [37], AgentFactory [15], Jason [10], simple application descriptors have been introduced, which at least enable a definition of the parametrized agent instances to start. With the LS/TS Developer also a tool exists, which simplifies the specification of agent applications in a similar way to J2EE deployment descriptors. It can be used to deploy the tool generated application in the agent platform automatically. Similarly, approaches like BlueJADE [17] and jademx[42] try to make agent

---

[42] http://jademx.sourceforge.net

platforms administrable similar to J2EE server environments, but do not consider the assembly of agent applications. In the following, the ASCML tool, conceived specifically for the deployment of agent applications, will be described.

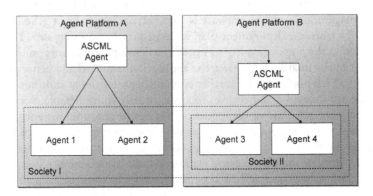

Fig. 9.11 ASCML refernce model (from [12])

The ASCML (Agent Society Configuration Manager and Launcher) is based on a generic deployment reference model for agent applications (cf. Figure 9.11) [12]. This reference model assumes that agent applications (here called societies) are controlled by dedicated manager (ASCML) agents. These agents have the responsibilities to start, supervise, and possible reconfigure the controlled societies. The concept of agent society here is recursively defined, meaning that it can be composed of a hierarchy of agent instances or sub societies possibly distributed across different network nodes. The ASCML tool allows defining agent applications in the form of society and agent descriptors, which are interpreted by the tool at runtime and lead to the instantiation of the specified software runtime configuration. It extends the basic facilities by constraint expressions, which can be used to state, in which cases the application needs to reconfigured, e.g. by restarting specific agents given that a necessary service is not available any longer.

9.7 Evaluation

The preceding sections have shown that numerous agent-oriented tools have been developed. Besides the phase-specific tools, which only address tasks of one development phase, mainly modeling tools and IDEs have been identified as important tool categories. In this section a coarse evaluation of these modeling tools and IDEs will be presented.[43] The main objective of this evaluation is an assessment of the state of the art of agent-oriented tools in order to highlight the strengths

---

[43] The phase-specific tools have been excluded from the evaluation due to the low number of representatives in each phase.

and weaknesses of the current tool landscape. The evaluation is based on the generic task requirements within the different phases of a development process (cf. Section 9.2.2). Each of the 10 modeling tools and 11 IDEs have been analyzed with respect to the identified tasks of the corresponding phases, i.e. modeling tools have been evaluated against task requirements from the analysis and design phase whereas IDEs have been tested against the task requirements from the implementation, testing and deployment phases. Cross-cutting activities like repository management and development coordination are not agent-specific and have not been evaluated. With regard to those cross-cutting tasks established tool support can be reused, e.g. the CVS (Concurrent Versions System) can be employed for version management. In case that agent-oriented tools build on established object oriented IDEs like eclipse, orthogonal support for those features is directly available via plugins for the IDEs. The aggregated results of the evaluation, which intentionally abstract away from the concrete tool representatives, are depicted in Figure 9.12. It is shown how many tools of each category (modeling tools vs. IDEs) support a given task.

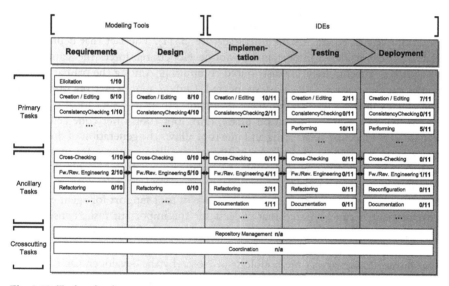

Fig. 9.12 Tool evaluation

Looking at the modeling tools, it can be seen that, in general, stronger support exists for tasks of the design phase, whereas only a few tools tackle tasks from the preceding requirements phase. The basic features for creating and editing requirements artifacts is supported by 5 of 10 tools. Further primary tasks are rarely supported in the requirements phase, i.e. only one representative handles the initial elicitation of requirements and consistency checking of requirements artifacts. Regarding the ancillary tasks, also only marginal tool support could be revealed. Two representatives allow the generation of design artifacts and one representative tackles cross-checking with generated artifacts. None of the tools addressed refactoring aspects. A similar support structure can be identified also at the design phase. Creating and editing of design artifacts is available by nearly all tools (8/10) and also the consistency checking of artifacts is supported by nearly half of the tools (4/10). When looking at the ancillary tasks, it can be seen that 5/10 tools include forward engineering features. Though, in most cases, only simple code generation facilities are available, which can produce initial code skeletons from design artifacts. Advanced features like reverse or round-trip engineering have not been introduced in any tool. Cross-checking and refactoring have not been addressed at all.

An agent-oriented IDE would ideally support all tasks from the implementation, testing and deployment phases. Among the IDEs, nearly all representatives (10 of 11) offer functionality for creating/editing implementation artifacts (i.e. agent code) as well as debugging running agent applications (i.e. the performing task in the testing phase). This reveals that tool developers consider programming and debugging agents as the most important tasks of agent developers. On the other hand, systematic creation of repeatable test cases is only supported by 2 representatives. A considerable amount of support is also available in the deployment phase, for the creation of deployment descriptors (7/11) as well as actually deploying agents to an existing infrastructure (5/11). The fact that deployment features are considered important by tool developers reinforces the significance of agents as a technology for distributed computing. Among the primary tasks, consistency checking is the least supported. Only 2 representatives offer some consistency analysis features for agent programs. Ancillary tasks are also seldom supported. In the implementation phase, only four tools offer code generation features, two support refactoring and one tool allows the generation of documentation. In the testing and deployment phases, ancillary features are mostly not addressed at all. Only one tool offers the forward generation of deployment descriptors from agent models.

Summing up this coarse evaluation of the state of tool support for agent-oriented development it can be noted that at least for the important tasks considerable support is available by most current development tools. This means the the most common development tasks are adequately supported by tools, regardless which specific agent language or methodology is chosen by the developer. On the other hand, no single tool is able to support all tasks. Especially in the area of the (probably less important) ancillary tasks, agent-oriented tools have considerable potential for improvement. As an example: even the most powerful agent-oriented IDEs only support at most 7 of possible 20 tasks in the implementation, testing and design phases. For comparison, a short analysis of state-of-the-art OO IDEs, such as eclipse or IntelliJ IDEA, indicates that these support up to 12-15 tasks out of the box and even more when using additional plugins. One notable feature in this area is refactoring, which becomes more and more important, the larger the developed applications grow. Therefore, improving agent-oriented tool support in this direction could be crucial for adequately supporting larger software projects.

9.8 Conclusion

This chapter has the purpose the give a systematic overview about the existing agent-oriented development tool landscape. Therefore, first the tasks of sofware development tools have been collected and categorized along the two dimensions: development phases and task importance. It has been identified as crucial that tools of all phases should enable the creation and editing as well as consistency checking of development artifacts. In addition, it is helpful when tools also cope with ancillary tasks like cross-checking, forward/reverse engineering and refactoring and also crosscutting tasks like repository management. Based on the existing surveys three major categories of tools have been identified: modeling tools, IDEs and phase-specific tools. For each of the categories the specific requirements have been described, an overview of existing tools has been given and finally one specific representative has been selected and described in greater detail.

The evaluation of the current agent tool landscape allows some general observations to be made. First, all development phases and all tasks are to some extent tool-supported, meaning that a variety of different tools are available for all possible use cases. Nonetheless, most of these tools suffer from the strong heterogeneity of the multi-agent systems field. This heterogeneity often leads to very specific approaches suitable only for one specific agent approach, e.g. a design tool for BDI agents only. Furthermore, the number of available tools is quite low compared to mainstream object-oriented solutions. In order to further improve the overall tool support it is necessary that at least the following future trends emerge. First, a general agreement on core concepts and a consolidation of the agent platforms would help concentrating on successful development branches. Second, tool support is generally dependent on the industry uptake of agent technology as a whole, because research institutions normally do not have enough resources for providing industry-grade tools, which typically demand high investments in terms of man-month of work (cf. the efforts for building an object-oriented IDE like eclipse).

The survey reveals that tool-support of agent technology is still a bit behind the currently available support in the predominant object-oriented paradigm. Nevertheless, the recent years have shown significant improvements in this respect. The analysis of the AgentLink directory highlights that some convergence has already happened in the area of agent platforms. The increasing maturity of agent platforms allows development efforts to also focus on secondary items like tool support. Moreover, agent-oriented tool support also profits from the fact that object-oriented tools have become more and more flexible and therefore many agent tools are not built from scratch but instead adapt existing object-oriented tools to agent-specific requirements. One reason for object-oriented tools becoming more flexible can be seen in the desire of supporting other post object-oriented technologies like model-driven development and web services. These technologies shift the focus to abstract modeling or the interaction of system components. Therefore, these technologies are conceptually much closer to the agent paradigm, which may foster an integration and convergence with agent concepts and tools in the future.

References

1. Alberti, M., Chesani, F., Gavanelli, M., Lamma, E., Mello, P., Torroni, P.: Compliance Verification of Agent Interaction: a Logic-Based Tool. In: R. Trappl (ed.) Proceeding of the 7th European Meeting on Cybernetics and Systems Research, Track AT2AI-4: From Agent Theory to Agent Implementation (AT2AI 2004), pp. 570–575. Austrian Society for Cybernetic Studies (2004)
2. Bartsch, K., Robey, M., Ivins, J., Lam, C.: Consistency checking between use case scenarios and uml sequence diagrams. In: M. Hamza (ed.) Proceedings of the IASTED International Conference on Software Engineering (SE 2004), pp. 92–103. ACTA Press (2004)
3. Bellifemine, F., Bergenti, F., Caire, G., Poggi, A.: JADE - A Java Agent Development Framework. In: R. Bordini, M. Dastani, J. Dix, A. El Fallah Seghrouchni (eds.) Multi-Agent Programming: Languages, Platforms and Applications, pp. 125–147. Springer (2005)
4. Bellifemine, F., Caire, G., Greenwood, D.: Developing Multi-Agent systems with JADE. John Wiley & Sons (2007)
5. Bitting, E., Carter, J., Ghorbani, A.: Multiagent system development kits: An evaluation. In: In Proceedings of the 1st Annual Conference on Communication Networks and Services Research (CNSR 2003), pp. 80–92. CNSR Project (2003)
6. Boehm, B.W.: A spiral model of software development and enhancement. IEEE Engineering Management Review 23 **4**, 69–81 (1995)
7. Boger, M., Sturm, T., Fragemann, P.: Refactoring browser for uml. In: M. Aksit, M. Mezini, R. Unland (eds.) Proceedings of the 4th International Conference on Objects, Components, Architectures, Services, and Applications for a Networked World (Net.ObjectDays 2002), pp. 366–377. Springer (2003)
8. Bordini, R., Braubach, L., Dastani, M., El Fallah Seghrouchni, A., Gomez-Sanz, J., Leite, J., Or'Hare, G., Pokahr, A., Ricci, A.: A survey of programming languages and platforms for multi-agent systems. Informatica **30**, 33–44 (2006)
9. Bordini, R., Dastani, M., Dix, J., El Fallah Seghrouchni, A.: Multi-Agent Programming: Languages, Platforms and Applications. Springer (2005)
10. Bordini, R., Hübner, J.F., Vieira, R.: Jason and the Golden Fleece of Agent-Oriented Programming. In: R. Bordini, M. Dastani, J. Dix, A. El Fallah Seghrouchni (eds.) Multi-Agent Programming: Languages, Platforms and Applications, pp. 3–37. Springer (2005)
11. Braubach, L.: Architekturen und Methoden zur Entwicklung verteilter agentenorientierter Softwaresysteme. Ph.D. thesis, Universität Hamburg (2007)
12. Braubach, L., Pokahr, A., Bade, D., Krempels, K.H., Lamersdorf, W.: Deployment of Distributed Multi-Agent Systems. In: M.P. Gleizes, A. Omicini, F. Zambonelli (eds.) Proceedings of the 5th International Workshop on Engineering Societies in the Agents World (ESAW 2004), pp. 261–276. Springer (2005)
13. Braubach, L., Pokahr, A., Lamersdorf, W.: Tools and Standards. In: S. Kirn, O. Herzog, P. Lockemann, O. Spaniol (eds.) Multiagent Systems. Intelligent Applications and Flexible Solutions, pp. 503–530. Springer (2006)
14. Braubach, L., Pokahr, A., Lamersdorf, W.: A universal criteria catalog for evaluation of heterogeneous agent development artifacts. International Journal of Agent-Oriented Software Engineering (IJAOSE) (2009). To appear
15. Collier, R.W.: Agent Factory: A Framework for the Engineering of Agent-Oriented Applications. Ph.D. thesis, University College Dublin (2001)
16. Cossentino, M.: From Requirements to Code with the PASSI Methodology. In: B. Henderson-Sellers, P. Giorgini (eds.) Agent-Oriented Methodologies, pp. 79–106. Idea group publishing (2005)
17. Cowan, D., Griss, M., Burg, B.: Bluejade - A service for managing software agents. Tech. Rep. HPL-2001-296R1, Hewlett Packard Laboratories (2002)
18. Dassen, J., Sprinkhuizen-Kuyper, I.: Debugging c and c++ code in a unix environment. The Object Oriented Programming Web (OOPWeb.com) (1999)

19. Dastani, M.: 2APL: a practical agent programming language. International Journal of Autonomous Agents and Multi-Agent Systems (JAAMAS), Special Issue on Computational Logic-based Agents 16(3), 214–248
20. DeLoach, S., Wood, M., Sparkman, C.: Multiagent systems engineering. International Journal of Software Engineering and Knowledge Engineering 11(3), 231–258 (2001)
21. Dix, J., Zhang, Y.: IMPACT: Multi-Agent Framework with Declarative Semantics. In: R. Bordini, M. Dastani, J. Dix, A. El Fallah Seghrouchni (eds.) Multi-Agent Programming: Languages, Platforms and Applications, pp. 69–94. Springer (2005)
22. Dröschel, W., Wiemers, M.: Das V-Modell 97 - Der Standard für die Entwicklung von IT-Systemen mit Anleitung für den Praxiseinsatz. Oldenbourg (1999)
23. Eiter, T., Mascardi, V.: Comparing environments for developing software agents. The European Journal on Artificial Intelligence (AI Communications) pp. 169–197 (2002)
24. Fonseca, S.P., Griss, M.L., Letsinger, R.: Agent behavior architectures - A MAS framework comparison. Tech. Rep. HPL-2001-332, Hewlett Packard Laboratories (2002)
25. Fricke, S., Bsufka, K., Keiser, J., Schmidt, T., Sesseler, R., Albayrak, S.: Agent-based telematic services and telecom applications. Commun. ACM 44(4), 43–48 (2001). DOI http://doi.acm.org/10.1145/367211.367251
26. Giorgini, P., Kolp, M., Mylopoulos, J., Pistore, M.: The Tropos Methodology. In: F. Bergenti, M.P. Gleizes, F. Zambonelli (eds.) Methodologies and Software Engineering For Agent Systems, pp. 89–106. Kluwer Academic Publishers (2004)
27. Gomez-Sanz, J., Pavon, J.: Agent oriented software engineering with ingenias. In: 3rd International Central and Eastern European Conference on Multi-Agent Systems (CEEMAS 2003), pp. 394–403. Springer Verlag (2003)
28. Gorodetsky, V., Karsaev, O., Samoylov, V., Konushy, V., Mankov, E., Malyshev, A.: Multi Agent System Development Kit. In: R. Unland, M. Calisti, M. Klusch (eds.) Software Agent-Based Applications, Platforms and Development Kits, pp. 143–168. Birkhäuser (2005)
29. Gotel, O., Finkelstein, C.: An analysis of the requirements traceability problem. In: Proceedings of the 1st International Conference on Requirements Engineering (ICRE 1994), pp. 94–101. IEEE (1994)
30. Grundy, J., Hosking, J.: Software tools. In: J. Marcin (ed.) The Software Engineering Encyclopedia. Wiley (2001)
31. Henderson-Sellers, B., Giorgini, P. (eds.): Agent-Oriented Methodologies. Idea group publishing (2005)
32. International Organization for Standadization (ISO): Ergonomics of Human-System Interaction-Part 110: Dialogue Principles, ISO 9241-110:2006 edn. (2006)
33. Jacobson, I., Christerson, M., Jonsson, P., Overgaard, G.: Object-Oriented Software Engineering: A Use Case Driven Approach. Addison-Wesley (1992)
34. Laird, J., Rosenbloom, P.: The evolution of the Soar cognitive architecture. In: D. Steier, T. Mitchell (eds.) Mind Matters: A Tribute to Allen Newell, pp. 1–50. Lawrence Erlbaum Associates (1996)
35. van Lamsweerde, A.: Goal-Oriented Requirements Engineering: A Guided Tour. In: Proceedings of the 9th International Joint Conference on Requirements Engineering (RE 2001), pp. 249–263. IEEE Press (2001)
36. Mangina, E.: Review of Software Products for Multi-Agent Systems. Tech. rep., AgentLink (2002). URL http://www.agentlink.org/resources/software-report.html
37. Mitkas, P.A., Kehagias, D., Symeonidis, A.L., Athanasiadis, I.N.: A framework for constructing multi-agent applications and training intelligent agents. In: P. Giorgini, J. Müller, J. Odell (eds.) Proceedings of the 4th International Workshop on Agent-Oriented Software Engineering IV (AOSE 2003), pp. 96–109. Springer (2003)
38. Morley, D., Myers, K.: The spark agent framework. In: Proceedings of the 3rd International Joint Conference on Autonomous Agents and Multiagent Systems (AAMAS 2004), pp. 714–721. IEEE Computer Society (2004)
39. Nwana, H., Ndumu, D., Lee, L., Collis, J.: Zeus: a toolkit and approach for building distributed multi-agent systems. In: Proceedings of the 3rd annual conference on Autonomous Agents (AGENTS 1999), pp. 360–361. ACM Press (1999)

40. Object Management Group (OMG): Deployment and Configuration of Component-based Distributed Applications Specification, version 4.0 edn. (2003). URL http://www.omg.org/cgi-bin/doc?formal/06-04-02

41. Object Management Group (OMG): Unified Modeling Language: Superstructure, version 2.0 edn. (2005). URL http://www.omg.org/cgi-bin/doc?formal/05-07-04

42. Odell, J., Parunak, H.V.D., Bauer, B.: Extending UML for Agents. In: G. Wagner, Y. Lesperance, E. Yu (eds.) Proceedings of the 2nd International Bi-Conference Workshop Agent-Oriented Information Systems Workshop (AOIS@AAAI 2000), pp. 3–17 (2000)

43. Padgham, L., Thangarajah, J., Winikoff, M.: Tool support for agent development using the prometheus methodology. In: Proceedings of the 5th International Conference on Quality Software (QSIC 2005), pp. 383–388. IEEE Computer Society (2005)

44. Padgham, L., Thangarajah, J., Winikoff, M.: The prometheus design tool ? a conference management system case study. In: M. Luck, L. Padgham (eds.) Agent Oriented Software Engineering VIII, LNCS, vol. 4951, pp. 197–211. Springer (2008). 8th International Workshop, AOSE 2007, Honolulu, HI, USA, May 14, 2007, Revised Selected Papers

45. Padgham, L., Winikoff, M.: Developing Intelligent Agent Systems: A Practical Guide. John Wiley & Sons (2004)

46. Pavón, J., Gómez-Sanz, J.: Agent oriented software engineering with ingenias. In: V. Marík, J. Müller, M. Pechoucek (eds.) Multi-Agent Systems and Applications III, 3rd International Central and Eastern European Conference on Multi-Agent Systems, (CEEMAS 2003), pp. 394–403. Springer (2003)

47. Pokahr, A.: Programmiersprachen und Werkzeuge zur Entwicklung verteilter agentenorientierter Softwaresysteme. Ph.D. thesis, Universität Hamburg (2007)

48. Pokahr, A., Braubach, L., Lamersdorf, W.: Agenten: Technologie für den mainstream? In: it - Information Technology, pp. 300–307. Oldenbourg Verlag (2005)

49. Pokahr, A., Braubach, L., Lamersdorf, W.: Jadex: A BDI Reasoning Engine. In: R. Bordini, M. Dastani, J. Dix, A. El Fallah Seghrouchni (eds.) Multi-Agent Programming: Languages, Platforms and Applications, pp. 149–174. Springer (2005)

50. Rao, A.: AgentSpeak(L): BDI Agents Speak Out in a Logical Computable Language. In: W.V. de Velde, J. Perram (eds.) Proceedings of the 7th European Workshop on Modelling Autonomous Agents in a Multi-Agent World (MAAMAW 1996), pp. 42–55. Springer (1996)

51. Rausch, A.: Componentware - Methodik des evolutionären Architekturentwurfs. Herbert Utz Verlag (2004)

52. Rausch, A., Broy, M., Bergner, K.: Das V-Modell XT. Grundlagen, Methodik und Anwendungen. Springer (2006)

53. Reticular Systems: AgentBuilder User's Guide, version 1.3 edn. (2000). http://www.agentbuilder.com/

54. Rimassa, G., Greenwood, D., Kernland, M.E.: The Living Systems Technology Suite: An Autonomous Middleware for Autonomic Computing. In: In Proceedings of the International Conference on Autonomic and Autonomous Systems (ICAS 2006) (2006)

55. Robbins, J., Hilbert, D., Redmiles, D.: Software architecture critics in argo. In: Proceedings of the 3rd international conference on Intelligent user interfaces (IUI 1998), pp. 141–144. ACM Press (1998)

56. Serenko, A., Detlor, B.: Agent Toolkits: A General Overview of the Market and an Assessment of Instructor Satisfaction with Utilizing Toolkits in the Classroom. Tech. Rep. Working Paper #455, Michael G. DeGroote School of Business, McMaster University (2002)

57. Shoham, Y.: Agent-oriented programming. Artificial Intelligence 60(1), 51–92 (1993)

58. Sturm, A., Shehory, O.: A Comparative Evaluation of Agent-Oriented Methodologies. In: F. Bergenti, M.P. Gleizes, F. Zambonelli (eds.) Methodologies and Software Engineering For Agent Systems, pp. 127–149. Kluwer Academic Publishers (2004)

59. Sturm, A., Shehory, O.: A framework for evaluating agent-oriented methodologies. In: P. Giorgini, B. Henderson-Sellers, M. Winikoff (eds.) Agent-Oriented Information Systems (AOIS 2003), pp. 94–109. Springer (2004)

60. Sudeikat, J., Braubach, L., Pokahr, A., Lamersdorf, W., Renz, W.: Validation of bdi agents. In: Proceedings of the 4th International Workshop on Programming Multiagent Systems: languages, frameworks, techniques and tools (ProMAS 2006). Springer (2006). (to appear)
61. Sunyé, G., Pollet, D., Traon, Y.L., Jézéquel, J.M.: Refactoring uml models. In: M. Gogolla, C. Kobryn (eds.) The Unified Modeling Language, Modeling Languages, Concepts, and Tools (UML 2001), pp. 134–148. Springer (2001)
62. Szekely, P.: Retrospective and challenges for model-based interface development. In: F. Bodart, J. Vanderdonckt (eds.) Design, Specification and Verification of Interactive Systems (DSV-IS 1996), pp. 1–27. Springer (1996)
63. Thangarajah, J., Padgham, L., M.Winikoff: Prometheus design tool. In: F. Dignum, V. Dignum, S. Koenig, S. Kraus, M. Singh, M. Wooldridge (eds.) 4rd International Joint Conference on Autonomous Agents and Multiagent Systems (AAMAS 2005), pp. 127–128. ACM (2005)
64. Tryllian Solutions B.V: The Developer's Guide, release 3.0 edn. (2005).   URL http://www.tryllian.com
65. Unland, R., Calisti, M., Klusch, M.: Software Agent-Based Applications, Platforms and Development Kits. Birkhäuser (2005)
66. Whitestein Technologies: Agent Modeling Language, Language Specification, Version 0.9 edn. (2004)
67. Whitestein Technologies: Agent-Oriented Development Methodology for LS/TS, A Comprehensive Overview, LS/TS Release 2.0.0 edn. (2006)
68. Whitestein Technologies: Core Agent Layer Concept, LS/TS Release 2.0.0 edn. (2006)
69. Whitestein Technologies: Message Dispatching Agent Logic Concept, LS/TS Release 2.0.0 edn. (2006)
70. Whitestein Technologies: Multi-Agent Reasoning based on Goal-oriented Execution, LS/TS Release 2.0.0 edn. (2006)
71. Winikoff, M.: JACK Intelligent Agents: An Industrial Strength Platform. In: R. Bordini, M. Dastani, J. Dix, A. El Fallah Seghrouchni (eds.) Multi-Agent Programming: Languages, Platforms and Applications, pp. 175–193. Springer (2005)
72. Winikoff, M., Padgham, L.: The Prometheus Methodology. In: F. Bergenti, M.P. Gleizes, F. Zambonelli (eds.) Methodologies and Software Engineering For Agent Systems, pp. 217–234. Kluwer Academic Publishers (2004)
73. Wooldridge, M., Jennings, N., Kinny, D.: The Gaia Methodology for Agent-Oriented Analysis and Design. Autonomous Agents and Multi-Agent Systems 3(3), 285–312 (2000)
74. Yu, E.: Towards modelling and reasoning support for early-phase requirements engineering. In: Proceedings of the 3rd IEEE International Symposium on Requirements Engineering (RE 1997), pp. 226–235. IEEE Press (1997)

Part III
Applications

Chapter 10
A Multi-Agent Environment for Negotiation

Koen V. Hindriks, Catholijn M. Jonker, and Dmytro Tykhonov

Abstract In this chapter we introduce the System for Analysis of Multi-Issue Negotiation (SAMIN). SAMIN offers a negotiation environment that supports and facilitates the setup of various negotiation setups. The environment has been designed to analyse negotiation processes between human negotiators, between human and software agents, and between software agents. It offers a range of different agents, different domains, and other options useful to define a negotiation setup. The environment has been used to test and evaluate a range of negotiation strategies in various domains playing against other negotiating agents as well as humans. We discuss some of the results obtained by means of these experiments.

10.1 Introduction

Research on negotiation is done in various research disciplines; business management, economics, psychology, and artificial intelligence. The foundations of negotiation theory are decision analysis, behavioral decision making, game theory, and negotiation analysis. The boost of literature on negotiating agents and strategies of recent years is in line with the continuous advance of ecommerce applications, such as eBay, and Marketplace in which negotiations play a role. In essence it focuses on the development of ever more clever negotiation agents, that are typically tested in one domain, against one or two other negotiation agents, almost never against humans. In our opinion, in order to become acceptable as negotiators on behalf of human stakeholders, negotiation agents will have to prove their worth in various domains, against various negotiation strategies and against human negotiators. In order to gain a better understanding of the negotiation dynamics and the factors that influence the negotiation process it is crucial to not

Koen V. Hindriks, Catholijn M. Jonker, and Dmytro Tykhonov
Man-Machine Interaction group, Delft University of Technology, Mekelweg 4, 2628 CD, Delft, The Netherlands, e-mail: {K.V.Hindriks,C.M.Jonker,D.Tykhonov}@tudelft.nl

---

R.H. Bordini et al. (eds.), *Multi-Agent Programming*,
DOI 10.1007/978-0-387-89299-3_10, © Springer Science+Business Media, LLC 2009

only mathematically evaluate the efficiency of negotiation outcomes but also to look at the pattern of offer exchanges, what Raiffa [30] calls the negotiation dance. In the remainder we present architecture of a formal toolbox to simulate negotiations and analyze patterns in offer exchanges and present some initial findings in the literature. The System for Analysis of Multi-Issue Negotiation[1] (SAMIN) is developed as a research tool, to improve the quality of negotiating agents, and as a training environment to develop negotiation skills of human negotiators. To that purpose SAMIN offers a range of analytical tools, a tournament tool, a preference elicitation tool, and a number of negotiation domains, negotiation agents, and user interfaces for human negotiators.

10.2 Application Domain

Negotiation is an interpersonal decision-making process necessary whenever we cannot achieve our objectives single-handedly [32]. Pruitt [28] emphasizes the process of negotiation and the fact that the outcome should be a joint decision by the parties involved. Typically each party starts a negotiation by offering the most preferred solution from the individual area of interest. If an offer is not acceptable by the other parties they make counter-offers in order to move each other closer to an agreement. The field of negotiation can be split into different types, e.g. along the following lines: (a) one-to-one versus more than two parties; (b) single- versus multi-issues; (c) closed versus open (d) mediator-based versus mediator-free. The research reported in this chapter concerns one-to-one, multi-issue, closed, mediator-free negotiation. A special case of one-to-many negotiation is considered. In this case, an auction mechanism [10] is approximated by a negotiation setup [16]. For more information on negotiations between more than two parties (e.g., in auctions), the reader is referred to, e.g., [31]. In single-issue negotiation, the negotiation focuses on one aspect only (typically price) of the object under negotiation. Multi-issue negotiation (also called multi-attribute negotiation) is often seen as a more cooperative form of negotiation, since often an outcome exists that brings joint gains for both parties, see [30]. Closed negotiation means that no information regarding preferences is exchanged between the negotiators. The only information exchanged is formed by the bids. More information about (partially) open negotiations can be found, e.g., in [20] and [30]. However, the trust necessary for (partially) open negotiations is not always available. The use of mediators is a well-recognised tool to help the involved parties in their negotiations, see e.g., [19, 30]. The mediator tries to find a deal that is fair to all parties. Reasons for negotiating without a mediator can be the lack of a trusted mediator, the costs of a mediator, and the hope of doing better. The SAMIN system is developed to support research into the analysis of negotiation strategies. The analysis of negoti-

---

[1] This negotiation environment, user manuals, and a number of implemented negotiation agents can be downloaded from http://mmi.tudelft.nl/negotiation.

ation strategies provides new insights into the development of better negotiation strategies.

Negotiation parties need each other to obtain an outcome which is beneficial to both and is an improvement over the current state of affairs for either party. Both parties need to believe this is the case before they will engage in a negotiation. Although by engaging in a negotiation one party signals to the other party that there is potential for such gain on its side, it may still leave the other party with little more knowledge than that this is so. Research shows that the more one knows about the other party the more effective the exchange of information and offers [30]. Furthermore, humans usually do have some understanding of the domain of negotiation to guide their actions, and, as has been argued, a machine provided with domain knowledge may also benefit from such domain knowledge [6]. It is well-known that many factors influence the performance and outcome of humans in a negotiation, ranging from the general mindset towards negotiation to particular emotions and perception of fairness. As emphasized in socio-psychological and business management literature on negotiation, viewing negotiation as a joint problem-solving task is a more productive mindset than viewing negotiation as a competition in which one party wins and the other looses [7, 30, 32]. Whereas the latter mindset typically induces hard-bargaining tactics and rules out disclosure of relevant information to an opponent, the former leads to joint exploration of possible agreements and induces both parties to team up and search for trade-offs to find a win-win outcome. Different mindsets lead to different negotiation strategies. A similar distinction between hard- and soft-bargaining tactics has also been discussed in the automated negotiation system literature where the distinction has been referred to as either a boulware or a conceder tactics [5]. Emotions and perception of fairness may also determine the outcome of a negotiation. People may have strong feelings about the "rightness" of a proposed agreement. Such feelings may not always be productive to reach a jointly beneficial and efficient agreement. It has been suggested in the literature to take such emotions into account but at the same time to try to control them during negotiation and rationally assess the benefits of any proposals on the table [7, 32]. Apart from the factors mentioned above that influence the dynamics of negotiation, many other psychological biases have been identified in the literature that influence the outcome of a negotiation, including among others partisan perceptions, overconfidence, endowment effects, reactive devaluation [25, 32].

10.2.1 The Added Value of the MAS Paradigm

Negotiation involves conflicting interests, hidden goals, and making educated guesses about the preferences and goals of the other parties involved. A system that supports closed negotiation needs to protect the integrity of the parties or stakeholders that participate in a negotiation and it is natural to provide every stakeholder with an agent of their own. It thus is natural to use the MAS paradigm to model the interaction between negotiating parties. Parties in a negotiation are autonomous and need to decide on the moves to make during a negotiation. This decision problem is particularly complex in a closed negotiation where negotiating parties do not reveal their preferences to each other. Moreover, other factors such as the complexity of the domain of negotiation may pose additional problems that need to be solved by a negotiating agent.

SAMIN contributes to the MAS paradigm as a research tool that facilitates research into the design of efficient negotiation strategies. The tool more specifically facilitates the evaluation of the performance of a negotiation strategy by means of simulating multiple negotiation sessions and feeding the results of the simulation to the analytical toolbox of SAMIN. We have found that the results of a well-defined negotiation setup may help analysing the strengths and weaknesses of a strategy and may be used to improve a negotiation strategy significantly. It has also been shown that strategies may perform quite differently on different domains. A variety of negotiation domains and agents is available in SAMIN to evaluate a negotiation strategy in different negotiation setups. The open architecture of SAMIN, moreover, facilitates the integration of new negotiation domains and agents.

10.2.2 Design Methods Used

An earlier version of SAMIN, see [2, 17], was designed using the DESIRE method [3]. Redesign was necessary to open the system for agents designed and implemented by others and to ease the definition of new negotiation domains. The redesigned version is implemented in the Java programming language that is supported my the majority of computer platforms.

The current version of SAMIN implements the architecture proposed in [13]. Figure 10.1 illustrates this architecture. The architecture is based on an analysis of the tasks that need to be supported by a generic negotiation environment that is capable of integrating a variety of negotiating agents and is able to simulate negotiations between such agents. The architecture provides a minimal but sufficient framework including all features necessary to simulate a wide range of negotiation scenarios and to enable integration of negotiation agents. The architecture consists of four main layers, a human bidding interface, and a negotiating agent architecture. The four layers include an *interaction layer*, an *ontology layer*, a *graphical user interface layer*, and an *analytical toolbox*.

The *interaction layer* provides functionality to define negotiation protocols and enables communication between agents (see Section 10.4.2 for details). The *ontology layer* provides functionality to define, specify and store a negotiation domain, and the preferences of the negotiating agents (see Section 10.4.3 for details). The architecture can also be used for education purposes and for the training of humans in negotiation. For that purpose, a *graphical user interface layer* is available that facilitates human user(s) to participate in a negotiation setup (see Section

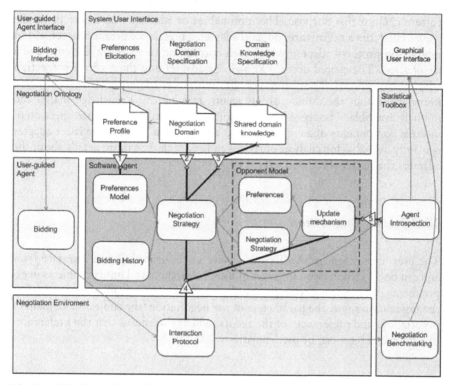

Fig. 10.1 The Open Negotiation System Architecture

10.2.3 for details). The *analytical toolbox* provides functionality to organize tournaments between agents, and to review the performance and benchmark results of agents that conducted a negotiation. It provides a variety of tools to analyze the performance of agents and may also be used to compute quality measures related to e.g. the quality of an opponent model [15].

The architecture that is introduced here identifies the main integration points where adapters are needed to connect a negotiating agent to this architecture. The agent architecture itself defines the common components of a negotiating agent. This architecture may be instantiated with various software agents, as illustrated below.

The integration points or interfaces to connect software agents to the negotiation environment which allows them to interact with other agents available in the environment are numbered 1 through 5 in Figure 10.1. To integrate heterogeneous negotiation agents, such agents have to be aligned with these integration points. Alignment by complete redesign of the agent typically requires significant programming efforts and may also cause backward compatibility problems. To minimize the programming efforts, a better approach is to use a set of adapters or wrappers which are used to wrap the agent code. We have used the adapter design pattern [22] for this purpose. The minimal set of adapters that has to be implemented includes a negotiation domain adapter, a preference profile adapter and an interaction protocol adapter, which each correspond to an essential element of a negotiation. The shared domain knowledge adapter and the agent introspection adapter are optional. The shared domain knowledge adapter provides additional knowledge about the domain to all agents, making this knowledge shared and publicly available. The agent introspection adapter facilitates the introspection of internal components of an agent, such as an opponent model. The latter adapter is mainly available for analysis purposes and research. For more details about the adapters the reader is referred to [13].

10.2.3 User Interaction

The user interaction in SAMIN takes place in the graphical user interface layer and can be divided in two categories of user: researchers and human subjects in experiments. We implemented a graphical user interface that enables a user to define the *negotiation game*. the parameters of the negotiation, the subject or domain of negotiation, and preferences of the agents (which also means that the preferences of a human subject can be predefined).

10.2.3.1 Negotiation Domain and Preference Profile Editor

The *Negotiation Domain and Preference Profile Editor* of SAMIN (see Figure 10.2) is used to create and modify negotiation domains and preference profiles. A *negotiation domain* is a specification of the objectives and issues to be resolved by means of negotiation. An objective may branch into sub-objectives and issues providing a tree-like structure to the domain. The leafs of such a tree representing the domain of negotiation must be the issues that need to be agreed upon in a negotiation. Various types of issues are allowed, including discrete enumerated value sets, integer-valued sets, real-valued sets, as well as a special type of issue used to represent a price associated with the negotiation object. For every issue the user can associate a range of values with a short description and a cost.

A *preference profile* specifies personal preferences regarding possible outcomes of a negotiation. The profile is used to convert any offer in that domain to a value indicating how the user would rate that offer, the so called utility value. The current version of SAMIN supports linear additive utility functions [30]. The profile is also called a *utility space*.

A *weight* that is assigned to every issue indicates the importance of that issue. A human user (see Figure 10.2) can move sliders to change the weights or enter their values by hand, which are automatically normalized by the editor. In the issue editor the user can assign an evaluation to every value of the issue. The

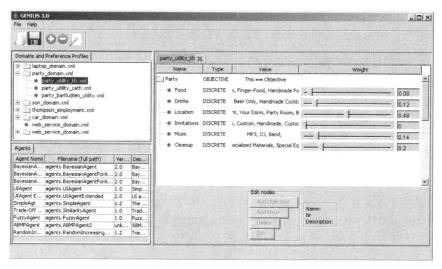

Fig. 10.2 A graphical user interface for preferences elicitation.

evaluation values are positive integers starting with 1. The evaluation values are automatically normalized for each issue to ensure they are in the range [0; 1].

10.2.3.2 Human Negotiator User Interface

A human subject playing in a negotiation game, is provided with a graphical interface for the bidding phase of the game. The bidding interface is implemented with a dummy agent that exchanges the messages between the graphical user interface (GUI) and the environment. Therefore, the GUI for the human negotiator is not hard coded in SAMIN. The GUI can be easily extended without modifications of the SAMIN code. Furthermore, the dummy agent can be replaced with an algorithm that would provide negotiation a support to the human negotiator. It provides, for example, an analysis of the opponent's behaviour or even advise the human negotiator upon the next offer to propose and an action to be taken. Figure 10.3 presents human player GUI that is currently available in SAMIN. This GUI has three main components: a bidding history table (top), a utility history plot (bottom left), and a bidding interface (bottom right). The bidding history shows all bids exchanged between the negotiating parties in a single session. The bids are represented by the values assigned to every issue in the negotiation domain. In addition, the utilities of the bids according to the human player's preference profiles are shown in the table. Note that in a closed negotiation the negotiating parties have no access to the preference profiles of each other and, therefore, utilities can be calculated only on the basis of own preference profile.

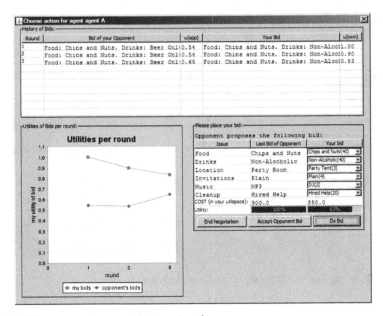

Fig. 10.3 Human negotiator graphical user interface.

The bidding interface has two main components: a table showing the last bid and a possible next bid and a row of buttons representing possible actions for the humans negotiator's. The table has three columns:

- the left column shows the names of the issues in the domain;
- the center column shows the values for the issues as proposed in the last bid of the opponent;
- the right column shows the current selected values for the issues. A user can edit the current bid by clicking on the fields, which will open the drop-down boxes in the fields.

The last two rows of the table show the cost and utility of the last opponent's bid and your current bid. The cost field will turn red if the bid exceeds the maximum cost. The utility is shown as a percentage and also as a bar of matching size. These values are computed according to the user's utility space because a user has no access to the opponent's utility space. The lower three buttons allow a user to submit the next bid as it is set in the right column, or to accept the opponent's last bid.

10.3 Agents

In this section we present an agent architecture in SAMIN and explain the state-of-the-art negotiation agents that are available in SAMIN.

10.3.1 Agent Architecture

The *software agent* component highlighted with the darker area in Figure 10.1 is a generic component that can be instantiated by a variety heterogeneous software agents. The components that are specified as part of a software agent in Figure 10.1 are the parts of the *conceptual design* of such agents but do not need to be actually present or identifiable as such in any particular software agent. These components are not introduced here to specify a requirements that need to be satisfied when developing an agent (although it could be used as such [1, 18, 21]). Here these components are introduced to identify integration points of agents with the system architecture. Five of such integration points, also referred to as *adapters*, were identified above.

In the reminder of this section we discuss every component of the proposed agent architecture.

Preference Model

The component models the agent's preferences with respect to the set of possible negotiation outcomes. The model can be based on various structures: utility functions, rankings, etc. This component can require additional processing depending on the complexity of the agent's preferences and the types of inquiries that can be made by other components, see e.g. [19]. Typically, the preferences model must be able to evaluate an outcome on a given scale, compare two or more outcomes, give a single or a set of outcomes that satisfy some constraints on the negotiation domain and preferences.

Negotiation Strategy

This is the core component of any negotiation agent. It makes decisions about acceptance of the opponent's offer, ending the negotiation, and sending a counter-offer. To propose a counter-offer the negotiation strategy can use various tactics [5]. Depending on the negotiation tactics used in the negotiation strategy the component can use information about the model of the agent's own preferences, the opponent's preferences and strategy (as far as known to or guessed by the agent), and, the previous offers made during the current, or even previous negotiation sessions.

Negotiation History

The negotiation history component keeps track of the bids exchanged between the agents in a negotiation. It can also have a history about earlier negotiations, the outcomes, identities of the opponents, and even opponent models. It can be used by the negotiation strategy component as an additional information source to improve its negotiation performance. For example, in repetitive negotiations with the same opponents this information can be used as a priori knowledge about the opponent to shorten the learning time.

Opponent Model

In the negotiation games we consider here, the preferences of negotiation parties are private [30]. Efficiency of a negotiation strategy can be significantly improved with information about the preferences of the opponent [33]. In the literature a number of learning techniques have been proposed to learn the opponent's preferences model from the offers exchanged in a single-shot negotiation, see e.g., [34, 13]. In [33] it was show that a successful negotiation strategy should make use of an opponent model.

Our generic component consists of three main subcomponents: *preferences, negotiation strategy*, and *update mechanism*.

The component *Preferences* contains specifications of the preferences of the current and previous negotiation opponents. As the opponent's preferences are typically private, the preference information has a certain degree of uncertainty. Depending on the agent developed on the base of the generic components information about the certainty of the preferences can be maintained or not.

The aim of the model of *opponent's strategy* is to predict negotiation moves that will be made by the opponent. It is important to know for an agent what the next move of the opponent would be. This knowledge can be used in the negotiation strategy to increase the efficiency of the agent's own offers and increase the chance of acceptance of its offer by the opponent.

Models of the opponent's preferences and strategy are typically learned by the agent from the evidence, such as negotiation agreements achieved in the previous negotiations [33], and offers sent by the opponent in multiple sessions of single-shot negotiations [13, 34, 18]. The learning techniques used in the agent can depend on the types of the models chosen to represent the opponent's preferences and strategy.

10.3.2 State of the Art Negotiating Agents

Interfaces and adapters have been developed to make it easy to integrate agents developed by others into SAMIN, see [13]. A number of the state-of-the-art agents have found a place in SAMIN: ABMP [17], Bayesian agent [14], Bayesian Tit-for-Tat [12], FBM [29], Trade-off agent [6], QO agent [24], Random Walker [11]. As they were developed by different teams, their design, architecture, and implementation varies.

Random Walker

The Random Walker strategy introduced in [11], also known as Zero Intelligence (ZI) strategy [8], randomly jumps through the negotiation space. It does not use own preferences or a model of opponent's preferences to make an offer. Random Walker accepts the opponent's offer if it has higher utility than the agent's own last offer. The Random Walker strategy can be run with a break-off point to avoid making offers below that utility and, thus, introduces some limited rationality in its behaviour.

It is difficult for the Random Walker strategy to achieve a better agreement than its break-off point as there is only a very low probability that it will be able to find bids close to Pareto frontier. Any efficient negotiation strategy that is capable of learning an opponent model and is able to use it efficiently would be expected to outperform the Random Walker strategy. For this reason, the Random Walker strategy may be used as a "baseline" strategy. In addition, as the Random Walker strategy does not derive its moves from its preference profile but only uses an acceptance strategy to avoid outcomes with a utility below its break-off point, it also provides a good test case to evaluate of robustness of a negotiation strategy.

ABMP Agent

The ABMP strategy is a concession-oriented negotiation strategy, see [17]. It selects counter-offers without taking domain or opponent knowledge into account. The ABMP strategy decides on a negotiation move based on considerations derived from the agent's own utility space only. It calculates a utility of a next offer, called *target utility*, based on the current utility gap between the last opponent's offer and the last own offer. To determine the next offer the target utility is propagated to the individual issues taking into account the weights of the issues in the agent's preferences profile. The ABMP strategy can be fine-tuned with a number of parameters, such as the negotiation speed, concession factor, configuration tolerance and others.

The original ABMP strategy was not capable of learning. A heuristic for adapting the ABMP strategy to the opponent's issue priorities was introduced in [18]. The results showed improvement of the negotiation outcome compared to the original version of the ABMP strategy.

The ABMP strategy was implemented in an ad hoc environment using the DE-SIRE method [3]. The environment facilitated negotiation about a Second-hand car domain [17] that was hard-coded in the implementation. Later, when the second Java-based version of the SAMIN was available the ABMP strategy was re-implemented in SAMIN. The results of the DESIRE-based ABMP implementation were reproduced in SAMIN.

Trade-off Agent

The effectiveness of using knowledge about the negotiation domain has been demonstrated in the Trade-off strategy introduced in [6]. In particular, this paper shows that domain knowledge (coded as so-called similarity functions) can be used to select bids that are close to the opponent's bids, thus increasing the likelihood of acceptance of a proposed bid by that opponent. In this approach, the knowledge represented by similarity functions is assumed to be public.

In [6], the Trade-off strategy is combined with several so called *meta strategies* that control the concession behaviour of the agent. The most interesting meta strategy, the *smart* strategy, consists of deploying a Trade-off mechanism until the agent observes a deadlock in the average closeness of own offers compared to that of the opponent as measured by the similarity function. In a case of the deadlock, the value of the previous offer is reduced by a predetermined amount (0.05), thereby lowering the input value of the Trade-off mechanism.

The Trade-off strategy was originally evaluated on the Service-Oriented Negotiation (SON) domain. The SON domain has four quantitative continuous issues, the price, quality, time, and penalty. Both, buyer and seller use linear functions to evaluate individual issues and combine them in a linear additive utility function using a vector of weights. It is assumed that the buyer and the seller have opposite preferences for every issue, that is, if buyer wants to maximize the quality then the seller wants to minimize it. Therefore, in this domain the differences in the weights are the key elements to consider for joint improvements of the offers.

The Trade-off strategy combined with the smart meta strategy showed good performance on the SON in the experimental setup of [6]. It was demonstrated that the Trade-off strategy is capable of producing very efficient offers resulting in agreements that are very close to the Pareto efficient frontier. Interestingly, the best performance the Trade-off strategy showed in negotiation against itself, while in negotiations against agents that used other meta strategies the utility of agreement was somewhat lower. This phenomenon will be discussed in details in Section 10.6.

Unfortunately, no implementation of the Trade-Off strategy was available. The strategy was implemented in the SAMIN from scratch. The results reported in [6] were reproduced for the Service-Oriented Negotiation domain.

Bayesian Agent

One way to approach the problem of incomplete information in closed negotiation is to learn an opponent's preferences given the negotiation moves that an opponent makes during the negotiation. A learning technique based on Bayesian learning algorithm was proposed in [14]. The opponent model in [14] is based on learning probability over a set of hypothesis about evaluation functions and weights of the issues. The probability distribution is defined over the set of hypothesis that represent agent's belief about opponent's preferences. Structural assumptions about the evaluation functions and weights are made to decrease the number of parameters to be learned and simplify the learning task.

The set of hypotheses about the evaluation function is defined using three types of shapes of the functions: (a) downhill shape: minimal issue values are preferred over other issue values, and the evaluation of issue values decreases linearly when the value of the issue increases; (b) uphill shape: maximal issue values are preferred over other issue values, and the evaluation of issue values increases linearly when the value of the issue increases; (c) triangular shape: a specific issue value somewhere in the issue range is valued most and evaluations associated with issues to the left ("smaller") and right ("bigger") of this issue value linearly decrease (think, e.g., of an amount of goods).

During a negotiation every time when a new bid is received from the opponent the probability of each hypothesis is updated using Bayes' rule. This requires a conditional probability that represents the probability that the bid might have been proposed given a hypothesis. Therefore the utility of bid is calculated according to this hypothesis and compared with the predicted utility according to the rationality assumption. To estimate the predicted utility value an assumption about the opponent concession tactics is used based on a linear function.

Authors propose two versions of the learning algorithm. In the first version of the algorithm each hypotheses represents a complete utility space as a combination of weights ranking and shapes of the issue evaluation functions. The size of the hypothesis space growth exponentially with respect to the number of issue and thus is intractable for negotiation domains with high number of issues.

The second version of the algorithm is a scalable variant for the first one. This version of the agent tries to learn probability distribution over the individual hypothesis about the value of the weight and shape of the issue evaluation function independently of other issues. The computational tractability of the learning is achieved by approximating the conditional distributions of the hypotheses using the expected values of the dependent hypotheses.

QO Agent

In [24] the authors propose a negotiation agent, called QO agent, that is based on qualitative decision making. The QO agent is designed for automated negotiations with multiple issues. The internal structure of the QO agent is similar to the agent architecture proposed in this article. The underlying assumption in the QO agent is that the opponent uses one of three preference profiles. The preference profiles of the opponent are represented in same way as QO agent's own preference profile. A probability is associated with each of the possible opponent profiles. An update mechanism interprets the observed offers from the opponent and updates the probability distribution according to the opponent strategy model. The opponent profiles have the same structure as the own preferences profile and the same preference profile adapter is used to load them from files.

The original implementation of the QO agent uses Java programming language. The interaction protocol, however, is more complex then the alternating offers protocol currently used by the SAMIN. The QO agent environment implements a rather complex interaction protocol that extends the alternating offers protocol. It does not have a clear turn taking flow and allows agents to exchange pre-defined textual messages between the agents, such as threats of breaking negotiation if the last offer is not accepted. It was decided to simplify it in the interaction protocol adapter. Only those functions of the agent were used that represent the core functionality: interpret the opponent's offer, generate next action of the agent, generate a counter-offer.

Fuzzy-based Model Agent

The other agent integrated into the negotiation system is the Fuzzy-based model (FBM) agent introduced in [29]. The Fuzzy-based agent is designed for negotiation where agents can exchange fuzzy proposals. The original FBM agent is designed for negotiations where agents can exchange fuzzy proposals. The original implementation of the FBM agent works only for one-issue negotiations but can be extended for multi-issue negotiations. As a result, the negotiation domain is defined using one issue that takes real values from a give interval. The agent adopts time dependent negotiation tactics from [5] and, thus, always makes concession towards opponent. The offers are defined using two values: the peak value and the stretch of the offer.

The FBM agent is implemented in an experimental setup using Java programming language. The experimental setup uses the alternating offers protocol [27]. The preference profile is hard-coded in the agent and based on a linear function. The experimental setup consists two agents that have opposed preferences over the issues.

Bayesian Tit-for-Tat Agent

In [12] a negotiation strategy is proposed that uses a model of the opponent's preferences not only to increase the efficiency of the negotiated agreement but also to avoid exploitation by the other party in a sophisticated Tit-for-Tat manner.Authors in [12] try to show that two important goals in any negotiation can be realized when a reasonable estimate of the preferences of an opponent is available.

For that purpose they combine the Bayesian learning technique as proposed in [14] with a Tit-for-Tat tactic, see e.g., [5], and the classification of negotiation moves as described in, e.g., [11]. As is typical for Tit-for-Tat, it avoids exploitation by a form of mirroring of the bids of the opponent. Bayesian learning is used to learn the opponent's preferences. The opponent profile together with the classification scheme is used to develop a sophisticated Tit-for-Tat Bayesian negotiation strategy.

Bidding of the proposed strategy can be understood by the opponent as signalling whether a move is appreciated or not (which is not as easy as it seems). Tit-for-Tat Bayesian negotiation strategy does not punish the opponent for making a move that can be understood as an honest mistake. The strategy is based on a rationality assumption, i.e., that an opponent would tend to accept more preferred offers over less preferred. In line with this assumption the strategy searches for Pareto efficient offers, i.e., offers that cannot be improved for both parties simultaneously. Pareto efficient offers increase the chances that an opponent accepts an offer, while protecting the agent's own preferences as best as possible. Finding such offers requires that the Pareto efficient frontier can be approximated which is only feasible if a reasonable model of the opponent's preferences is available.

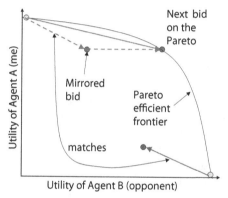

Fig. 10.4 Bayesian Tit-for-Tat Strategy

The basic idea of Tit-for-Tat in multi-issue negotiation is to respond to an opponent move with a symmetrical one, as depicted in Figure 10.4. Typically, a rational negotiation strategy would try to make concession moves at some points during the negotiation. The most reasonable response to a concession move would be a concession move of approximately the same concession size. This is called "mirroring" the move of the opponent.

Mirroring simply in this manner would imply that an unfortunate move (an offer that decreases utility for both parties compared to the agent's previous offer) of the opponent would be answered with an unfortunate step. However, it is not rational to consciously make unfortunate steps. Therefore, authors conclude that the pure tactic by mirroring the opponent moves is too simplistic. Instead they use an approximation of the Pareto frontier computed using the learned opponent model and the agent's own preference profile to add an additional step.

The Bayesian Tit-for-Tat strategy is constructed on the basis of the assumption that by maximizing the opponent's utility in every offer, the chance of acceptance increases as well. Therefore, if after mirroring the opponent's move the efficiency of the agent's own next move can be increased by selecting an equivalent offer (with respect to the agent's preference profile) on the Pareto frontier the strategy will choose to make that offer. Important is that this approach makes the Bayesian Tit-for-Tat negotiation strategy less dependent on the efficiency of the opponent's strategy. The opponent might intend to make a concession but in fact make an unfortunate move. By selecting a bid on the approximated Pareto frontier, while mirroring the concession intent of the opponent, the strategy is able to maintain a high efficiency of the outcome, no matter what mistakes the opponent makes.

10.4 Multi-Agent System

The organisation of SAMIN as a multi-agent system and as research environment is introduced in [13].

10.4.1 Organisation

Negotiation, in fact, can take place in a distributed environment. To support distributed negotiation a Web-based interface to the system will be introduced in the next version. This will enable negotiations between humans that are physically distributed. In addition, the Web interface will allow researchers to upload their code from different locations and participate in a tournament.

To setup a negotiation a negotiation template is created. Negotiation template specifies all details of the negotiation: number of agents (currently only bilateral negotiations are supported), names of the agent's classes that implement negotiation strategies, negotiation domain and preference profiles of the parties. This setup is static through single negotiation session.

The structure of the multi-agent system and organisation of the negotiating agents in SAMIN is determined by the negotiation protocol that is used. The interaction of agents is also fully controlled by the environment and negotiation protocol used. All agents are required to comply with the protocol, which is enforced by the environment.

10.4.2 Interaction

The interaction layer manages the rules of encounter or protocol that regulate the agent interaction in a negotiation. Any agent that wants to participate in such a negotiation protocol must accept and agree to conform to these rules. An interaction protocol specifies which negotiation moves and what information exchange between agents is allowed during a negotiation.

The current version of SAMIN focuses on bilateral negotiation. A centralized interaction engine is used, which facilitates the control over the negotiation flow and the enforcement of rules on the negotiation process. The interaction engine also feeds information to the advanced logging capabilities of SAMIN. Logs are used by the analytical toolbox to assess the performance of negotiation strategies and algorithms, see [11, 13]. Interaction protocols are implemented in the negotiation environment as a separate component to allow the use of a variety of protocols. Implementation of a new interaction protocol in the negotiation environment is a relatively easy task and has no or minimal effect on the agent code.

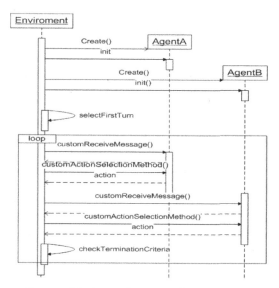

Fig. 10.5 A sequence diagram of the interaction protocol

An example of one of the best known negotiation protocols, the alternating offer protocol [27], is illustrated in Figure 10.5. The alternating offers protocol in a bilateral setting dictates a simple turntaking scheme where each agent is allowed to make a single negotiation move when it is its turn. Apart from turntaking a protocol may also dictate whether exchange of complete package deals is required or that alternatively the exchange of partial bids is allowed. In addition a protocol may manage deadlines, or timeouts that are fixed by the environment.

The interaction protocol is initialized with the information provided by the user. There is no need for a yellow pages mechanism as the agents are made aware about the identity of each other and thus are able to keep track of previous negotiations with the same partner if multiple negotiation sessions are played.

In [16] an alternative protocol involving multiple agents is introduced that is also available in SAMIN. The motivation for introducing this protocol is that it can be used to simulate an auction mechanism. [16] shows that a particular auction mechanism, called the Qualitative Vickrey Auction (QVA) [10], can be simulated with the protocol.[2]

The QVA mechanism can be thought of as consisting of two rounds. In the first round, the buyer publicly announces her preferences, potential service providers (sellers) submit offers in response, and a winner is selected by the buyer. The winner is the seller who has submitted the best offer from the point of view of the buyer. After establishing the winner, in a second round, the buyer determines the second-best offer (from its perspective again) it received from another seller, announces this publicly, and then the winner is allowed to select any agreement that has at least the same utility to the buyer as the second-best offer (which can be determined by the winner since the preferences of the buyer are publicly announced). It is assumed that the bids proposed in the first round are all monitored by a trusted third party.

The negotiation protocol of [16] provides an alternative to the QVA mechanism. An advantage of using a negotiation setup instead of the QVA is that in that case the buyer does not have to publicly announce its preferences. The negotiation protocol is structured in two rounds to match the structure of the mechanism. In the first round negotiation sessions are performed between the buyer and every potential seller using the Alternating offers protocol (see Figure 10.5). Moreover, the negotiation sessions are assumed to be independent. At the end of the first round, a winner (one of the sellers) is determined. Before starting the second round, the agreement between the seller and buyer that is second-best from the perspective of the buyer is revealed to all sellers, in particular to the winner. In the second round an agreement between the winner and the buyer is established. In section 10.6 we present some experimental results received for the proposed negotiation mechanism.

10.4.3 MAS Environment

The MAS environment in SAMIN is a negotiation environment that controls some aspects of the agent's behaviour, such as the setup and initialization of a negotiation session(s), compliance of the agents with a selected negotiation protocol, etc. The layers with corresponding components of the negotiation environment are shown in Figure 10.1 and have a lighter background. First of all, the negotiation environment provides a negotiation ontology to the agents. The ontology specifies concepts, such as a negotiation domain, a preference profile, and shared knowledge.

A *negotiation domain* is a specification of the objectives and issues to be resolved by means of negotiation. It specifies the structure and content of bids or offers exchanged, and of any final outcome or agreement. An outcome determines a specific value for each issue, or, alternatively, only for a subset of the issues. Ob-

---

[2] The QVA is a generalization of the well-known Vickrey auction to a multi-issue setting where payments are not essential. In QVA a buyer has complex preferences over a set of issues.

jectives allow to define a tree-like structure with either other objectives again or issues as children, in line with [30]. Various types of issues are allowed, including discrete enumerated value sets, integer-valued sets, real-valued sets, as well as a special type of issue called *price* issue. Additionally, a specification of a negotiation domain may introduce constraints on acceptable outcomes. For example, costs associated with a particular outcome may not exceed the available budget of the agent.

A *preference profile* specifies the preferences regarding possible outcomes of an agent. It can be thought of as a function mapping outcomes of a negotiation domain onto the level of satisfaction an agent associates with that outcome. The structure of a preference profile for obvious reasons resembles that of a domain specification. The tree-like structure allows to specify relative priorities of parts of the tree. This allows, for example, to ensure that all issues relating to travelling combined are weighted equally as all issues relating to the actual stay at a particular location.

In a *closed* negotiation an agent is not informed about the preferences of its negotiating partner. In that case an agent can at best use a reconstruction (using e.g. machine learning techniques) of these preferences to decide on the negotiation move it should do next. It is typical, however, that with a domain comes certain public knowledge that is shared and can be used to obtain a better negotiation outcome. For example, common preferences such as preferring early delivery over later (though not always the case) may be common knowledge in a given domain. Such knowledge allows agents to compute the preferences of their negotiation partner e.g. using the time interval between two dates. This type of knowledge, labelled *shared domain knowledge*, is modelled explicitly as a separate component that can be accessed by all negotiating agents.

The *analytical toolbox* layer of the negotiation environment a set of statistical analysis methods to perform an outcome analysis on negotiation sessions as introduced and discussed in e.g., [11, 30]. Furthermore, the toolbox contains methods for the analysis of dynamic properties of negotiation sessions as discussed in e.g., [11]. The methods for both outcome and dynamics analysis were used to produce a number of performance benchmarks for negotiation behaviour and for the agent components [13]. The analytical toolbox uses the optimal solutions [30], such as the Pareto efficient frontier, Nash product and Kalai-Smorodinsky solution for the negotiation outcome benchmarking. The benchmarks in the negotiation system can be used to analyze the performance of opponent modelling techniques, the efficiency of negotiation strategies, and the negotiation behaviour of the agent. The result of the analysis can help researchers to improve their agents. The output of the analytical toolbox is presented graphically (see e.g., Figures 10.6 and 10.8).

10.5 Execution Platform

The system is implemented as a stand-alone application running on a single computer. The negotiation settings, such as role and types of the agents, negotiation domain, and preference profiles are predefined by an script. A tournament is a typical experimental setup for negotiating agents [11]. Therefore, the system has a utility to generate scripts for a tournament setup and can automatically run a sequence of negotiation.

SAMIN is currently focused on the closed negotiations, where negotiating parties have no access to the preference profiles of each other. In addition, agent's own preference profile is supposed to be static during negotiation and cannot be changed during the negotiation. Few security precautions were implemented in SAMIN to meet these requirements and avoid situations where agents would improve their performance by means of software hacks. This is especially important when SAMIN is used as a testbed for negotiating agents or in an educational setup. Negotiating agents in SAMIN as any imperfect software product can fail. All errors and exception raised by the agent's code are properly logged by the SAMIN to allow the agent's developer to improve it. SAMIN uses multi-threading mechanism to assure responsiveness of the SAMIN's GUI during negotiation sessions. Agents running into a deadlock can be stopped by the user by means of the GUI without fatal consequences for the negotiation environment.

The algorithms used in the negotiation strategies can have high computational complexity [19] and, thus, require significant computational power from the execution platform and essential time slot to perform necessary computations to process opponent's offer or select the next action. Negotiation typically, take place under time constraints [5]. Therefore, a timeout mechanism is implemented in SAMIN.

The agents are notified by the negotiation environment about the time left until the deadline using the real-time clock. The timeout mechanism can be switched off by the user when SAMIN is used as a research tool.

10.6 Results

The main advantage of the proposed MAS architecture is to allow for integration of heterogeneous agents and to facilitate comparison of their negotiation. SAMIN can be used as a testbed to perform experiments with various negotiation domains, preference profiles and negotiating agents. Thus, it contributes to automated negotiating agents research by providing a tool that is able to show new insights about such agents. Here we shortly present the most interesting results received with SAMIN for negotiating agents that have been implemented and/or integrated in it.

10.6.1 Experimental Setup

A tournament is a typical experimental setup for evaluation of negotiating agents It enables analysis if the behaviour and effectiveness of an agent compared to that of others. Multiple negotiation domains and preferences profiles can be selected for a tournament. To test sensitivity of a strategy to its internal parameter the value of the parameter can be varied in a tournament. Every session can be repeated a number of times to build a representative sample of negotiation results for a statistical analysis in case of non-deterministic negotiation strategies.

A number of negotiation factors influencing negotiation behaviour have been reported in [11]. We reuse these factors in our method.

Size of the negotiation domain. Complexity of the negotiation domain and preference profiles is determined by the size of the negotiation domain. Size of the domain can influence learning performance of the negotiation strategy and, thus, the outcome reached by the strategy [14]. The size of the domain is exponential with respect to the number of issues. Therefore, to be able to test scalability of a negotiation strategy the experimental setup should have a set of domains ranging from low number of issues to higher number of issues.

Predictability of the preferences. Negotiation strategies can try to exploit the internal structure of the preferences in order to improve one's own efficiency. I.e., the Trade-off strategy assumes that distance measures can be defined using domain knowledge for the preferences of the opponent. These measures combined with the opponent's offers allow the Trade-off strategy to predict opponent preferences and as a result improve efficiency of the bidding. In [11], however, it has been shown that in case of a mismatch of the domain knowledge and the actual structure of the opponent's preferences the performance of a strategy can drastically drop. Therefore, we introduce the notion of the predictability of the preferences into our method.

Issues are called predictable when even though the actual evaluation function for the issue is unknown, it is possible to guess some of its global properties. For example, a price issue typically is rather predictable, where more is better for the seller, and less is better for the buyer, and the normal ordering of the real numbers is maintained; an issue concerning colour, however, is typically less predictable.

Opposition of the preferences. The results of analyzing negotiation dynamics presented in [11] revealed that some negotiation strategies are sensitive to preference profiles with compatible issues. Issues are compatible if the issue preferences of both negotiating parties are such that they both prefer the same alternatives for the given issue. Negotiation strategies may more or less depend on whether preferences of the negotiating parties are opposed or not on every issue. That is, using some strategies it is harder or even impossible to exploit such common ground and agree on the most preferred option by both parties for compatible issues (humans are reported to have difficulty with this as well; cf. [32]). A selection of preference profiles should therefore take into account that both preference profiles with and without compatible issues are included.

To measure the opposition between two preference profile we use ranking distance measure proposed [16]. The measure is based on the conflict indicator proposed in [9]. The conflict indicator function yields 1 when the ranking relation of two arbitrary outcomes based on the utility space of one agent is not the same as the ranking relation based on the utility space of the opponent; if the rankings based on both utility functions match the conflict indicator takes the value of 0. The conflict indicator is calculated for all permutations in the negotiation domain and normalized over the domain. The higher the value of the ranking distance the stronger opposition between the preference profiles.

Another measure for the opposition of preferences proposed in [15] uses Pearson's correlation coefficient for that purpose. This coefficient represents the degree of linear relationship between two variables. The Pearson's correlation coefficient takes a real value from the interval $[-1; 1]$. A value of $+1$ means that there is a perfect positive linear relationship between variables, whereas a value of -1 means that there is a perfect negative linear relationship between variables. A value of 0 means that there is no linear relationship between the two variables.

The following negotiation domains and preference profiles are available in SAMIN (see Table 10.1 for summary):

- The *Second hand car selling* domain, taken from [17], includes 5 issues. Only the buyer's preferences and the price issue are predictable, in the sense that an agent can reliably predict the other agent's preferences associated with an issue.
- The *Party* domain is created for negotiation experiments with humans. It is a rather small domain with 5 discrete issues with 5 possible values each. All of the issues are unpredictable. In this domain, the preference profiles used are not as opposed to each other as in the other domains.
- The *Employment contract negotiation* domain, taken from [26] with 5 discrete issues. All issues have predictable values. The preference profiles are strongly opposed, i.e. both negotiators dislike outcomes that the other prefers most.
- The *Service-Oriented Negotiation* domain, taken from [6], includes 4 issues. All issues are predictable, i.e. based on available "domain knowledge" preferences can be reliably predicated.
- The *AMPO vs City* domain, taken from [30], includes 10 issues, of which 8 are predictable. Information about the opponent's issue priorities, i.e. the weights agents associate with issues. This is a large domain with more than $7,000,000$ possible outcomes.

Domain	Utility spaces		Weights		Domain size	Number of predictable
	Ranking	Pearson	Ranking	Pearson		
AMPO vs. City	0.662	-0.482	0.422	-0.139	7,128,000	3 (10)
Party	0.540	-0.126	0.467	-0.276	3,125	0 (5)
SON	0.669	-0.453	0.833	-0.751	810,000	4 (4)
2nd hand car	0.635	-0.387	0.600	-0.147	18,750	1 (5)
Employment contract	0.698	-0.584	0.600	-0.241	3,125	5 (5)

Table 10.1 Summary of the negotiation domains and preference profiles

10.6.2 Experimental Results

Here we present the most interesting results we received for the state-of-the-art agents described in Section 10.3.2.

Trade-off and ABMP Agents

Figure 10.6 shows typical runs in the AMPO vs City domain. Figure 10.6a shows a run of Trade-Off, representing the City, versus Random Walker (with break-off set to 0.6), playing AMPO. The Random Walker strategy is insensitive with respect to its own preferences. This fact, combined with the lack of information of relative importance of issues (weights) causes the unfortunate moves (an offer that decreases utility for both parties compared to the agent's previous offer, see [11]) produced by the Trade-off strategy.

Figure 10.6b shows Trade-off (as City) vs ABMP (as AMPO) in which ABMP is rather insensitive to the behaviour of the opponent, and Trade-off is sensitive. In this domain Trade-off really exploits the available domain knowledge. Figure 10.6c shows Random Walker (City) vs ABMP (AMPO). ABMP always concedes on all issues, determining the size of the concession on the difference between the utilities of its own bid and that of its opponent. It does not use previous opponent bids to get insight into the opponent's preferences and, as a result, does not adapt much to the strategy of the opponent.

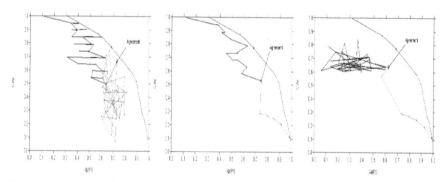

Fig. 10.6 Dynamics of negotiation process for: a) Trade-off (City) vs Random Walker strategy (AMPO), b) Trade-off (City) vs ABMP strategy (AMPO), c) Random Walker (City) vs ABMP strategy (AMPO).

This analysis shows a direct link between the correctness and/or completeness of the domain knowledge and opponent preferences sensitivity. The Trade-off strategy is very sensitive to opponent preferences given complete information. In that case, the similarity functions exactly match the opponent's preferences and the weights exactly represent the issue importance factors of the opponent.

The SON domain does not have information about weights of the similarity functions and thus opponent preferences sensitivity of the Trade-off strategy decreases but it is still more sensitive to the opponent preferences than ABMP. Similarity functions for the Second hand car domain were defined in such a way that they often do not match the preferences of the negotiation opponents. In addition, the weights of the similarity function do not match the opponent's importance factors of the negotiation issues. This leads to under performance of the Trade-off strategy while ABMP shows more robust negotiation behavior. The experiments show that if less domain knowledge is available, Trade-off makes more unfortunate steps.

In general, when issues are predictable, the chance of making an unfortunate step becomes small. This aspect becomes clear in the car domain, where the seller's preferences are rather predictable, but the buyer's preferences vary a lot.

We conclude that it is impossible to avoid unfortunate steps without sufficient domain knowledge or opponent knowledge. Indeed, the similarity criteria functions used in the Trade-off Strategy provide general information about the negotiation problem, but do not take into account the specific attributes of the negotiating parties. In any particular case, a negotiator may deviate from the generalized domain model in various ways. Approaches as reported in [4, 23, 32] apply techniques to learn more about the opponent.

Bayesian Agent

In small domains such as the SON domain, the Bayesian agent is very efficient in learning issue weights and evaluation functions of the issues that is indicated by the fact that the negotiation trace almost coincides with the Pareto frontier, see [14] for the details. Here we demonstrate the effectiveness of the scalable version of the Bayesian Agent on larger domains. The results on the AMPO vs City domain presented in Figure 10.7 show, as is only to be expected, that it becomes harder to stay close to the Pareto efficient frontier. The performance of the Bayesian learning agents is now similar to that of the agent based on the Trade-off strategy and both stay close to the Pareto frontier. The ABMP strategy shows similar behaviour as on the other negotiation domains, and is outperformed by the other strategies. The results thus are still very good. Also, note that the agreement reached by the Bayesian agents has a higher utility than that reached by the other strategies and that both the Bayesian agent without domain knowledge as well as the Trade-off agent make quite big unfortunate steps.

QO Agent

Figure 10.8 presents the results of the negotiation experiment. A small and simple negotiation problem, called "Party" [14], is used to analyze the performance of the QO gent within our negotiation framework. This domain has been created

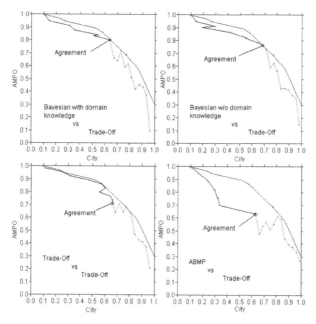

Fig. 10.7 Negotiation dynamics for the Bayesian agent on the AMPO vs. City domain

for negotiation experiments with humans, which also explains its rather limited size. The charts show the space of all possible negotiation outcomes. The axis represent the utilities of the outcomes with respect to the utility functions of the negotiating agents. The charts show the negotiation paths of the agents marked by arrows with the names of the agents.

The Bayesian agent starts with an offer that has maximum utility. It tries to learn the opponent preferences from the offers it receives and uses this model when it makes a concession towards the opponent. As a result, it stays close to the Pareto Efficient frontier. The QO agent in this domain has more difficulty to propose efficient offers. This is a result of limitation of the opponent model of the agent. The QO agent accepts an offer of the Bayesian agent as soon as such an offer has a utility level for the QO agent that is higher then utility of the QO agent's own offer.

Fuzzy-based Model Agent

The other agent integrated into SAMIN is the FBM agent introduced in [29]. The FBM agent was tested in a setup where it has to negotiate against the Bayesian agent about a single issue defined on real values ranging from 10 to 30. The original FBM agent is designed for negotiations where agents can exchange fuzzy proposals. The implementation of the FBM agent we used is able to negotiate about one-issue negotiations but can be extended for multi-issue negotiations. The agent

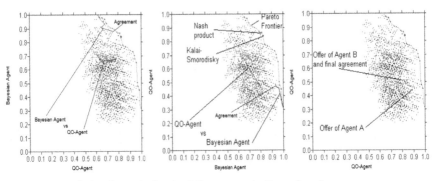

Fig. 10.8 Negotiation dynamics for the QO agent on the Party domain

adopts time dependent negotiation tactics from [5] and, thus, always makes concessions towards opponent. The offers are defined using two values: the peak value and the stretch of the offer. The preference profiles of the agents used were in complete opposition: the FBM agent wants to minimize the value of the issues and the Bayesian agent tries of maximize it. In the experiments we performed, the β parameter that defines whether an agent makes bigger concessions in the beginning of the negotiation (Conceder) or at the end (Boulware) was varied, see Table 10.2.

Agents	Utility						
	$\beta=0.02$	$\beta=0.1$	$\beta=0.5$	$\beta=1$	$\beta=2$	$\beta=10$	$\beta=50$
FBM Agent	0.898	0.897	0.734	0.585	0.449	0.193	0.060
Bayesian Agent	0.102	0.103	0.266	0.415	0.551	0.807	0.940

Table 10.2 Utility values of the FBM and Bayesian agents

In a single issue negotiation there is no possibility for a "win-win" outcome and all negotiation outcomes are Pareto efficient. One of the more important aspects of a negotiation strategy for a single issue negotiation is how fast it concedes to the opponent. As a result, for $\beta > 1$ the FBM agent implements a Conceder tactic and the FBM agent under performs with respect to the Bayesian agent that makes linear concessions in this case because no moves towards the Pareto frontier are possible. When the FBM agent employs a Boulware tactic ($\beta < 1$) the Bayesian agent starts conceding significantly and the result is a much lower utility for the Bayesian agent.

Bayesian Tit-for-Tat Agent

As discussed, the main objective associated with a negotiation strategy is to gain the best agreement possible in a negotiation. Utility of an agreement, therefore, measures the efficiency of a strategy. For every negotiation domain and preference profile the utility of agreements achieved by a strategy were averaged over

Negotiation Domain	Negotiation Strategy			
	ABMP	Trade-Off	Bayesian Smart	Bayesian Tit-for-Tat
Car	16%	12%	13%	14%
Party domain	13%	9%	13%	14%
Service-Oriented	14%	17%	25%	38%
Employment contr.	11%	40%	44%	47%
AMPO vs City	10%	13%	14%	20%

Table 10.3 Increase in utility for the Bayesian Tit-for-Tat strategy relative to the Random Walker strategy

all opponent strategies in the tournament. We assume that an efficient negotiation strategy should perform better than the Random Walker strategy. Therefore, we calculate the percentage of the utility increase compared to the utility of the Random Walker strategy (see Table 10.3).

The results show that on all domains the Bayesian Tit-for-Tat strategy performs better than all other strategies currently available in the negotiation repository. Only on the 2nd hand car negotiation domain the Bayesian Tit-for-Tat strategy is outperformed by the ABMP strategy. As in this domain a concession-based strategy is very efficient, and ABMP aims to concede on all issues, this strategy does particularly well in this domain.

The most significant increase in the efficiency of the reached agreement is shown on the Employment contract negotiation domain. This negotiation domain is rather small and evaluations of the issue alternatives are predictable in this domain. Learning in such a domain is relatively simple and, as a result, the Bayesian Tit-for-Tat strategy shows excellent performance. The Trade-off strategy shows good performance as well, however, it does not perform as well as the Bayesian Tit-for-Tat strategy. The ABMP strategy is significantly less efficient than the Bayesian Tit-for-Tat and the Trade-off strategies due to presence of issues with compatible preferences.

Similar results are obtained for the Service-Oriented Negotiation domain. This domain is much bigger than the Employment contract domain in terms of the possible agreements but has less issues. In addition, weights of the issues in the SON domain have bigger variation then in the Employment Contract domain where importance of the issues is more uniform. This explains the much lower efficiency of the Trade-Off strategy that is not capable of dealing with the weights of the issues. The Bayesian Tit-for-Tat strategy learns weights of the issues in the opponent preference profile and therefore shows a better performance.

AMPO vs City domain is the biggest domain in the repository. As is to be expected, the performance of the learning technique used in the Bayesian Tit-for-Tat strategy degrades in such bigger negotiation domains. This explains the lower relative increase in Table 10.3.

10.6.3 Approximating Auction Mechanism with Negotiation

In Section 10.4.2 we introduced a one-to-many negotiation protocol that approximates an auction mechanism. Here we present experimental results received for the proposed negotiation protocol. Figure 10.9 shows the histograms of the differences in utilities between the outcomes received with the original auction mechanism and the negotiation protocol.

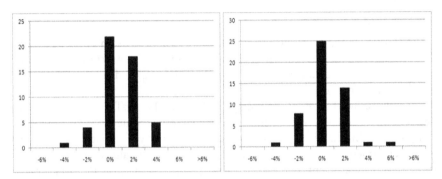

Fig. 10.9 Histograms of the differences in the utilities of experimental and theoretical outcomes for the buyer (left) and the seller (right).

The winner predicted by the mechanism and the negotiation protocol coincide 100%. This means that the negotiation protocol does not change the results of the first round in which a seller is selected as winner. Moreover, in the second round, in general the outcomes obtained by negotiation are also quite close to those determined by the mechanism. That is, in 78% of the experiments the deviation is less than 5%. The standard deviation of the difference between the mechanism outcome and the experimental results is 4%, and in 94% of the experiment the deviation did not differ with more than 10%, indicating that overall outcomes were reasonably close to the mechanism outcome with a few exceptions. This means that the negotiating agents that can learn are able to approximate the outcome determined by the mechanism quite well.

10.7 Conclusion

SAMIN, the system for analysis of multi-issue negotiation introduced here, has proved to be a valuable tool to analyse the dynamics of human-human closed negotiation against a number of dynamic properties. Our analysis shows that humans find it difficult to guess where the Pareto Efficient Frontier is located, making it difficult for them to accept a proposal. Although humans apparently do not negotiate in a strictly Pareto-monotonous way, when considering larger intervals, a weak monotony can be discovered. Such analysis results can be useful in two different ways: to train human negotiators, or to improve the strategies of software agents. Clear from our research so far, is that five key factors shape the outcome of a bilateral negotiation with incomplete information: (i) knowledge about the negotiation domain (e.g. the market value of a product or service), (ii) oneŠs own and oneŠs opponentŠs preferences, (iii) process attributes (e.g. deadlines), (iv) the negotiation strategies, and (v) the negotiation protocol.

The use of agent technology for negotiation systems has been a big help in both the design and the implementation of the SAMIN system. Principled design methods for agents and multi-agent systems such as DESIRE ensured a transparent design that properly reflects the interests of the stakeholders (researchers) and negotiators (human and software agent). The organization makes it easy to run tournaments with any number of agents, and over a number of negotiation domains. The interface and adapters to connect agents to the negotiation environment have been clearly specified which enable an easy integration of heterogeneous negotiating agents. The graphical user interfaces support both researchers and human subjects participating in experiments.

A good start has been made in the development of a toolkit for analysis in SAMIN, but more work needs to be done. Additional research on ontologies for negotiation is required to make this feasible; for example, we cannot currently formulate associated constraints on the domain of negotiation that must be satisfied for an agreement to be acceptable. More technically, components for web integration as well as extensions of adapters need to be developed, e.g., in order to handle more generic ontologies.

Acknowledgements This research is supported by the Dutch Technology Foundation STW, applied science division of NWO and the Technology Program of the Ministry of Economic Affairs. It is part of the Pocket Negotiator project with grant number VIVI-project 08075.

References

1. Ashri, R., Rahwan, I., Luck, M.: Architectures for negotiating agents. In: The 3rd Int. Central And Eastern European Conf. on Multi-Agent Systems (2003)
2. Bosse, T., Jonker, C., Treur, J.: Experiments in human multi-issue negotiation: Analysis and support. In: Jennings, N., Sierra, C., Sonenberg, L., Tambe, M. (eds.) Proceedings of the Third International Joint Conference on Autonomous Agents and Multi-Agent Systems, AAMAS'04, p. 672 Ú 679. IEEE Computer Society Press (2004)
3. Brazier, F., Dunin-Keplicz, B., Jennings, N., Treur, J.: Formal specification of multi-agent systems: a real world case. International Journal of Co-operative Information Systems, IJCIS **6(1)**, 67–94 (1997)
4. Coehoorn, R., Jennings, N.: Learning an opponent's preferences to make effective multi-issue negotiation tradeoffs. In: Proceedings of the 6th International Conference on E-Commerce, pp. 59–68 (2004)
5. Faratin, P., Sierra, C., Jennings, N.R.: Negotiation decision functions for autonomous agents. Int. Journal of Robotics and Autonomous Systems **24**(3-4), 159–182 (1998)

6. Faratin, P., Sierra, C., Jennings, N.R.: Using similarity criteria to make negotiation trade-offs. Journal of Artificial Intelligence **142**(2), 205–237 (2003)
7. Fisher, R., (and for the latest edition B. Patton), W.U.: Getting to Yes: Negotiating Agreement Without Giving In. Penguin Books (1981, 1992, 2003)
8. Gode, D.K., Sunder, S.: Allocative efficiency in markets with zero intelligence (zi) traders: Market as a partial substitute for individual rationality. Journal of Political Economy **101**(1), 119–137 (1993)
9. Ha, V., Haddawy, P.: Similarity of personal preferences: Theoretical foundations and empirical analysis. Artificial Intelligence **146**(2), 149–173 (2003)
10. Harrenstein, P., Mahr, T., de Weerdt, M.M.: A qualitative vickrey auction. In: Endriss, U., Paul W, G. (eds.) Proceedings of the 2nd International Workshop on Computational Social Choice, pp. 289–301. University of Liverpool (2008). URL http://www.st.ewi.tudelft.nl/.pdf
11. Hindriks, K., Jonker, C., Tykhonov, D.: Negotiation dynamics: Analysis, concession tactics, and outcomes. In: Proceedings of the IEEE/WIC/ACM International Conference on Intelligent Agent Technology (IAT'07), pp. 427–433 (2007)
12. Hindriks, K., Jonker, C., Tykhonov, D.: Using opponent models for efficient negotiation (extended abstract). In: Decker, Sichman, Sierra, Castelfranchi (eds.) Proc. of 8th Int. Conf. on Autonomous Agents and Multiagent Systems (AAMAS 2009) (2009)
13. Hindriks, K., Jonker, C.M., Tykhonov, D.: Towards an open negotiation architecture for heterogeneous agents. In: Proceedings of 12th International Workshop CIA 2007 on Cooperative Information Agents, Lecture Notes in AI. Springer-Verlag (2008)
14. Hindriks, K., Tykhonov, D.: Opponent modelling in automated multi-issue negotiation using bayesian learning. In: Proceedings of the AAMAS 2008 (2008)
15. Hindriks, K., Tykhonov, D.: Towards a quality assessment method for learning preference profiles in negotiation. In: Proceedings of the AMEC 2008 (2008)
16. Hindriks, K.V., Tykhonov, D., de Weerdt, M.: Approximating an auction mechanism by multi-issue negotiation. In: Hindriks, K.V., Brinkman, W.P. (eds.) Proceedings of the First International Working Conference on Human Factors and Computational Models in Negotiation (HuCom2008), pp. 33–38 (2008)
17. Jonker, C., Treur, J.: An agent architecture for multi-attribute negotiation. In: Nebel, B. (ed.) Proceedings of the 17th International Joint Conference on AI, IJCAI'01, pp. 1195–1201 (2001)
18. Jonker, C.M., Robu, V., Treur, J.: An agent architecture for multi-attribute negotiation using incomplete preference information. Journal of Autonomous Agents and Multi-Agent Systems **15**(2), 221–252 (2007). DOI http://dx.doi.org/10.1007/s10458-006-9009-y
19. Klein, M., Faratin, P., Sayama, H., Bar-Yam, Y.: Negotiating complex contracts. Paper 125 of the Center for eBusines@MIT. http://ebusiness.mit.edu. (2001)
20. Kowalczyk, R., Bui, V.: On constraint-based reasoning in e-negotiation agents. In: Dignum, F., Cortés, U. (eds.) Agent-Mediated Electronic Commerce III, Current Issues in Agent-Based Electronic Commerce Systems, Lecture Notes in Computer Science, pp. 31–46. Springer Ü Verlag (2003)
21. Lai, G., Sycara, K.: A generic framework for automated multi-attribute negotiation. Group Decision and Negotiation **18**(2), 169–187 (2009)
22. Larman, C.: Applying UML and Patterns: An Introduction to Object-Oriented Analysis and Design and Iterative Development. 3 edn. Prentice Hall PTR (2004)
23. Lin, R., Kraus, S., Wilkenfeld, J., Barry, J.: An automated agent for bilateral negotiation with bounded rational agents with incomplete information. In: Proc. of the 17th European Conference on Artificial Intelligence (ECAIŠ06), pp. 270–274 (2006)
24. Lin, R., Kraus, S., Wilkenfeld, J., Barry, J.: Negotiating with bounded rational agents in environments with incomplete information using an automated agent. Artificial Intelligence Journal **172**(6-7), 823–851 (2008)
25. Mnookin, R., Peppet, S., Tulumello, A.S.: Beyond Winning: Negotiating to Create Value in Deals and Disputes. Harvard University Press (2000)

26. Nadler, J., Thompson, L., van Boven, L.: Learning negotiation skills: Four models of knowledge creation and transfer. Journal of Management Science **49**(4), 529–540 (2003)
27. Osborne, M.J., Rubinstein, A.: A Course in Game Theory. MIT Press (1994)
28. Pruitt, D.: Negotiation Behavior. Academic Press (1981)
29. Raeesy, Z., Brzostwoski, J., Kowalczyk, R.: Towards a fuzzy-based model for human-like multi-agent negotiation. In: Proc. of the IEEE/WIC/ACM Int. Conf. on Intelligent Agent Technology, pp. 515–519 (2007)
30. Raiffa, H., Richardson, J., Metcalfe, D.: Negotiation Analysis: The Science and Art of Collaborative Decision Making. Harvard University Press (2003)
31. Sandholm, T.: Multi-agent Systems: A Modern Introduction to Distributed Artificial Intelligence, chap. Distributed rational decision making. MIT Press (1999)
32. Thompson, L.: The Heart and Mind of the Negotiator. Pearson Prentice Hall (2005)
33. Zeng, D., Sycara, K.: Benefits of learning in negotiation. In: Proceedings of the Fourteenth National Conference on Artificial Intelligence (AAAI-97) (1997)
34. Zeng, D., Sycara, K.: Bayesian learning in negotiation. International Journal of Human Computer Systems **48**, 125–141 (1998)

Appendix A
Language Summaries

This appendix provides summaries of the main features of the programming languages presented in the first part of this book. The first section shows a list of questions that the editors posed to the contributing authors of chapters about agent programming languages. The following six sections provide the answers given by the authors of the respective chapters. This can be useful for quick reference and comparision of the languages, for example in searching for the best approach for a particular application.

A.1 Comparison Criteria

1. **Agent-Oriented Programming Language**

   a. **Functionality**
   Does the language support various agent concepts such as, mental attitudes, deliberation, adaptation, social abilities, and reactive as well as cognitive-based behaviour?

   b. **Communication**
   Does the language provide high-level (i.e., speech-act based) primitives for communication (as well as general addressing mechanism such as broadcast and multi-cast)?

   c. **Underlying Computational Model**
   Does the language support the design of mobile agents, and if so, which kind of mobility (week and/or strong)?

   d. **Simplicity**
   How easy it is to use and understand the language?

   e. **Preciseness**
   Does the language have clear and precise semantics? How has it been formalised?

R.H. Bordini et al. (eds.), *Multi-Agent Programming*,
DOI 10.1007/978-0-387-89299-3_BM2, © Springer Science+Business Media, LLC 2009

f. **Expressiveness**
Is the language suitable for the implementation of a variety of agent-oriented programs and applications or is it purpose-specific?

g. **Extensiveness**
Does the language allow the definition of new language components from the basic constructs in a systematic way?

h. **Verification**
Does your approach provide a clear path for the (formal) verification of programs written in this language?

i. **Software Engineering Principles**
Have Software Engineering and Programming Language principles, such as abstraction, inheritance, modularity, overloading, information hiding, error handling, generic programming, etc., been considered or adopted within design of this language?

j. **Language Integration**
   i. Does your approach deal with the possibility of integrating the language with existing (well-known) programming language (e.g., Java)?
   ii. Can the language be interfaced with other programming languages, or does it allow the invocation of methods/programs built using other (classical) programming languages?

2. **Platform**

   a. **Deployment and Portability**
      i. Does the platform provide material, such as documentation, tutorials or training of any kind, installation and deployment guidelines, to help users in deploying their systems?
      ii. Does the platform require a specific computing environment (computer architecture, operating system, libraries, etc.) to be used / deployed?

   b. **Standards Compliance**
   To what extent does the platform adhere to the standards (FIPA, MASIF, etc.) with respects to: general architecture, naming service, white- and yellow-page services, mobility services, agent-life cycle management, etc.?

   c. **Platform Extensibility**
   Can the platform be extended with additional functionality, for example through Open Source collaboration?

   d. **Available Tools**
      i. What tools are provided by the platform for the management, monitoring, logging and debugging of applications?
      ii. What documentation for on-line help, and manuals for the platform's installation, use, and maintenance are available?
      iii. Are there tools for administration, management, and configuration of the platform? Is an IDE provided?

e. **Tool Integration**
In existing applications, what tools (e.g., JESS, web services, JSP) have been integrated or are known to work well with applications running on this platform ?

f. **Technical Interoperability**
Is an application aimed at running on this platform tied to a specific programming language, specific architectures (e.g., .NET, J2EE), or are there special operating system requirements?

g. **Performance Issues**
 i. What number of agents can be expected to run efficiently within a single instance of the platform, what scale of number of messages can be handled by the platform, etc.?
 ii. What is the current state of the platform (simple prototype, available as a commercial product, stable Open Source distribution, etc.)?

h. **Multi-Agent Systems Features**
 i. Does the platform support open multi-agent systems and heterogeneous agents?
 ii. Does the platform provide centralised or distributed control, and hierarchical structure of agents?
 iii. Does the platform offer libraries for programming multi-agent systems (libraries of interaction protocols, agent or group templates, reusable agent or organisation components, etc.)?

3. <u>**Applications Supported by the Language and Platform**</u>

a. **Typical Examples**
What types of application have already been developed with this platform (toy problems, real-world applications, industrial applications)? What are the most prominent examples?

b. **Targeted Domains**
Is any particular domain of application (e.g., simulation, resource allocation, mobile computation) targeted by your approach?

A.2 MetateM

1(a) Cognitive deliberation is the abstraction that best describes the behaviour of METATEM agents, specifying reactive behaviour is also possible though less intersting. Adaptation is supported by the ability agent have to modify their plan-base and deliberation preferences at run-time. A variety of social abilities can be built on top of METATEM's agent grouping mechanisms, which provide the programmer with the flexibility to define their own social behaviour.

1(b) Multi-cast is the default messaging mechanism. METATEM does not rely upon a centralised addressing service but one-to-one messaging is, of course, possible between agents known to each other and broadcast messaging can also be achieved by a series of recursive multi-casts. Speech-acts are not explicitly supported, but the logical nature of the language allows their semantics to be built-in.

1(c)   METATEM does not have a built-in mobility framework, however it does have some reflection constructs and as agents can be extended with arbitrary Java code, weak mobility is possible.

1(d)   Founded, as it is, on temporal logic and composed of just four simple rule types (start, present, next and sometime), we believe the language is intuitive and easy to use.

1(e)   The semantics of METATEM and some of its extensions have been formalised in [12, 9] by way of both temporal and operational semantics.

1(f)   METATEM is a general, high-level and flexible language for the specification of multi-agent behaviour.

1(g)   All METATEM constructs use the language of classical first order logic, including complex terms. Creating new language components, for example the "tell" informative, is achieved by employing complex terms. For example;
`receive(From, tell(Message)) => ...`

1(h)   The clear semantics make METATEM amenable to automated verification by model checking [3].

1(i)   A similar notion to that of object-oriented inheritance in which agents receive behaviours (goals, preferences, beliefs) from other agents at run-time is supported. Modularity and re-use of code is supported by the `include` pre-processing insruction.

1(j).i   Yes, the developer can define executable chunks of Java code that are denoted by ability predicates in the METATEM specification.

2(j).ii   The language only supports direct integration with Java, but of course one can use Java as a wrapper for many other languages and/or services.

2(a).i   Language documentation, example programs and API documentation is provided. Tutorials are planned.

2(a).ii   The METATEM download is a self-contained Java archive that contains no platform dependent libraries. It requires a Java runtime version 1.6 or later.

2(b)   Standards have not been considered during the development of METATEM, though this does not preclude their future compliance.

2(c)   The developers of METATEM welcome suggestions for its improvement and, whilst the source code is not currently available, it is planned to release the source under an open-source license.

2(d).i   METATEM has an agent visualisation tool which monitors agents during execution, it provides a graphical representation of the structure of a multi-agent system and allows the inspection of an individual agent's states and access to their logs.

2(d).ii   Basic documentation for installation is provided. METATEM is not intended for real-world deployments that require long-term maintenance.

2(d).iii   No tools for administration, management, and configuration of the platform at present, though an Eclipse plug-in (or similar) would be considered if requested.

2(e)   Since Java code can be accommodated, any tool that can be accommodated by Java can be integrated with METATEM, however this has not been done in any existing application.

2(f)   The only requirement is a Java runtime environment (see item 2(a) above).

2(g).i   Whilst no performance statistics are available, each agent consumes its own thread in the Java virtual machine, thus scaling of the number of agents is related to the thread management employed by the host virtual machine.

2(g).ii   METATEM should be regarded as a stable prototype language.

2(h).i   Open-systems are not currently supported, although new agents can be spawned at run-time. Heterogeneous agents can only be accommodated by wrapping them inside a METATEM agent with a Java interface.

2(h).ii   Control is truly distributed whilst agents can form social structures of many kinds including groups and hierarchies.

2(h).iii   It has a mechanism to create and draw from libraries of agent definitions and behaviours. Some social protocols are being worked on.

3(a)   The language has only been used for simple examples so far.

3(b)   METATEM targets application areas that require high degree of clarity at a high-level of abstraction, particularly where temporal constraints feature prominently in the specification.

A.3 IndiGolog

1(a)   The language supports agents with complex beliefs about their environment and its dynamics, specified as a situation calculus action theory. The beliefs are automatically updated based on the model when actions are performed or events occur. The agent can perform sensing actions to acquire additional knowledge. It can perform means-ends reasoning to generate a plan that will achieve a goal or find an execution of a "sketchy" nondeterministic program. Specifying reactive behaviors is also supported. However, there is no built-in support for declarative goals, or for reasoning about other agents and their mental states.

1(b)   The language does not provide built-in support for speech act based communication. However, communication in FIPA ACL and FIPA coordination protocols (e.g. contract net), as well as interfacing with the JADE [8] multiagent platform are supported by the IG-JADE-PKSlib library [69, 68]. The framework been extended to incorporate a rich model of multiagent beliefs and goals and speech acts based communication in [95, 94]; but the resulting formalism is no longer a programming language but a specification language that supports verification of properties.

1(c)   No specific built-in support for mobile agents is available so far.

1(d)   The language is easy to understand and learn, as it combines a classical Algol-like imperative language for specifying behavior with a well known action description language for specifying the application domain dynamics. The whole language has a classical logic semantics.

1(e)   The language has a very solid formal foundation. The semantics of programs is specified through a transition system account defined on top of the situation calculus (the latter is used to specify the application domain, primitive actions and state-dependent predicates). Thus the language is fully formalized in classical predicate logic. One can make statements about offline executions of programs within the logical language, and one can reason about properties of programs in the logic. Online executions of programs are formalized metatheoretically in terms of entailment in the situation calculus theory.

1(f)   The language is very rich and expressive. Complex domain models can be specified declaratively and the agent's beliefs are automatically updated. Complex tests about the state of the world can be evaluated. Behavior can be fully scripted, or synthesized through planning, with the program constraining the search. A rich set of procedural constructs is provided, including concurrent programming facilities. Reactivity and online sensing are also supported.

1(g)   The declarative language definition supports the easy addition of new programming constructs. The underlying situation calculus framework supports many extensions in the way change is modeled, e.g. continuous change, stochastic effects, etc. The language has been extended numerous times.

1(h)   Given its strong formal foundations, the language is highly suited for formal verification. The CASLve verification environment [95, 94], which is based on the PVS theorem proving/verification system, has been developed to support verification of programs in an extended version of ConGolog.

1(i)   The language supports procedural abstraction, but not modules. However, very complex agents can be decomposed into simpler agents that cooperate. The agent's beliefs are automatically updated based on a declarative action theory, which supports the use of complex domain models, and helps avoid the errors that typically occur when such models are manually updated.

1(j)   Our platform is implemented in SWI-Prolog, which provides flexible mechanisms for interfacing with other programming languages such as Java or C, and for socket communication.

2(a).i   The platform provides documentation and examples that, though simple, have allowed new users to learn how to effectively develop new applications.

2(a).ii   The current implementation of the platform requires SWI-Prolog, a sophisticated Prolog implementation which is actively supported and available free for many architectures and operating systems (including MS-Windows, Linux and MacOS X).

2(b)   The basic language and its current platform do not per se adhere or conform to any standards. However, a library, IG-JADE-PKSlib [69, 68], has been developed to support communication in FIPA ACL and FIPA coordination protocols (e.g. contract net), as well as interfacing with the JADE [8] multiagent platform.

2(c)   The platform is designed in a modular way and is easily extensible, though this requires expertise in Prolog. It is currently hosted as an open source project at SourceForge (http://sourceforge.net/projects/indigolog/).

2(d)   Currently, there are no CASE tools developed specifically for the platform. For debugging, tracing facilities are provided; Prolog facilities can also be used.

2(e)   The platform is integrated with Prolog (more specifically SWI-Prolog) and all the facilities it provides can be used (e.g. socket communication, calling C or Java procedures). The IG-OAAlib library [49] supports the inclusion of IndiGolog agents in systems running under SRI's Open-Agent Architecture (OAA) [67]. As mentioned earlier, another library, IG-JADE-PKSlib [69, 68] supports the inclusion of IndiGolog agents in systems running under JADE [8].

2(f)   The platform is implemented in Prolog and requires SWI-Prolog (http://www.swi-prolog.org/).

2(g).i   No detailed analysis regarding the number of agents that could be run efficiently or the number of messages that could be handled has been performed so far. For use in robotic architectures or workflow management, performance has not been a problem.

2(g).ii   The current state of the implementation is as an advanced stable prototype that is available through open source distribution.

2(h).i   The language itself does not provide specific facilities for multi-agent programming (though it and the underlying theory are expressive enough to allow the design of multi-agent systems). It is intended primarily for the implementation of individual autonomous agents. Multi-agent programming (including open systems) is accommodated through the interfaces with the JADE and OAA platforms.

2(h).ii   The language provides a centralized control architecture.

2(h).iii   As already mentioned, the IG-JADE-PKSlib library [69, 68] allows IndiGolog agents to be integrated in systems running under the JADE [8] multi-agent platform; it supports the development of IndiGolog agents that use FIPA ACL communication and coordination protocols. Another library [49] supports including IndiGolog agents in systems running under the OAA platform [67].

3(a)   So far, the language and platform have been used to program high-level controllers for several real robotic platforms (as part of a larger control architecture). Moreover, the language (or variants), and the platform, have been used as part of larger systems to develop advanced applications, for instance the museum guide robot of [16], the process/workflow management system for pervasive computing applications of [52], the automated web service composition/customization systems of [70, 72], etc.

3(b)   The language is not targeted at any particular application domain. However, it is primarily intended for developing complex autonomous agents that do reasoning and planning. It provides good support for interfacing with robotic control architectures/platforms.

A.4 Brahms

1(a)   Brahms agents include mental attitudes, deliberation, adaptation, social abilities, and reactive as well as cognitive-based behaviour.

1(b)   Brahms provides two types of communication capabilities: 1) a built-in belief communication activity, 2) a FIPA-based Communication Library for sending/receiving Communicative Acts.

1(c)   Brahms, currently, does not support any mobility service.

1(d)   Brahms is easy to learn. Brahms users include not only computer scientists, but also cognitive scientists, psychologists, economists and even an architect.

1(e)   Brahms has a precise syntax and semantics. The syntax is specified in EBNF. The semantics is currently not formalized, but is descibed as part of the Brahms language document.

1(f)   Brahms is suitable for the development of agent-based work practice, orgazizational, work flow and cognitive simulations, as well as the implementation of a variety of agent-oriented programs and applications.

1(g)   Brahms allows for extention and definition of new language components through the definition of Java activities using the JAPI.

1(h)   Although the Brahms semantics is currently not formalized, Brahms does allow for a clear path for the (formal) verification of programs (also called models).

1(i)   Software Engineering and Programming Language principles, such as abstraction, inheritance, modularity, overloading, information hiding, error handling, generic programming, have been adopted within the design of the Brahms language.

1(j).i   Brahms can be integrated with the Java programming language, using the JAPI, in both simulation and real-time execution mode.

1(j).ii   In real-time execution mode, Brahms agents can communicate with other general Java or C++ agents, using the agent Collaborative Infrastructure (CI).

2(a).i   The Brahms website (http://wwww.agentisolutions.com) provides Java docs of the JAPI, a detailed Brahms language specification, both EBNF syntacs and semantics, a Brahms tutorial that includes excercises and documentation, and a web-based discussion forum. The BAE installation is done with an easy to use installation wizard. The Brahms website includes a readme file with some additional information on configuring MySQL.

2(a).ii   Brahms requires the Java Runtime Environment (version 6), and is currently supported on Windows 2000/XP, Linux, OS X, Solaris. The AgentViewer tool requires MySQL 4.1, 5.1.51 or later to be installed.

2(b)   In real-time execution mode, Brahms uses a custom agent collaborative infrastructure (CI). Both Brahms and the CI use Communicative Acts, loosely based on FIPA. The CI provides a custom naming/directory service and custom agent life-cycle management for managing the starting and stopping of distributed agents running in one or more Brahms Virtual Machines (BVMs).

2(c)   Brahms is not Open Source, but does allow for being extended with additional functionality. Using the JAPI, it is possible to add new services, external agents to interact with, external systems, and java activities to add additional activity behaviors.

2(d).i Brahms logs history events that are used post-execution in the AgentViewer tool, for the display of all agent events (new beliefs, workframe/activity and thoughtframe execution, movement in the geography model, and communication).

2(d).ii Brahms is installed as the Brahms Agent Environment using an easy install wizard. The Brahms web-site provides a web-based discussion forum through which the Brahms developers can be contacted http://www.agentisolutions.com/cgi-bin/Ultimate.cgi). There is no specific maintenance provided to external users, however, the Brahms team is regularly updating the BAE with new releases for download. Any bugs in the BAE that are reported will be resolved in the next release, or provided as updates on the website.

2(d).iii The BAE does not include specific tools for management or real-time monitoring. However, there are two separate IDEs provided: 1) the Composer is an IDE through which Brahms models can be designed, implemented, compiled, and executed, 2) there is also a Brahms Eclipse Plugin. The Composer includes the Agentviewer, which is can be used as a post-execution debugger. Both the compiler and the BVM has configuration files that can be set outside the Composer in a text editor, or within the Composer using property editors.

2(e) Existing tools and applications integrated are JacORB CORBA, E-mail Client, FTP Client, IM Client (Jabber), GPS, Biosensors, digital cameras, MS Excel (J-integra), MS Word (J-integra), RIALIST speech dialoque system, LEGACI astronaut metabolic calculation algortithms, Compendium.

2(f) Brahms requires Java Runtime Environment (version 6) and MySQL version 4.1, 5.1.51 or later

2(g).i Currently, there are no specific performance metrics available. However, depending on the complexity of the agents, one BVM can easily simulate 150 Brahms agents and objects. In distributed real-time execution mode, the number of BVMs is unlimited, and depending on the complexity of the agents, each BVM can easily run 10 to 20 agents.

2(g).ii The BAE is a thoroughly tested and stable agent environment. It is used to execute a MAS application 24x7 in NASA's International Space Station Mission Control. A free release is available for research purposes only. Brahms is not Open Source.

2(h).i The new version of Brahms will support open multi-agent systems and heterogeneous agents through the use of the Collaborative Infrastructure (CI). Other ways are to develop proxy agents using the external agent JAPI.

2(h).ii The BAE, through the CI, provides distributed control. The Brahms language provides hierarchical structure of agents. However, the directory service for distributed agents does not.

2(h).iii The BAE provides a Communicative Acts library and templates for programming multi-agent systems (both in Brahms and Java).

3(a)   Brahms has been used to develop research, real-world and industrial applications both for simulation and for MAS development. The most prominent application is the OCA Mirroring System (OCAMS) in NASA's International Space Station Mission Control and Mobile Agents, a planetary exploration MAS workflow framework for robots and astronauts.

3(b)   Brahms is a domain-independent simulation and MAS language. It can be used for agent-based simulation, as well as for MAS development and execution. Brahms is not geared towards any specific domain, but has mostly been used in the space mission operations and exploration domain. It is particularly useful for simulating work practice and organizations, and developing intelligent agent-based workflow services and applications.

A.5 Goal

1(a)   GOAL has been designed to support rational agents that derive their choice of action from their *beliefs* and *goals*. Two types of knowledge or beliefs of an agent are distinguished: conceptual or domain knowledge stored in a *knowledge base* and dynamic beliefs to represent the state of the environment stored in a *belief base*. Goals are declarative representations of *what* a GOAL agent wants to achieve not *how* to achieve it. The language supports action selection (i.e. decision making) using so-called *action rules*, which provides for the programming of flexible agents capable of cognitive as well as reactive behaviour. Additional constructs to structure action selection by agents are provided by means of *modules*.

1(b)   Multi-agent GOAL systems are supported by communication primitives that enable agents to exchange declarative messages derived from their mental state. The current implementation of GOAL runs on top of the JADE infrastructure [2] to facilitate communication between agents but abstracts from most implementation details that need to be specified when using JADE communication primitives (such as the requirement to specify the knowledge representation language in which message content has been specified). Communication in the current implementation is based on a simple "mailbox semantics" as in 2APL [12]. Messages received are stored in an agent's mailbox and may be inspected by the agent by means of queries on special, reserved predicates sent (*agent,msg*) and received(*agent,msg*) where *agent* denotes the agent the message has been sent to or received from, respectively, and *msg* denotes the content of the message expressed in a knowledge representation language.

1(c)   GOAL does not support explicit constructs to enable the mobility of agents. The main concern in the design of the language is to provide appropriate constructs for programming rational agents whereas issues such as mobility are delegated to the middleware infrastructure layer on top of which GOAL agents are run.

1(d)   One of the main concerns in the design of GOAL has been to design a language that provides intuitive programming constructs related to common sense concepts used everyday by humans to explain and justify their actions in ordinary language, including in particular the notions of belief and goal (see also 1(a)) as well as a basic notion of action. To facilitate understanding, the architecture for running GOAL agents is a simple instance of the sense-plan-act cycle [36]. At the core of this architecture is the action selection mechanism based on action rules. The main additions to this action selection mechanism concern connecting GOAL agents to the environment. These include exchanges with the environment of *percepts* (received from the environment and processed just before action selection), *messages* received from other agents and *actions* (to be executed by the environment).

1(e)   GOAL has a formal, operational semantics defined by means of Plotkin-style transition semantics [33]. A formal verification framework exists to verify properties of GOAL agents [3]. This verification framework allows for compositional verification of GOAL agents and has been related to Intention Logic [20]. The language GOAL is firmly rooted in agent theory as well as the practice of agent programming.

1(f)   GOAL is a general-purpose agent-oriented programming language. The language has been designed such as to enable declarative specifications of the mental states of agents using high-level concepts such as beliefs and goals. It thus aims at designing programs at the *knowledge level* [31].

1(g)   GOAL allows programmers to specify user-specified actions using a STRIPS-style notation [17]. The main concept for structuring agent programs in GOAL is the notion of a *module*. Modules allow a programmer to structure the agent and facilitate a modular development of an agent. More specifically, modules allow a programmer to locate and combine the beliefs and actions relevant for achieving particular goals inside a module. Modules allow an agent to focus on a particular goal and to choose the relevant actions to achieve that goal within the context of a module.

1(h)   GOAL provides a verification framework that facilitates compositional verification of GOAL agents. A Maude [9] implementation for the GOAL language has been provided which facilitates model checking of GOAL agents. Maude has been used to verify the Blocks World agent discussed in this chapter.

1(i)   The GOAL language supports reusability by providing a mechanism for including belief base files and goal base files as well as by providing a module construct (see also 1(g)).

1(j).i   The GOAL language is designed to facilitate writing agent programs that derive their choice of action from beliefs and goals. GOAL, however, does not commit to any particular knowledge representation language to represent the beliefs and goals of an agent. The current implementation has integrated Prolog as the technology for knowledge representation. In principle, however, Answer Set Programming [1], expert system languages such as CLIPS [26], database languages such as SQL [7], or a language such as PDDL [17] could have been used as well.

1(j).ii   The main interfaces the GOAL platform offers concern interfaces connecting GOAL to a middleware infrastructure on top of which GOAL agents are run (see 1(b) and (c) above), to a knowledge representation technology (see 1(j).i), and to an environment. The interface to an environment is generic and abstracts from the implementation language used to run the environment. Currently, Java is used to connect GOAL agents to an environment.

2(a).i   The GOAL language can be obtained by downloading the GOAL installer. GOAL comes with documentation discussing the language, IDE and some examples that are distributed with the language as well. For the most up to date information about the GOAL system the reader may visit the page http://mmi.tudelft.nl/~koen/goal.html where it also can find references to GOAL-related publications. The development of a tutorial is planned.

2(a).ii   The implementation of GOAL has been tested and runs on most well-known platforms. The GOAL language has been implemented in Java and requires Java version 1.5 or higher. In addition, a middleware infrastructure layer on top of which GOAL is run must be supported (see also 1(b)).

2(b)   The *Goal* agent programming language provides a framework for programming rational agents and has been designed to support basic notions associated with such agents (see also 1(a,b,d)).

2(c)   The GOAL language is aimed at providing a general-purpose programming language for rational agents at the knowledge level. It does not commit to any particular knowledge representation language, domain or middle-ware infrastructure (see also 1(j)). The main extensions and variations that can be created are by implementing other KR technologies or environments to run agents in. It is planned to distribute *Goal* under the GPL open source license.

2(d).i   GOAL is distributed with a simple Integrated Development Environment which includes the main functionality for monitoring, logging and debugging agents. A sniffer is available to monitor message exchange between agents. Debugging can be used to trace the operation of an agent at various levels of granularity, e.g. at the inference level which allows tracing belief and goal inferences as well as at higher levels which allow tracing of action selection only.

2(d).ii   A manual is provided for GOAL, including a discussion of the main language features, the IDE, installation and some advice on troubleshooting, and can be obtained from http://mmi.tudelft.nl/~koen/goal.html.

2(d).iii   GOAL comes with a simple Integrated Development Environment.

2(e)   In the GOAL framework a number of interfaces have been defined for integrating knowledge representation technologies and environments. The current implemented version of GOAL is implemented in Java and it should be relatively straightforward to integrate various tools that provide a Java interface or are easily accessible from Java.

2(f)   Applications written in GOAL require the Java Virtual Machine since GOAL has been implemented in Java. In addition, the current implementation runs on top of JADE (which is distributed and installed with the GOAL interpreter by the installer for GOAL). The implementation has been tested and shown to run on several operating systems including the main versions of Windows, OSX, as well as Unix.

2(g).i   The number of agents that can be run efficiently and the number of messages handled depends on the underlying knowledge representation technology (currently we use SWI Prolog [42]) as well as the middleware infrastructure (currently we use JADE). For example, it turns out that SWI Prolog does not allow to start up more than 100 threads simultaneously restricting the number of agents we can simultaneously run. For small-scale agent systems most choices do not pose any restrictions but the development of large-scale agent systems would require to carefully consider the choice of knowledge representation technology and middleware infrastructure.

2(g).ii   The current state of the platform is still a prototype. We are putting continuous effort in developing a stable release. The core of the GOAL framework is stable and well-defined in several papers [3, 19, 21, 22].

2(h).i   The GOAL framework does not itself provide support for open systems nor heterogeneous agents. GOAL agents are particular agents defined by their beliefs, goals and action rules that facilitate decision making. GOAL agents may nevertheless interact with other types of agents whenever these agents run on top of the same middleware infrastructure and exchange messages using the facilities provided by this infrastructure to this end.

2(h).ii   The GOAL language does not itself provide a centralised or distributed control but depends on the middleware infrastructure on top of which GOAL agents are run to provide such control. Although GOAL does not provide support for hierarchical structuring of agents it does provide a construct to define modules within agents that define agent-like substructures of such an agent.

2(h).iii The GOAL framework does not provide libraries yet.

3(a)   GOAL so far has been illustrated by means of classical examples such as the Blocks World discussed in this chapter and has been used in education by students to program rational agents.

3(b)   GOAL is a general purpose agent programming language. It is most suitable to developing systems of rational agents.

A.6 JIAC

1(a)   JIAC V supports three different types of agents that build upon each other. The first type is a simple reactive agent with no mentalistic attributes. The second type uses a BDI metaphor and explicit knowledge to enhance its decision making and the third type extends the agents with learning and planing capabilities.

1(b)   JIAC V agents support communication via Inform messages. Agents have individual messageboxes as well as the possibility to join agentgroup channels which are used for delivery of these messages. Furthermore, interaction can be realised via services for a more structured approach.

1(c)   The architecture is designed to support strong mobility for agents. However, as we perceive mobility rather as an action on the part of a management entity (likely an AMS), JADL++ has no distinct support for it.

1(d)   As the procedural part is simple scripting language with C-style syntax, most programmers should be familiar with it. However, due to the integration of OWL ontologies, a programmer should be familiar with the OWL concepts and their usage.

1(e)   We have tried to formalise most of the scripting elements of JADL++. The formalisations of OWL and OWL-S are of course publicly available. However, our formalisation of the use of OWL in JADL++ is still incomplete, as we are still experimenting with the precise semantics.

1(f)   The language JADL++ is tilted towards service composition, and as it is a scripting language it is not as powerful as a full programming language. However, the easy inclusion of Java allows for any programs to be implemented in JIAC V.

1(g)   The scripting part of the language is rather static. However, due to the inclusion of OWL, the knowledge description part of the language is freely extensible (as long as the ontologies are OWL-lite conform). Furthermore, the language can be expanded by arbitrary services, which by means of the agent architecture can be implemented with multiple technologies.

1(h)   So far, verification was out of scope.

1(i)   As the language uses OWL for knowledge representation, all features of OWL are also useable within JADL++. Furthermore, JADL++ supports modularity with its concept of service invocations.

1(j).i   The language uses OWL for knowledge representation and allows the invocation of actions and services that are implemented in arbitrary languages via an abstract description.

1(j).ii   Due to the invocation mechanism that allows actions and services to be implemented in any language, Yadl has a clearly defined interface to other languages. Moreover, as JIAC V is implemented completely in Java, thus Java-Methods can easily be used as actions in Yadl and vice versa.

2(a).i   Currently, JIAC V is supported by a programmers guide, an extensive maven site documentation for developers, a tutorial document and a list of small examples that display certain features.

2(a).ii   JIAC V is implemented with Java 1.6, using a list of openly available libraries such as the Spring-framework and ActiveMQ. Thus we are able to provide a complete release than can be run with any installation of Java 1.6.

2(b)   While the platform adheres to the FIPA life cycle management, it currently does not natively support any other FIPA standards.

2(c)   Currently, licensing issues about JIAC V have not been fixed. However, collaboration on development can be discussed on request.

2(d).i   JIAC V currently features an interaction monitor for monitoring and demonstrations, a standard conform JMX interface for management (that can be used with e.g. JConsole). Logging is handled via the commons-logging api, for which free tools are publicly available. We are currently working on an invocation monitor for services and service chains. Future plans include a JADL ++-debugger as well as a tailored management tool for the management api.

2(d).ii Currently the JIAC V documentation consists of a short tutorial, a list of example applications and a maven-site documentation for developers. Detailed documentation about the architecture is currently in the works.

2(d).iii As the architecture is based on Java, we recommend to use Eclipse to programm java-based components for JIAC V. As for JADL++, we have not yet implemented any tool support, though it is possible to use the VSDT tool to design workflows. We plan to provide an extended Eclipse plug-in for the scripting part. The OWL part is well covered with Protégé. To support configuration and deployment of multi agent systems in JIAC V, we are currently adapting the JIAC IV agent role editor.

2(e) JIAV V supports and provides webservices, and has connectors for UPnP services. Each node provides a webserver which can be used to easily deploy JSPs and therby provide user interfaces for the agents. The communication technology is based on JMS, and it comes with an extensive management interface that is based on JMX.

2(f) With the basic JIAC V platform, any system that has Java 1.6 installed can run it. However, certain extensions, e.g. webservice or IMS-support may have additional requirements.

2(g).i Currently we are able to run about 10000 Agents on a standard workplace machine without notable performance issues. However, this is of course subjects to the individual agents workload.

2(g).ii The core of JIAC V is stable, though not yet publicly released. The BDI-extension and the service-matcher are currently in the prototyping phase. Further extensions are in development with varying degrees of completion.

2(h).i The platform supports three different scalability levels for agents (with the highest level open to extensions). Furthermore, agents have a well defined interface for interaction with other software systems, including agent- and SOA-platforms.

2(h).ii The platform provides methods of group communication which can be used to create groups. It does not however support hierarchical groups. Each platform consists of any number of nodes, each of which controls agents on them. It therefore provides distributed control of agents.

2(h).iii We are currently in the process of providing libraries for different applications, such as a webserver, usermanagement and an integration to the IP-Multimedia-Subsystem(IMS).

3(a) JIAC V has been used as a service execution environment within the context of a german funded research project. It is currently used in a number of further projects ranging from simulation, and service execution, to energy control and home automation.

3(b) While the platform is domain agnostic it is tilted towards service oriented structures and telecommunication environments in that it provides services to deal with IMS and other telecommunication technologies. Its extensive management interface allows the use in industrial applications.

A.7 Agent Factory

1(a)   The language supports mental attitudes and specifically beliefs and commitments. Reactive behaviour is encoded imperatively in Java.

1(b)   The language supports speech act based primitives for communication. Wildcard pattern matching is used to broadcast messages to multiple agents, for example a message sent to Ja* would be received by Jack and Jay, but not Frank.

1(c)   Support is provided for the construction of mobile agents. Truly strong migration is not possible in Java. With Agent Factory, the agents' mental state and code are transferred. With AFME, only the mental state is transferred.

1(d)   The language is easy to understand for someone who has experience of declarative/logic programming.

1(e)   The language has clear and precise semantics. The original language was formalised in Collier's thesis [10]. Work is underway on formalising more recent enhancements/alterations.

1(f)   The language is intended for the construction of a variety of agent programs.

1(g)   The language enables the reuse of agent designs through roles, but does not enable the definition of new language components.

1(h)   At present a clear path to formal verification is not provided.

1(i)   Software Engineering principles have been considered in the design of the language.

1(j).i   The language is integrated with Java and was previously integrated with Smalltalk-80.

1(j).ii   The language allows the invocation of methods written in classical languages.

2(a).i   Detailed instructions on how to install and use the framework (including Javadoc) are available from http://www.agentfactory.com.

2(a).ii   In its current form, the framework requires either Java Standard Edition or Java Micro Edition to execute.

2(b)   The general architecture of the framework is consistent with the FIPA specifications. Agent Factory provides FIPA compliant communication through a message transport service. With AFME, FIPA communication is facilitated through a combination of a TCP (binary) message transport service and a "translator message server" that operates on a desktop machine. Support is also provided for yellow and white page services.

2(c)   The platform can be extended with additional functionality through open source collaboration.

2(d).i   An agent mental state debugger is provided along with a logger.

2(d).ii   Extensive documentation including Javadoc is available from agentfactory.com.

2(d).iii   A Netbeans IDE plugin is provided.

2(e)   Existing applications have been integrated with JSP, Java Servlets, and Struts.

2(f)   An application running the platform would require Java.

2(g).i   Agent Factory is quite an efficient and practical system and is capable of executing a large number of agents subject to the number of commitment rules the agents have and the hardware on which they are operating.

2(g).ii   The platform is a stable open source distribution.

2(h).i   The platform supports open multi-agent systems and heterogeneous agents.

2(h).ii   The structure of the agent community is dependent on the design of the individual agents that form the community. As such, centralised, hierarchical, or distributed control can be catered for.

2(h).iii   The platform does not provide libraries of interaction protocols. Agent templates are supported and reuse is facilitated through the use of roles.

3(a)   The platform has been used for the development of applications in several disparate domains, including E-Commerce [26], Ubiquitous Computing [36], Mobile Computing [38], Robotics [19], Wireless Sensor Networks [37], and Mixed Reality [17].

3(b)   The platform does not target a specific domain.

Index